The New Thinking Man's Guide to PRO FOOTBALL

by

Paul Zimmerman

Simon and Schuster
New York

Copyright © 1984 by Paul Zimmerman

Published by Simon and Schuster
A Division of Simon & Schuster, Inc.
Simon & Schuster Building
Rockefeller Center
1230 Avenue of the Americas
New York, New York 10020
SIMON AND SCHUSTER and colophon are registered trademarks of
Simon & Schuster, Inc.

Designed by Irving Perkins

Manufactured in the United States of America

1   3   5   7   9   10   8   6   4   2

Library of Congress Cataloging in Publication Data

Zimmerman, Paul Lionel.
The new thinking man's guide to pro football.

Rev. ed. of: A thinking man's guide to pro football.
Rev. ed. 1971.
Includes index.
1. Football—United States. I. Zimmerman, Paul
Lionel. Thinking man's guide to pro football.
II. Title.
GV954.Z56   1984   796.332′64′0973   84-10688
ISBN: 0-671-45394-7

TO
SARAH,
MICHAEL
AND
FROGGY

Contents

Introduction

I WROTE the first version of this book after the 1969 season. Joe Namath, Joe Kapp, Merlin Olsen and Joe Don Looney were the reigning heroes. Hank Stram was the current genius and everyone was talking about his Football of the Seventies concept. I revised the book a year later and changed some things, but the basic ideas held. In the 13 seasons that have gone by since then, many of the observations, and practically all of the people who made them, have been rendered obsolete, so this, in a sense, is an entirely new book.

A little bit has been retained. Marion Motley remains the greatest player I've ever seen, so that chapter is virtually untouched. Olsen's philosophical and technical ideas about defensive line play remain fresh and pointed; as an NBC broadcaster he's still on top of the game, so I've kept many of his quotes. Elsewhere a whole new generation of players and coaches has given rise to a new set of reflections about a world that is ever-changing.

Football of the Seventies, with Stram's ideas about the quick, agile quarterback operating from a "moving pocket," turned out to be an era of defense, until the rule makers stepped in after the 1977 season and opened up the passing lanes and artificially created an entirely new trend. Until then, football had been a process of natural evolution.

Some of the things you will read about will already have changed in the few months between writing and publication. The chart on drafting proficiency between 1973 and 1983, for instance, will not reflect trades in the late spring and early summer.

It's a bigger book now, and for economy's sake two chapters have been dropped, "The Medics" and "TV." Something had to go, to make room for the mass of new material, and these were the victims. Maybe they'll return in a subsequent book. You will see 49er coach Bill Walsh quoted far more than anyone else, not because he's got an edge on his fellow coaches . . . it's just that his quotes and observations crystallized much of my own thinking, and he said it in a better way than I could.

I would like to give particular thanks to those members of the business who gave me so much of their time when it was precious, who helped me step back and take a longer, more philosophical look at the game . . . Art Rooney, Jr., George Young, John Riggins, Lyle Alzado, Bobby Beathard, Mike Giddings, John McVay, Bill Walsh, John Madden, and, of course, Merlin Olsen and Weeb Ewbank from the old days . . . and I'm sure I'm forgetting many more.

Finally . . . special thanks to my wife and children for the day-to-day sacrifices that enabled me to get this book written.

Paul Zimmerman, March 1984

HAPTER ONE

A Violent Game

Thus ended the memorable field of Ashby-de-la-Zouche, one of the most gallantly contested tournaments of that age; for although four knights, including one that was smothered by the heat of his armor, had died upon the field, yet upward of thirty were desperately wounded, four or five of whom never recovered. Several more were disabled for life; and those who escaped best carried the marks of the conflict to the grave with them. Hence it is always mentioned in the old records as the Gentle and Joyous Passage of Arms at Ashby.

—Ivanhoe, Ch. 12

I always got a special kick out of playing against Bill Bradley, the Eagles' defensive back. Once, after a long gain, I was walking by the Eagles' huddle and I reached out and pinched him as hard as I could on the arm. He ran to the referee, screaming that I had pinched him and the ref told him they didn't have a penalty for that. Another time he tried to get inside my face mask, so I stuck my fingers in his. I was trying to pull his eyes out. That's when I realized that I might be insane.

—Conrad Dobler

FOR years Conrad Dobler, who played guard for three professional teams, was everyone's favorite capsule of violence and craziness in the NFL. TV's isolated cameras would catch him going for the face mask, the knees, the groin, and the announcer would say, "I think he's gone a little too far this time." But they couldn't stay mad at him for long. The guy was just so loose and friendly and talkative off the field.

11

Merlin Olsen, the great defensive tackle for the Rams, hated Dobler intensely. He does to this day; that's right, Merlin, who plays all those gentle giants on TV, whose style on the field was always one of extreme honor and sportsmanship.

"I hate to admit it," Olsen says, "but Dobler bugged me so much that I once got together with a teammate to figure out a way to put Conrad out of the game. I'm ashamed of it. It's the only time I ever did anything like that in 15 years. I worked it out with Jack Young-blood, the end next to me, that I'd get Dobler stood up and Jack would crash down from his blind side, right into his ribs. Except that we weren't very good at it. Dobler'd been over the course before. He smelled it coming, and turned at the last minute and Jack wound up hitting me, and Dobler just laughed at us."

"I told Merlin, 'We've got to practice that thing a little more before we use it in a game,' " Youngblood says.

Dobler was the symbol of an older, and rarer, species in the NFL, the big, rough guy who didn't spend much time in the weight room but could get by on natural meanness and determination. Every now and then you hear somebody labeled a "throwback" . . . Lyle Alzado and Matt Millen of the Raiders, Jimbo Covert, the big offensive tackle for the Bears . . . but violence in the NFL, which was, is, and always will be the major selling point of the game of football, has an added element today. Speed. Nowhere in any sport will you find people so big who can move so fast. Anabolic steroids and weight training have swelled them to unnatural size, synthetic turf has given them a faster track to run on. Collisions are violent and spectacular. (Some years ago a physicist figured out that if a 250-pound lineman running a 5.0 forty collides with a back who runs a 4.6, the kinetic energy equals 66,000 inch-pounds, or enough to move 33 tons one inch.) They're spectacular by the very nature of the game now. The ordinary roughness in the pits is a constant factor, but it doesn't attract the TV replays.

Mean people still exist in the NFL, but they are not as fashionable as they used to be. Cosmetic rule changes work against the head-hunters. The defensive lineman's head slap was outlawed, and I always thought that was ironic . . . that it's against the law to slap someone on the side of the helmet with an open hand, but perfectly legal to play the game on a surface as hard as concrete. Contact above the head is carefully scrutinized, shots to the knees not so carefully.

Once the players took care of cheap-shotters in their own way, but now the feeling seems to be: There's so much more money to be made in the game, why bother with this nonsense? No one on the Bengals, for instance, went after the Steelers' Keith Gary in 1983 after he buggy-whipped quarterback Ken Anderson by the face mask and put him out of action for a month—and then drew a roughness penalty by spearing the backup QB, Turk Schonert, while he was on the ground. The two cheapest shots of 1982—Detroit's Leonard Thompson's frightening blow to the head of the Giants' Leon Bright (after a fair catch), and New England's Don Hasselbeck's spearing of the Jets' Joe Klecko, while Klecko was lying on the ground, gripping his wrecked knee—drew no retaliation.

"I'm surprised no one put out a contract on Hasselbeck after he went after you on the ground," someone said to Klecko a few weeks later.

"I've got my own contract on him," Klecko said.

In the old days there was always a get-even syndrome in pro football. I remember hearing Sid Youngelman, the tackle for the old N.Y. Titans of the AFL, talking about how he was going to take care of the Oilers' Al Jamison, who had been nicknamed Dirty Al, for obvious reasons.

"How can you?" someone asked. "With the face bars and equipment and everything now, how can you get a guy?"

"Lots of ways," Sid said. "The easiest is in a pileup. You pick your spot, and then you get his helmet off . . . and kick his damn head in."

"The big mistake players make is trying to pull the helmet off," says Alzado, the throwback. "They try to wrestle with it and get nowhere. The trick is to snap it off. It's as easy as removing the cap on a Dr. Pepper."

Alzado actually got the league to put in a new rule, after he had heaved a helmet at the Jets' Chris Ward in an '83 playoff game. (He was annoyed because Ward had tried to shove him over a pileup.) The new rule, which drew a few smiles by its language, called for "automatic disqualification of a player who uses a helmet he is not wearing as a weapon."

Alzado's point, which he made a little too forcefully for some tastes, was that life's tough enough in the NFL without the sneaky stuff. And there has always been a clear difference between a rough player and a diry one.

"Larry Eisenhauer of the Patriots is a rough player," the Jets' former tackle, Winston Hill, once said. "He comes at you clawing, and he yells and screams and slobbers at the mouth. He even bit me once, right here on the arm. But he's not dirty. When a guy hits you after the whistle blows or when your back is turned, or when he tries to kick you in the groin, that's a dirty football player."

"When you come right down to it, your life is at stake out there," Olsen said toward the end of his career. "I'm not a weak man, and I've had quarterbacks bent under me in such a way that I'd only have to twist them a little to end their careers. I don't do it because I don't want to and I don't want it done to me.

"They don't call the middle of the line The Pit for nothing. We really do get like animals, trying to claw one another apart in there. It is very hard in The Pit. No matter how it seems, no matter what the score shows, it's always hard. We get so bruised and battered and tired we sometimes wind up playing in a sort of coma. By the end of the first half your instincts have taken over. By the end of the game you're an animal."

Memories of one violent hit often stay with a player for his whole career. Dan Dierdorf, who retired after 13 years with the Cardinals, remembers his first week with the club, sitting on the sidelines watching a preseason scrimmage against the Bears.

"A Chicago receiver went out for a pass and caught it," he says, "and Larry Wilson knocked the guy completely out. It was the hardest hit I'd ever seen in my life. I said, 'Oh my Lord, welcome to the NFL. This is the way it is.' "

The very language of football is designed to further the violent image. Analogies have been made to religion and life itself and the family, but war and the military have given the game its liveliest vocabulary: the bomb, the blitz, attack, offense and defense, platoons, even rookie, which is short for "recruit." The Giants call their punt coverage men "bullets." The desperation pass play that gave Atlanta a win over the 49ers in 1983 used to be called Big Ben; the Falcons changed its name to "rocket." A typical press release has a team going to Detroit to "battle" the Lions. "It's going to be a war," a coach will promise. In 1983 Baltimore coach Frank Kush got upset at a couple of TV announcers for giggling and laughing in the back of the plane bringing the team home from a loss.

"I don't want levity to overflow to the troops," he said. "They came from a war and got shot and were dying."

In the late 1960s antiwar sentiment triggered a revolution among

America's youth, or maybe it was the other way around. Anyway, traditional values were being uprooted, and pro football also went through its rebel stage.

"If you don't believe that people in America have a need for pro football, you writers should sit in the stands more and hear what goes on," St. Louis Cards right linebacker Dave Meggyesy told the *Philadelphia Inquirer*'s Sandy Padwe. "Football is just short of war for some of those people. It brings them right up to the edge. The fans can really get their hostilities off. There's mayhem but no killing. It's a titillation.

"Football is an archaic ethos. The black athletes know more than anyone who's kidding whom. Face it, football's passe. It's a game for the Yahoos. It's like the old Roman sports. Throwing the bomb, blitzing—now what the hell does that mean? If this society changes like I hope it will, football will be a dead issue. The people will be able to get their hostilities off in a healthier way.

"The top football players are psychos. They are very unhealthy people, but society views them as some of our healthiest people. When you have men perpetuating violence in sports, in television, or anything of that nature, you can't call that sane. You can't call the people who do it sane. You can't call me sane."

Meggyesy got it all off his chest a year later in a book called *Out of Their League:* the racism in pro football, the everyday indignities, the hypocrisy that began with the payola back in his college days at Syracuse—everything got worked over. The establishment turned on him with ferocity, but some of the players looked at their way of life with a new kind of introspection.

"I felt terribly threatened, I was almost afraid to read the book," said Baltimore center Bill Curry, who's now the coach at Georgia Tech. "I thought it might force me into giving this game up, that it might show me things I was too stupid to see. There are some dark corners in my mind that I don't understand. Violence is one of them. When I had read what he had written, though, I found contradictions in his logic. I didn't agree with him, but he made me think."

In 1970 a very promising young linebacker for the Oakland Raiders, Chip Oliver, dropped out and joined a Berkeley commune. "I was tired of just being another slab of meat," he said. An organic food diet dropped his weight from 230 to 175. ("I feel great now. What did I need all that weight for?")

They were easy targets. Meggyesy had diluted his argument by admitting he was an occasional drug popper. Oliver was written off as a wheat-germ and yoga freak. The game, people argued, was stronger for their absence. The game discouraged oddballs. But then in April 1971 George Sauer, the Jets' two-time all-pro wide receiver, quit at the age of 27. Sauer was not a freak. His dad had coached at Navy and Baylor, and George grew up as a football brat. He said he still loved the game, but he didn't like what it had become—a mirror of the commercialism and success-at-any-price philosophy that was diluting modern life.

He said you could play at top efficiency without hating the man across the line from you. But people wouldn't let you. Vince Lombardi's "winning is the only thing" credo had taken too strong a hold. Pro football destroyed your sense of values as a human being, Sauer said. So he quit.

But here's the funny thing. They all came back. Meggyesy returned as an officer in the Players Association. Oliver tried a comeback with the Raiders. And Sauer stayed out for three years and then tried it again with the New York Stars of the World Football League, catching passes in the dim off-lighting of Randalls Island, before 5000 fans.

Why? The game hadn't changed, but they found that they couldn't really leave it. Something in it was stronger than their logic.

"Honesty," said Joe Kapp, ex-quarterback for the Vikings and Patriots and currently the coach at the University of California. "It was an honest thing we were doing out there. I'm not talking about all the hype and hoopla surrounding it. I'm talking about what went on down on the field itself."

Strangely enough, it is the undercurrent of violence that gives football its own special brand of honesty. "Men travel side by side for years, each locked up in his own silence or exchanging those words which carry no freight—till danger comes," wrote Antoine de Saint Exupery in *Wind, Sand and Stars.* "Then they stand shoulder to shoulder. They discover that they belong to the same family. They grow and bloom in the recognition of fellow beings. They look at one another and smile."

No one feels it more than the men in The Pit, the linemen. They have their own kind of dignity, and when the Jets' defensive end Mark Gastineau first started doing his sack dance a few years ago, linemen on both the offensive and defensive sides of the ball showed their disgust. "Hey, that stuff's OK for the wide receivers and defensive backs, the pirouettes and dances in the end zone, but we should be above that," they would say. "We should have more class."

All of them understand what they do on the field—the violence, even the brutality—and every now and then they are shocked at what they see.

"I don't really realize how brutal the game is until the off-season, when I go out to banquets and watch movies of our games," the old Packer guard, Jerry Kramer, wrote in *Instant Replay*. "Then I see guys turned upside down and backwards, and hit from all angles, and I flinch. I'm amazed how violent the game is, and I wonder about playing it myself."

"The first time I saw a game live, from a TV booth," San Francisco tight end Russ Francis says, "I looked at one particularly vicious hit, and I said to the guy next to me, 'My God, do I really do that?' Somehow the game films the coaches show us, those little figures in black and white, never get that across. They're like KGB films. You get the feeling something's held back."

"My mother," says Dolphin guard Ed Newman, "watches our games on TV through a crack in the closet door."

Many of them are haunted by the image of the Dumb Football Player.

"I'm not trying to suggest that pro football players, as a group, are the intellectual equals of, say, the staff of the *Paris Review*," Kramer wrote. "But I've sat with lawyers and politicians and with writers, and frankly, when I want an interesting conversation, I'd just as soon chat with a bunch of pro football players. At least the players are willing to discuss something besides football."

Time magazine once sent a stringer out to get information on Raider linebacker Ted Hendricks for a possible feature story. This was when Hendricks was a senior at the University of Miami and a finalist for a Rhodes Scholarship.

"The guy's no dummy," the stringer wrote. "His favorite authors are William Blake and Oscar Wild [*sic*]." Hendricks snorted when someone mentioned the report to him, including the variant spelling. "Maybe he meant Wild Oscar," he said.

Often they find their lives incongruous. Pat McInally, Cincinnati's punter and a Harvard graduate, once talked about a two-a-day session on a hot and humid afternoon back in college.

"They had this weird deal where all the offensive people would line up and the defensive people would line up," he said. "You'd get down on one knee with a cup in your hand and a manager would come through and give you one squirt of water in the cup. I remember looking around me at all these guys who were going to be senators, who were going to run companies all over the world, and there they were, sweating, breathing hard, on one knee waiting for their cup of water."

Once, in the course of a 1981 interview, Jet quarterback Richard Todd said, "I'm more confident because we're winning." Then he paused for a moment. "Strange way to measure your happiness, isn't it?"

"The two worst things in football," former Dallas safetyman Cliff Harris says, "are, one, they think that a 30-year-old professional athlete has to be locked up in a hotel room, with a curfew, the night before a game, and, two, they're right."

Sometimes the establishment's view of pro football borders on the ludicrous. A decade ago the league office sponsored a contest in which schoolchildren were supposed to submit essays on "The NFL's Role in American History." Chicago sportswriter David Israel wrote a piece for which he called up 10 leading American historians and asked them the same question. Their answer—it has meant zero.

Fans are being brought to new levels of awareness, from the heavy narration of the NFL film segments to the slow-mo and instant replays and reverse-angle shots of the TV cameras, and they are bombarded with a never-ending torrent of hype. This, from the league's publication, *Pro Magazine,* March–April 1982 issue: "The healthy unrealness of the whole phenomenon carries a powerful residue of emotion into Sunday night, and from that feeling the anticipation for next week's game seems to build. Person-to-person, electronically and in print, Topic A claws a tighter and tighter hold on community spirit."

Some pro football people take a more cynical view.

"What's your greatest thrill in football?" *Pro Magazine* once asked Art Rooney, the 83-year-old owner of the Steelers.

"Making the payroll on Mondays in the old days," he said.

Bill Walsh, the 49ers' coach, was asked what he thought about the hype surrounding his Super Bowl game against Cincinnati.

"They want to be able to stage the Epic Game," he said. "They want it to be Army versus Carlisle. That way they can sell more T-shirts."

In their news telecasts the networks deplore violence. But when they do a game they'll replay a particularly vicious hit three or four times.

"We're all guilty of it," ABC's Don Meredith says. "We zoom in. . . . 'Oh, isn't it awful . . . let's look at it again in slow motion . . . whoops, there goes his head.' I'm told by the people in the trucks at all three networks that if the fans don't get to see those things, man, the switchboard lights up."

"We are the gladiators," Miami guard Bob Kuechenberg says. "What we do is a great substitute for war, a violent chess game. All the wide receivers run a 4.5. All the linemen run a 5.1 and bench-press 450 pounds. Where do you use your pawn? Where do you move your rook?"

Psychologists have made inroads into the game. Dallas built a sensory isolation tank three years ago, and Philadelphia countered with its Mood Room, complete with a sunset picture on the wall, in front of comfortable chairs, underneath soft lights. Detroit fooled around with biorhythm charts, and almost everyone has experimented with team hypnotists.

Old-timers look at the modern game and sneer. "Today you ask a guy if he plays football," said Leon Hart, the Lions' former All-Pro end, "and he says, 'No, I play left linebacker.' "

"The size of the players is much greater now," former Ram half-back Dick Bass says, "and I think a lot of that weight lifting is cute, and they look good in their clothes, but give me a guy who'll go four quarters chewing tobacco."

Some things, though, don't change. The average life expectancy in the game is still a little over four years. Coaches still ask players to sacrifice everything for team success, to use their bodies with "reckless abandon," but then cut them on the basis of individual skill, or loss of it, when the machine shows a few knocks. They're released and traded at random; sometimes they become football gypsies.

"I felt like the American Gigolo," linebacker Joe Federspiel said after the Saints cut him and he spent the next six weeks trying out for different NFL teams around the league. "You fly here, run around there, head back home and do it again."

Gypsies, paste-up figures on the big board in the personnel office, chessmen to be moved and removed, waived and traded and dangled as bait. Seldom is there any regard for the effect it might have on the people themselves, or their families.

In the mid-1970s the Eagles had a defensive end named Blenda

Gay. He had graduated from Fayetteville State College in North Carolina with a bachelor of arts in sociology. What it got him was a few weeks in the Oakland Raiders' camp in 1972 and then a year of semipro football for a team called the Model City Diplomats. The Raiders brought him to camp again in '73, then released him, and the Jets picked him up a year later. They traded him back to Oakland for a draft choice, and the Raiders released him a third time. San Diego picked him up in December and he played the final two games of the '74 season with the Chargers. In 1975 they traded him back to Oakland, as a throw-in in a five-player deal, and the Raiders cut him for a fourth time. He finally caught on with the Eagles and played 14 games for them, eight as a starter at both defensive end positions, and stayed on the squad the next year. He had a wife named Roxanne and one child.

You might remember the name, Roxanne Gay. And you might remember her testimony at the trial in which she was accused of fatally cutting the throat of her husband, "former Philadephia defensive end Blenda Gay."

She said she had lived in constant fear for herself and her baby, that her husband had turned into a different person; he had finally cracked under the strain of the job.

"Toward the end," she testified, "he started telling me what it was like, how much stress and strain a player is under. He's like a puppet in the organization—a piece of meat, that's all he is—and when they're through with you they cut you and let you go. And he got banged up more as he tried harder, and after the games he'd come home so full of tension and mad. He became so mean and hard I was scared of him."

The nonfootball public wrote it off as just another horror story in a world full of them. Maybe there had been drugs involved, alcohol. Who knows what makes crazy people do what they do? But a deep shudder went through the football community, where so many livelihoods are hanging by a thread, by a whim.

Dave Herman, the old New York Jets' guard, used to say, "Football is like life. You come in crying and you go out crying."

With very few exceptions the end is sudden, and devastating—and perhaps that is the ultimate violence in the violent game.

"Yeah, you're at the top, people give you all this attention, everybody recognizes you," Tony Dorsett says. "But you know it's going to disappear. It's scary."

"For 13 years I lived a fantasy, full of life and dreams-come-true, emotionally, physically, spiritually," former Ram defensive end Fred Dryer said when he was finally released. "You know, of course, that it isn't going to last. There's a part of you, way down deep inside, that's always uneasy about that. And it does end so fast. It all went by in a heartbeat."

CHAPTER TWO

Offensive Line (Anonymous)

I've compared offensive linemen to the story of Paul Revere. After Paul Revere rode through town everybody said what a great job he did. But no one ever talked about the horse. I know how Paul Revere's horse felt.

—Gene Upshaw

It's a very interesting game. They have big bears up front and little rabbits in the back. The idea is for the bears to protect the rabbits.

—Viktor Tikhonov, National Soviet hockey coach, seeing American football for the first time

IN the beginning there were linemen—not offensive and defensive linemen, just linemen. Linemen and backs. There were no linebackers; they were called roving centers. There were no cornerbacks; they were called halfbacks. There were no situation players or designated sackers or pass blocking specialists. It was a simple age, and people blocked for the run, then turned around and tried to stop it on the next series. The fans brought flasks to the games and enjoyed a dim awareness of what was going on, because maybe they'd seen a movie about football. In the movies the backs were played by Dick Powell or Ronald Reagan and the linemen by Jack Oakie.

Writers in those days never talked to linemen until they became coaches. They were never quoted. Why, for goodness sakes, would any reader want to know the intricacies of a crab block? Of course, in those days writers talked to very few players anyway. They sat in the press box and smoked their pipes and created marvelous, swirling prose—without quotes, or if there were a few, they were generally piped, made up.

When the two-platoon era arrived a few linemen started making names for themselves, but they were defensive linemen—Ernie Stautner, Leo Nomellini, Arnie Weinmeister, Gino Marchetti, Big Daddy Lipscomb. Smashing through the line to make a tackle could capture one's fancy. Blocking couldn't.

Remember the famous Giants-Colts sudden-death game for the NFL championship in 1958? It was the game that supposedly lifted football into every American living room. The names of the stars spill out like salt crystals . . . Unitas, Conerly, Gifford, Moore, Ameche, Huff, Berry, Marchetti. How many starting offensive linemen can you name? New Yorkers knew about Rosey Brown, because he was fast . . . he pulled out to lead the sweeps . . . and in Baltimore they were very proud of a young, second-year tackle named Jim Parker, later to earn great fame as a guard. But eight more offensive linemen started that day, and can you name one of them? OK, I'll do it for you: Preas, Sandusky, Nutter, Spinney, Barry, Wietecha, Mischak and Youso. Why are you shrugging?

They say that the famous Ice Bowl game between Green Bay and Dallas for the '67 championship marked the first time an offensive lineman was awarded recognition, when the instant replay cameras caught Jerry Kramer driving Jethro Pugh over the goal line (a double-team block, incidentally . . . center Ken Bowman did the more difficult job of setting Pugh up). I think it had happened before. In the '58 championship the cameras consistently caught Parker in his near-perfect day, pass-blocking on the Giants' Andy Robustelli. Up till then a pass blocker got about as much acclaim as an ice fisherman.

The first professional game I ever covered was the 1960 Green Bay–Philadelphia championship, won by the Eagles, 17–13. My paper, the *New York World Telegram & Sun*, had sent me down to Philly to get losing dressing-room quotes for Joe King, our regular pro football man. I was assigned to the Packers, who had gone down following Lombardi's reversion to what the columnists considered Stone Age football in an era of the high flyers. One man, I remember, began his Monday column: "They should have parked a Stutz'-Bearcat outside of Franklin Field yesterday. . . ."

But the Packers had gained 223 yards on the ground against the

Eagles that day, and even from my seat in the skyscraping Franklin Field press box, where you lived in mortal fear that a strong wind would blow the whole thing over and drop it, *plop*, right on the 50-yard line, I could see that right guard Jerry Kramer and left guard Fuzzy Thurston and center Jim Ringo were doing terrible things to the middle of the Eagles' defensive line. The Eagle tackles had been nullified, and even the great Chuck Bednarik was having trouble getting out of the way of Ringo's precise cutoff blocks.

My interest was somewhat personal, too, because that was a year in which I had been spending my Saturday nights playing offensive guard for the Paterson (N.J.) Pioneers of the semipro Eastern Football Conference. And when I hit that Green Bay dressing room, I wanted to hear from Kramer himself—and Thurston and Ringo—how they called their audibles and what the Philly tackles were doing on their pass rush.

Yes, a lot of pass-block pressure was relieved by the runs, Kramer patiently explained, and any one of the three of them had the option of making calls, and why was I bothering to talk to an offensive lineman, anyway?

Pretty soon Ringo and Thurston came out of the shower—pleasant, friendly men who were amused at the idea that a reporter seemed interested in their world, even if it was only one reporter.

The four of us had a nice little chat, and I came away from that dressing room thinking, gee, covering the pro football beat must be a real breeze. And, of course, then the awful realization came that I was totally blank on Starr and Hornung and Lombardi quotes, and Joe King nearly heaved me out of the press-room window, with a few carefully delivered words to help get my mind off option blocking and audibles and the whole subject of offensive linemen.

Next day I was back covering the high schools, where I couldn't get in trouble, and it was a full two years before I set foot inside a pro football dressing room again.

The stories that came out of that game were all Philadelphia: quarterback Norm Van Brocklin and coach Buck Shaw, ending their careers in a wondrous blaze; and, of course, Chuck Bednarik, a 60-minute center and linebacker after 12 years in the game. Still, Vince Lombardi had shown people a slight peek into the future.

Someday the former offensive linemen of the world might sit down and pool their pension money and decide to erect a monument to Lombardi, because if any man could be called the Great Emancipator of the offensive line, it would have to be him. He gave them a better way of life, a more sensible way of earning a day's pay. He freed the great masses of congestion in the middle of the line, and, indirectly, he helped bring them what small measure of publicity has come their way.

He came to the New York Giants as Jim Lee Howell's assistant in 1954, his head full of Jock Sutherland's sweeps and Earl Blaik's finesse. And when he got there he found a world in which the blocking linemen performed their work like gladiators, digging away at the tightly packed defenses, occasionally straightening up to take their punishment on the pass blocks.

Lombardi put in his old St. Cecilia's High School end-run stampedes, and the same blocking principles carried down to his Green Bay Packer and Washington Redskin days. He lifted a Giant running game that had been last in the league in 1953, averaging less than 90 yards a game, into respectability in that first season, and a year later, when Alex Webster and Mel Triplett joined Frank Gifford in the backfield, Lombardi knew he had something unique.

He had three big backs who could run with power and speed. Best of all, they could block. All of them. Lombardi pulled his guards on the sweeps, and used the blocking ability of his backs, and the whole thing put unbelievable firepower on the defensive flank men.

He employed the exceptional talents of Roosevelt Brown as a pulling tackle. And he took the heat off the center by moving the guards out wider, creating splits in the middle of the line and rendering obsolete the huge defensive middle guards, such as Detroit's 350-pound Les Bingaman or Washington's 275-pound Jim Ricca or Green Bay's 290-pound Ed Neal, whose 19-inch forearms had left a trail of unconscious centers around the league.

But Lombardi's biggest contribution in those Giant years (1954–58) was his option system of blocking. Now the linemen had the option of moving the defensive man in either direction, riding him the way he was going, using his own momentum against him. It was a tremendous break for the blockers, who had grown old before their time trying to move out 260- and 270-pounders planted squarely in the hole like sequoias. It was the start of a system that became famous in Green Bay as "Run to Daylight."

Face bars on the helmets helped. The bars, which became mandatory in the mid-1950s, provided the lineman with a new blocking weapon, his head. Now he could drill a man with his forehead, reassured by the knowledge that a defender's blow that once would have caved in his face now would give him only a hell of a headache.

But Lombardi gave his offensive linemen some respite from the tedium and the abuse of pass blocking, a highly specialized form of masochism in which a man's ability is graded by the ways he absorbs punishment—and the duration of time that he can stand it.

Lombardi's offensive linemen got some recognition, but they were hardly famous. The sight of Kramer and Thurston pulling to lead the Packer sweeps, a rare combination of precision and power, like a pair of perfectly matched Percherons, became a trademark of the Green Bay teams. And in Kramer, Thurston, Ringo and tackles Forrest Gregg and Bob Skoronski, those early Lombardi teams probably had the finest line ever put together, a unit of five All-Pros. But Kramer had been in the league 10 years before he got real notoriety, and that was from one block.

"One of the Cleveland Browns once told me," he wrote in his book, *Instant Replay*, "that if he ever had to go on the lam from the law, he'd become an offensive lineman."

Occasionally the draft will whet people's interest in offensive linemen, but that seldom lasts past the first round. The recent success of the Redskins and their Hogs up front, blocking for John Riggins, gave the Washington fans a new set of heroes to cheer for, but part of that was freak appeal. I mean, who ever heard of winning in the modern, pass-happy NFL by grinding it out in the old-fashioned way? It was quaint.

Veteran beat writers know that if you want to find out what's going on, you ask the offensive linemen. Usually they're the most introspective and articulate members of the team. One NFL personnel director, who tests hundreds of college seniors every year, says that the positions that grade highest on intelligence testing are (1) offensive tackle, (2) center and (3) quarterback, with offensive guard a close fourth.

"They're the real thinkers of the team," Rams' coach John Robinson says. "The receivers just say, 'Throw me the ball.' The runners say, 'Hand me the ball.' But offensive linemen stop and say, 'Why are we doing that?' "

As defenses got trickier, with multiple stunts and blitzing, and in an effort to cope with the new pass-blocking rules, offenses began placing greater emphasis on intelligence in linemen drafted out of college. If an offensive lineman misses a call, or if he messes up on a read or an automatic adjustment—many of which aren't even called (you've got to make the adjustment by what you see in front of you)—the quarterback goes down for the count. The complexities of a system have bent the minds of many promising rookies. Mike Oriard, former center for Notre Dame and the Kansas City Chiefs, wrote in *The End of Autumn* about his first taste of an NFL playbook:

> I looked at a typical play, one called "Red right X, 52 full pop G-O inside," and tried to figure out what all the codes meant. Red was the formation, right the direction to which the strong side of the formation lined up, X an indication to one of the wide receivers to split out, 52 meant the fifty-series run through the two hole (around right end); full signaled a switch in assignments between the fullback and halfback; pop told a back to block the defensive end while the tight end hooked the outside linebacker; G-O indicated both guards pulled; and inside dictated that the wide receiver would block the inside man forcing the play from the secondary, while the lead puller blocked the outside man. What it amounted to, then, was a sweep to the right with the combination of blocks clearly specified. I studied the center's assignments on this play, against the half-dozen primary defenses we were likely to see, and discovered that I would have to be able to recognize the defense and make the proper calls to set the blocking for my fellow offensive linemen. If I called even, I would reach out to tie up the defensive tackle lined up over my pulling right guard, while my own tackle came down to block the middle linebacker. If I called odd because the defensive man was lined up too wide, I would exchange assignments with my right tackle. If a defensive player lined up in the gap between myself and my left guard, I would have to make the proper call that would tell the guard either to pull as the play dictated or to stay at home and block the man in his gap. My eyeballs were rolling after looking at only one play.

That was 14 years ago. Imagine what it's like now.

There's no way you can lean on statistics for help when you're writing a story about offensive linemen, because they aren't covered by any. Passers, runners, receivers, interceptors, kickers, punters, returners—they all work their way into the stat sheet. Even defensive players have come into some statistical recognition, and after the game you're handed sheets marked "tackles and assists," with "pass deflections" thrown in as a special concession to defensive backs.

Fans who crave numbers can locate statistics for every other man playing a professional sport in the United States—at every position. Hockey, basketball, baseball; everyone winds up with either saves or assists or put-outs or shots taken—something statistical. Only football's offensive linemen remain uncovered, except in a reflected sense—the number of times their quarterback was sacked, defensive stats for the men they played against, etc. So the fan thinks of offensive linemen in nebulous terms—a magazine piece he once read, the All-Pro teams at the end of the season, a sensational downfield block he once saw and remembered, a TV commentator's hypnotic repetition: "So-and-so's playing a whale of a game."

"We don't have any statistics to be remembered by," Gregg said in 1970, "so I don't want anyone to overlook the fact that I haven't missed a game since I came into the league in 1956."

The meat-and-potatoes blocks on running plays—tackle on end, guard on tackle, center on nose guard or middle linebacker—are so difficult to isolate and analyze that the statisticians never have considered devoting any effort to them. The head coach can't help much, because his horizontal view of the game doesn't give him any kind of perspective on the work in The Pit. He can tell if a man is getting beaten on pass protection, and if it gets too brutal he'll yank the lineman and talk things over. And if he doesn't like the way the conversation is going, there will be a different guard or tackle on the next series of plays. The hard-core analysis is handled by the coaches in the booth next to the press box—and they're very hesitant to discuss what they've seen—and of course by the movie camera. The coaches reach their verdicts on the offensive linemen in a dark room, running the plays over and over and over.

That's when the linemen finally get their shot at the statistical tables, but it's a very private affair. The coaches grade the blockers on every play. The grades are sometimes on a percentile basis (pass blocking is expected to draw a lower score than blocking for the run), sometimes on an aggregate score system. And they're a secret between coach and player, but the grades always make a reappearance during next year's contract talks.

"I've always felt," Kramer said, "that the real value of grades is to provide a helluva good lever for them during next year's contract talk."

It takes discipline to get into the habit of watching the line when you're looking at a football game. For some unknown reason everybody seems to want to watch the rather boring routine of quarterback taking the snap, quarterback either dropping back to throw or handing the ball off. It's hypnotic, and sometimes I catch myself doing it too, but really, you're not going to see much in those first two seconds if you watch the quarterback.

"It's crazy, I know," Gregg said when he was a player, "but when I'm just watching a game on TV, I start off looking at the offensive linemen, but then, if it's an exciting game I'll react just like any other fan and look at the quarterback. Or sometimes I just get lazy and start off by watching him right away."

If you're sitting in the stands, with no instant replay camera at your side, you occasionally might want to watch the wide receivers and how they run their routes, if it's a passing down. But if you're looking at the game on TV there's nothing much else to watch but the tackle-to-tackle battle, because the receivers move out of the picture after the first few steps. Not to worry. Your security is the replay, which will probably pick up anything dramatic that happens downfield. So if you can tear yourself away from watching the quarterback take the snap and hand the ball off, a whole new world will open up to you.

I get excited about the one-on-one matchup between great offensive and defensive linemen. When New England plays Dallas I can't watch much of anything else except the battle between the Patriots' left guard, John Hannah, the finest blocker in the game today, and the Cowboys' Randy White, the best interior lineman on defense. Guards always get help when they're trying to block White; sometimes two men will just lay all over him at the snap of the ball, sometimes he'll get pinballed from guard to center to running back. But the Hannah-White matchups always have been one-to-one things, and it's a rare sight, almost like a heavyweight championship bout.

I still have very clear pictures of a memorable battle I saw between Gregg and the Rams' great pass-rushing end, Deacon Jones, in the 1967 NFL Western Division Championship Game. Jones had won the first bout in Los Angeles early in December, but this time the decision went to Gregg, who was giving away speed, 15 pounds in weight and five years in age (he was 34, Jones 29). He kept Jones off Bart Starr that afternoon by using leverage, body control and a complete knowledge of Jones's attacking techniques.

"We were all waiting for that battle," Kramer said. "Deacon kind of tore into Forrest the first time we played them, and Forrest had gotten bawled out by Mr. Lombardi. The second time they met Forrest was ready. He'd taken those game films home and run them over and over, all by himself. He could tell you more about Jones' moves than Jones could. After the game everyone knew what kind of a job Forrest had done. Even the reporters knew."

If you took careful note of the line play in the 1970 Super Bowl you were an eyewitness to a historical event, the end of the small, agile "greyhound" center that had become fashionable in the NFL. The Vikings' 235-pound Mick Tingelhoff had made All-Pro six straight years, cutting off middle linebackers in the NFL-style 4–3, which squared up the tackles on the offensive guards and left a linebacker in the middle. But in that Super Bowl the Chiefs lined up in stack-overs and -unders, placing a defensive tackle directly over the center and "stacking," or hiding, their linebackers behind the linemen. It was an AFL-style defense; Tinglehoff played head-up against either 6'1", 260-pound Curly Culp or 6'7", 275-pound Buck Buchanan, and either way he was overmatched. The days of the greyhound centers became numbered.

At one time, the offensive guards would provide your clue as to where the play would go. They were the tea leaves of football; you could use them to see into the future.

If they fired out, straight ahead, the play usually would be a run inside. If they fired out low and cut-blocked their man, it could be a "quickie" pass over the middle. If they set themselves in a pass-blocking stance, the play would be a regular pass or a draw (a delayed handoff to a back coming through any area of daylight between the tackles). And if they did a pivot and pulled out, running parallel to the line of scrimmage, the play would be an end sweep and you'd be an eyewitness to one of football's classic dramas.

Many things could happen to a guard on his journey from his set position on the line to the final destination—the corner linebacker or defensive back. You could get a whole chronicle of success or failure. If one guard was half a count late getting out, his man might get a piece of him, upsetting his rhythm and causing the other pulling guard to run him down. Stripped of his two interference men, the runner would find himself rounding the corner into a mob, since the middle linebacker, watching all movement along the line for tip-offs, would race over to meet the sweep, bringing his gang with him.

Or maybe both guards would have pulled out in textbook fashion and were well on their way, say, around right end. But the offensive right tackle, or perhaps the tight end, whose duty it was to block straight ahead and contain, had been pushed back, into the path of the guards—those dutiful guards who always worried about losing the speed necessary to beat their runner to the corner.

So there would be a stack-up along the scrimmage line, and the only place the runner could go would be down. Ninety percent of the fans watching the game would ask, "What the hell's the matter with that back?" And the other 10 percent, the ones who picked up the picture from the beginning, would smile and recite their expertise— "Well, you see, the defensive end beat the tackle and got penetration, and this knocked off the pulling guards, so the ballcarriers' interference was stripped away. . . ."

The old Lombardi Sweep is pretty much a thing of the past these days, but sometimes it can reappear in dramatic fashion. If a team goes into a nickel (five backs) or dime (six) defense on a passing down, the offense just might run an old-fashioned power sweep at them . . . big guys blocking little guys. That's what the San Francisco 49ers did to Dallas in their classic 87-yard march in the dying moments of the 1981 NFL Championship Game. They made a hero out of Lenvil Elliott, a 30-year-old warhorse of a halfback who had been cut and then activated eight days before the game—which led to Dallas safety Charlie Waters's classic remark: "They were beating us with guys we didn't even know who they were."

The guards aren't the tip-offs anymore. The 3–4 defense did that. Nowadays the guards can spend much of their time misdirecting . . . moving away from the play to give the inside linebackers a false read, getting them to take that one fatal step in the wrong direction. Watch Dallas and you'll see a lot of that, and you'll also see the tackle on the off side (the side away from the play) pull out and come back to trap-block, or turn upfield and lead the play, an almost impossible assignment. I still don't see how he can get there in time.

If you watched Washington's offensive line, the Hogs, in 1983, you might have noticed they were capable of a lot more than grunting and snorting and rooting straight ahead. Joe Jacoby, the 6'7", 298-pound left tackle, was adept at pulling to his right. In the old days if

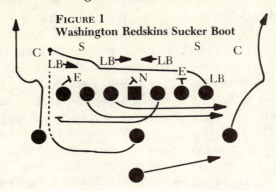

FIGURE 1
Washington Redskins Sucker Boot

a coach had drawn up such a play for a big guy like Jacoby, there would have been a lot of head scratching, and probably a straight-jacket on the field. The Hog guards, Russ Grimm and Mark May, were very adept at a technique called "fold-blocking," waiting for the center to make his move and then folding around him and block-ing the other way—a short-trap, actually, or "step-around and cross block," as we called it in the old days. And the Hog linemen were parties to a play involving the utmost deception, the Sucker Boot (Fig. 1), one of the stranger things I've seen on a football field and a maneuver that CBS-TV's John Madden calls "my favorite play in football—ever."

The guard and tackle on one side pull one way, and the tailback, John Riggins or Joe Washington, follows them. Then the guard on the other side pulls in the reverse direction from the other two Hogs, a deeper pull—behind them. Joe Theismann rolls out behind the sin-gle puller, the last guy, and either keeps running or throws a pass to a receiver occupying an area vacated by the thoroughly confused de-fense. It's been a big yardage-gainer for the Skins, a "key-breaker," Washington coach Joe Gibbs calls it, and a play that I guarantee you will be widely copied. The danger, of course, is that all those pulling linemen may run into each other—which is what happened when the Giants, who'd been burned by it, copied it and tried it against St. Louis. There was a huge traffic jam in the middle, the tackle found himself staring at the center, and poor Scott Brunner wound up run-ning for his life and throwing a jump pass over everyone's head.

"The only trouble with it is we're laughing so hard while we're running it," Grimm says. "I mean I've seen the two inside linebackers run into each other. Of course I wouldn't be laughing if I bumped into Mark.

"It hasn't happened yet," he added, touching his knuckles to wood.

Watch the offensive line and you'll see who handles his man alone, or who needs help. If it's a tackle you're watching, and the tight end or the second ("motion") tight end is always hanging around to chop away at his man and give him help, then you've learned one of two things: either the tackle is weak or the end he's facing is deemed uncontrollable by one man alone. So that should give you a picture of how highly regarded that tackle is—or the defensive end.

Watch the center, if you can pick him out in the middle of The Pit. The good ones, such as the Steelers' Mike Webster or the Dolphins' Dwight Stephenson, will wind up going head-to-head on the nose guard, without any help. Most of the others will get assistance from a guard or two. Obviously, if a center works the nose man alone for an afternoon, his guards will be freed up for other duties—such as blocking the inside linebackers or blitz pickup—and the offense will be a lot healthier.

Right now we're in the Golden Age of NFL centers. They've never been better, because the nose guards across from them have become so good. Practically every team has a good center, a man capable of making All-Pro in the old days. The list is endless—Stephenson, Webster, Joe Fields of the Jets, Jeff Bostic of the Redskins, Jeff Van Note of the Falcons, Pete Brock of the Raiders, the Browns' Mike Baab, the Chargers' Don Macek, the Packers' Larry McCarren, the Broncos' Billy Bryan, the Seahawks' Blair Bush . . . and I'm probably leaving off four or five.

Once upon a time it was the hideout position on the offensive line—"A place where you hide a weak brother," the Chargers' All-Pro tackle Ron Mix used to say. "A racket."

"Yeah, I've heard that theory," said Jim Otto, who made All-AFL and then All-Pro for the Raiders for a dozen years. "If it's so easy, how come nobody wants to play there?"

The Raiders keyed their defensive operation around Cincinnati's rookie center, Dave Rimington, in their 1983 opener. They changed their base 3-4 defense to a 4-3 and put in a set of loops and stunts involving their tackles and inside linebackers, all designed to increase the firepower up the middle. The result was a comfortable win and, for the Bengals, just seven yards more than their lowest offensive output of the season.

The actual task the center performs is unnatural. He snaps the ball backward at the same time he charges forward, and the quarterback has to retreat at the same time his hands ride forward to get the ball. Centers don't tape their hands as heavily as the guards and tackles do; the tape would take away their feel of the ball. So the result is usually a set of badly mangled fingers each Sunday.

And there's always the traditional mental picture players have had about centers: poor fools who are busy snapping the ball while the sadists across the line wind up and deliver their blows to that most wonderful target of all—the helmet. In the old days, when "bird-cages" were for sissies and helmets were made of leather, and the center always had a middle guard playing directly over him, it was truly a position for martyrs.

You used to be able to tell a center by his nose. The longer he played, the less cartilage it had.

"I guess it's something you've got to get used to, like olives," the Giants' old star, Mel Hein, once said, pointing to his own flattened nose.

"I remember one day I was playing against the Bears, and their middle guard, George Musso, 270 pounds and mean as they came, kept slugging me on the helmet.

"Finally on one play I brought my fist up and got him under the chin and it dumped him on his back, but you know what, he didn't even get mad. He just said, 'Gee, I didn't think it was bothering you.'"

"When they first put in the 5-4 defense in the forties," recalled the Bears former center, Bulldog Turner, "they put the biggest, toughest guy they had right over the center, and he'd let you have it in the face as soon as you snapped the ball. Green Bay had this 290-pound guy, Ed Neal, with an arm as big as my leg and just as hard as that table.

"You didn't have a face guard then, and so Ed Neal broke my nose seven times. No—he broke my nose five times. I got it broke seven times, but five times he broke it."

But when face bars became mandatory, the battle between the center and the middle guard became more even. The head became a blocking weapon.

"Every man has a slight fear for his face," Ringo said. "God made you that way. When I first came up to the pros, a face mask was the sign of cowardice, but when it became standard equipment, you could stick your head into a block. Thank God for the face bars. I don't think I could have made it without them."

Ringo, whose specialty was cutting off the middle linebacker, would have a tough time against today's nose guards, whose styles and shapes run the entire spectrum, from the Bengals' boisterous 290-pounder, Jerry Boyarsky, to the Dolphins' lean and agile Bob Baumhower. Even when a team is in a four-man defensive line, either on passing downs or as their base defense, it's likely to line up one of the tackles over the center in the old AFL odd-front style.

Finally, there's one more job a center has to perform, and that's so difficult and so loaded with disaster potential that I can't even conceive of a man doing it and retaining his sanity—the long snap, on punts and placekicks. Some teams keep a specialist on the roster for that purpose alone, freeing the regular center from a job that can age him before his time. The long snapper is under a double strain here, because he must devote his full concentration to making his pass absolutely accurate, and at the same time getting the ball back as swifly as he can. (Watch the field goal or punting drill in practice and you'll usually see a coach measuring every tenth of a second with a stopwatch.) A mistake here is dramatic; the result can be the instant loss of points. And in back of the center's mind is the knowledge that for one long moment his head is unguarded, an inviting target for a fist or a forearm, anything that will shake his concentration, along with other things.

"It's a right awful feeling," said former St. Louis center Tom Goode. "It's like trying to sink a putt for a $50,000 championship in golf and not even being able to see the hole.

"It's like there are only two people in the world, you and that guy who has to get the ball. You have to put the ball right on the button for him, and you'd better get your head up in time or you're liable to catch a killin' lick."

The Raiders' Otto preferred to handle the long-snapping chores himself. It was a point of honor. He took pride in his art, and had his own theory about the raps in the head a center has to take.

"It sounds funny, but I firmly believe that your head gets in shape like any other part of your body," he said one year toward the end of his career. "Early in training camp I always get headaches after practice. My head isn't in shape yet. But later on in the season it's not so bad. I wonder if you can toughen and condition the material around your brain? Anyway, the headaches always go away after a few beers."

For the guards, the world is constant movement. The days when a man could just gear himself for the battle against the tackle opposite him have become more complicated, and now a guard never knows what he'll have to face—a tackle, an end looping over on a stunt, an inside linebacker in a base 3-4 defense, maybe two of them if they're loading up for a particular stunt, or possibly even a safetyman, cheating up for a blitz.

His basic assignments used to be fourfold: on the run straight ahead, dig out the man across from him and drive-block; be able to do a short pull and execute the trap block; get out of his stance in a hurry and get outside on a sweep or screen pass; and hold his position and nullify the rusher on pass blocks. But since he's playing in space so much now—playing against the "bubble," or the open area in front of the linebackers—he must be a mover and a thinker. He must be able to react to switches and execute a whole number of nifty-footed nuances—"scoops" and "shovels" and "do-dad" blocks, all of which involve agility. He might spend almost a whole day using cross blocks and short traps, with very few straight-ahead shots. He must be able to think on the move, and he has to be sturdy enough to handle one of the monster defensive tackles on a head butt or straight-ahead bull rush. Some teams prefer their guards tall, 6'4" or 6'5", able to fight the leverage of a tall opponent; other teams, like the Steelers, who run a trap-block offense, like them quick and smart and don't care much about their height. But one thing every scout looks for in a guard—or in any offensive lineman—is quick feet.

"I'm not a great fan of the Cowboys," says John Wilbur, who played guard for them, and a few other clubs, "but they did straighten out my game for me. After my first year with them they said I'd never make it if I didn't work on my agility, if my feet weren't quicker, and they gave me an off-season program that concentrated on racquetball and stuff involving getting up on my toes and moving my feet. It was the best thing that ever happened to me."

In every team's defensive game plan there's a short critique of the players on the enemy offense. In evaluating the linemen, special attention is paid to a man's balance, the way he sets up, how he comes out of his stance, and if he favors one particular side and move. The defense hones in and then attacks it. A small technical weakness could become a disaster.

A veteran defensive lineman has his own scouting report, though, and often it helps him as much as the technical stuff—I'm speaking of a knowledge of the personality of the guy across from him. If a guard is young and aggressive, a fire-eater, a man prone to fly off the handle, he'll get needled, and the skill that suffers will be his pass blocking.

"On pass blocking, you've got to be patient and you've got to let the man come to you," says ex-Jet Sam DeLuca, who played seven years in the AFL.

"You've got to resign yourself to the fact that you're going to take punishment from those big tackles. If he wants to stand there and slug, it's OK, because he's not rushing the passer while he's doing it. A younger player has trouble understanding this, and he'll get impatient and fire out and pop his man. That might work for a while, but when he does get beaten, he gets beaten quickly, and that's the worst thing that can happen to an offensive guard, because the pressure on the quarterback will come up the middle."

DeLuca's teammate Dave Herman was one of the few guards who could control the Steelers' Joe Greene when he was in his prime. Their temperaments seemed geared for a standoff—both highly strung, emotional players, both battlers. As with fighters, it's often a matter of comparative styles. A man will always seem to do well against a certain opponent, but a lesser opponent will always seem to have his number. Herman, for instance, never had an easy day against the Patriots' Earthquake Hunt, whose game was built on quickness and finesse, and he had nightmares about the Bengals' Mike Reid, a flash of lightning on the inside.

"I've had games against him," Herman says, "when I can swear I never touched him once."

The new blocking rules, though, by liberalizing the use of extended arms, have nullified a lot of the great one-on-one battles, and to survive today a guard first has to figure which of the various stunts and tricks are coming his way. And then he has to react to them.

A tackle must also be a thinking man, but often a mass of deficiencies can be covered by one attribute—a good pair of arms. When Woody Hayes was building his Ohio State offense around tackles who could come off the ball in perfect form and drive-block their man low and hard, when Pappy Waldorf was building dynasties at

Cal around tackles who could "move the pile," as he'd say, they never thought the game would come to this, but it has. Offensive tackle versus defensive end has turned into a shover's game. The 1978 rule changes allow the offensive linemen to extend their arms and use their hands. Man beats you off the ball and takes a wide rush? No problem. Give him a shove and send him into right field. Man beats you inside? Push him into the pile. Time to block for a run? Stay up high and shove. Pulling out to lead a sweep? Why throw your body and get all dirty when you can shove 'em out of the way? It's ugly football; high school coaches cover their linemen's eyes so they won't have to watch it, but it's what the rules have created. A tackle still has to have quick feet, to position himself for the push-off, and he has to recognize and react to the most dangerous trap he can fall into—getting so securely pinned inside by a defensive end that he's late in making the switch and getting out on the defensive tackle stunting around him. But a set of arms with the necessary length and strength can blast him out of trouble.

The Browns love offensive linemen with long arms. Their style is to get two fists to the throat and clamp.

"It's effective and frustrating as hell," Raider defensive end Howie Long says. "Cody Risien of the Browns is the best at it. Once he gets those hands in there, all your rip-ups and maneuvers are useless because his arms are so long. It's a race to see who can get his hands up first."

Once upon a time Ohio State was the breeding ground for NFL tackles. It seemed that every year one or two of them would go in the first round of the draft. Then USC took over, with the big fulcrums in the power sweeps of John McKay and John Robinson. Now Pitt is Offensive Tackle U, with Mark May, Jimbo Covert, and this year's edition, Bill Fralic, all drafted in the first round. The reason is that they teach the pro style there—get those arms up and sock it to 'em.

Traditionalists in the game, who remember some of the formful, drive-blocking tackles of yesteryear, still feel that the key to a sensible running game is a tackle tandem that can move the pile.

"If you want to start building a team, start with a pair of pillars at the tackles," Gregg says. "You say, which way do you want to run? Doesn't make a difference; either way won't be wrong." '

Conversely, the erosion of a team's offense often can start with a slow leak at the tackles. It wasn't only the loss of tailback Freeman McNeil that crippled the Jets in 1983. The club suffered from a great loss of efficiency in Marvin Powell and Chris Ward, a pair of tackles that once had been the stabilizing force in a fine offensive line. Powell's decline was the most apparent and most shocking; his strength and balance seemed to go all at once, and Richard Todd, once able to operate secure in the knowledge that his protective pocket wouldn't break down around the edges, became unhinged under steady pressure from the outside. He hadn't been used to it. The fact that Powell was voted to the 1984 Pro Bowl is the ultimate mockery in a system that bases its awards more on memory than merit.

In his younger days Powell was one of the league's prettiest drive-blocking tackles, able to get off the ball in a low dip charge and lift his man and drive him. Here and there you find a few others who have the old skills—Mike Kenn, Anthony Munoz, Joe Jacoby (although he does it more on brute power than on form). Tackles are called on to do more trapping than they used to, a salute to agility rather than technique, and quick-footed tackles are still highly prized in the draft. Power and strength and muscle mass can be added; the weight room, plus anabolic steroids (widely used, seldom discussed), will take care of that; but quick feet are God-given, according to some coaches.

Others feel they can be developed. In 1982 Redskins line coach Joe Bugel put the 6'7", 298-pound Jacoby on a program of rope jumping, plus the speed bag. "Fast hands, fast feet to survive," Bugel would say.

"They also had a thing called the Dot Drill," Jacoby says. "Five dots on the floor, 18 inches apart. You had to keep switching your feet to hit the right dots."

In the old days there were only two types of tackles. Trim 245- to 250-pounders such as Gregg and Mix based their game on speed, moves and technique. At the other end of the scale—if you could find a scale big enough—were the mountains, the massive tackles who used the body as a great wall between the defensive end and the passer. The epitome of this breed was the Jets' 330-pound Sherman Plunkett.

Sherm never lifted weights and seldom watched his own. God had blessed him with an unusually quick pair of feet, and he used them to keep his ample body constantly positioned in front of his man. He was effective enough to make the All-League team one year, and there is a memorable film clip of the 1967 AFL All-Star Game, in which the West's coach, Hank Stram, watches Plunkett and sighs to one of his defensive linemen, "Getting past him is like taking a trip around the world."

"In pro football," Mix used to say, "if you're a tackle who can protect the passer—you can't do anything else but protect the passer—you can make the team. You may even make the All-Star team.

"You can be worthless as far as the rest of the game is concerned. Your downfield blocking can be nonexistent. Your blocking at the point of attack can be below average. But if you can pass-protect, you are considered an excellent football player, not only by your contemporaries, but by the fans."

In Plunkett's prime, there were few tackles better at maintaining the vacuum inside, which is the key to the passer's protective pocket, or cup. An inside rush against Plunkett was almost useless, since he could lean on a man and cave him into the logjam in the middle of the line. Plunkett knew how to practice the subtle arts, too. His hands and arms were always busy, always flirting with a 15-yard holding penalty. A quick push with both hands, a quick grab of the jersey; he knew all the tricks. But his best technique was a short, jolting punch to the midsection, not enough to cause any real injury, but sufficiently distracting to destroy timing. It used to be fun watching someone play against Big Sherm for the first time, to see the look of shock and amazement when he tasted that first solar plexus blow. It was as if a great canvas dummy had suddenly struck back, or the faithful family Labrador retriever had suddenly turned and inflicted upon its owner a deep, painful bite.

When the end came for one of the big fellows, it came suddenly and without warning. During the 1967 season Plunkett started losing his quickness afoot—and this was coming off an All-Pro year in 1966. The word went out to the defensive ends, via movie projector, that Plunkett could be beaten to the outside.

Moves were laid aside, and every battle became a footrace to the outside between the defensive end and Sherm, a race Sherman wound up losing too often.

"Twisting him was like twisting a building," said Kansas City left defensive end Jerry Mays. "But his legs eventually went on him. Legs are so important. Even if you're properly conditioned, you usually can't get anywhere against a blocker for three quarters. Then his legs tire and he can be had."

It's not very often that you see a tackle beaten to the outside these days. The push-off is too convenient a weapon. Usually, if he loses the battle it will be a stunt or a technique that did it. And if you have a tackle who's a weak pass-protector, then you've got a real problem with your offense, because most of his help will have to come from the tight end or the motion tight end, thereby removing one receiver from your patterns. And unlike the guard, who has a smaller, more heavily trafficked area in which to operate, the tackle is often alone on his man on the outside—"on an island," the coaches say.

The old offensive tackle two-class society, the monsters and athletes, has broken down because weights and steroids have created a new set of dimensions . . . "Rubber-stamped 6′6″, 280-pounders," the Rams' defensive end Jack Youngblood says. A 245- or 250-pounder in the old days would weigh 270 or so now. In 1983 the average size of the 56 NFL tackles who started most of the way was 6′5¼″, 271. Only four of them were shorter than 6′4″ (all at 6′3″), and only seven weighed less than 260—the lightest being the Browns' 6′5″, 252-pound Doug Dieken, who is blessed with long enough arms to keep the uppercuts and elbows away from his rather skinny physique. He's a good strangler.

I don't know when coaches first started teaching the use of hands in pass blocking. I know Chuck Knox taught it to his offensive linemen on the Jets in the early sixties, and veterans such as DeLuca would shake their heads in admiration and say, "The man's 10 years ahead of his time. He's going to be a great head coach some day." While Jet players such as Winston Hill, a marvelously agile and graceful 270-pounder, were positioning the opposition with their hands, and then steering them where they wanted them to go, the Giants across town were still using the old techniques of the 1940s— fists in tight to the chest, elbows out; wingless birds.

There really hasn't been much of a study done on pass blocking. I recently looked at my first primer on the game, Bernie Bierman's *Winning Football,* published in 1937. In his section on blocking ("close line blocking" he called it) there were intricate instructions on how to execute the crab block and tie-up block, the body and reverse body blocks. But pass blocking? Nothing. Zip. Not a word. It was just something that was supposed to come naturally, I guess, like coughing.

My high school coach was Charley Avedisian, who had been a starting guard for the wartime Giants, playing between Mel Hein and Al Blozis. "Pass blocking," he'd tell us, "is like two guys trying to go through a door, walking toward each other. One guy steps one way, the other guy steps in front of him, he goes the other way, he steps in front of him again." He let us work out the details of stopping that other guy ourselves.

I used to enjoy watching the Cleveland Browns when I was in high school. Pro football was a passing game, especially in the old AAFC, and Otto Graham was one of the best. I remember a story I once read, that every time the Browns broke the offensive huddle their linemen would chant, "Nobody touches Graham." So I would watch that line for a while, and it was pretty boring. They'd form a semicircle, a kind of cup, and nothing would happen. Nobody would get through.

The line coach was Weeb Ewbank. He seemed to make a habit of being around great quarterbacks—John Unitas at Baltimore, Joe Namath with the Jets—and great quarterbacks needed protection. Passive pass blocking was the best way. Step back and absorb the blow, dance with them, steer them with your hands, Ewbank and his line coach, Knox, would say, but don't commit yourself too early. Don't get beaten quickly. Offensive line became a position for masochists, placid temperaments and, often, strange shapes.

I remember when I covered the Jets in the sixties I used to like to watch the offensive linemen go through their drills in camp. One year they drafted a pair of guards, Gene Bledsoe from Texas and Randy Rasmussen from Kearney State in Nebraska. Bledsoe, nicknamed The Blade, was a tightly wired 240-pounder. He'd hit the dummies and they'd pop. Rasmussen was a sleepy-looking 255-pounder, heavy-legged, bottom-heavy, built like a night watchman. He'd been a math major in college.

"Which one's the player?" Weeb asked me once.

"Bledsoe," I said. He shook his head.

"Rasmussen," he said. I thought he was nuts. Rasmussen became a 15-year starter for the Jets. Bledshoe never made it through camp.

Brains, quick feet, techniques, plus the ability and desire to absorb an inordinate amount of punishment without flinching—those were the attributes of the pass blockers. The Jets used their hands. Around the league they were known as holders, but they got the job done. They escorted the practically immobile and stiff-kneed Joe Namath into the Super Bowl. The Raiders were early masters of the push-off technique. They made it to the Super Bowl in '67.

You had to know the tricks to get the job done. Pass rushers were getting swifter, and nimbler, but there were still enough of the old head-bangers around to remind people of the way it used to be. John Schmitt, Namath's center on the Jets, has special memories of Ray Jacobs, a 6′3″, 285-pound defensive tackle from Texas, who drifted around the AFL for a while, finally settling with the Boston Patriots as a reserve.

"Everything was going OK, it was a nice sensible game," Schmitt said after one Jets-Patriots game in Shea Stadium. "Then they called time out and I saw Number 87 coming onto the field, and I said, 'Boys, fasten your chin straps, here comes the head crusher.' He had got that forearm shot to your left ear down pat, and about the sixth time he hit me, I didn't see the huddle anymore.

"I told the ref, 'Watch him, he's winding up. You're not allowed to wind up on a blow.' The ref kind of looked at me like he felt sorry."

"Jacobs," said Dave Herman, "caused a lot of offensive linemen to celebrate when he retired. One year, when he was playing in Miami, Jeff Richardson was in at center for us. Jeff came back to the huddle, tugging at his helmet. It was twisted all the way around and he was looked out of the ear hole.

" 'I didn't know Jacobs was in the game,' I said to him.

" 'Yeah, he just came in,' he said."

I remember once asking Herman how his wife enjoyed coming to the games.

"All she looks for," he said, "is to see whether I get up or not."

The thrill of letting one's body go wild in a sudden mad urge of abandon—the wild rush of the blitzing linebacker, the ferocious bull-elephant charge of the defensive tackle—they're all practically unknown to the offensive lineman. Even on his open-field work, when he pulls out and leads a ballcarrier downfield, he must be in control, always in control. But there are moments for revenge.

"This is football, this is what football should really be like," Rasmussen said one year, after the Jets used 43 running plays and only 21 passes to defeat the Patriots.

"Four yards and a cloud of dust. Vince Lombardi football. God, I love it. Now I know why the Packers loved to play this game so much."

They have their own terminology; they speak a strange language, these offensive linemen, and old-timers who practiced the crab and reverse body blocks would look at them blankly if they heard them talking about "scoops" and "shovels" and "hoes," which are offensive line stunts to combat the trickery of the defense. Some terms are pretty much universal throughout the league. For instance, on a scoop block a guard releases inside one man and then cuts off the man on his outside, while the tackle next to him cuts off the man playing on the guard. A shovel is a maneuver against a 3-4 defense; the tackle blocks the inside linebacker and the guard comes around and blocks the end in. On a hoe, the tackle blocks the linebacker out and the guard blocks the end out. An area block is the same as a zone block, in which the lineman takes whoever is in his area, instead of going for one particular man; it's the technique to counteract defensive stunts. A do-dad is an area block against a stack—a linebacker positioned, or "stacked," directly behind his lineman. A peel block involves coming around from the blind side and peeling back on the target, a sprint block is a tackle pulling out, an "easy" involves a tight end releasing on the side where the run is going and blocking the safety or cornerback. And so on, and so on.

Often linemen have their own trademarks, their own particular techniques. Before the Browns played New England in Foxboro in 1983, Cleveland's nose guard, Bob Golic, who used to be a Patriot, was briefing defensive end Elvis Franks about John Hannah.

"Watch out for his turtle block," Golic said.

"His what?"

"Turtle block. He'll pull his head down into his pads, like a turtle, so only his eyebrows are showing. Then when he's blocking he'll pop his head out into you. It's effective."

Some take great pride in one special skill. With Cleveland's right guard, Joe DeLamielleure, it's the trap block. In 1981 his trap blocks put three 49er defensive ends out of action in one game. He got them all with the hat, the helmet. Fred Dean went down with a bruised sternum and esophagus. "My pads slipped up," he said. "It felt like an iron ball hit me in the chest." Larry Pillers got a cracked rib, Dwayne Board a shoulder injury. On Monday after the game, San Francisco guard Randy Cross passed the three of them lined up outside the trainer's room.

"Old Joe D can still trap, can't he?" he said.

Some coaches teach a cut-blocking technique, used mostly by tight ends blocking down on defensive ends, as a way of controlling pass rushers who are on a roll, chopping down on the outside of their knees. The bigger tight ends, such as the 49ers' 6'6", 242-pound Russ Francis, feel it's a point of honor not to indulge in that technique, no matter what the coaches tell them. Besides, all sorts of strange things can happen to you once you hit the dirt. When Tommy Hart, the great pass rusher, became an assistant coach with the 49ers last year he sought Francis out.

"He told me, 'You're one of the few guys who never cut-blocked me,' and he thanked me for it," Francis said. "I just didn't believe in it. When I was with the Patriots they used to get on me all the time . . . 'Why didn't you cut him, like we told you to?' I'd say, 'Hey, did the man make the tackle?' "

Sometimes the terrain has something to do with it. Last year I asked Patriots' inside linebacker Steve Nelson if he'd watched Dwight Stephenson much that season and if he's noticed anything different.

"Yeah, he won't cut-block on artificial turf this year," Nelson said. "Last year he would. Not many guys like to cut you on artificial turf. On grass you hit the ground and bounce, on artificial you slide—and you get burns."

San Francisco coach Bill Walsh foresees a day when specialization will become so complete that even the offensive line will indulge in situation substitutions. "One right guard for running plays, another for passing," he says. I saw a hint of it with the Redskins in '82. When they hit the second round of the playoffs they had one starting right guard for 4-3 defenses, Mark May, a bonafide Hog at 288 pounds, and another, lighter one (255), Fred Dean, for the 3-4's. The theory was that May was better equipped to handle a tackle playing him head-up, while the more mobile Dean was better suited to attack the bubble. Dean was the 1983 Super Bowl starter against the 3-4 Dolphins, but during the 1983 season May went full time.

Size seems to be taking over now. Weight training has produced offensive lines at Washington and New England that average close to 280 . . . weight training and, of course, steroids. No one will ever convince me that pumping iron alone will add 30 pounds over the course of a year, but very few players will ever admit that they're on steroids, which can do infinite harm over the long run. Only one ever told me he was taking them, and that was off the record.

The Patriots are hipped on heavy weight training, on the development of great bulk. "I want our line to be like a massive, unstoppable force," coach Ron Meyer says, but not all his players agree—particularly Hannah, who seldom agrees with coaches about anything.

"You can get carried away by that weight training stuff," Hannah said last year. "I really think you don't need 450- to 500-pound bench-press strength . . . 350 is enough as long as you've got agility and quick feet. They wanted me to play at 285 this season. Actually I lost weight, down to 265, and I feel better."

Even Tom Landry, who deplores the new pass-blocking rules and the push-pull nature of the game, has made concessions. In 1982 the first offensive lineman the Cowboys drafted was 6'9" Phil Pozderac of Notre Dame. The next season the first two were 6'8" Chris Schulz of Arizona and 6'6", 284-pound Eric Moran of Washington.

"There's a movement in the league now for size because of the holding rule," Landry said. "With a little more pull and a lot more pushing, a bigger guy is going to be able to take advantage of the rules. Some of these linemen are just massive, though. They're mountain men."

On the other side of the issue is Chuck Noll at Pittsburgh. Maybe it's because the Steeler offense is based on movement and trap-blocking along the line, maybe it's because he was a small, smart lineman himself when he played for the Browns, but his style seems to be linemen created in his own image. Last year the Steelers had the most banged-up offensive line in football, but people such as 6'1" Emil Boures and 6'3" Tunch Ilkin and 6'2" Rick Donnalley came off the bench and filled in where needed, often switching positions from week to week. The Steelers finished at 10–6 and made the playoffs, and for most of the year they had an offensive line that averaged 6'2" in height, in an era of 6'5" lines.

"All those years he used to get on the scouts," Pittsburgh's director of scouting, Art Rooney, Jr., said. "All those years he'd say, 'I don't want any dumbbells. I want guys who can think and play more than one position.' Well, it's finally paying off. Look at all the great linemen we've had who could play two or more positions . . . Jim Clack was a guard and center, Gerry Mullens was a guard, tackle and tight end, Mike Webster was a guard and center when he came up, Larry Brown was a tight end, now a tackle.

"I remember sitting in here, in this scouting room, at a meeting, and our assistant coaches would say, 'I want big, strong, mean guys,' and I'd ask Noll, 'Have you changed?' And he'd say, 'No, I want guys who are fast, who can think on their feet . . . I don't care if they're 6'1" or 6'0".' "

"We're looking for guys who can play," Noll says. "We're looking for speed, strength, intelligence and a lot of adjustments. Leverage is so much. I've seen a lot of big guys who can't get down and tuck. It's always a struggle, getting the big guys to break down."

The Steelers have also been a good pass-blocking team through the years, but statistically the best over the last half-dozen seasons has been San Diego, with an offensive line that averaged 272, tackle to tackle, in 1983. Since Don Coryell took over as coach in 1978 the Chargers have allowed only 4.79 sacks per 100 passes thrown, with Buffalo the runner-up, at 5.94. Some of it is the system—many of Dan Fouts's patterns are quickies, off a three-step drop—and some of it may be Fouts himself, his ability to unload in a hurry. But in 1983, with Ed Luther playing most of the way at quarterback, the Chargers led the league again, with a 4.41 sack ratio. The linemen are smart, they adjust well. In 37-year-old Ed White and 37-year-old Doug Wilkerson they have one of the finest guard tandems ever to play the game, and Don Macek, their 30-year-old center, is one of the league's most underrated pivot men.

A couple of years ago Fouts and his linemen were honored at a postseason dinner. When it was Fouts's turn to speak, he moved and stood behind the linemen, who were seated according to the way they lined up on the field.

"I feel more comfortable behind my guys," Fouts said.

When historians look back on this era, though, they will probably point to the offensive line and see a decline in skills, a reliance on the new pass-block rules to help them win what was becoming a losing battle.

"All you have now is pushing and shoving and holding," Weeb Ewbank said from his home in Oxford, Ohio. "It reminds me of intramural football years ago."

"It's not football anymore," 49er linebacker Jack Reynolds says. "They tackle you, they throw their arms out, the game has been ruined for the sake of passing. All the rules are on their side. It's like Great Britain against Argentina."

"When we had the head slap," says Viking nose guard Charlie Johnson, "that's when they had some real football. Blood and stuff trickling down your legs. You don't hardly see no snaggle-toothed linemen anymore. Everything's changed. All of 'em got teeth."

From his broadcast booth at NBC, Merlin Olsen, perhaps the finest defensive tackle ever to play the game, looks at the NFL sadly.

"I'd have a lot of trouble playing the game under today's rules," he says. "My whole thrust was to try to make some initial contact with the offensive lineman, but now he'll grab you and you'll never get away. Nowadays the whole idea is to avoid contact. You need stunts and tricks and designated pass-rushers. The new rules have destroyed one of the finest parts of the game, the integrity of one-on-one battles on the line. You don't get that anymore. It's a wrestling match now, a joke. If you went back to the rules of seven or eight years ago, very few offensive linemen today could play the game. You can get any big, strong guy off the street and teach him to pass-block.

"I'm sad. They've taken an art form and destroyed it. Some people are very Machiavellian. They look at the scoreboard, they look at the dollar sign. Does that mean happiness?"

Offensive linemen have heard this complaint since 1978. They have their own answers.

"Let's face it, the pass rushers were getting to be just too good athletes," says Dave Lapham, who played left guard for the Bengals for 10 years before migrating to the USFL in 1984.

"Guys are coming up now who are 6'5", 270, and they can run a 4.7 forty. My clocking's on the sundial somewhere. They could just rush the passer at will if we couldn't extend our hands and lock our elbows.

"Besides, they have all the momentum. We're going backward, retreating, giving ground—grudgingly. They're going forward. You've got to have something to equalize that.

"What these rules have done is to take a lot of pressure off the umpire, who has to call most of the holding. A lot of it was going on before, anyway. Personally, I might grab a little cloth every now and then; it can't be helped, but I try to let it go.

"I've heard complaints about us clamping down on guys' arms, but say you extend your arms and the defensive lineman throws an uppercut to get your arms off him. Well, then the blocker is allowed to clamp down on the defensive guy's arms. It's strength versus strength, and it really bothers defensive linemen a lot, but as long as you don't take 'em down it's OK—I mean you can't use a sumo-wrestler move where both of you hit the dirt.

"But don't think that the defensive guys don't get away with a lot of stuff, too. On end-tackle games or tackle-tackle games, where one defensive lineman penetrates into the gap and the other one loops around him, well, often the first guy will just reach in and grab enough cloth to nullify both the guard and center. That'll free his partner, the looper. It should be a five-yard penalty for defensive holding, but I've never seen it called.

"The old Baltimore Sack Pack team was great at it. The Steelers were real good at it, too. Joe Greene was great at grabbing and consuming two guys. Teams that use zone blocking, as we do, are hurt most by this. When you're blocking man-to-man you just follow your man when he loops, but a zone- or area-blocking team is shafted.

"One thing that saddened me, though, was when they outlawed the head slap. An offensive lineman paid his dues with the bell ringers. Some of those head slappers just wanted to stand there and beat you up; they forgot about rushing the passer. It wasn't the bell ringers and bull rushers that gave me problems; it was the guys who combined speed with strength.

"But you still see head slaps. A lot of guys use the shoulder slap now, and that can be almost as effective in stunning you and getting your body weight moving one way. But sometimes they'll miss the shoulder and get your head. They'll say, 'Sorry, I was aiming for your shoulder,' but in the meantime you're getting a long-distance phone call and there's nobody home to answer it."

When Frank Kush came into the NFL in 1982 after a year in Canada and more than two decades at Arizona State, he looked at the offensive linemen and what he saw shocked him.

"The first thing I noticed," he said, "was that the poor backs were getting killed. The linemen just use too many finesse techniques, not enough root-'em-out. They can't bend their knees. The worst thing pro football did for the offensive linemen was to let 'em use their hands so much. It erodes their run-blocking skills. If you're a big belly-bumper, 290 pounds, you can get by pushing people out of there. Everything's a pushing contest.

"It's happening in college, too. A lot of linemen are coming into pro ball now with very little conception of what the shoulder block is all about. I have to teach them all over again. They're so used to using their hands and pass blocking that they've forgotten almost all their drive-blocking skills. That's why you see so many teams having trouble getting it in on goal-line and short-yardage situations, tackle to tackle. It's a pushing contest.

"Of course it goes both ways, and you see defensive linemen who don't want to work at stopping the run, either. You have to tell them, 'Left foot here, right foot there, fight the pressure.' It's like a return to high school."

Watch the replays on television and you'll hear, "Great block on this run . . . I hope the camera caught it . . . yep, there it is." And when you look for that great block you'll see one guy shove another one out of the way, and you'll wonder if the announcers are watching the same game you are. I'll see a tackle, a great big imposing fellow who fills out a uniform nicely, pull out to lead a toss play, but when it comes time to commit himself, he'll wave at his man, or maybe stick one hand out for a shove—while on TV you hear, "So and so's out there leading the play in fine style."

"We have an expression for that," says Miami's pro personnel director, Charley Winner. "We say, 'Give him the ball.' He should be carrying it."

"The art of run blocking is one of the most underrated skills there is," says Mike Giddings, director of Pro Sports, Inc., a scouting service for eight NFL teams, and himself an old Cal guard. "Unfortunately it seems to be a dying art. Watching a Hannah or a Wilkerson come off the ball . . . that excites me as a movie grader. It's a thing of beauty . . . dip the shoulder, turn up, ride the linebacker, hook block, with their feet perfect. I love that."

Maybe we'll see more of it. There's a new wave of college coaches in the NFL, men who had powerful running games in school—Kush, Meyer, Robinson. They seem to want to get back to old drive-blocking principles.

"We teach a power-block system, as opposed to trapping, shielding or misdirection," Robinson says. "When you have a quick, darting type of guy, you can block sideways and just open a little crease, but we bring our back, Eric Dickerson, in more slowly, so our linemen have to hold their blocks longer. We want them to knock people back.

"The Raiders are like that, too, with Marcus Allen. It's a Raider tradition. For years John Madden refused to run a trap block, for psychological reasons. Power blocking takes stubbornness. You have to have a stubborn, Lombardi mentality. By God we'll make this go.

"I like that power mentality . . . if you're not ready for a fight, don't show up. If you can't stop it, you're going to see nothing but. The Raiders always talked about their long passing, but if they had a lead late in the game they could pound you. You'd never get the ball back."

Sometimes the linemen change on their own and start reviving old techniques. In a world in which everyone was packing on mass and weight Mike Webster decided to shed some poundage last year. He said that in camp he went back to old techniques, coming off the ball lower, lifting and driving, instead of staying high and wrestling, as he did in '82. The result was perhaps the finest season an NFL center ever had. I watched one Steeler game on TV in which he kept blocking his man entirely off the screen, out of the picture—literally.

The 49ers went from 28th in the NFL in running in '82 to 8th in '83. The addition of Roger Craig and Wendell Tyler was crucial, naturally, but the linemen had a lot to do with it.

"When Wendell joined us we became more concerned about run blocking," right tackle Keith Fahnhorst said. "I've got to admit, going into training camp, well, it was the first time I'd worked on the run in a long time. I used to figure that if I didn't get beat on pass protection I'd be here forever, but when a good runner comes you know you've got to work on blocking for him. You know damn well that if a running back like that isn't making his yardage it's not his fault."

Merlin Olsen says the integrity of the old one-on-one battles has been lost, but even with the grabbing and shoving, a lineman still tunes in to the man in front of him, and there have been some classic confrontations. I always used to enjoy watching the Eagles' left tackle, Stan Walters, play his precise, unemotional game against the Redskins' Coy Bacon, whose style often bordered on the maniacal.

"A hot dog, a nut," Walters used to say. "With a hot dog like that you have to be very careful about letting him get an early sack or he'll become damn near uncontrollable. He screams, yells, talks gibberish. Half the time you can't even understand what he's saying. He's the only one of them who ever got to me on a personal level. Nuts. One day we were killing them, and at the end of the game he's still ranting and raving . . . 'You ain't crap, you ain't nothing!' . . . that kind of stuff. Finally I said, 'Hey fern brain, look at the scoreboard.' "

Some are talkative, some never say a word.

"What's there to talk about?" the Jets' All-AFL defensive end Gerry Philbin used to say. "You do your job, he does his."

I asked him if he'd ever said anything to an opponent on the field.

"Just once," he said. "The week after we won the Super Bowl, I played in the AFL All-Star Game in Jacksonville. I played against Ron Mix, who always gave me more trouble than any tackle in the game. On one pass play he caught me just right and knocked me on my back. I mean it was a helluva shot. I got up and as I was walking back he said, 'Gerry, that was a great Super Bowl,' and I said, 'Thanks.' I think that's the only time I ever talked to a guy. But you'll notice that he did his job first, before he said anything."

The Redskins' old center, Len Hauss, figured that, counting college games, he must have played against the Cowboys' middle linebacker, Lee Roy Jordan, 30 times. "Over all those years the words between us were full of animosity," he says.

"But toward the end of his career he actually said something nice to me, and that's when I knew he was getting old. After one play he patted me on the butt and said, 'Nice block.' I said to myself, 'He's winding it up.' "

Respect across the line is a funny thing. Often it approaches awe.

"When I was growing up my favorite player was Merlin Olsen," Cross says. "In '76 I was one of the captains when we played the Rams. Merlin was one of their captains. At the coin toss the referee introduced us, 'Captain Cross, Captain Olsen,' and I said, 'Pleased to meet you, sir.' "

The day before a Dallas game in 1981 I asked Walters about the respect the two teams had, or didn't have, for each other. He looked at me as if I were crazy.

"Do you think I really care about whether they respect us or we respect them?" he said. "Do you think players really care about that stuff? I care about the guy I'm playing against, Harvey Martin, and winning the game."

"Respect," defensive end Claude Humphrey grumbled from a nearby locker. "Respect is something a father wants from his kids. I don't want their respect. I want to beat them."

EPILOGUE: In 1982 I wrote a piece in which I called John Hannah the greatest offensive lineman of all time, an explosive drive blocker, a dominating force for years. When I called people who had been around football for a while, their responses were mixed. Most of them preferred Jim Parker, who started as a tackle with the Colts, then moved to guard, earning All-Pro honors at both positions for eight years. I polled 25 NFL old-timers and asked them to name their candidates for "best ever" offensive linemen, and these are the ones that kept coming up, the products of serious reflection as well as fleeting memories—a perfect afternoon, a great year or two. Many fine players may have been omitted simply because the experts momentarily forgot them. The players are listed in no special order.

Jim Parker. Ran a 4.9 as a 264-pounder right out of college, weighed as much as 285 during his NFL career and ran a 5.1–5.3 at that weight. The best pure pass blocker who ever lived. Knew all the tricks—the quick push-off, the short jab—that are legal now. Says that watching the techniques of today's linemen "gives me a terrible headache."

Bucko Kilroy's Monsters of the Midway. Kilroy broke in as a tackle and guard with the 1943 Steagles, the Philadelphia-Pittsburg merger, and played for the Eagles until 1955, when he retired to become one of the league's first player personnel men. He says the Bears were the one team everyone measured himself against in the 1940s. "I lined up against *Bronko Nagurski* in my fourth game as a pro. He'd been out of football for five years, but the Bears brought him back, as a tackle, during the war. I stared at him like he was Jim Thorpe. What kind of a player was Nagurski? Strong. Not much finesse but you couldn't muscle him. He grabbed a little. The Bears were always great for that. *George Musso*, the guard, was the guy you had to watch out for. He was one of the real early speed-and-size guys, 260 and fast—and mean. That's putting it nicely. The game was mayhem then, and the Bears weren't called the Monsters for nothing. *Joe Stydahar* was past his prime when I played against him. So was *Danny Fortmann.* He was just a little man, a technique guy, cross blocks, body blocks, like that. *Lee Artoe* and *Chuck Drulis* were guys who could wire you real good—block you and stick to you. I thought *Ed Kolman*, the tackle, had the most technique. *Bulldog Turner* was a bull, a great strength guy, but *Mel Hein* of the Giants was more skillful."

Fritzie Heisler's Finest Five. Heisler was the Cleveland Browns' line coach for 24 years, through the entire Paul Brown and Blanton Collier eras. The All-America Conference Browns of the 1940s represented one of the first teams to specialize in pass blocking: "*Mike McCormack* and *Lou Rymkus* at the tackles. *Gene Hickerson* and *Abe Gibron* at the guards, *Frank Gatski* at center. *Lou Groza, John*

Wooten and *Jim Ray Smith* just a shade behind." *McCormack* is Paul Brown's choice as the best he ever coached. Consistently handled the Colts' Gino Marchetti better than any tackle in the game. Power combined with great intelligence and 4.8 speed. "I've seen him have games," Kilroy says, "where if you were grading him he'd score 100. Not one mistake, and his guy would never make a tackle." *Gibron* was a mean, low-slung fire-blocker who caught them underneath and crumpled them. Huge upper body, thin legs, blazing speed. At 4.75 perhaps the fastest of any of them.

Jerry Kramer. His college coach told the scouts he'd never play at more than 225. At the College All-Star Game they weighed him in at 263, with no fat. With *Fuzzy Thurston* at Green Bay he formed one of the finest pulling-guard tandems in history, along with Wooten and Hickerson of the Browns, Bob Kuechenberg and Larry Little of the Dolphins and Joe DeLamielleure and Reggie McKenzie of the Bills. Tremendous pride and courage. A shade behind Hannah and Parker in straight-ahead firepower. Ran a 4.9.

Forrest Gregg. Vince Lombardi said he was the best player he ever coached. Master of the dance. A position blocker who made people go where he wanted them to.

Jim Ringo. Master of the cutoff block; played between eras of the nose guard.

Bob Kuechenberg. Another teeth-gritter. Tenacious. Dirt tough. Switching from guard to tackle cost him at least two years of All-Pro. Not quite the booming straight-ahead blocker that teammate *Larry Little* was.

Bob Brown. The Doug Atkins of offense for the Eagles, Rams and Raiders. Annoy him and he'd split your helmet. Only weakness was game-to-game inconsistency, but against big-league opponents he was terrifying.

Ron Mix, Jim Tyrer. The AFL's all-time tackles, with, respectively, eight and nine years of All-Pro credentials. San Diego's Mix was the pure technician, the Forrest Gregg of the AFL, a tackle who pulled to lead sweeps. Tyrer and *Ed Budde* ranked as the intimidators on an oversized and highly feared Kansas City line.

Billy Shaw. Old AFL men will tell you this Buffalo guard was as good as anyone who ever played. Great strength and savvy, a shade behind Hannah and Parker in speed.

Walt Sweeney. Played guard next to Mix on the Chargers. Oakland's Al Davis says he was the AFL's most underrated.

Stan Jones, Leo Nomellini, George Connor, Chuck Bendarik. Defensive legends for Chicago, San Francisco, Chicago and Philadelphia, respectively, who turned around and made All-Pro on offense. Jones was one of the earliest disciples of weightlifting.

Al Blozis. A relative stringbean at 6'6½" and 250 pounds who was famous for his defensive work with the Giants, but Kilroy says his real future was on offense. "He had the quickest feet I've ever seen on a guy that size." Killed in World War II. He had played pro ball three years. At Fort Benning he set an Army record by heaving a grenade 94 yards, 2 feet, 6½ inches. At one time he held the world indoor shotput record at 56 feet, 4½ inches.

Al Wistert, Vic Lindskog. 1940-era Eagles. Smaller guys, precision blockers, stars in training manuals.

Roosevelt Brown. Eight-time All-Pro tackle for the Giants. Greyhound type. Eye-catching on the sweeps or downfield. Quick rather than overpowering.

Bob St. Clair. A 6'9" 49er who was the prototype of the crusher-type tackles later personified by St. Louis's *Dan Dierdorf* and Oakland's *Art Shell*.

Dick Stanfel, Bob Reynolds. Started as big, raw-boned kids for Detroit and St. Louis, respectively, and ended as great finesse and position blockers.

Gene Upshaw. Knew tricks they hadn't even invented yet, even in Oakland.

Jim Otto. Twelve All-Pro years. Incredible iron man. Never missed a game in 15 years as Oakland center. *Mike Webster* and *Dwight Stephenson* are the best of the modern centers.

Joe Jacoby. The heir apparent. Needs to string a few All-Pro years together.

CHAPTER THREE

Quarterbacking for Fun and Profit

If you can count to 11 you'll have no trouble playing football. Count to 22 and you can play quarterback.

—Daryle Lamonica

"NEVER mind how many passes he throws and what his completion percentage looks like," my old high-school coach, Charley Avedisian, used to say. "My quarterback's got to be the guy who can take you in in the last two minutes, when it's getting dark and the fans are booing and the wind is blowing and there's so much ice on the ball he can't grip it."

Charley, who had once played guard for the old Giants, had a sense of the dramatic, and we used to chuckle at him behind his back—"Win it for the Gipper," and all that. But when you look it all over, is there anything else to being a quarterback?

Well yes, there is, of course: There's reading defenses and knowing how to decipher the defensive flimflam of the masked zones and "combinations"; and, naturally, when a guy reaches the pros he can't have a weak arm. But what it all comes down to is those last few minutes, with the fans booing and the wind blowing, etc.

Joe Namath could do it. In the Jets' Super Bowl year, Namath brought them from behind in the dying minutes of four games, including the AFL championship against Oakland. Y. A. Tittle could do it; it seems that he always could. Even in his diaper days with the Baltimore Colts of the old All-American Football Conference. He could leave you for dead in two minutes.

Bobby Layne had it, and John Unitas, and Otto Graham. And of course the Dutchman, Norm Van Brocklin; in those last two years at Philadelphia, he might have been the best of them all.

"The year we won the championship in Philly, we trailed at half-time in five games, sometimes by 24 points," Tommy McDonald says. "But each time, between halves, Van Brocklin went to the black-board, explained what the defense was doing, and we came back to win in the second half." Which makes you wonder what coach Buck Shaw was doing while Van Brocklin was chalk-talking, but that's the way it goes.

I can't comment on Sammy Baugh's style as a quarterback. I saw him through a kid's eyes, and he was merely the guy who scared you to death while he was beating your Giants. I remember him throwing bull's-eyes while he was falling all over the place, but I also remember that he could bring the team down the field in a hurry and beat you.

One of the sad things about the new rules is that they've cheapened the two-minute drive. Almost anyone can get one going nowadays. In the past, when the cornerbacks mugged the receivers downfield and defensive linemen headslapped their way to the quarterback and roughed him up and hit him late, two-minute quarterbacks were something special. So we look for consistency now, for the guy who can do it not once in a while but most of the time. We look for the quarterback who can do it in the money games, in the playoffs, the man who won't choke when things aren't going right.

Joe Theismann is Old World. "Give me 50 seconds and two time-outs and I'll put something on the board," he says. Yep, that's him all right. Cocky, brash, likes to ride in limos and wear fur coats and collect a bundle in endorsements. Not well loved by his teammates, but the Jets were divided into pro- and anti-Namath factions, too. And none of it carries over to the field.

I took a good look at him up close at the Pro Bowl workouts last season. He was coming off a downer, the Super Bowl blowout, and a whole season of triumph had been erased by the memory of that one disastrous pass at the end of the first half. But by God he had a hungry predator look to him, broken nose, wrinkles starting to show around the mouth and eyes, raw-looking bruise on the chin. I think that's the kind of face I'd like to look across the huddle and see if I were down by six in the last minute.

Roger Staubach, spanning the eras of old rules and new, had it. Sometimes I used to hear him get booed in the first quarter, when his timing wasn't down and his passes would sail, but there were very few times when he didn't perform down the stretch, when the game was on the line.

"I honestly used to feel sorry for the other team's defense sometimes," former Dallas safetyman Cliff Harris says. "You'd put yourself in their position and realize the feeling of utter helplessness. There was really nothing you could do to stop him when he was on."

"The whole idea," Tom Landry says, "is to have the poise when it's fleeing away from you."

Staubach spoiled some of the older veterans for the man who replaced him, Danny White. Not that White isn't a competent quarterback. The Cowboys made it to the playoffs four straight years with him running the show—and never made it to the Super Bowl. But do you know what the vets complain about? White won't take Landry on.

Unitas once said, "A quarterback doesn't come into his own until he can tell the coach to go to hell." Not as a steady diet, of course, or he'd be quarterbacking under different colors. But there are subtle ways. Staubach was always looking to stretch the play that had been called; he was always looking downfield. In the huddle he'd tell Drew Pearson or Tony Hill to take the pattern five or ten yards deeper. He was always greedy, hungry. White does as he's told.

The players know it, and in the Cowboy system, any spark of originality seems to light people up. One of their happiest moments was when Clint Longley, a rookie without a down of NFL experience, came off the bench and threw the 50-yard pass that beat the Redskins with 28 seconds left in 1974, prompting right guard Blaine Nye's immortal line: "The triumph of the uncluttered mind."

White's meticulous approach has produced the second-highest career completion percentage in history, and in his overall efficiency rating, a system that's wired to percentages, his numbers are slightly higher than Staubach's. But I can close my eyes and see Staubach putting the ball on the money 20 yards downfield, and when I think of White I see an eight-yard completion on third-and-10.

In his blunt style, author and former cowboy Pete Gent discussed the decline of the team last year and he summed up White this way: "The guy's got a year's supply of dried food in his basement. He's got phone numbers to call when Armageddon arrives. That's the kind of guy you want quarterbacking your team, down 17 points with time running down? Hell no, man. Too logical. He knows you can't come back."

In 1979, the first of the Browns' Kardiac Kids years, Brian Sipe was the ultimate two-minute quarterback. Len Dawson covered five of the Browns' games as an NBC analyst, and the former Chiefs' quarterback says he saw Sipe pull four of them out at the end. The key, he said, was confidence—by both Sipe and the team around him.

"I talked to the Cleveland players," Dawson said, "and they really believe he can get it done. The receivers feel he'll get them the ball if they get open. So the linemen are going to try to hold their blocks for that one extra split second. Now you've won it. Everything's a sales job when you get that many people involved."

I wonder what Doug Williams would have been like if he'd had a real quarterback coach working with him from the beginning. I've never seen a player get hot so quickly, or put on a greater long-ball show, than he did in the second half against Oakland in 1981. In the first half he was 2-for-10 for 10 yards, and the Bucs were down, 15–0. In the second half he went crazy, 14-for-20 for 325 yards, and all of a sudden the Raiders were fighting for their lives, finally winning it, 18–16, on a blocked field goal at the end.

Once I ran into Fran Tarkenton in the off-season in Vegas, and we were talking about some of his big days, and I told him the best game I'd ever seen him have was in a Monday-nighter against Dallas in 1971, a 20–13 loss, when he was playing for the Giants. "It's my favorite, too," he said.

The Giants ended up 4–10 that year. Dallas was the Super Bowl champ. The receivers Tarkenton had to work with that night were Clifton McNeil and Dick Houston, his running backs were Bobby Duhon and Junior Coffey. But Tarkenton managed to keep that motley assortment in the game almost through sheer will, scrambling, dodging bullets, making big plays out of nothing, finally seeing the thing fizzle at the end when he tried, in desperation, to lateral to a lineman. That's the picture of Tarkenton that I'll always remember, a quarterback in a competitive frenzy.

I wonder how history will evaluate Terry Bradshaw. Mike Giddings, who runs a special pro scouting service for eight NFL teams and sees more game films that any man alive, calls Bradshaw "the most productive quarterback of this generation." He has it all, the arm, the courage, the instincts. He has the knack of elevating the people around him and getting them playing on a higher level. In 1983 he saw action in only one game—against the Jets in December, the game the Steelers needed to clinch the division title, after three straight losses. He played for a little more than a quarter and threw two touchdown passes with an arm so sore it could barely push the ball, but those two TDs were all the Steelers needed to win the game, and the remarkable thing was how much better everyone around him played. The blocks were sharper, the backs and receivers were more finely tuned, there were no penalties. It seemed that his mere presence had put the team on a higher plane.

I hope Bradshaw's arm isn't finished. I'd like to see him as the Comeback Player of the Year in '84, because if ever a guy has gotten a bum rap by the media it's been him. One year they asked him what he thought about Pat Haden being a Rhodes Scholar. "I never did like hitchhiking myself," he said, and a few guys wrote what a dummy he was.

"Oh man, I was just kidding and those guys didn't even know it," he said.

He's had his disputes with Chuck Noll. He brooded about them.

"I saw him at the Pro Bowl one year," Cliff Harris said, "and he started telling me his troubles. He was leaning real close, the way he does, and his head was down and he was staring at the ground, and I was thinking, 'Is this really the guy that whipped our ass in two Super Bowls?'"

Super Bowl XVI . . . 49ers against the Bengals . . . offered quarterback students a unique opportunity to watch the finest pair in the game that year going head-to-head, Joe Montana of the 49ers and Cincinnati's Ken Anderson. Both, incidentally, were developed by Bill Walsh, probably the best QB coach in the business. Both were high completion percentage/low interception passers (Montana now ranks number one in pro history in each category) and each had a good day, statistically. The difference was that Anderson was intercepted twice in that '82 Super Bowl and Montana zero.

Their personalities are fairly close. Neither is very flamboyant. "Kenny likes to play football and drink beer and be with his family," his former tight end, Bob Trumpy, says. "He should have been a hockey player."

Before the Super Bowl someone asked Bengal guard Dave Lapham what he learned from rooming with Anderson on the road. "Clean linens," he said. "He's very neat, very meticulous; my wife loves the idea that I room with him. He taught me to pick up after myself. He's the kind of guy who always hangs his socks on a hanger. Nothing's ever out of place. He's computerlike in everything he does, and to my mind, no one dropping back can recognize his progression of receivers downfield like him."

Walsh personally scouted Anderson at Augustana College—by accident. He was there to look at someone else. "Anderson was the second biggest guy on the field," he said. "The only guy bigger was the fella with the tall hat in the other team's band."

He compared Anderson, whom he had coached for five years in Cincinnati, with his own quarterback, Montana, before the Super Bowl: "Anderson throws from a firmer base; he's more muscular, he has a stronger arm. Montana's a lithe, quick, almost sensuous-moving athlete. He throws on the run while avoiding a pass rush, and he doesn't have to be totally set. He's not a moving platform, like some quarterbacks who are mechnical and can only do well when everything's just right. Joe performs just as well under stress."

Stress. At Notre Dame Montana brought the Irish back to win the 1979 Cotton Bowl with 23 points in the last seven and a half minutes—"The greatest comeback in Notre Dame history," athletic director Moose Krause said. In his second year with the 49ers he engineered, statistically, the greatest NFL comeback ever, a 38–35 win over New Orleans after the 49ers were down, 35–7, at the half.

Tackle Keith Fahnhorst said, "Joe's like the guy who spots you five baskets in a one-on-one game, just so he can come back to beat you."

"It's not so much that I relish pressure," Montana said. "I just don't fear it."

Nevertheless, by the Super Bowl, his teammates were already calling him a legend. Randy Cross, the right guard, said he was "eerie . . . totally detached . . . it's almost like he does it in the third person." Fahnhorst remembers watching a game film one day with John Ayers, the left guard. "Joe had just done something incredible," he said, "and Ayers looked up and said, 'You know, maybe he *is* all we have.' "

"A legend?" Montana said. "I can't believe legends do the things I do. I mean every afternoon I go to the barn and shovel it out. Do legends do that? I go to the store to buy milk and I forget the bread. I try to hammer a nail, I hit my thumb. Do legends do that?"

Life-styles often lend legendary qualities to certain players. In some sections of the country ex-Raider, ex-Oiler and current New Orleans Saint Ken Stabler is considered a legend. To me he's always been an enigma. I'm not talking about his drinking and carousing off the field; lots of great NFL players have had a wild side. What's always puzzled me is the way he could be in absolute control of a game, zipping neat, precise passes through the tiniest of holes—he always was a great "touch" passer—and then see the whole thing come unraveled.

"When we played in the '77 Super Bowl, I was the quarterback coach under John Madden," Raiders' coach Tom Flores says. "One day in practice before the game Kenny threw for an hour and the ball didn't hit the ground once. Madden came over to me and said, 'What do you think?' I said, 'Put a blanket over him and send him in . . . this is scary.' "

"I always admired the absolute disdain he showed for the other team, for the guys rushing him, even when they got to him," said Oakland defensive end Pat Toomay, who roomed with Stabler in camp. "It's like they weren't even worth thinking about. But then after being around him for a while I had different feelings. The way he lived . . . the lack of effort he put into his job . . . well, I just couldn't respect it."

Once, when the Oilers played in New York and Stabler had already been traded, a kid from a local college newspaper asked Dave Casper for his opinions about Stabler. Casper had been his tight end with the Raiders and Oilers, and the off-the-cuff comments he gave that young interviewer were things I'd never seen written before.

"He set coaching back 50 years," Casper said, as he was knotting his tie. "He knows everything there is to know on a football field, but when they give him his game plan on Wednesday he probably takes it home and throws it in the waste basket. No one ever suspected how little he knows about the game plan on a particular week. He's fooled 'em all his life and he continues to fool 'em.

"I don't think he ever cared about losing. Winning is fine. Losing? So what? He'd rather win the gamble and force a pass in there. A bluffer, a gambler . . . he'd rather do it the hard way."

The way the game is played today, a quarterback had better be sharp, because the guy on the other side will probably be on target. Defense can't carry offense like it did in the old days. Football's like tennis now. Hold your service and you'll win the set. You score on your possession, they score on theirs. Break service, stop the other team on its possession, and you've got an edge. It was refreshing to see the Raiders win with defense in the '84 Super Bowl, but that was a rarity. You outscore people these days, you rarely stop them. And if you don't have a quarterback who's capable of a 300-yard, four-touchdown game every now and then, you're in trouble. In 1983 the Steelers, for instance, had the best defense since their Super Bowl years but they also had Cliff Stoudt at quarterback, and when they got to the playoffs they were blown out. San Diego lost five of the six games in which Ed Luther replaced the injured Dan Fouts.

"Today's game is a space game," Giddings says, "and the quarterback position's almost doubled in importance. In the old days you could win with a 'winner' at QB, a Joe Kapp or Billy Kilmer type . . . throw when he had to, get the other guys to play well . . . but you can't anymore.

"A guy who has reading problems, for instance, cripples his team. Y. A. Tittle used to say that if you can't read where you're going to throw the ball when your left foot moves—in other words, by your second step—it's too late. And if you're fundamentally not right the whole thing breaks down, even if you read right.

"Being a great athlete doesn't have anything to do with it, either. Look at Fouts. He looks funny on his setup. He kind of waddles. But he gets back there, sets, and *bammo*, the ball's on target."

The quarterback gets the biggest share of the cheers, and naturally, the boos. "Any quarterback who's gone through his career without being booed . . . I'd like to know about it," Anderson says.

"I told my wife and parents," Stoudt said, "that the way to stay popular as a QB in the NFL is never to play."

On a team that's struggling, the most popular player with the fans is the quarterback on the bench—or as Don Meredith once said, "How they love backup quarterbacks." Meredith sat on the bench when Eddie LeBaron was the quarterback and the Dallas fans booed Eddie and called for Meredith. Then they booed him and cheered Craig Morton. When Morton became the starter they booed him and demanded Roger Staubach. When things were going bad Staubach got booed for Danny White. And now White is getting booed for Gary Hogeboom. You can't win.

In Ron Jaworski's second year in Philly the Eagle fans, perhaps the finest booers in the NFL, gave him the business in an early season game. Jaworski remembers coach Dick Vermeil yelling in his ear on the sidelines, "Forget all that! I'm not going to jerk you! You're my quarterback!" Later Vermeil told reporters, "Fans have been changing quarterbacks here for years, which is one reason they've always lost. That's over."

The worst kind of a pressure situation is one in which a team has two quarterbacks of roughly the same age and close to the same ability fighting for the job. It seldom works. The best situation is to have an established starter, and behind him an old pro who can take over and work a game, a Don Strock type, and behind *him* a youngster with potential, a guy who doesn't mind waiting, and learning, for a while. The situation on the Giants, with Phil Simms, Scott Brunner and Jeff Rutledge, was the worst. Richard Todd still bears the scars from the days he and Matt Robinson were fighting for the Jets' job. In his first couple of years he was the darling of the Shea Stadium fans, who'd grown tired of the old and immobile Namath, but when Robinson made a run at his position they turned on Todd and subjected him to some of the worst abuse in the NFL.

"Now if I went out and got cheered I wouldn't know what to do," he said. "They boo you during the introductions. They boo you when you throw a pass away because you don't want to take the sack or let your running back get killed. I'd really like to have the fans on my side, but by now I just don't give a damn. The only ones I care about are my teammates. A wide receiver might get booed once every 30 plays or so if he drops the ball. A quarterback gets booed every play. He'd better have ice water in his veins. Booing on the road's OK. With your own, it's a little different."

I remember Dan Pastorini's early years with Houston—a bright young quarterback on the worst team in the NFL. He'd get sacked five or six times a game, get his nose broken, teeth knocked out, wrists and fingers mangled—and the crowd would boo him.

"It's like being in a street fight with six guys," he said, "and everybody's rooting for the six."

One of the sad things about the draft system is the way it throws the best young quarterbacks onto the worst teams, which often rush them into combat before they're ready and put them behind inferior lines. The 1971 draft is remembered as the Year of the Quarterback. Jim Plunkett, Archie Manning and Pastorini were the first three picks, right off the top. In the College All-Star camp the following summer, Eagles' backfield coach Charlie Gauer watched Pastorini practice and came away raving about him.

"Damn, what an arm," he said. "And listen to that kid shout the numbers. He's a leader." Three months later Pastorini was fighting for his life.

Manning, considered the greatest quarterback prospect ever to come out of the South, played for the Saints for 10 years and part of another, never knowing what a winning season was like. He's been a solid NFL quarterback, and he's probably been sacked more than any QB in history. Who knows what he would have been like on a decent team? And Plunkett? He became a physical wreck in New England, quarterbacking losing teams for each of his five years there. His career was rescued by the Raiders' Al Davis, but if Al would have gotten him early, before those shoulder operations, he might have set records.

Perhaps the saddest story of a career burned out before it really began is that of Greg Cook, who had what Walsh called "the greatest single ability I've ever seen at that position." He was 6'4" with a cannon for an arm and a great head for the game. He played for the Bengals as a rookie in 1969 and led the entire NFL in passing, the first rookie to do it since Parker Hall in 1939. But he banged up his arm against the Chiefs that year, came back and played on it four weeks later, and eventually strained a deltoid muscle. He was finished. His arm never came around.

At the other end are the tough-guy quarterbacks, the guys who get banged up but always manage to stay in the lineup. I've always admired Fouts, who started every Charger game for four years until a damaged shoulder finally took him out of action in 1983. He was playing with his left thumb and wrist in a cast at the time. One of the most underrated through the years has been the Bills' Joe Ferguson, who hasn't missed a start since 1976. And then there's Unitas, to my mind the consummate NFL quarterback, the greatest who ever lived.

He started 158 of his first 163 games with the Colts, spanning a 13-year period. Anyone who ever played with or against him speaks of his great courage.

"Against the Bears one time," said Jim Parker, who was playing left tackle, "my man, Doug Atkins, got through and smashed Unitas across the nose. Blood squirted out all over the place and Alex Sandusky scooped up some mud and stuffed it up John's nose to stop the bleeding. When I came into the huddle I almost got sick at how he looked."

"The ref stuck his head in the huddle and said, 'Take all the time you need, Unitas,' " center Buzz Nutter said. "You know what John said to him? He said, 'Get the hell out of here so I can call the play.' "

"You can't intimidate him," said the Rams' defensive tackle, Merlin Olsen. "He waits until the last possible second to release the ball, even if it means he's going to take a good lick. When he sees us coming, he knows it's going to hurt and we know it's going to hurt, but he just stands there and takes it. No other quarterback has such class.

"I swear that when he sees you coming out of the corner of his eye, he holds that ball a split second longer than he really needs to—just to let you know he isn't afraid of any man. Then he throws it on the button. I weigh 270, myself, and I don't know if I could absorb the punishment he takes. I wonder if I could stand there, week after week, and say, 'Here I am. Take your best shot.' "

And in the old days, some of those shots were horrendous. In 1968 the injury rate for quarterbacks hit an all-time high: Eighteen of the 26 starters were lost for all or part of the season. Pass rushing was becoming a sophisticated art. Blitzing had become fashionable, and every member of the defensive line was a pass rusher. Once only the ends put a real rush on the quarterback, and that was only if they were "crashing," instead of playing their normal "boxing" game, containing the sweep. The three men in the middle, two tackles and a middle guard, were run stoppers. They thought more about beating up the guys in front of them than getting to the QB, and there was a kind of unwritten rule, anyway—anyone who treated the quarterback too roughly would get his from one of the policemen on the offense. But eventually the interior linemen became agile, pass-rushing types, and retribution became almost unknown, except of course on teams like the Raiders, who have always believed in the old biblical "eye for an eye" approach.

At the end of the '68 season, when he was addressing a pre–Super Bowl banquet, Namath was asked who was the most important member of the team.

"The doctor," he said, "because the name of the game is Kill the Quarterback, brother."

The off-season talk was all about new rules to make the position safer. Defensive linemen laughed.

Alex Karras, the Detroit defensive tackle, once had a radio show in which he answered fans' questions. The phone rang one night and an effeminate voice asked, "Don't you think a quarterback should get more protection from the linemen?"

And Karras answered, "Really now, they get more money than we do, sweetheart."

Another time he said, "If you took a survey of most quarterbacks, you'd find that they go to the Presbyterian Church and the cafeteria afterward, and there they drink ice tea and eat a hog dog with a dab of mustard. They're all milk drinkers and they're all alike . . . pretty boys, all in the same image. The only one I know who isn't is Sonny Jurgensen."

There's always been a fundamental difference in the life-styles of a quarterback and a defensive tackle. One is slim and the other is not. One gets the girl and the other one doesn't. And if the quarterbacks don't like the pounding they have to take, then the hell with them.

Unless a quarterback can stand back there and say, "The hell with you too, Jack," he's in trouble. There are different ways of saying it. He can curse and snarl at the defensive linemen, as Bobby Layne used to do. (He snarled at his own, too.) Or he can keep his mouth shut and beat them to death with his passes. No matter what his style, his teammates must believe that he knows he can do it, or they'll give him a funny look when he claps his hands and says, "Let's go, gang!" They'll ask themselves who's kidding whom.

"There's a difference between a quarterback coming away from the center and saying to himself, 'I hope I find my receiver,' and a quarterback coming away saying, 'You better stop this one, pal. I'm putting it right there in his gut,'" former Giants' coach Allie Sherman once said.

The league has stepped in. First they outlawed the defensive linemen's head slap. Then they gave the quarterback an easier read downfield with the one-bump rule for pass defenders, then they gave offensive linemen freer use of their hands. The result was a drastic drop in sacks, but now they're coming back. More blitzing, more defensive line stunts, more all-out rushes in situations when the enemy used to lay back in a "prevent" defense, and, of course, many more pass plays called.

It's a hazardous position once again, from both a physical and intellectual standpoint. Only nine NFL teams started the same quarterback throughout the 1983 campaign. Some, such as the Vikings' Tommy Kramer and New England's Steve Grogan, went down through injury, but 1983 was also the year in which young quarter-backs got the hook and had their confidence deeply shaken. The Dolphins gave up on David Woodley in favor of rookie Dan Marino. The Giants never did figure out who their starter was. Chicago went from Jim McMahon, who loomed as the savior in '82, to Vince Evans and then back to McMahon. John Elway got the hook in Denver. So did Mike Pagel, briefly, in Baltimore.

Naturally, all this had an unsettling effect on the teams, except in Miami, where Marino exploded onto the scene like a skyrocket. Jerry Kramer, in his *Farewell to Football,* described rookie Billy Stevens stepping in to quarterback the Packers in 1968 in a game in which they were beating the 49ers.

"He called a play I'd never heard before. It must have been a play from his college days. He tried to pass a couple of times and the 49ers hit him late and turned him on his head and stomped him into the ground and just about killed him."

The very act of quarterbacking a team takes an unusual set of skills.

"It took me three months to learn to ride a chariot for *Ben Hur,*" said Charlton Heston, who played the part of a quarterback in the movie *Number One.*

"I learned enough about painting in a couple of weeks to do *The Agony and the Ecstasy.* Parting the Red Sea, with the help of De Mille and God, took no time at all. But I've been trying to learn to play quarterback for eight months, and I find it incredibly diffi-cult, by far the toughest preparation I've ever had for a film."

Heston said the toughest part was learning to step up into the pocket in the face of an all-out pass rush.

"This is going against every instinct in the human animal. Every nerve in your body is saying, 'Keep going, keep going, get rid of it, get rid of it!' "

Rookie quarterbacks seldom take a team all the way. Green Bay won the championship in 1930 on the wings of Arnie Herber's passes, but he was more of a single-wing tailback. Ditto Sammy Baugh in 1937. The Cleveland Rams won the '45 title with Bob Waterfield as quarterback, but this was the wartime era and Waterfield, 25 years old with a tour of duty at Fort Benning, Ga., behind him, wasn't your everyday rookie. And that's it. Marino looked like the best shot for it last year, but in the playoffs he ran afoul of Seattle's seven-back pre-vent defense and he was overmatched.

Nope, it takes time; time until the young QB can figure out everything that's going on in front of him, time before the veterans adjust to him and feel confident, especially when he's making more money than they are. Even quarterbacks who've been around for a while aren't accepted by a new team right away.

"I thought he was crazy," Eagle tackle Stan Walters said when Jaworski joined the team on a trade in 1977. "He had this goofy porkpie hat on, and he was yapping away a mile a minute. Every other quarterback I'd played with had been a loner or very businesslike. Jaworski wasn't like that. He was laughing and yelling and telling us we're going to be winners. We're coming off a 4–10 record and he's talking about winning a title. Crazy!"

Now if a rookie came on like that the veterans would just laugh at him. Most rookies have the good sense to keep their mouths shut. Tony Eason, drafted out of Illinois in the first round by the Patriots last year, said he even had trouble in college, getting the grasp of Mike White's system.

"Your first year, your grasp of the passing game is like a tree trunk," he said. "The second year you learn about branches, even twigs."

And in the pros he learned another thing—the people are different.

"I guess the biggest surprise came on the interception I threw," he said after Steeler linebacker Brian Hinkle had picked off one of his passes in the first exhibition game. "I don't think a college linebacker would have gotten it. They are two different games."

"My coach at Arizona State was Bob Baker . . . he's with the Rams now," Pagel says. "Every day he worked on my reads . . . if the inside is jammed, go from here to here, like that. It took me until the 10th game of my junior year to get it down, but then I got so fluid. I mean I just *knew*. From then on it was just like stealing. We led the nation in total offense my senior year; we averaged nearly 500 yards a game. I knew when they were in a coverage, exactly what they were going into. I thought I was better than I really was when I came into the NFL. I was waiting for it to develop. It didn't. Why?

"One—different system and offensive philosophy.

"Two—athletes on this level can disguise things much better. The cornerbacks can bump your receiver, man to man, and then drop off into a zone. In college not a lot of teams have the talent to do that.

"Three—because the defensive guys are such great athletes the holes are smaller. It looks big but by the time you go to throw the ball it closes up. They're so much quicker.

"Four—the pass routes and reading philosophy are different. It's the reverse order from college. At ASU you read short to deep—to your backs, then downfield. Here you read longer to shorter—downfield first, then short patterns.

"Five—there are so many more routes and variations here. In college we basically ran two receivers. Here there are three or four guys I could go to."

Before the 1983 Super Bowl, the Dolphins' 24-year-old David Woodley, the youngest QB ever to start a Super Bowl, brooded and worried.

"There is no way I can sit here and make you understand how difficult it is to grasp the things you have to learn to play this game," he said. "You play a different team every week. It puts a lot of pressure on you. I just wish I had better knowledge of the game.

"People ask me about leadership. No, not yet. It comes from years and years of experience. Bob Kuechenberg, Nat Moore, they're leaders. You don't become a leader overnight. When I got to the Dolphins I didn't know anything. My first game was against New Orleans. I threw three interceptions in the first half. They hadn't won a game. I thought, 'This is gonna be tough.' "

When Elway came to Denver last year he was joining a team that had never drafted a quarterback that even became competent, let alone a star. He was heralded as a messiah. His every utterance was etched in stone, with 28 Denver reporters assigned to a permanent "Elway watch." One evening, after a training camp meal, two writers got into a heated argument over whether the uneaten vegetable on Elway's plate was peas or beans. After five games, in which Elway had compiled the lowest efficiency rating in the NFL, Dan Reeves sat him down for Steve DeBerg, about whom his ex-coach, Bill Walsh, once had said: "He plays just well enough to get you beat."

Nevertheless the veterans breathed a sigh of relief. So did Elway.

"It's taken 5000 tons of bricks off my back," he said. "Sitting on the bench now I've stopped memorizing the offense and started learning it."

"The whole mechanics of the thing were wrong," said Jim Turner, the old Jet kicker and a Denver radio and TV man now. "Reeves used that complicated Dallas system and he had alternating wide receivers bringing in the plays. When Elway called a play in the huddle he had to give all the assignments. I had him on my radio show once. I asked him to call a sample play, and I timed it. It took 12 seconds. By then he's fighting the 30-second clock and there's no time for an audible."

Reeves tried simplifying the offense for Elway, but by then it was too late. And the veterans on offense felt handicapped. Which goes to show that there has always been something about the quarterback position that has mystified the most astute coaches. In 1971 Tom Landry was so puzzled about his quarterback situation, about whether to go with the physically gifted Staubach or the more experienced Morton, that he started alternating them on every play, a system that pleased nobody. Finally he realized that at 29 Staubach had leadership. It was called Vietnam.

Jim Hart, who joined the Cardinals as a free agent, was in and out of the lineup for four years, until Charlie Johnson was traded. Fouts struggled for three seasons in San Diego until he got to work with Walsh for a year in '76. Tarkenton was traded twice before he finally settled in at Minnesota, where he proceeded to complete more passes for more yards than anyone in history. Van Brocklin was traded from the Rams to the Eagles, whom he led to a title. The coach who traded him was Sid Gillman. The GM was Pete Rozelle. Tittle was traded to the Giants, even-up, for guard Lou Cordileone. ("Me . . . just me for Tittle?") He led them into the championship game in his first three years, and is now in the Hall of Fame. Yep, the position mystifies them all right.

"The best thing about having Unitas as your quarterback," Ewbank said at Baltimore, "is that it keeps you from making a fool of yourself for 10 years."

Even the great Unitas hung around Walt Kiesling's 1955 Pittsburgh camp like a lost soul until he got his release.

"I don't think coach Kiesling knew I was in camp—literally—until the AP put out a picture of me showing a Chinese nun how to hold a football," Johnny U said.

The scouts don't always have better luck. Marino was the sixth quarterback picked in the '83 draft, and there were severe questions about his arm and his attitude, yet he proved to be the best of all of them. Montana was a hot quarterback at Notre Dame, but as draft day approached his stock dropped noticeably. Scouts questioned his arm; they said he was uncoachable. The 49ers stole him in the third round.

"I can't find any negatives about either his arm or his attitude," Walsh said. "Maybe the so-called experts can."

Often coaches will malign a young quarterback to make themselves look better. The Rams' Vince Ferragamo was one of the bright young talents in the NFL in the late seventies. Everyone praised his heroic performance in the '80 Super Bowl, keeping the mighty Steelers on their heels for most of the afternoon. But next season when he walked out of camp for a day in a salary dispute, Rams coaches privately told reporters that if Pat Haden had been healthy they would have beaten Pittsburgh.

"Seven times he screwed up in that game," one of them said, "either calling a play we didn't have or totally missing a wide-open receiver."

"It's funny that people said that," Ferragamo said. "Maybe if I hadn't taken chances we wouldn't have been in the Super Bowl in the first place."

Two years later the Rams gave up a first- and a second-round draft choice to bring in Bert Jones to play ahead of Ferragamo. But last year, when injuries forced Jones out of the game, rookie coach John Robinson settled on Ferragamo, and he did just fine.

Coaches and quarterback are often miles apart, philosophically. Former 49er QB John Brodie once explained it this way: "We're playing Atlanta, and we're up by four points with something like six minutes to go, and Dick Nolan sent me out with instructions to run the clock. Hell, there's no way we're gonna hold onto the ball for six minutes. Gene Washington came back to the huddle and said, 'The cornerback's cheating up. I can get deep on him.' So next play I hit him on a bomb. Boom, six points and the game's over, just like that. I caught hell when I came back to the bench. Very few coaches think like a quarterback in a situation like that."

It's always amazed me why there are so few qualified quarterback coaches around. I remember talking to Brian Sipe in 1979, his second year working with Jim Shofner at Cleveland. He said, "After all the quarterback coaches I've played for here, all with new ideas, new theories, this is the first real one I've ever had." Next season the Browns were 11–5 and Sipe, with Shofner coaching him, was the starting Pro Bowl quarterback. His efficiency rating had soared to 91.4, the best in his career. Then Shofner moved on to Houston and Sipe crashed. His rating fell more than 23 points, he threw the most interceptions in the NFL and the Browns dropped to 5–11.

"When I was at Kansas City in the sixties," said Pete Beathard, a former AFL quarterback and the brother of Washington GM Bobby Beathard, "Don Klosterman brought in a quarterback coach—Bobby Layne. It was revolutionary. No one had done it before. All Bobby wanted to do was drink and play cards with the writers until 4:00 A.M. Then he'd need dark glasses and eye drops to get through practice the next day. The game had passed him by six or seven years. He still didn't know there were such things as zones. All his coaching was how to attack the man-to-man."

Quarterbacks called their own plays in those days, and every now and then a scouting report on a particular QB would note: "Smart. Good play-caller." I still remember one of the most masterful play-calling jobs I've ever seen, Namath dissecting the Colts' strong-side rotating zone in Super Bowl III, and most of the time he never even called a play in the huddle. It was, "Check with me," which meant he wouldn't call a play until he got to the line of scrimmage—almost a total audible system, the ultimate in brainwork. Unfortunately, the play-calling quarterback has gone the way of the head slap and tear-away jersey. It was nice to see the Raiders win the Super Bowl with a quarterback who called his own plays; Pittsburgh still does it with Bradshaw, and maybe there are one or two others, but that's it. The Paul Brown messenger system, once deemed so authoritarian and dictatorial, has now taken hold. Almost every NFL quarterback gets his plays from the sidelines, through either messengers or a wig-wag signal system. Even an old-timer like Raider coach Tom Flores admits that his method might be doomed.

"Quarterbacks coming up now, from high school and college, have never called a play," he says. "It's going to be tougher, letting them call them from now on. You might have to send everything in in the future. In '81 I sent in too much. They got confused. Now I'll send in the first play of each series; it's a bench call. I'll send in goal-line and short-yardage stuff. But we'll discuss things between series.

"I'll say, for instance, 'This is what I like, what do you think?' And Jim'll say, 'Well, I like this.' Usually I'll go to his way. He has confidence in it and he's comfortable with it. If he looks at you, all of a sudden, with a tilt to his head, he's not that confident, and the chances of things working out are not that good."

Plunkett has lived in a schizophrenic play-calling world ever since his Stanford days. "When I was a junior and sophomore the plays were sent in," he says. "The players didn't know they came from the sideline. In my senior year I called my own. In '71 I called my own under John Mazur on the Patriots. Then Chuck Fairbanks called them, except for one year.

"When I was younger I was more defiant, but now I can fit into just about any system. But I hate to wait for a play from the sideline. You're looking at the 30-second clock with high anxiety. You get in the huddle, you're rushing. You don't call your plays with authority. As the players are walking to the line of scrimmage they're saying, 'What was that play?' "

The Raiders' tight end, Todd Christensen, says their huddle is like no one else's.

"Gregg Pruitt will come in, for instance, and he'll say, 'Tom wants 19 flip.' Henry Lawrence'll say, 'Nah, that won't work.' I'll say, 'Jim, you're the quarterback.' Jim'll say, 'Henry's right. Forget it,' and he'll call something else. Do you know how valuable that is to a team to have a huddle like that? As John Madden says, 'The coaches are the theoreticians. The guys in the huddle are the combat troops.'

"Yet . . . the other side of it is, when Marc Wilson was breathing down Jim's neck, Jim called lousy games. He kept trying to get the ball deep, to be the hero himself. He'd say, 'Well, they want me to go long. . . .' "

According to Ken Anderson you can't win, no matter how you feel about it. "If you don't mind when the plays are called in you're a nothing," he said. "If you do, you're a militant."

When Manning joined the Saints, someone asked Bum Phillips if Archie would call his own plays.

"No," Phillips said, "he'll call our plays. We ain't gonna let him make up any."

"During the 1941 season, we were away out in front in one of the games," the old Bears' quarterback Sid Luckman once said. "I decided to try something. I asked the linemen if they would like to call the plays, to see how far the team would go without the quarterback doing it. The plan was to let each lineman call one play—the one he liked best.

"They all thought it was a great idea and we started in. We started on the 20 and five plays later we scored. That beat one tackle and an end out of their turn to call a play."

"Reading," not play-calling, is the measure of a quarterback's intellect these days. According to the Patriots' vice-president, Bucko Kilroy, the first read is man or zone, and the most basic calls in foot-

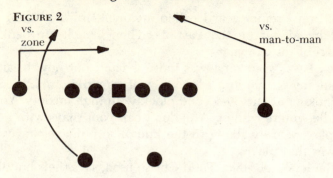

FIGURE 2
vs.
zone

vs.
man-to-man

ball, "the ones they teach a high school quarterback on his very first day," are diagrammed above.

It's not that easy, of course, but it's a starting point. The whole idea of reading begins as soon as the quarterback gets the snap from center. As he drops back, his eyes are following his primary receiver, although he might look the other way for an instant—to throw the defender off. His brain is working like a computer: receiving, digesting and discarding information as it is recognized. This all must be done in the space of 2.7 seconds or so, 3.5 tops. Namath used to say he would throw to his primary receiver 75 percent of the time, "Either that or your game plan is no good—or you're not reading well." Then comes a quick look at the secondary receiver, and against some defenses the second man will automatically become the primary target. Then there might be time for a quick peek at the third one, and then the three-second gong goes off, and it's time to unload the ball or have your head taken off.

If everyone is covered, the rookie quarterback will stand there and take his loss, like a good little soldier, or try and scramble for some yardage. The old pro will throw the ball away, unload it out of bounds or into the ground, where no one can intercept it. This usually sets up a round of booing in the crowd, especially if money has been wagered on the game. And up in the press box, the writers are saying, "Gee, he's really off today."

There's a danger in throwing the ball away, though. Houston's player personnel director, Mike Holovak, says, "You can't do it too much. It's a question of courage. People might feel you're not looking long enough. Then, you can get in the habit."

"It depends on the down," Brodie says. "One fault I find with Marc Wilson of the Raiders is that he takes the sack too much on first down. He gets 'em in too many second-and-20 situations. You're better off not having the ball. First down is the one you cannot get sacked on. Throw it away. On third down it doesn't matter. You can hold it."

All the reading in the world, though, won't help if a passer doesn't have the knack of hitting his receiver at just the right time—hitting him on the break, if the pattern calls for it. A lot of it comes from pure dog-labor, the after-practice stuff, or "specialty work," as Ewbank liked to call it.

Unitas and Ray Berry got to know each other during Ewbank's hours of specialty work. Montana got firmly acquainted with Dwight Clark that way, too. If the passer is in perfect harmony with his receivers' moves, he can snap off his throw in less time, putting less of a burden on the offensive linemen and considerably improving their outlook on the game of football.

If a passer develops the knack of hitting his receivers on the break—or if he is born with it—he won't get intercepted as much.

The late Paul Christman once drew a diagram for newsman Murray Olderman in which the old Cards' QB showed a receiver where the line veered, and another one where it stopped.

"If a receiver is covered," Christman said, "the passer can't hit him here [pointing to the first circle], because he hasn't shaken free yet, or here [the second circle] because by then it might be too late. The defensive back might have caught up to him. He has to hit him here [a point between both circles]. That's where the receiver has made his break and that's when he's open for a fraction of a second.

"A hundred kids today can throw the ball as well as Sammy Baugh did. In practice. They've got the arm and the strength. And they can fire it on a line, overarm, sidearm, any way you name it. But what makes a passer is this—the ability to hit his man on the break. Some of them never develop it."

OK, so assume your receiver is breaking off his pattern 20 yards downfield and you have three seconds to get the ball to him, and in front of you a panorama of shifting zones and switches is unfolding. You have to make sure to look the defenders off so they can't read your eyes and know exactly where the ball is going—so how do you ever pick your man out in all the traffic? "You do it by watching him," says former Cleveland QB Frank Ryan.

"Suppose you're in a crowded railroad station, and you look across the waiting room at a nondescript man and you want to watch him

walk across the room. If you watch him all the time, it's easy to follow him as he makes his way through the crowd. But if you look
away for a second, you won't be able to find him again. It's the same
with receivers."

Ah, but what about that moment when you have to look the defense off him? The question is unanswered. It's just something you
have to do if you want to win big in pro football, which might give
you an idea why Heston said it was easier to split the Red Sea than
play quarterback.

As for this business about a quarterback having peripheral vision,
how he can look at the left sideline and see out of the wee corners of
his eyes what's going on on the right side, former Colt QB Gary
Cuozzo says it's a myth.

"When I was young, I used to read about quarterbacks with peripheral vision," he says, "and I honestly believed they could see the
whole field. But it's impossible. Don't believe it. I've asked several
players about that, and I've never found one of them who told me he
could see all the way across the field at the same time. You look here
and you look there. This peripheral vision thing is one of the mis-
leading things you read. A quarterback has to have good vision, period."

I've heard of only one athlete who could truly see things beyond
the normal periphery. Dr. Henry Abrams, a Princeton ophthalmolo-
gist, tested Bill Bradley when Bradley was an All-American basketball player for the Tigers. He found that sideways, Bradley could see
15 degrees more than what was considered perfect, and five more
degrees straight down. His upward vision was particularly astounding. The perfect eye could see 47 degrees upward. Bradley could see
70. Dr. Abrams doubted whether a man could expand his peripheral
vision through exercise, but Bradley told him that when he was a
young boy he'd walk down the main street of Crystal City, Mo., and
keep his eyes focused straight ahead and at the same time try to
identify objects in the windows of the stores he was passing.

But mere mortals, such as quarterbacks, are better off watching
their targets.

"People have said to me," Jaworski said, " 'You always look at
your primary receiver before you throw to him.' I've never seen a
quarterback yet who could throw to his receiver without looking at
him."

"You've got three seconds, and you're not only reading your receivers but coverage, too," Ferragamo says. "Plus there are so many route adjustments now. My tight end, Mike Barber, for instance, never runs the same route twice. You can read three receivers, tops ... you're not looking at guys, 1-2-3, but you're reading the coverages on the move. Once you leave a primary receiver you can't get back to him. He's really gone."

Sometimes the whole thing gets a bit too complex. Cliff Harris said he stayed awake nights worrying about the way Bradshaw shredded the Cowboy defense in the '79 Super Bowl, when he set the passing record.

"Finally I couldn't stand it any more, and I called him up," he says. "I asked him, 'What did you see? What were your primary reads—the free safety, the weakside linebacker, or what?' He said, 'Well, I'd look for Swann, and if he was covered I'd look for Stallworth, and if he was covered I'd look for Franco.' He was serious. I said, 'Oh no. There's got to be more to it than that.'"

I used to do the same thing, more or less, when I'd interview Bob Griese after the Dolphin QB had just carved somebody up. He'd drive me wild. The shutters would come over his eyes, and he'd blink twice and say, in that bland way of his, "I just took what the defense gave me." It drove me crazy.

Finally I caught up with him when he was with NBC, when he'd been retired for a couple of years, and I said, "You were lying, right? You were always working on someone." And he gave me that same heavy-lidded look, and blinked, and said, "Of course I was lying. You always say to writers, 'Take what the defense gives you,' especially when you have to play that team again.

"I always looked at the two or three guys in a defense who could hurt me most, the pass rusher who could hurt me, so I'd know where to give help, the feisty guy in the secondary who'd say, 'Throw here and I'll pick it off.' With New England, for instance, it was Haynes, Clayborn and Nelson; those were the guys who could hurt you. Then you turn it around and look for the pigeon. There's always someone."

Griese probably wouldn't be drafted very high today. The computer would say he was too small, barely six feet. Ditto Tarkenton. Scouts are always drafting for height. Often an inch or two can mean $100,000 or so in a rookie's contract. Once I asked a scout why he didn't stop worrying so much about height and just take the guy who could play, and he said, "Name a quarterback under 6'0" who's ever led a team to a championship." I couldn't, but I couldn't name one over 6′3″, either, and neither could he. It might involve the correlation of height and coordination with the speed of impulses between brain and arm, arm and ball, ball and receiver, or something like that. But we'll never be sure until a shrimp or a stork produces a championship.

The art of pure passing has been dissected and put together many times. Tittle says you can teach a poor thrower to be OK, but you can never make the so-so guy great. What a pro coach can do, though, is to take the untamed arm of the college quarterback and teach it subtleties.

Walsh says that the greatest thing a young QB has to learn is patience, that he doesn't have to do it all at once. "The number one mistake they make is to try to be the hero, to do it themselves, and they seldom do," he says.

OK, so how do you teach a young passer touch?

"Touch is part of the system," Walsh says. "It's repetition. You have to teach it very carefully, every part of it. On a three-step drop, I want three big steps; on a seven-step, three big and four small. You have to teach them where to put the swing pass to the fullback, how to drop it over the linebacker's head. And through repetition will come touch."

Many quarterbacks scoff at the idea that the ideal NFL passer must be able to knock down buildings. Most kids coming out of college have to have their delivery softened, anyway. "There are high school quarterbacks with a stronger arm than mine," Sipe says. And Tarkenton adds, "Throughout my career, my backup always had a stronger arm than I did."

Some of the most successful long passes have been deliberate underthrows. Unitas and Namath both perfected it. A receiver goes deep, turns and comes back for the ball, at which point the defender gets his feet crossed and falls down, and the offense is six points richer. In the press box we're saying, "What luck!" but often it's planned.

"If your timing is down, it's the best way to beat bump-and-run," Namath said. "When your man goes long the cornerback has to run like hell to keep up with him, the deliberate underthrow, the comebacker, will get him all screwed up."

As far as gripping the ball and releasing it, no one style is perfect.

"Our assistant coach, George Sefcik, has pictures of every quarterback in the league gripping the ball," Anderson says, "and everyone is different. So's their release. You do what's natural for you. Bradshaw throws with his index finger on the point of the ball. Who'd try to copy that? A lot of it is determined by hand size, anyway."

Even in this era in which the pass offense controls so much of the game, pure passing doesn't always equate with success. Here, for instance, is a list of pro football's all-time top 14 performances for completions in a single game.

Sept. 21, 1980: The Jets' Richard Todd went 42-for-59 vs. San Francisco.

Dec. 20, 1982: The Bengals' Ken Anderson went 40-for-56 vs. San Diego.

Nov. 29, 1981: The Vikings' Tommy Kramer went 38-for-55 vs. Green Bay.

Dec. 14, 1980: Kramer went 38-for-49 vs. Cleveland.

Oct. 9, 1983: The Bills' Joe Ferguson went 38-for-55 vs. Miami.

Nov. 1, 1964: The Oilers' George Blanda went 37-for-68 against Buffalo.

Sept. 25, 1983: Todd went 37-for-50 against the L.A. Rams.

Sept. 5, 1981: The Vikings' Steve Dils went 37-for-62 vs. Tampa Bay.

Dec. 5, 1948: The Giants' Charley Conerly went 36-for-53 vs. Pittsburgh.

Dec. 15, 1974: The Colts' Bert Jones went 36-for-53 vs. the Jets.

Dec. 16, 1979: Kramer went 35-for-61 vs. New England.

Sept. 19, 1982: The Falcons' Steve Bartkowski went 34-for-56 vs. the L.A. Raiders.

Dec. 20, 1964: The Broncos' Mickey Slaughter went 34-for-56 vs. Houston.

Oct. 18, 1970: The Jets' Joe Namath went 34-for-62 vs. Baltimore.

Those are the 14 passingest performances in history, and in 11 of those games the passer's team *lost*—repeat, *lost*—the contest. And all three of the victories were iffy . . . Todd against San Francisco and Ferguson against Miami were both overtime victories, and Kramer pulled out the win over Cleveland on the last play of the game.

In 1982 the NFL put out a release extolling all the 300-yard games Fouts had had, 27 in all, and 25 since Air Coryell arrived in 1978. The Chargers' won-lost in those 25 Air Coryell-Dan Fouts extravaganzas was 14–11, but like most statistics in NFL releases, they don't go far enough. During that same five-year span, the Chargers' record in games in which Fouts did *not* throw for 300 yards was 32–12.

Here are some more interesting stats: No team that led the NFL in passing ever won the Super Bowl; and big days for quarterbacks are so spread around in this era that of the 14 individual high-yardage performances in 1983, you find only one repeater, Lynn Dickey.

If there is one new trend in quarterbacking styles nowadays, it's the drop-and-roll. "Yeah, I know all about that," Griese said. "I perfected it in my first four years at Miami, when we had new offensive linemen every week. It's called running for your life."

"Actually Shula did put it in as a deliberate thing in the early 1970s," Walsh says. "It's popular with smaller quarterbacks. I'm not talking about what Tarkenton did or Len Dawson, with Hank Stram's moving pocket in Kansas City. Those were straight rollouts. I'm talking about when a quarterback takes a drop and then rolls. We did it in '81. It's the whole key to Montana . . . he has to be able to avoid the first rusher all by himself, make him miss, and think on the move. You see it with Anderson and the bootleg concept. Dan Henning does it in Atlanta; you see it in San Diego and in Washington with Thiesmann. You don't want your quarterback standing immobile in the pocket anymore."

If there is one remark that will stay with me following the 1983 season it's something Theismann said during the Pro Bowl week in Hawaii. We were talking about the Super Bowl, and how the Raiders' man-to-man defense was shutting everything down, and how tough it was to go deep because of the swirling winds. I asked him why he didn't try to get the ball to his close-in tight end, Don Warren, on the right side, to try to get Ted Hendricks running with him. Theismann's jaw set and his words became very bitter.

"I don't put in game plans," he said. "I don't even think about them anymore. I am an instrument. I don't get involved in the process. I've totally given up on that aspect of it. I've become a tool of the game."

Somehow quarterbacking should be more than that.

CHAPTER FOUR

Divers and Survivors: The Runners

Many shall run to and fro, and knowledge shall be increased.

—Daniel, 12:4

Halfbacks are born. Some coaches take a lot of credit for having developed certain halfbacks. What is generally meant by that is that a man with a lot of talent comes to a coach, and the coach does him no particular harm.

—Knute Rockne

THEY come into pro football all instinct and nerve, without the surgical scars on the knees or the knowledge of what it's like to get hit by a 230-pound linebacker. They burn brightly, and by the time they're 30 or so they might still be around, but they're different players. They know how to pass-block, and they can run their pass routes without making any mistakes; they can block in front of a ballcarrier, and they run just well enough to be considered runners. They dive— and survive.

Running back is a position governed by instinct, and many of the great ballcarriers were never better than they were as freshman pros. It's the most instinctive position in football, the only one in which a rookie can step in with a total lack of knowledge of everything except running the ball, and be a success.

Ask Red Grange to detail the moves he made on that 60-yard touchdown against Michigan and he'll look at you blankly.

"I was never taught to do what I did, and I know I couldn't teach anyone else how to run," says the great halfback. "I don't really know what I did, and I'd have a hard time telling you what I did on any individual run, even if it's one of the runs that everyone always talks about.

"I read about my change of pace, and it was news to me that I ran at different speeds. I know I used to have a crossover step, and I had an instinctive feeling about where the tacklers were. I read that I had peripheral vision. I didn't even know what that meant. I had to look it up."

All right, you say. Grange was running around in the Dark Ages of football, when everyone was 185 pounds and slow, and no lineman pursued downfield, etc. Listen to Donny Anderson, the former Green Bay halfback who set a pro record for bonus money.

"I think running ability has to be bred in you. You can't learn, and I did something back at Texas Tech, against Texas A&M in my junior year, that I couldn't do again in a thousand years if I tried to show you.

"I was supposed to go off left tackle, but it was closed up. I must have seen an opening to the right out of the corner of my eye. My left foot was already planted to the left. Then somehow I put my right foot about five or six inches to the right and changed directions.

"Teddy Roberts, our safetyman, and I were looking at the films and he said, 'How'd you do that?' I said, 'I don't know.' We ran it back and forth six times, and I still couldn't tell him."

It's the kind of quote you hear repeated many times. Eric Dickerson on a run he made at SMU: "I ran up in the hole, stopped, jumped back and ran the other way. It was one of the most amazing moves I've ever seen, but when I saw the film it was like I was watching another guy do it."

Billy Sims, sophomore year at Oklahoma, Vanderbilt game: "I started right and things were closed off, and I leaped to my left—five yards into the end zone. The guy who was watching the film with me said, 'Damn, how'd you do that, Billy?' and I couldn't tell him. I just did it."

A lot has been written about runners' styles, analyzing their moves, their techniques. Seldom does it capture the person himself. It's like pinning butterflies under glass. You've read that old limp-leg quote that's attributed to Jim Thorpe—"I just give 'em the leg and then take it away again." The quote probably originated with Walter Camp, and then was tacked onto any decent runner until it became a cliché. Thorpe probably gave them the leg, and took it away, and gave it to them again—hard, plus the knee and the boot and anything else to let them know the old Indian was not to be messed with. He liked to punish people.

Each runner has his own style, and if the coach likes what he sees he doesn't do any editing. No heavy pencil. "A great runner is like a Picasso," ex-San Diego coach Sid Gillman once said. "No one's going to tell him, 'This is the way to paint.' "

They put their own brush strokes on the canvas, and each one leaves his own memories. The first great runner I remember is Steve Van Buren, 200 pounds and 9.5 speed for the 100. He'd run the sweep and lower his shoulder and scatter bodies. O. J. Simpson and Gale Sayers—wisps of smoke, a surgeon's probe, the glide and then the quick incision, overdrive to shoot them out of trouble. Walter Payton, a little package of fury, Larry Csonka, a wrecker's ball knocking down a wall. I remember Marion Motley as a gathering avalanche, and, of course, Jim Brown, the power and grace of a lion on the hunt, all instincts and moves and strength. If I'd pick an all-time backfield I'd put Brown at running back and Motley at fullback, and I'd spot-substitute Simpson and Sayers. If I needed one play on third-and-20 I'd have Y. A. Tittle throw that reverse screen pass to Hugh McElhenny, the King.

Tittle would sprint out to his right and look downfield, and at the last minute he'd turn and throw crossfield to McElhenny, way over on the left side. Opponents would call it a "garbage play," and it would either lose five yards or pick up 30, and I can close my eyes now and see McElhenny whirling and dodging and high-stepping in that crazy-legged way he had of running, the Willie Galimore style.

Galimore made some of the most incredible runs I've ever seen on a football field, bouncing out of a mass of tacklers long after he should have been down, and I never knew how he did it. Dick Bass, now an L.A. radio man and a great halfback for the Rams in the 1960s, says, "Galimore once told me that when you're hit, there's a moment in there when the tackler relaxes and his arms come open, like a clam shell. That's when you can pop it."

The quickest takeoff I've ever seen belonged to little Buddy Young, the 5'4" halfback for the old AAFC New York Yankees. He was a wingback in the Yankees' single wing, and he'd only carry seven or eight times a game, but every time he did the crowd would be on its feet.

The best series I ever saw a runner have came in a game between the 49ers and the old AAFC Buffalo Bills in 1949, Joe Perry's second year with the Niners. Perry had been tackled, and after the play Rocco Pirro, a player as mean as his name, walked by and casually gave Perry a little kick in the head. It took three guys to hold him back, and Frankie Albert, clever little devil that he was, gave Perry the ball eight straight times, and I've never seen such uncontrolled violence in a runner.

People forget quickly. Who remembers the 49ers' Ken Willard, one of the dominating big backs in the game for years, or the great, unsung, and largely forgotten year Bass had in 1962, gaining 1033 yards for a 1–12–1 team? Does anyone remember Dick Hoak of the Steelers, or Tom Woodeshick or Billy Barnes of the Eagles? They were all powerful forces for a while.

"Billy used to call himself the most exciting two-yard runner in the league," his old Philly teammate, Tom Brookshier, says. "He once said, 'Our offensive line is so good our own backs can't even get through it.' "

The sadness of runners who burned themselves out before their time, of the Redskins' great Larry Brown, who "played too tough for his body," as the scouts used to say, and retired a physical wreck at age 29, of the 49ers' slashing halfback, Paul Hofer, who went down with a knee injury. Even sadder are the careers that never got off the ground because they happened to be on the wrong team at the wrong time. No one ever remembers Bill Butler, who played for the Saints in their dismal years, a "boisterous blocker," the press book called him. I saw him have some heroic games in absolutely hopeless situations.

There were, and are, players who get the utmost out of their bodies, and after the game there is nothing left . . . Dave Preston of the Broncos, Rocky Bleier, who played for the Steelers. There is a tendency to downgrade Bleier as a man who got lucky, fitting in with a four-time Super Bowl champion, but his production in big games, and over the course of a career, was consistently high. In the intricate balance of an offense there is sometimes a perfect mesh, and Bleier, blocking for Franco Harris, catching third-and-eight swing passes out of the backfield in precise, disciplined routes, running in straight, short bursts ("Rocky gained 1036 yards in 1976 without ever making a cut," the Steelers' center, Ray Mansfield, used to say) was the perfect counterpart to Franco. The Steelers' offense has been trying to recapture that same balance ever since he left.

Some qualities seem universal in a running back. The great ones usually run with their feet close to the ground—Sayers, Brown, Jimmy Taylor, Perry; they all did it. Even Lenny Moore, who was noted for his high knee action, brought his feet down when he got near the line. The reason is balance. And they were all quick starters, even the seemingly slow men like Taylor and Alex Webster (who ran about a five-flat 40). They all got off the mark in a hurry.

Pure speed is nice to have, especially in this era of space-age football, but it doesn't mean much in itself, without the runner's instincts. The three fastest running backs in pro football are Tony Dorsett of the Cowboys, Curtis Dickey of the Colts and Herschel Walker of the New Jersey Generals of the USFL. Dickey and Walker were track men, world-class level. Dorsett has competitive speed, football speed, and he's the most productive of the three. After his freshman year at Pitt he probably could have made it in the NFL.

"If I were that kid," said Tom Keating, a defensive tackle for the Steelers, after he had seen the young Dorsett perform, "I'd go into hiding for three years and live in a cave somewhere and then come into the NFL with fresh legs."

Dickey is an up-and-downer, an exploder who can have good games or bad, depending on his mood. Walker is an enigma. Coming out of college as a junior he looked like the finest running back prospect in history, the greatest combination of speed (4.3) and size (6′2″, 224) the game had ever seen, but after his first few games with the Generals he seemed disappointing.

"He's missing one ingredient that the great runners have, but he was so explosive in college that no one noticed it," said Mike Giddings, the director of Pro Sports, Inc., a private scouting service for eight NFL clubs. "He's not an avoider. He can't make the first man miss him; he can't go side to side, like a Chuck Muncie can. He breaks his long runs by running over the first guy, and I don't know whether he could do that in the NFL."

Sour grapes, said the USFL. We've got him, and wouldn't they just like to have him?

"We had one like him," says Jack Faulkner, the Rams' director of operations. "Elvis Peacock. He had the same fault Walker does. He's a one-way runner, right side. When he goes left he cuts off the wrong foot and slips, especially on artificial turf."

"I'm amazed by his stats," Simpson said, after Walker had gained 1812 yards in his first USFL season. "Herschel has the physical ability, but sometimes he looks like he doesn't have a clue about how to run."

One thing always surprised me about the breakaway backs. You'll see them caught from behind, often by slower people, by linebackers and safeties. The answer is that the actual mechanism of carrying the football slows people down.

Marty Glickman, the radio and television announcer, once did a study of it. He had been an Olympic sprinter who doubled as a halfback for Syracuse.

"I was timed for a 100 in a track suit, and then I was timed for that 100 again, only this time I was carrying a football under my arm," Marty said. "The conditions were the same each time. I was wearing the same clothing, the same spikes. I repeated it a few times, and each time I was one to two seconds slower when I carried the ball.

"The arms play a part in pure running. Coaches always show the sprinters how to use their arms for balance and power while they're running. Anything that impedes that free arm movement—like a football—is going to cut your speed."

Pure track athletes who pop up in the pro football drafts come in as wide receivers, occasionally as defensive backs, but seldom as running backs. Their speed is used for running *without* the football, and, once they've got it, they slow down. In the old days you'd even see a sprinter such as Dallas's Bob Hayes caught from behind.

But the good runners all have the quick start and the knack of avoiding objects, and a rookie can use exactly the same skills he had in college. And if he's got the physical qualifications, he will make a good, often a sensational first-year pro. He hasn't learned fear—or self-defense. The repeated hammering hasn't yet taken the zip from his legs. Everything else can be taught, the faking and blocking and pass routes, provided he has the desire to learn and the courage to execute some of these more tedious jobs. But if he's a pure and gifted runner, a club will sacrifice the other traits to keep him in the lineup. He's going to draw people into the stadium, and football is still a moneymaking proposition. People have never yet paid to see a great blocker.

Many of the fine running backs made All-Pro their first year— Gale Sayers, Jimmy Brown, Alan Ameche, Hugh McElhenny, Doak Walker, Steve Van Buren, Bullet Bill Dudley; all had arrived by the time they put on a pro uniform. Marcus Allen made All-Pro as a rookie in 1981. George Rogers had made it the preceding year.

Scouts generally have a better percentage when they recommend rookie runners. Occasionally there are failures. No one can scout the future. But the percentage rate on running backs is high. Four runners were drafted in the first round in 1983. Two of them, Dickerson and Seattle's Curt Warner, made All-Pro. The other two, Detroit's James Jones and Philly's Michael Haddix, were starters, although Haddix was later demoted.

College blocking backs don't scare the scouts any more. At Auburn William Andrews blocked for Joe Cribbs and James Brooks, but when he came to the Falcons they gave him the ball and he blossomed. Mosi Tatupu was strictly a head-knocker at USC, but last year the Patriots learned that he could be a devastating force with the ball under his arm. Ditto Andra Franklin at Miami. Pass blocking, once an integral part of the education of an NFL back, is less important than it used to be. Offensive coaches realize that hardly any back, no matter how big, can handle a Lawrence Taylor or a Chip Banks on a blitz. The new style, in the two-tight-end, one-back offense, is to assign one of the tight ends blitz-control duty, as the Bills did with 235-pound Mark Brammer in their overtime victory at Miami in 1983.

"Mark swatted them away like flies," said Buffalo quarterback Joe Ferguson.

Most pro backs can catch the ball, and they always could, even though their college coaches didn't know it. So they're getting plenty of work as pass receivers now. Andrews's pass-catching stats in college were so minimal that the Falcons' press guide doesn't even list them, but he caught 59 balls last year, and an amazing 81 in 1981. Cribbs caught 30 passes in four years at Auburn, 57 for the Bills' '83 season; Payton caught 27 in his entire Jackson State career, 53 for the Bears in '83. Sims is the strangest story of all.

"At Oklahoma they threw two passes to me in five years, four years varsity and one year redshirt," Sims says. "I caught both of 'em. Actually it was two passes in nine years, because they threw zero to me in high school."

And yet in his first season with Detroit he caught 51.

"In camp I could tell right away he was a natural receiver," Lions quarterback Gary Danielson said. "Some guys fight the ball; with him it was smooth and easy. I have a theory about that. He played in the wishbone at Oklahoma, and I think wishbone tailbacks have an advantage as receivers because they get so many pitchouts. They're used to seeing the ball in the air. A guy who spends his college career taking handoffs doesn't get that."

Last year Dickerson gained 1808 yards rushing, the fifth highest total in history, but to appreciate his entire contribution you have to look at his pass-catching stats—51 for 404 yards. Simpson, Earl Campbell and Jim Brown had the three greatest rushing seasons ever. Their combined pass receiving output for those three years was 41 for 385 yards. And what kind of a receiver was Dickerson in college? Nineteen receptions in four years.

Sometimes a runner will do things in college that would get him in trouble in the NFL. Outside of Sayers' most electric moves, I'd never seen a better cut executed than one I saw Dick Bass make against Stanford when Dick was a senior at the College of the Pacific. It was a sideline move. He had turned the corner and the tacklers were running him out of bounds, and he gave it one of those sharp, full-stride cuts to the inside, knocking one man over and gaining 10 more yards before he was dragged down. It was a move of a man who's much better than the competition, and knows it; a confident, almost disdainful move. And it was one you'd practically never see in pro football, for the simple reason that it violates all the instincts of survival.

It brought him right back into the flow of traffic, and laid him open to blind-side contact. But the Stanford boys weren't the Packers, and in the pros the runners give up those extra few yards to keep in mind the long-range picture, the preservation of a career.

"I watch some ballcarriers fighting along, long after the issue is closed," the Browns' Leroy Kelly once said. "That's how a back gets hurt. There is a time to give that second effort you read so much about, and there is a time to find yourself a soft spot."

Or a sideline. I've never seen as many runners ducking out of bounds as they did last year. Maybe it's the higher payrolls that have done it. Maybe it's the knowledge that the 16-game season and the one-back offense and all the added pass-catching responsibilities have increased the work load so much that all unnecessary hits are to be avoided. But some of the old-timers are disgusted by it.

Last year there were only 11 running backs who were 30 or older when the season began. Only four were starters, Franco Harris, John Riggins (the oldest, at 34), Chuck Muncie and Mark van Eeghen. Only five players in history have ever had a 1000-yard season after passing their 30th birthday—Franco, Riggins, John Henry Johnson,

Tony Canadeo and Bleier. The game does not treat 30-year-old runners very kindly.

"The thing about age doesn't bother me," Franco says. "But what you have to watch out for is, does it bother the organization, or the coach? I never was much for turning it on in preseason. I probably wouldn't have made the club, based on my preseason play of the last nine years."

His style is unique. You never know what you're watching. He doesn't look like he's moving very fast, but you seldom see him caught from behind. "Competitive speed," Chuck Noll calls it. He's a different runner on first and 10, when he'll dance and fake, then on third and four, when he'll put his head down and drive. He'll make some of the most incredible four- and five-yard runs you'll ever see, stutter-stepping his way up to a hole that doesn't seem to exist, then all of a sudden bursting through it with a quick slash, and you wonder what he saw there, how he did it.

"He thinks out everything," his ex-teammate Joe Greene said. "You watch him run, he's not dancing, he's making decisions."

"I could run the 19-straight play 10 times and each time it's going to be different," Franco says. "The hole is never where it's supposed to be."

When he came out of Penn State, the scouts didn't know what to make of him. "Could be a great pro," one of them wrote, "but might not even be a good one." In his senior year he'd been benched in favor of Tommy Donchez for the Cotton Bowl because of a disagreement with his coach, Joe Paterno. "Bad attitude," the scouts wrote in their books.

He weighed 225, but he never looked very imposing. "I sat next to him in the meetings," Bleier said, "and I thought, 'Little, thin arms . . . he's undeveloped. What does he have that I don't have?'"

A knack, a talent, an instinct, who knows? Dorsett talks about seeing "flashes of color" when he runs, mere impressions of enemy jerseys that steer him through trouble, like warning lights. He talks about one run he broke a couple of years ago, when it seemed as if he were pinned three or four times.

"I don't know what I saw on that play," he says. "It wasn't even color flashes. Sometimes it's just this feeling for everything that's happening around you, almost like an outside force. I knew people were coming and I stepped back in a spin, and . . . it was incredible."

The Cowboys have tests for everything. No one has run their agility test, a course dotted with cones and hurdles, faster than Dorsett. They have another one, developed by their conditioning coach, Dr. Bob Ward, called the Agility–Speed–Unexpected Visual Stimulus Test, which uses flashing lights to direct runners through a route. No one has ever come close to Dorsett in that one, either. "Dorsett's ability to perceive the unexpected is extraordinary," Ward says.

Rams coach John Robinson, who says he loves to "talk about running backs . . . to compare their styles," says that for all his agility the greatness in Dorsett is his toughness.

"Sitting back there in that I-formation, eight yards deep, he's great, running for the tough yards," Robinson says. "I don't know what he weighs, 190 maybe, but he hits like he weighs 220 . . . shoulders level . . . God, he's a great player. I like to think that our guy, Dickerson, is going to be like that. You watch the finish of Eric's runs. He'll always get something extra. He's a tall man, 6'3", and eventually he'll play at 227, 228, and a tall man will look bad on some hits, the same as Franco and O.J., but they're seeing something. Our guy is so smooth, though . . . he'll destroy angles, like O.J. did. Guys like William Andrews and Walter Payton have a power in them, a kind of ferociousness . . . they run like they're possessed."

Landry's philosophy always has been that successful offense is predicated on being able to run the ends. His approach is keyed on misdirection, making the defense commit itself one way, and then socking it to them in the opposite direction. To set up a sweep left, for instance, he'll have Dorsett make a positive setup step to his right, which goes against a runner's natural instincts—he wants to get the ball and take off. Landry says Dorsett's ability to do a good acting job on that misdirected setup step is what makes the play go, to give the right tackle time to pull to his left and lead the blocking—an almost impossible job without the extra time.

Some runners are very happy being stationed deep in the I-formation, or in a one-back alignment. "You see more from back there," the Patriots' Tony Collins says. "The one-back is also better in sloppy weather. There's so much room that you don't have to worry about slipping and bumping into someone."

The Jets' Freeman McNeil even goes so far as to say, "I'm not only an I-formation tailback, I'm an I-formation *person*. My personality isn't geared to splitback, quick-opener type of running. I like to feel my way around, look for the options, choose my route, in life as well as football."

Walt Michaels took the Jets' favorite running play, 19-straight, a fullback read-and-delay that Weeb Ewbank brought from Baltimore in 1963, and redesigned it for the halfback, for McNeil.

"Paul Brown ran that play with Marion Motley and Jimmy Brown," says Michaels, the caption of Brown's old NFL championship teams in Cleveland. "Alan Ameche ran it for Weeb in Baltimore, and Matt Snell and John Riggins ran it for him here. Now it's handed down to Freeman."

McNeil had a so-so first year with the Jets in 1981. But a year later he was the NFL's leading ground gainer and a unanimous All-Pro. He has said he never really knew what he was doing that first year, plus he played too heavy.

"I was 227," says McNeil, who's 215 now. "I thought you had to bulk up for pro football. I thought that's what it was all about, power and endurance. It limited my effectiveness. The system was tough to pick up, too—the refinements, the little things.

"The defense would play games—you'd check inside and see if anything was coming; if not, then you'd check outside. But the defensive men might be exchanging, the inside man going outside and vice versa. I felt like I was 10 years old again. I felt I was in with a bunch of people who were a lot older than me, who knew the game. I felt the vibes of not being as good as the rest of them. It was like going to a place, and they give you the directons but not the right address. They tell you it's on this street, and they draw a little square, but the rest of it you have to find yourself."

McNeil missed seven games with a separated shoulder his third season. Bruce Harper, the Jets' fine little pass-catching halfback, missed another seven the same year. Deprived of their possession game, the Jets' offense came apart, and a team that was a winter book Super Bowl choice finished 7–9.

Frank Gifford once called durability a prime requisite for greatness. At times it feeds on itself. A runner proves durable, so a coach isn't afraid to use him—or overuse him. Payton, a small, compact back at 5'10", 202, has missed only one game in his nine-year career. He has started 120 straight. "There's nothing he can't do," his teammate Doug Plank, the free safety, said. "I'll bet he could even make a good football." In 1981 the Bears signed him to a three-year, $2 million contract, and someone asked general manager Jim Finks if the dollars weren't a bit extravagant for an organization as conservative as the Bears.

"For another player, maybe," Finks said, "but Walter's got the skins on the wall."

"It's like he runs with a fever," Bear defensive end Al Harris said. "You have to wonder what drives him."

In the 1977 playoffs Dallas safetyman Cliff Harris, one of the game's most punishing hitters, nailed Payton as he was turning to catch a pass. "One of the hardest blows I've ever delivered," Harris said, "and he just bounced up and tapped me on the helmet."

"The shots he takes and bounces up from," said the Bears' defensive coach, Buddy Ryan, "would put anybody else in intensive care."

In 1981 he was the only weapon on a 6–10 Bear team that finished 26th in NFL in offense. He gained 1222 yards behind minimal blocking. During the course of his career he had averaged more carries per game than anyone except Earl Campbell. His body was starting to feel it.

"I used to try to run away from tacklers," he said. "Now I've got to attack them, because there's no place to run." He pointed to his scarred helmet. "I've been using it," he said.

A new coach, Mike Ditka, drafted a new quarterback in the first round the next year and promised to take some of the load off Payton's back. The following season they got a couple of sprinters as wide receivers, Willie Gault and Dennis McKinnon, to open up the offense. But by the end of the season Payton still had more carries than all except six NFL backs, and he closed out the campaign with a 30-carry, 148-yard performance.

How does he do it? His off-season workouts are part of the answer. He runs up a sandbank on a 65-yard course he developed himself, a stretch of land by the Pearl River near his hometown of Columbia, Miss. He found a landfill hill of packed black dirt near his Arlington Heights, Ill., home, and he started running it. No one could keep up with him. He burned them all out.

"Running alone is the toughest, but I like it best," he says. "You keep pushing yourself. You stop, throw up, push yourself again. There's no one around to feel sorry for you."

Sometimes a person's durability is totally unexpected. Few people thought that John Riggins could come back to the Skins after his lay-off in 1980, but he did. In 1981 he set a club record for touchdowns, a record he broke last year when he ran for 24, the best ever in the NFL. Going into the playoffs after the '82 season he told his coach, Joe Gibbs, "gimme the ball," and the result was a Super Bowl ring and a fistful of records for Riggins, for postseason and Super Bowl yardage and carries. The pattern in the playoffs was the same—Joe Theismann set the defense up with his passes, got the defensive linemen tired out from pass rushing, and then the 235-pound Riggins finished them off.

By 1983 it was assumed that his duties would lessen, thanks to the return of the alternate tailback in the one-back offense, little Joe Washington, an unusual, scatter-type runner who was capable of plenty of big days of his own—e.g., the 147-yard afternoon he had against Detroit.

"He broke one 41-yard run, and in the middle he stopped and turned around," the Skins' general manager, Bobby Beathard, says. "I thought maybe he'd dropped something."

"I had a brainstorm," Washington said.

But by the end of the season the 34-year-old Riggins had 375 carries, the third most in NFL history—and this was a man whose durability had been questioned 11 years before, when he was a young fullback with the Jets.

"At the beginning of the year I didn't think I was gonna make it," Riggins said. "In the last exhibition game, against Buffalo, Sherm White clotheslined me and damn near broke my neck. I started the season wearing a three-inch collar. I felt like Frankenstein. Then it dropped to a two-inch, then I got rid of it. A few weeks later, against Green Bay, I popped something in my back, and I wound up in traction for three days. I was a big ship that was floundering. I'd had my hull punctured a few times. Time to seal the compartments off. I'd lost a few sailors. I thought, 'Ooh, the big guy ain't gonna make it to the end of the tunnel.' "

It's on the minds of all of them, the disabling injury that will put them out for keeps. Eagles coach Dick Vermeil was always fond of reminding people that his little halfback, Wilbert Montgomery, was "not an avoid runner," but last year a knee injury put Montgomery out for most of the season. A year earlier Montgomery said he could see it coming.

"Whoever we played," he said, "their game plan was to take me out of the game. When we played the Giants, they hit me when I had the ball and they hit me when I didn't have it."

In 1967 the Jets' fine halfback, Emerson Boozer, was lost for the season with torn ligaments in his knee. He came back and had many good years, but he said his outlook had changed.

"Just watching football games now," he said in camp the following season, "I see things I never saw before—like pain. It startled me. I never looked at footgall games with that in mind. I always heard fans *ooh*ing and *aah*ing when someone was really hit, and I couldn't understand it. It had no meaning to me. A solid shot was just a solid shot. It was never painful. But now I look at games the way fans do."

"I hear guys saying, 'I can make it another year, another two years,'" Payton says. "They don't know that they're just dragging it out. They can't see it, and often those are the people who get hurt. I'll know it. I won't let it happen to me. Never."

Earl Campbell is 28. He says he feels like 40. He has averaged 22 carries a game for his entire six-year career with the Houston Oilers, and last year someone suggested that it might be a good idea to run out of bounds to avoid taking the extra hit.

"It's not a bad idea," he said, "but I just don't think I could let myself get away with it, especially if there was only one guy in front of me."

As complicated and as wide-open as football gets, there will always be a place for the big backs, the one-yard runners, such as the 240-pound Campbell.

"A few years ago, when I was still with the Oilers," Giant fullback Rob Carpenter says, "we beat the Bears in Chicago, 10–6, with Earl just pounding at them. I think he had 31 carries, and on the 30th he broke five tackles. The Bears were so tired they couldn't wrap him up. And he was so tired he couldn't cut."

When the Dolphins' 5'10", 225-pound Andra Franklin came into his own in 1982, Don Shula could return to the old Larry Csonka–Jim Kiick, ball-control game he so dearly loved, and Miami wound up in the Super Bowl. People in Miami started calling Franklin the new Csonka.

"Zonk was uglier," veteran guard Bob Kuechenberg said. "But there's no telling how ugly Andra will be in four or five years."

Some of the big backs were amazing athletes in their younger days. San Diego's 230-pound Chuck Muncie was a 6-9 high jumper in high school. Riggins was a Kansas high school sprint and long jump champion, and in his senior year at Centralia High he averaged 48 yards per punt return and 61 yards per kick return.

"On some of those returns John just went straight down the field," his high school coach, Lennie Mohlman, said. "He didn't have to cut or zigzag. They guys on the other team just fell back away from him. Too many of them had been hurt trying to stop him."

When the Bengals' 270-pound Pete Johnson, the biggest of the big backs, returned after his four-game suspension in 1983, his first start was a 112-yard game against the Packers. "When you have 270 pounds of inertia going, it's hard to stop," Green Bay defensive end Bryon Braggs said. When I heard the quote I thought it was a misuse of the word *inertia,* so I looked it up in *Webster's:* "*Inertia:* The property of matter by which it will remain at rest, or in uniform motion in the same straight line or direction unless acted on by some external force."

That's Pete all right, uniform motion in the same straight line. And that night the Packers weren't the external force that was going to stop him.

The big guys will always be around, like the dinosaur exhibits at the American Museum of Natural History, but the new passing rules and the wide-open nature of the game have produced a new type of player, the quick, speedy little halfback—"scatbacks," they used to call them. As players grew bigger they were shifted to the wide receiver or defensive back positions. Now they've returned as setbacks—Impact Players, in the scouts' terminology, guys who can make a quick impact on a game. The Vikings' 5'9", 180-pound Darrin Nelson is an example. The late Joe Delaney (5'10", 184) of the Chiefs was the best of them. They run wide, but they're also used on quick hitters inside the tackles. They keep the defense from going into a nickel or six-back pass-prevent alignment too early, and they're especially effective on the faster artificial turf.

In 1983 the average NFL running back listed on the 28 opening-day rosters stood 5'11⅝" tall and weighed 210 pounds. In 1941, when pro football was starting to gain momentum, a swing that was halted by World War II, the average back was taller . . . he measured 5'11¾" (and weighed 198). In the succeeding years he was bigger. Running backs are heavier now—a 190-pounder of 25 years ago would now be 200 to 210, thanks to weight training—but perhaps a

better gauge is a comparison of the average heights and weights of
the top 15 ground gainers in the league. They haven't changed much
in the last 20 years. At five-year intervals, plus each of the last five
years, and including the prewar year of 1941, the average size of the
15 leading NFL rushers was as follows.

1941 (NFL) . . .	5'11⅞", 196
1948 (NFL and AAFC) . . .	6', 199
1953 (NFL) . . .	6'¼", 198
1958 (NFL) . . .	6'¼", 204
1963 (NFL and AFL) . . .	6'½", 212
1968 (NFL and AFL) . . .	6', 213
1973 (NFL) . . .	6'¼", 211
1978 (NFL) . . .	5'11½", 204
1979 (NFL) . . .	6'¼", 210
1980 (NFL) . . .	6'¼", 210
1981 (NFL) . . .	5'11¾", 210
1982 (NFL) . . .	6'¼", 213
1983 (NFL) . . .	6'¼", 212

Vince Lombardi has been credited with restoring the running game
to favor. Actually it had never been out of favor. There was one brief
period in the early 1950s when the Los Angeles Rams drove everyone
crazy with their passes, and analysts were brooding that the defense
would never catch up. The team everyone points to was the 1950
Rams: Bob Waterfield and Norm Van Brocklin throwing to a covey
of receivers—Elroy Hirsch, Tom Fears, Glenn Davis, Vitamin Smith,
and others. But the Rams that year threw 453 passes and called 404
running plays. And next year, when they won the NFL title with an
aerial attack that was only slightly less productive, the Rams' runs
outnumbered their passes, 426 to 373.

There has *never* been a team that won an NFL championship or a
Super Bowl by passing more times than it ran. Never. The AFL had a
few in its formative years, but the teams that gave the young league
its first two victories over the NFL—New York and Kansas City—
both ran the ball more than they threw it. That's right, the Jets, the
Joe Namath Jets, ran more than they passed.

The running back always has been an important figure, even in
this wide-open era, when it seems that the pass-catch operation will
sweep the game into the skies. And the running back has always
taken his share of the lumps. Twenty years from now people will
have trouble remembering their names.

"I've got a rookie linebacker named Jeff Davis," Tampa Bay coach John McKay said in 1982. "The first time he touched the ball he ran for a touchdown. The last person to do that was Red Grange. When I told my players that, no one knew who Red Grange was."

CHAPTER FIVE

Catching the Football

Strength thrills, speed kills.
When he's even, he's leavin'.

—The language of the swift

In my fourth year with the Patriots, Raymond Berry be-
came the receivers coach. The first time he saw me he tossed
me a football, standing about two feet away. I thought
maybe there was a message written on it, like a note in a
bottle someone finds washed up on shore. So I turned it
over and looked at it on all sides. Nope, just a plain old NFL
football. So I tossed it back to him. He tucked it away. Then
he moved a step back and underhanded it to me. I tossed it
back and he tucked it away. Pretty soon we were playing
catch, overhand, and every time he got the ball he tucked it
away. I got the message. He never said a word, but nothing
he could have said would have been as effective as that lit-
tle game of catch we had. From then on I tucked the ball
away, even when someone just handed it to me. If some-
body would have tossed me a bomb I'd have probably
tucked it away and blown myself up. Even now, if some-
one spills a drink I'll catch the ice cube and tuck it away.

—Russ Francis

IT was in Kezar Stadium in San Francisco 25 years ago, and the Baltimore Colts had a second down, goal to go, on the 49ers' seven-yard
line, right below where I was sitting.

It must have been ESP that made me decide to hold my binoculars
steady and unwavering on split end Raymond Berry, neglecting
everything else on the field. Or maybe it was just the law of averages.
But in the next 2.7 seconds or so I saw a tableau that is still vivid in
my memory as the perfect coordination of passer and receiver.

Berry cut straight down toward Abe Woodson, the 49ers' right cornerback, and launched himself at Abe's knees in a straight head and shoulder block. Abe, figuring some sort of sweep was on the way (there must have been some play action simulating a sweep), fought to get Berry off him. Then, in an instant, Berry turned and hooked to the inside and John Unitas's ball was right there as he hooked. TD. Six points. And the 49ers' fans gave poor Abe a tremendous booing. What the hell was he doing a yard away from Berry anyway?

To me, there's no higher standard of excellence in the art of pass receiving than this intricate knowledge of timing, a knowledge of the workings of someone else's body as well as of those of your own. There have been many great passers and many fine receivers and quite a few good combinations of both. But to me, the Unitas-Berry combination was the greatest of all. Berry's biggest numbers came in 1960, when he caught 74 passes, and in '61, when he caught 75. That was over a 12-game season. Project that 75 over today's 16-game schedule and you have a 100-catch year. The year he caught 74, the Colts completed 196, the most in the league, by far. He caught 37.7 percent of their completed passes. A receiver catching 37.7 percent of the passes of 1983's leading completion team would have had 139.

History awards a special place to the Arnie Herber–to–Don Hutson pass-catch combination that exploded onto the NFL scene when the league was still tuned in to Bronko Nagurski and Tuffy Leemans. It was daring and spectacular—"You go long and I'll throw the hell out of the ball"—and the defense wasn't ready for this stuff yet. But Unitas and Berry arrived when the defense had gone into a careful study of guarding against the pass, after suffering through the wild passing orgies of Los Angeles, and any receiver who got troublesome was quickly awarded double or triple coverage.

This chapter is a study of the pass catchers, but a receiver is negated without a good arm to get him the ball, and vice versa. Unitas and Berry fed off each other, and the greatness of one was a mirror of the greatness of the other. It helped that both were of the same emotional makeup—careful, meticulous and (a word that has become almost a cliché now) dedicated.

Berry in practice was a Colt legend. He would always show up in full pads. He would spend time checking the field for hidden holes and impediments. He would leave nothing to chance. He had a set of moves that he would painstakingly rehearse every day, mentally checking them off as he did.

The year after Berry retired from the Colts he joined the Cowboys as an assistant coach. One day he stepped out on the practice field, ran a couple of routes, to get the feel of it again, and suddenly announced: "There's something wrong with this field. It's too narrow."

The Cowboys figured he had to be kidding; they'd been using the field for years. But Berry, who knew his sidelines, insisted. So to humor him they brought out tape measures and stretched them from the center of the field to each sideline. The field turned out to be four yards short on one side and two and a half on the other.

The many Ray Berry chronicles have pointed out that he had no outstanding speed, but this could have been an aid rather than a hindrance to his development.

You can generally divide receivers into two groups—workers, who are known as "possession" receivers now, and flyers. Berry was a worker, and perhaps if he had been born with a sprinter's speed, life would have come easier and he never would have developed his scientist's approach to the game. It's a nebulous argument ("if Namath had had the good knees, it would have taken him two or three more years to learn to stay in the pocket"), but a man without the flyer's speed cannot stay in the league without moves and a well-disciplined knowledge of patterns, while a flyer can make it with little brainwork but a lot of leg. Or at least he'll get a long look from a lot of teams before he's sent packing.

The flyer will terrify the defensive backs, and he'll draw the bulk of the double coverage. He's like an exotic jewel you bring out on display. But the possession receivers pay the rent—the guys who can make the third-and-eight catch in traffic, who won't break off their patterns a yard short.

The Oakland Raiders won the Super Bowl in '76 with an offense centered around not one but two great possession receivers, Freddy Biletnikoff and tight end Dave Casper, but as Biletnikoff grew old and declined, so did the Raiders. In 1980 they finally found one to take his place, Bobby Chandler, a terrific—and vastly underrated—possession receiver for a decade, and back they came as Super Bowl champs. Injuries ended his career, and for two years the Raiders didn't smell the roses, but in '83 tight end Todd Christensen blossomed into one of the best possession receivers in the game, and the Raiders were in the Super Bowl once again.

Among the wideouts, the best possession receiver of the eighties is the 49ers' Dwight Clark, who averaged 77 catches a season through 1983, including the nine-game season of '82. And yet his speed was so marginal at Clemson that he wasn't drafted until the 10th round.

"Clark is the kind of receiver most teams don't have," his coach, Bill Walsh, says, "and don't realize they need. We're not so much interested in the 4.4 sprinter as the man who holds the key pass in the key situations."

And yet the 49ers shelled out big bucks in '82 for Reynaldo Nehemiah, a world class hurdler with little knowledge of football. You can't get away from it, the flyers are seductive.

The best wide receiver combination is a burner on one side and a possession guy on the other. If you've got a man who's a combination of both, then you've got something special, but that's a very rare breed. The outlook is usually different. A flyer wants to fly, a worker wants to give you the first down—"keep the chains moving," as Walsh says. The combination of two burners at the wideouts looks good on paper, but it seldom works.

The Jets gave up 2 number-one drafts to move into position to get Lam Jones, a world class sprinter, in 1980, and pair him with Wesley Walker, another flyer. The combination has never clicked. It seldom does. Too many things can go wrong. When the Jets ran into an off track in the '82 AFC Championship Game in Miami, there was no one to move the chains. Ask any defensive coach who was the most respected receiver on the Jets and they'd tell you Bruce Harper, the little free-agent halfback, who was the closest thing to a possession man the club had.

Backs can fill that role, but there also has to be some firepower on the flanks to go with it. Rocky Bleier was a fine possession man for the Steelers, running his precise routes out of the backfield. The Cowboys' Preston Pearson was one of the most amazing. In 1979, when he was 34 and getting ready to wind it up, he caught 26 passes, 23 of them for first downs. Sixteen of 17 passes turned a third down into a first down, and the 17th gained nine yards on a third-and-10 . . . and that's with everybody in the place knowing he was going to get the ball.

Harper, Bleier, Pearson . . . they've never drawn big salaries, and these kinds of players never will. All they do is win ball games for you. Mostly they're self-taught. They've got to do something to stick with the club, so they become familiar with the passing game. On the other end of the scale are the pure sprinters, the collection of inexperienced "World's Fastest Humans" who deluged the league after Olympic sprint champ Bob Hayes made it big with the Cowboys . . . Frank Budd, Jimmy Hines, John Carlos, etc.

I once saw the Jets keep a guy for three years on the basis of one overthrown pass. His name was Harvey Nairn. He'd been a hurdles champ in college, and one night in an exhibition game against Detroit he blew by the Lions' All-Pro cornerback Lem Barney and left him flatfooted on his way to a ball that was overthrown by five yards. Weeb Ewbank was on the sidelines, right next to the play, and he got a good look at Barney's face as the kid left him for dead. Ewbank never forgot it. Harvey hung around the Jets for three years, never catching a pass in a game, until Ewbank finally decided he simply couldn't play.

They're the pampered athletes of football. You see them every year, coach-breakers, guys who stay around long after more talented players are cut, guys who get that extra-long look, and then another; great for anchoring the NFL's 400-meter relay but duds as football players. And God forbid if one of them should actually catch a bomb or two in a game. Then he'll last for years, shuffled off from one team to another. Speed, always the search for speed.

The Patriots' Stanley Morgan came into the league as a pure flyer, but he's learned the game. After the 1982 season, his sixth in the NFL, he had a career average of 22.5 yards per catch, the best in history. The following year he was called on to be more of a possession receiver, though, and his average of 14.9 cut his lifetime mark to 20.9 (second on the all-time list to Homer Jones's 22.4). But he still caught 58 balls, 13 more than his single-season high.

"The first couple of years you're in the league," he says, "you just run downfield as fast as you can, hoping to catch the ball. You really don't understand what's going on around you. You haven't learned to study it. You can make some plays like that, but you can also get yourself killed."

Morgan ran a 4.36 forty when he first came in, and it takes a lot of work with the quarterback to adjust to that kind of speed. Often there are a lot of interceptions along the way. Roger Staubach said he had a hell of a time getting in sync with Hayes's speed.

"I couldn't wait the extra couple of seconds with him," he said. "I couldn't look the defensive man off, because if I did he'd be out of range of my arm."

"There's no substitute for raw speed," says Dan Fouts, "but, and it's a very big *but*, the ability to use it, to be where the quarterback expects you to be, is so much more important than speed."

The San Diego system, Air Coryell, is based on timing, Fouts taking a three-step drop and throwing to his receivers at a given spot. Occasionally he'll take a deeper drop and gun one downfield, but every team has to do that to keep the cornerbacks from crowding too close.

"Sometimes you'll go along all season and never get your long passing game going," Berry said when he was an assistant at Dallas. "But you have to keep going to it. You have to use it like a club over the defense's head or they'll shut off everything else."

There are many elements that make Air Coryell one of the most devastating passing attacks in history, ranking right up there with the Rams of the early 1950s and the 1961 Houston Oilers: a fine offensive line, an intelligent and courageous quarterback and a magnificent set of receivers.

It's fun to look at the great receiving tandems of history. In the old days it would be a twosome—Lavelli and Speedie on the Browns, Hirsch and Fears on the Rams (aided and abetted by a whole set of nifty little backs who would come swooping off the flanks to catch passes . . . Glenn Davis, Vitamin T. Smith, Tommy Kalmanir, etc.), Berry and Mutscheller on the Colts. Then it became a threesome, as the third back became a flanker and the bigger of the ends stayed close to the line as "tight end"—Berry, Mutscheller and Moore, later Berry, Orr and Mackey; Maynard, Sauer and Lammons on the Jets; Biletnikoff, Wells and Chester, later Biletnikoff, Branch and Casper on the Raiders; Dowler, McGee and Kramer on the Packers; and currently, Jefferson, Lofton and Coffman on the Packers. Statistically, though, the Chargers' trio of J. J. Jefferson (later replaced by another All-Pro, Wes Chandler), Charlie Joiner and Kellen Winslow was the best.

In 1980 Jefferson, Joiner and Winslow caught 242 passes for 3762 yards (more yards than 21 NFL teams, total) and 26 TDs (only seven NFL teams had more). All three made the Pro Bowl. Jefferson was the acrobat, able to make the impossible catch; the 250-pound Winslow was the dominating force on the inside routes, although he was—and is—more of a slot man than a pure tight end; but Joiner was the man who made the whole thing work, the possession receiver.

I wonder what kind of a place history will award him. He's only made the Pro Bowl twice in a 15-year career, but last season he moved into fourth on the list of all-time pass catchers, and as he nears 37 he's showing no signs of slowing down. The unusual thing about him is that he's one of the few men to have made a successful, and very smooth, transition from flyer to possession receiver, a tough task for a little guy who stands 5'11" and weighs barely 180.

"He came to the Oilers as a rookie in '69 when I was their quarterback," Pete Beathard says. "Right away we knew he was the best receiver on the squad. He was devastating. No defensive back could cover him man-to-man. But our receivers coach, Fran Polsfoot, tried to change him. He took away all his fluid moves and coached him to stop and square off his cuts. He nullified all his speed. You see it happen to some receivers in a certain system."

It happened to Washington's Art Monk in his first year, when Joe Walton, the offensive coach, worked Monk into a more precise style, toning down his freer instincts.

Bobby Beathard, the Skins' general manager, had made Monk his number one draft choice. Beathard's wife, Christine, said Bobby would come home from practice "depressed, with his head down to here. He'd say, 'They're telling me my number one draft can't play in their system.'"

Joiner drifted to Cincinatti and then San Diego. In his first seven seasons as a regular he was a flyer. He averaged only 29.6 catches a season, but 18.9 yards per catch, putting him right up there with the league's long-range threats. Then he changed. The Chargers drafted Jefferson. Air Coryell needed a possession guy, a worker, and Charlie was it. In his last seven years he has averaged 54.5 catches a year, with the yardage dropping to 15.6 per reception. Last season, at age 36, he caught 65 balls.

"He's deceptive," the New Jersey Generals' Gary Barbaro said when he was the All-Pro free safety for the Chiefs, facing Joiner twice a year. "He's not a blinder any more, but he's more consistent than Jefferson. He's more defined and he runs more exact routes."

"Probably the smartest receiver in the league," the Rams' left cornerback, Gary Green, said. "He reads a zone or man coverage as well as anyone . . . he sees a zone so quickly."

"It's his toughness that amazes you," Barbaro said. "He takes the shot and bounces right up. But the thing about him is that he's not arrogant. None of this jumping up, high fives, spinning around in the air, pirouettes. He catches the ball and goes back to the huddle."

All the great ones have their own trademarks. I can close my eyes and see Joiner making the 10-yard catch for the first down, taking a hit and flipping the ball to the referee. I can see Paul Warfield running the slant-in pattern, the Quick-I they call it, making a back miss him and breaking it long. Or the incredible timing between Unitas and Berry, or Joe Namath zipping the ball downfield on precise, eight-yard square-outs to George Sauer and Don Maynard, and then cranking up and letting one go to Maynard 50 yards downfield. I can see Dwight Clark fighting to make a catch in double coverage, and his incredible leap that brought the 49ers an NFC championship against Dallas; and I can see the animal acts of the great tight ends, Mike Ditka, John Mackey, Ron Kramer, Casper, as they dragged a mauling, cursing mass of tacklers downfield.

But the one who left the most breathtaking memories, the prettiest of them all, was Lance Alworth, "Bambi," reaching high to pluck one out of the San Diego sunshine, diving and scooping one off the grass.

I remember once telling him something Sauer had said to me. I'd seen him catch five straight square-out passes on one drive, and I wondered what was to keep him from catching 20 of those six- and seven-yard outs in a game, as long as the cornerback was playing off him.

"Oh, I probably could," Sauer said, "assuming the linebacker didn't start dropping back in the area to help out, and even then we could probably run some stuff at him that would get him back where he belonged.

"But I don't think a wide receiver could stand it physically. When you reach up for that ball you stretch and leave your whole side open. All the cornerback would have to do would be to lay back, wait until you catch the ball and crack you with his helmet each time. It's perfectly legal; it's good, hard football. Your ribs wouldn't hold up for a whole game, and even if they managed to, you couldn't get through a season like that."

I told Alworth what Sauer had said, and his boyish, child's face lit up and he said, "I wish they'd throw *me* 20 passes a game."

"He always wanted the ball," his coach, Sid Gillman, said. "He never got it enough. He was like a virtuoso, a violinist, playing his own music out there."

"He first showed up at our office in June, looking for an apartment," says the Raiders' Al LoCasale, who worked for the Chargers in the AFL's early days. "He had a skinhead haircut . . . he looked 15 years old. Barbara, my secretary, said, 'We're not giving you the money because we're not getting the paper.' She thought he was the newspaper boy.

"Dr. Cureton of Illinois used to run all those tests. He got Alworth in a 36-inch spot jump. He was amazed. Lance stood 5'11". It was like a 6'9" high jump. Dr. Cureton told me it was a record. Lance had run track and played basketball and baseball at Arkansas. They said he was a better infielder than Don Kessinger, who'd gone from Arkansas to the majors. I used to love to watch Alworth line up, his off-hand shaking . . . all that adrenaline . . . waiting to explode."

Alworth's most devastating pattern was the post, termed by Gillman "the long and the short of it," in which he headed straight downfield for 10 or 15 yards, then broke inside, angling toward the goal posts. It's the route most feared by cornerbacks, since their primary responsibility is the outside. When a receiver is running a post pattern, his body is between the defender and the passer. An interception is almost impossible, unless the pass is misthrown. The cornerback gets no help from the sideline.

"One of the few things in football that hasn't changed," Don Hutson says, "is pass patterns. I suppose they never will. What more can anybody do?"

"The post was Hutson's best pattern," said former Green Bay halfback Tony Canadeo, whose career bridged the Hutson years and the dawn of the modern era. "But he could run the outs, too. The routes were the same as now, but they just had different names, such as Z-in and Z-out. Clark Shaughnessy gave them the terms *post* and *corner*."

The old Browns' receiver Mac Speedie, who was an assistant coach at Houston and Denver and head coach of the Broncos until 1966, says that the pass patterns he coached in the AFL were the same ones that he and Dante Lavelli ran 15 to 20 years before that with Cleveland.

"The only difference," he says, "is that now the players are bigger and stronger and faster."

The basic patterns, also called the passing "tree," are listed in Figs. 3–5. Different clubs use different names. A sideline pass could also be called a hitch or a square-out or just an out, a deep pattern could be called a fly or a go or an up, etc.

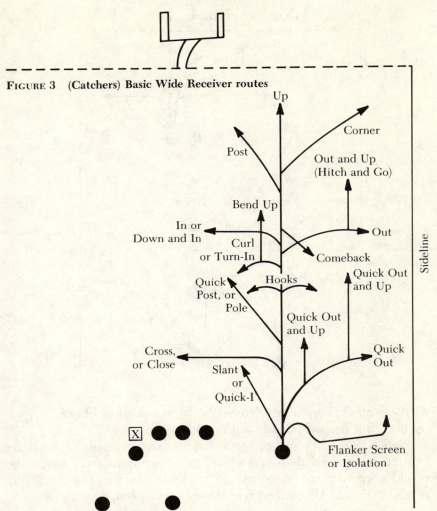

FIGURE 3　(Catchers) Basic Wide Receiver routes

Every receiver has his own style of running these routes. Sauer would run his outs with geometric precision, everything sharp-angled. Maynard would round the pattern off, making it more of a circle-out. Alworth would come off the line hard, pushing the cornerback deep, and then circle back for the ball. He caught a lot of short outs because the defenders were playing so far off him.

A great cornerback—with speed—generally has an easier time with the young flyer who hasn't yet learned to adjust to the ball than

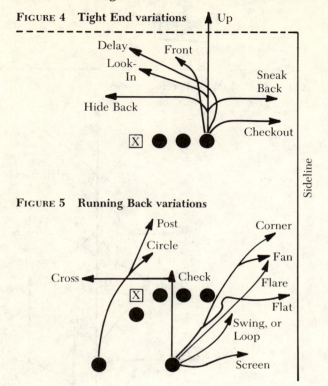

FIGURE 4   Tight End variations

FIGURE 5   Running Back variations

with a worker. Raider All-Pro Willie Brown used to blanket a lot of burners, but he had trouble with Sauer.

"When you come out of a game after covering Sauer," he'd say, "you're more tired than you would be covering a faster guy. Sauer would keep working on every play, whether he was the designated receiver or not. All the receivers should do it, but they don't."

You hear the same quotes from cornerbacks who have worn themselves out covering the 6'4", 210-pound Clark, who fights for everything, and makes himself universally disliked in the secondary by diving at knees and ankles on running plays.

In 1982 his teammates voted him the Len Eshmont Award for Most Inspirational Player. "They don't usually give this award to a wide receiver," former 49er linebacker Matt Hazeltine said at the presentation ceremony. "That's because wide receivers don't block. They have something written into their contract that says, 'I don't block.' But Dwight is the finest blocking wide receiver in the game today."

"He never coasts or rests, like some of them do when it's time to block," 49er line coach Bobb McKittrick said. "Every time you look at a game film you see Dwight in the middle of some kind of near-fight with a defensive back over a three-yard gain up the middle. He's just battling every minute."

The pass catchers have fancier numbers now, thanks to the 16-game schedule and the heavy emphasis on passing, but I really don't think they're as good as they used to be. The new rules, which limit the defenders to one bump, within five yards, have cut down the receivers' escape skills. Practically anyone can come off the bench and catch four or five passes now. In the old days, when receivers got bumped all the way down the field, they had to work for every ball. The good ones caught a lot, the poor ones caught very few, but now everything is spread around. Out of the top 22 single-game performances in 1983, passes caught and number of yards, there were 22 different names. Not one repeater. There's enough wealth for everybody.

"In the old days," says CBS announcer Tommy Brookshier, an old defensive back, "receivers spent an awful lot of time working on individual moves. Now a receiver starts off, and if they go into a certain defense he just runs straight and he might get open. Nobody running straight would have caught a ball years ago. We would have killed him."

One thing that bugs me is the increased use of gloves. I remember once hearing Tommy McDonald, the Eagles' fine little long-ball threat, talking about how important it was to get skin contact with the ball. McDonald used to rub his fingertips on a concrete wall before a game. The idea was to give them sensitivity, like a safecracker sandpapering his fingers. He'd bite his fingertips to get the blood circulating, and he played in shirtsleeves, no matter how cold it was.

"The bare skin of your forearm is sensitive," he said. "But your jersey isn't. It binds you. It can take an inch off your reach. And when the ball hits your bare skin, the immediate reaction is to grasp it."

You don't see as many of the great fingertip catches nowadays. How can you fingertip the ball with gloves on? I remember O. J. Simpson sitting in the Bills' locker room after they'd lost to the Jets on a cold day in Buffalo and ripping all the receivers on his team who were wearing gloves.

"It's time to take the gloves off and play football," he said.

It isn't only the cold. I've seen receivers come into the Orange

Bowl wearing gloves on a 75-degree day. Something about playing under conditions they're used to. The TV announcers also seem to have forgotten what real pass catchers used to look like. I've seen plays in which a receiver had to make a slight adjustment to a ball and he dropped it, even though it hit both hands, and the analyst (that's TV, not psycho) said, "It wasn't his fault. The ball wasn't on the money."

The rise of artificial turf fields has turned the scouts' eyes to their stopwatches when they check out wide receivers. A flyer will fly quicker on synthetic, but by the same token the cornerbacks will be faster, too. Some of the biggest days I've seen receivers have were on slippery grass fields, when defenders lost a step making a quick cut and slipping.

Generally speaking, a team using a two-back offense, with one tight end, will designate one wide receiver as the split end and the other as the flanker. The flanker plays on the tight end's side, and he'll generally be the smaller and swifter of the two. The split end has to do more blocking, mostly on weak-side running plays, and he's easier for the cornerback to jam.

The new rules have made a place in football for the midget receiver, the Smurf. Last year's opening day rosters showed 51 of the 138 NFL wide receivers under 6' and 32 below 180 pounds, with three under 170. In 1942, Hutson's top year as a receiver, there were only four sub-six-footers and only one end who weighed less than 180. The little guys, what there were of them, were scatbacks. The tall fellows were the pass catchers, and on defense they'd have to turn around and stop the sweeps. Hutson was an exception. He was a halfback on defense. Receivers, both wide and narrow, were a heartier breed in those days.

No one can quite explain Hutson. He came up at a time when defense ruled with an iron fist. The leading passer in the league, Ed Danowski of the Giants, averaged less than five completions and 70 yards a game; and the leading runner, Doug Russell of the Chicago Cards, averaged just over 40 yards a game. The NFL single-season record for pass receiving was 26.

All of a sudden it was *whoosh* and *whoosh*, Arnie Herber cranking up like a javelin man and letting 'em go to Hutson, while 13,000 fans in the stadium gasped. Ty Cobb once saw Hutson play and he called him "the second-best judge of a fly ball in athletic history," which makes you wonder who Ty considered number one—himself, or Tris Speaker, or maybe Arnie Herber.

There was no one to take the pressure off Hutson, either, no secondary receiver. In 1937, the year he shattered the record with 41 catches, the second leading receiver on the Packers was the other end, Milt Gantenbein, with 12. In 1942, when Hutson caught 74, all the other Green Bay ends, combined, caught 24. Hutson's catches were more than the total completions of four different NFL teams.

"He was so difficult to defend against," said old Bear halfback Luke Johnsos, "because half the time he didn't know himself where he was going. He'd signal the passer how he was going to break."

It's interesting that when Hutson and Sammy Baugh teamed up in various All-Star games, they never quite managed to click. Baugh was a spot passer, great at hitting a man on the break, *provided* the receiver showed up where he was supposed to be. But Hutson was a free-lancer who took no orders from a playbook. He was an early-day Don Maynard.

At Green Bay, Cecil Isbell and Hutson did manage to work out one devastating pattern later on. It was the original tag-out, in which Hutson did a hook, or stop move, dropped to his knees, and caught Isbell's low pass. It was impossible to intercept.

"Hutson would have been the same today," Canadeo says. "They didn't time people in the 40 then, but he was about as fast as James Lofton."

One final Hutson note. Edmond F. Rovner, a lawyer from Bethesda, Md, says he will take a lie detector test that he once saw Hutson catch a low pass, one-handed, in full stride, with the palm of his hand facing *downward*. Sorry, but this I don't believe.

Hutson was exceptional, but for ordinary mortals, the Berry training probably was the best: learn your routes, learn to tuck the ball away, keep working on fundamentals.

"I was lucky," Francis says. "At New England I had two of the greatest teachers ever, Berry and Ray Perkins. The day after I was drafted in the first round I went out to the stadium for a press conference. Perkins took me down to the locker room, got me a pair of shorts and shoes and took me to the field to work me out . . . the whole package, left foot here, right foot there, the sled, the dummies. After he had run me through techniques for about an hour he said,

'Don't worry, we're filming the whole thing so you can see your mistakes.'

"Once he was looking across the stadium during practice and he said, 'I want to die here.' I said, 'What?' and he said, 'Right here. This is where I want to die and be buried.' "

Sometimes the receivers develop techniques by their own peculiar methods. Sauer said he learned by bouncing off trees.

"We had about 13 trees in our backyard when I was a kid in Waco, Texas," he said. "My dad would throw the ball to me close to the trees, and I'd bounce off 'em after I caught it. I remember my father telling my mother one time, 'With his hands he should be an end.'

"In the NFL, when I would catch a pass, sometimes it was like I was still bouncing off those trees in our big ol' backyard in Waco. Except that those trees were chasing me."

Great quarterbacks and their favorite receivers usually have their own thing going. The pass that beat Dallas in the '81 NFC Championship Game, San Francisco's Spring Right Option, had a schoolyard look to it. Joe Montana, chased by three Cowboys, let the ball go into the end zone before he went out of bounds. Clark climbed into the sky and grabbed it before it went into the seats. He had gone from his right to his left, and then back to his right again, just inside the far stripe in the end zone. There are people who still think Montana was merely trying to throw the ball away. Sam Wyche, the 49ers' quarterback coach, said no, it was something they'd worked on together since day one at the Rocklin training camp. Dallas safety Charlie Waters said it went a little deeper.

"They've got a ticket going, Montana and Clark," Waters said the day before the game . . . words that were to prove prophetic. "Clark always has an option on every play. On a basic slant he can break it back outside. It's sandlot stuff . . . just get open and I'll hit you . . . like Tarkenton and Rashad on the Vikings."

"In the huddle Fran would call a play," Ahmad Rashad says. "Maybe some combination of receivers, maybe a bomb. Then he'd add, 'Ahmad, you go ahead and do what we talked about on Tuesday.'

"I'll give you an example. He'd call one play that had three receivers going to the right side. I'd be on the left. He'd scramble to the right, but all the time I'd just stand there at the line of scrimmage. So he'd be scrambling all over the right side, and everybody in the stadium would be saying, 'Look at this guy improvise,' because, see, that's what he wanted them to think. But the truth was, it was all planned, a planned scramble. He'd come running back to the left, and there I'd be, all alone. He'd throw me a two-yard pass and I'd run for 30."

Practically every sophisticated passing attack has a set of automatic adjustments for the receiver, off every pattern. If the defensive back plays you this way, you break off the pattern and go to point B. Vince Lombardi, whose offenses seemed very basic, built around the power sweep, had a very advanced concept of the passing game, and he was one of the first coaches to put in a system of automatic reads and adjustments.

Of course, if a quarterback has a set of dumb receivers it won't work, and all he'll have will be a high interception rate. Hence the value of a Charlie Joiner, working with Dan Fouts.

"I know what he'll do," says Fouts, who had the same thing going with Rashad when they played together at Oregon. "He'll do the right thing. I know if I get the ball to him he'll catch it. What more can you say?"

The new rules have helped all of this, and cut down the two- and three-car accidents in the passing lanes. "Legalized muggings" is how Paul Brown used to describe the way some of the defensive backs would attack receivers in the old days. The Rams would dive for receivers' knees as they started their pattern; they'd cut them down. The Ax Technique, they called it. The Chiefs' Fred Williamson, a big, strong guy with marginal speed but a knowledge of karate, would chop them across the helmet and face. His nickname was the Hammer.

"Pass defense," Weeb Ewbank would snort. "It's nothing but mayhem."

One of today's favorite patterns, the long crossing route, which is practically unstoppable if the quarterback has enough time, was rare in the old days, because a receiver traveling through the picket line of linebackers would never make it to the end of his journey. A receiver's courage was judged by his willingness to go over the middle.

"You know, even to this day, and I'm 53," Kyle Rote said in 1981, "I still have nightmares in which I'm going over the middle on a pattern. Your ribs begin to hurt even before you leave the ground, because you know as surely as you're standing there that they're going to crack you.

"I wake up so many nights panting and out of breath with that experience. I left football a long time ago, but that part of the game just won't leave me—that terrifying moment of being right in the middle, knowing that if you do your job you're going to pay heavily for it."

Tight ends take the most punishment. They're getting hit by bigger people, such as linebackers, and by more of them. A wide receiver often finds himself one-on-one with a cornerback, with a sideline next to him. The tight end works in traffic. One guy tees him up, another one finishes him off.

"After an offensive team meeting in camp we break up into groups to see films," Francis says. "The receivers coach tells me to go with the linemen. The line coach says no, you go with the receivers. I'm in each group, and I'm not in them. I block with Keith Fahnhorst, the tackle, but I'm not involved with him that often. Every once in a while Joe Montana throws me a pass, but I'm not a receiver.

"I'm the tight end. They've never been able to label the tight end. It's the story of my life."

They come up with fire in their legs and they like seeing themselves in the NFL Films highlights, dragging linebackers, running over safetymen. In a few years, though, they've learned. They catch the pass, get the first down and hit the dirt.

"When I was 23 or 24, guys used to warn me that I'd begin to feel the beating I was taking," Ditka says. "I just laughed at them. I never missed a game in Chicago—84 straight. By the time I was 28 I felt like an old man, a physical wreck."

The best tight ends were usually big, tough guys, like Ditka and the Packers' Ron Kramer. Occasionally you'd get a big guy who could also fly, like the Cards' Jackie Smith or Mackey of the Colts, but they were rare. Nowadays there's room for both. The double zones that are so popular today (two defenders on each wide receiver, covering him short and long) create a hole in the deep middle, so you want at least one tight end on your roster who can move, such as Ozzie Newsome of the Browns or the Vikings' Joe Senser, an ex-basketball player. But you don't want to sacrifice in-line blocking, or the short, possession reception, so there's room for the big guys, too.

The new one-back offense puts two tight ends on the field at the same time. Most of the two-back teams have a lot of two-tight-end formations, as well. At one time a team kept only two tight ends on its roster; now some of them, such as the Redskins, keep four.

Washington calls the ones who play on the line, such as 242-pound Don Warren and 251-pound Mike Williams, their "close" tight ends. The slot men, set out wider and often sent in motion, are their "move" guys—Rick Walker and Clint Didier, a mobile 240-pounder who was a wide receiver at Portland State and then moved inside, "where the thunder is," as Norm Van Brocklin used to say.

The keynote slot, or move–tight end of the eighties, is the Chargers' Winslow, 250 pounds, fast, remarkably coordinated, sure-handed and arrogant. He likes to shove the defenders around, muscle them, showboat a little. Consequently he takes his share of hits.

"They might start out with a light, quick linebacker on me," he says. "Then they'd change to a bigger linebacker to work me over at the line of scrimmage and cheat up with a safetyman. A couple of years ago it became more physical. The more balls I caught, the harder the opposition tried to hit me. After a while it was getting ridiculous. I'd catch a pass, go down, and guys would still be flying over the pile trying to get a piece of me."

Giants' safetyman Pete Shaw, an ex-Charger, says Winslow "doesn't think like a tight end. He thinks, 'I'm going to catch the ball and run,' while most of them are looking for a place to fall down." Pure tight ends, such as the Raiders' Christensen, resent slot men like Winslow. They think the All-Pro pickers should create a new position for them and leave tight end to the guys who do the dirty work.

"I don't feel any remorse for lining up wide," Winslow says. "I know I'm resented for it. Defensive backs call me a sissy and say, 'Get back in there where you belong.' But it's like telling Earl Campbell he can't run because he's too big."

"I don't know what they're saying about Winslow's toughness," says New England defensive coordinator Rod Rust, who coached the Kansas City defenses for years, "but he's always been plenty tough against us. Whenever a gifted athlete comes along, particularly if he's big, someone always says, 'Well, he's not tough.' I guess they want to show he's mortal."

Great receivers like Winslow and Alworth and Sauer all seem to have the same thing—a great hunger for a thrown ball.

"I love the physical act of catching a ball properly," Sauer once said. "When it's thrown in my direction, I know it's my ball, not the man's covering me, not the ground's—but mine. I follow it into my hands with such concentration that I can see the grain. I can even see the printing.

"It says JSV on it—I think."

CHAPTER SIX

Defense

Defense is the stronger form with the negative object, and attack the weaker form with the positive object.

—Karl von Clausewitz, *On War*

Tackling is more natural than blocking. If a man is running down the street with everything you own, you won't let him get away. That's tackling.

—Vince Lombardi

THE defensive troops are football's counterpunchers. They can score knockouts, but they don't lead. When they've stunned the enemy, when they've got him on the ropes, the offense takes over.

They've never been as sorely tested as they are now, thanks to the new, liberalized passing rules of 1978. Defensive people are sleeker now, built more for speed, to counter the quick, flashy offense. Defenses have never given up more yards, but they've never scored more touchdowns, either. It's a space game.

The history of defense reads like a conditioned reflex, a reaction to new offenses, to new trickery, deception and power. (See Fig. 6 for the history of defensive evolution.) The defensive formation that has held the longest reign in history has been the 4-3 . . . 34 years since its inception, 28 years since it became a base alignment. Its father was Steve Owen, but Tom Landry is its eldest son; he first explained it, drew it up on the blackboard. Is it any wonder that he is hesitant to join the herd and move to the 3-4 these days, as 19 NFL teams already have done?

FIGURE 6

7-Diamond
The defense of the
twenties looked like this

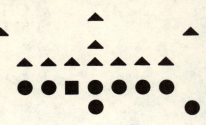

6-2-2-1
But for increased
mobility it changed to
this (early thirties)

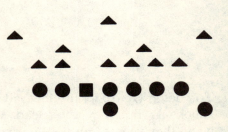

When the T formation
with man-in-motion
came in

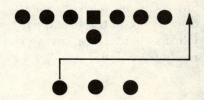

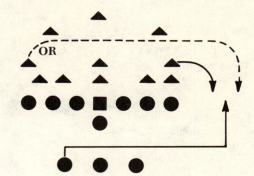

The defense did this
(Steve Owen's 5-3-2-1)

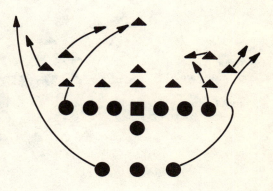

When the halfbacks
started catching passes
and outrunning the
linebackers

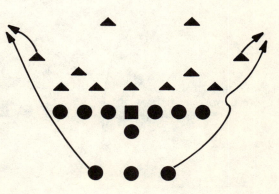

The defense did this
(Greasy Neale's 5-2-4
"Eagle" defense—
mid–late forties)

So in 1950 Paul Brown's
Cleveland Browns beat
Neale's Eagles doing
this

(Spread ends Lavelli and
Speedie and sent Motley
up the middle through
split line)

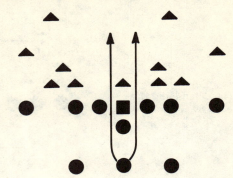

And this
(Sideline passes to
spread ends)

(Flat passes to
backs)

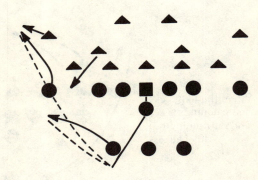

And the L.A. Rams
spread everyone and
did this

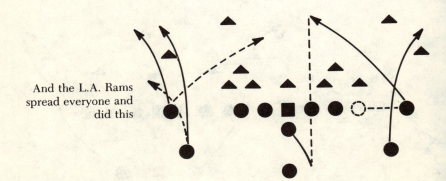

So in 1950 the Giants lined up
in this
(6-1-4 "Umbrella")

And "Flexed," or
dropped the ends back
into the wide flat zone
like this

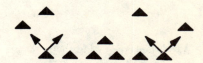

And wound up
with this modern 4-3
defense

Which was also achieved
when the Eagles dropped
middle guard Bucko
Kilroy back into a
"stand-up" position

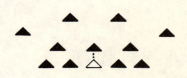

AFL teams began
shifting their lines
into "odd" fronts, with a
tackle over the center,
creating an "over" (strong-
side shift)

Or an "under" (weak-side shift)

And "stacked," or hid their one or two linebackers (Jets' 4-4 stack)

Or all three (K.C. stack vs. Minnesota, Super Bowl IV)

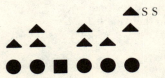

When the offense brought in an extra wide receiver

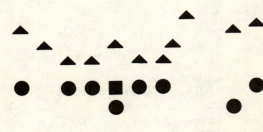

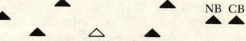
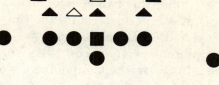

The defense pulled a lineman, or middle linebacker, creating a five-back "nickel"

Dime Defense

Or a "dime" (six backs) or even a "seven penny" (seven backs) to counter four wide receivers

And the base defense has now become the 3-4, used by 19 NFL teams last year, especially against the two-tight-end, one-back offense

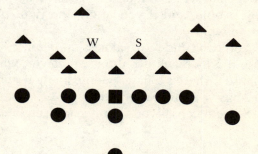

Landry brought the 4-3 to its highest degree with his Doomsday Defense of the 1970s, reaching the ultimate in containment, covering every gap, offsetting two linemen in a "Flex" to control the traps and counters. It was perfect against the run, but football's a passing game now, so Landry has modified his 4-3, bringing in extra backs early, blitzing more than anyone ever thought was sane or healthy, shifting his line into odd fronts. Containment won't do it any more. The rules aren't built for it. Nowadays a defense must attack.

"Before the coin toss, our offensive guys on the sidelines are saying, 'Win it, win it,'" Raiders defensive end Lyle Alzado said. "And our defensive guys are saying, 'Lose it, lose it.'"

The Raiders attacked in the '84 Super Bowl. They lined up in a 3-4, but they played an old-style attacking defense consistent with their operation since the 1960s. Their inside linebackers were set close to the line and they attacked the Redskin guards, the Hogs, before they could get their hooves churning. The Raider pass coverage was basically man-to-man, with the cornerbacks playing bump-and-run, denying the receivers the short stuff—and everything else.

"You're going to hit some big ones against them," said Joe Theismann, who did manage to connect on a 60-yarder to Charlie Brown, after the game was out of reach. "But they'll pick off a couple and disrupt your rhythm."

What brought the Raiders' defense together was the addition of All-Pro cornerback Mike Haynes, a classic man-to-man cover guy, who came to them in an October trade and gave them the opportunity to play their style of defense. After Hall-of-Famer Willie Brown retired in the late 1970s, they tried all sorts of people at the right corner, but the formula was never right. With Haynes in the lineup their postseason success was keyed on their pass defense, almost unheard of in this era. In the three games—playoff, championship and Super Bowl—they held each team under 50 percent in completions and under 200 yards. Which just goes to show that defense is still basically people, and if you've got the right players you can make any system work.

"You can't hide a weakness on defense," Bill Walsh says. "On offense if a halfback is out, or a receiver, you can cover for it, but on defense if there's a flaw, people know it and every attempt to hide it weakens you somewhere else.

"Some defenses you simply can't run because your people can't do it. Coaches forget that, which is more common than uncommon. People tend to do what's safe and expected."

The birth date of the 4-3 defense was officially Sept. 24, 1950, but the idea was planted on Saturday night, Sept. 16, when Giant coach Steve Owen drove down to Philadelphia to scout the AAFC champion Cleveland Browns, making their NFL debut against the Eagles, the defending champions. He had to play the Browns in Cleveland eight days later. Owen watched the Browns humiliate the Eagles, 35–10, shredding Greasy Neale's 5-2-4 Eagle defense with as fine a collection of talent as pro football had ever seen.

Paul Brown split his ends, Mac Speedie and Dante Lavelli, and Otto Graham hit them on sideline and comeback patterns in front of the defensive halfbacks (they weren't called cornerbacks in those days). He threw to his halfbacks, Rex Bumgardner and Dub Jones, in the flat, and the Eagle linebackers couldn't cover them. Their angle of pursuit was wrong. When the linebackers loosened up, the Browns ran 238-pound Marion Motley up the middle on trap plays. The results were devastating.

How to stop this monster? Owen loved to tinker with defenses. The 5-3-3 had been his baby. Occasionally, when he faced a power team, he'd go with a 6-2-3. But that year he'd been awarded three excellent defensive backs from the defunct AAFC Yankees, Landry, Harmon Rowe and Otto Schnellbacher, to team with Emlen Tunnell. He'd never had this kind of talent in the secondary before, so he'd decided to use four men at the deep backs. Landry and Rowe were the corners, Tunnell and Schnellbacher the safeties. (Programs of those days still listed them in offensive terms—i.e., QB, LH, RH and FB, and John Cannady, a linebacker, was the C.) Owen decided to put a 6-1-4 on the field against the Browns, but the switch was that he'd "flex" his ends, Ray Poole and Jim Duncan, and drop them back as linebackers, to join the middle man, Cannaday.

"Steve was a great guy on concepts but he wasn't a great detail man," Landry said. "He just drew the thing up on the board and handed me the chalk and left it to me to explain it. I remember it to the day. It's where my coaching started. I was 25 years old.

"They called it the Umbrella Defense because it had the effect of an umbrella opening. It worked very well. Emlen played next to me. We sort of worked things out on our own, on the field. Graham didn't complete a pass on our defense in the first half. We intercepted three. We had both Speedie and Lavelli double-covered. In the second half Brown had Graham rolling out and throwing underneath the retreating defensive ends. So the ends started blitzing and the cornerbacks rolled up, and it gave them more problems."

The Giants won, 6–0, the first shutout in Paul Brown's pro career. When the teams met again in November the Giants came out in a 5-1-5, with five defensive backs. Five and six defensive backs had been used that year, to combat the Rams' aerial circus, but no one had ever opened a game with such a formation before. The Giants won, 17–13.

"Paul Brown was such a meticulous coach," Landry says, "that if you gave him something he'd never seen before, he became flustered."

For the next few years the Giants alternated the 5-2-4 and 6-1-4, sometimes flexing, sometimes not. Here and there the 4-3 popped up around the league. The Eagles got into a form of it when they had their middle guard, Bucko Kilroy, stand up, although at 258 he hardly had true middle-linebacker responsibilities. The Redskins tried it, lifting middle guard Ron Marciniak and substituting a linebacker, Charley Drazenovich.

Landry graduated from player to player-coach to defensive coach under Jim Lee Howell. Vince Lombardi ran the offense. In 1956 the Giants drafted a tackle from West Virginia, Robert Lee Huff, nicknamed Sam, who'd been born to play middle linebacker in the 4-3, and that became the Giant's official, standard defense. By 1957 everyone was in it.

Landry watched Lombardi work out his Run to Daylight concepts. The Giants' bitterest rival, the Browns, were keyed around the running of Jim Brown. Landry had to figure out a way to contain all that power, so he came up with his gap-defense, mixing in some Flex principles.

"Green Bay made us do it, with Lombardi's Run to Daylight and power sweeps," Huff says. "We coordinated all four guys up front with the linebackers, in military terms. You had your own platoon. I had a three-man platoon, me and the two tackles. We used an Outside 4-3 and an Inside 4-3. On the Outside 4-3 the tackles charged on the outside shoulder of the guards, and I had inside responsibility. On an Inside 4-3 the tackles played the inside shoulder and kept them off me and I'd go with the flow.

"Nobody knew how to block it. I'd always be in the face of the ballcarrier. No one blocked me. All we did was play the strength of the formation—split backs and we'd go Outside 4-3; Brown formation, where the backs are strong to one side, we'd play an Inside 4-3.

"Green Bay caught up with us. Lombardi had taken our defensive playbook with him. He started running counters and cutbacks. So how do you stop that? Your strong-side tackle had to hit and control. Some called it playing the piano. Your weak-side tackle was flexed. Anyway, it took care of Lombardi's counters and Run to Daylight theory. With the Flex there is no daylight."

The birth of the 3-4 is a little harder to pin down. In the 1960s the Oakland Raiders featured a "rover," Dan Birdwell, who would line up at either tackle or end, most of the time in a down position but occasionally up, which would give the alignment a 3-4 look, although Birdwell didn't have much coverage responsibility. When Bob Matheson, an oversized linebacker, joined the Dolphins in 1971 he gave them a pure 3-4, but it was only in passing situations. He'd replace Bob Heinz, a tackle, and he'd float, sometimes playing it as a linebacker, sometimes set in a down stance. At 6'4", 235, he was big enough to handle it. The defense was called the "53," in honor of Matheson's number, which was the same one Birdwell had worn. Bill Arnsparger, until this year the Dolphins' defensive coach, was always partial to swing players, who could line up as either linemen or linebackers. The current one, 248-pound A. J. Duhe, is a Matheson in reverse. He started as a defensive lineman, was converted to a linebacker in the base 3-4 defense ("my whole world changed when I got my hand off the ground"), but goes back to the line in passing situations. Gets complicated, eh?

For a while three-man lines were very popular in what used to be called "prevent" situations, when you tried to prevent the offense from completing passes by rushing three people and dropping eight back into coverage. I always hated those things. So did the fans. Usually they prevented nothing. All they did was waste three linemen, who hadn't a prayer of reaching the quarterback. Given the luxury of time, he could complete any number of passes. Coaches were a little late in catching on to this. They figured that if they stopped the bomb they had it made.

"I'd rather pass against a prevent than a hard rush any time," Brian Sipe said. "Coaches just don't seem to realize that three me-dium passes come out to 60 yards, the same as one long one. But I really shouldn't mention this too often or I might be out of a job."

You still might see it at the end of a game, when the offense is in a Hail Mary situation, but generally it's been junked in favor of a four-man rush in passing situations, sometimes even a five-man rush, counting a blitzer. And the 3-4 is the base defense most commonly used.

The 3-4 was first installed as a first-down defense in 1974, by a pair of Big Eight coaches. Chuch Fairbanks, newly arrived to the Patriots from Oklahoma, used it in his second year at New England, with Sugar Bear Hamilton as his nose guard. Bum Phillips, who took over as Houston's defensive coach after a tour of duty at Oklahoma State, went 3-4, with Curly Culp in the middle. The 3-4, or 5-2 with the ends occasionally playing "soft" and dropping back, was, and is, the standard Big Eight defense.

When Bum became head coach at Houston he stayed with the 3-4. His reasoning was simple: "I've got better linebackers than defensive linemen." Which might be some coaches' subconscious reason for using it, anyway.

"College trends influence a lot of what you do," Cincinnati's former defensive coach, Henry Bullough, says. "There aren't as many good defensive linemen coming out nowadays as linebackers. They're harder to find. Look at the draft. There are probably more mistakes made with defensive linemen than any other position. One goes and then everyone says, 'We've got to get one, too.'"

The trend now is to rush three linemen on first down, but to keep a linebacker in reserve as a potential delayed rusher, a designated blitzer, a Lawrence Taylor type. The trick is to keep the offense guessing. Will he come or will he drop back into coverage? Standard NFL 4-3s are more predictable.

"I've made my living against 4-3s," Walsh says, "using the old Sid Gillman concepts . . . force the linebackers into certain coverages, lock them in, no flexibility."

Everyone blitzes these days. You've got to. You can't sit back and let the new rules eat you up, unless you're as talented, defensively, as the Raiders are. Then you can afford to play the old one-free, man-to-man, with the free safety as a pure rover. You'll see a team blitz most when it's backed up inside its 20.

"It's tough to play any kind of zone when you're that close to your own end zone," Cowboy assistant Ermal Allen says, "so since you're stuck in a man-to-man anyway, you might as well blitz. You've got nothing to lose."

It's a guessing game. On Dec. 26, 1982, the Cardinals drove 70 yards in four plays to beat the Giants, 21–17, at the wire. New York stayed with a three-man rush and dropped everyone back into coverage. On the same day the Packers' James Lofton caught an 80-yard touchdown, the longest play of the weekend, against Atlanta when the Falcons went into a four-linebacker blitz. You take your chances. Personally I prefer the quick death to the slow burn. I'd rather try to rush the passer into an errant throw. Of course, a lot of it depends on the quality of the people you've got rushing.

Fourteen years ago, when I wrote the first version of this book, I spent a few pages showing how a flashy offense was no formula for success, how the top defenses always made it to the playoffs. It's still a pretty good rule of thumb, but last year that formula was jolted. Cincinnati and New Orleans finished 1–2 in defense and neither of them had a winning record. That's never happened before. It only means that in this era, no matter how good your defense is, you're not going to stop people forever, and you'd better be able to put points on the board.

For many years most of the head coaches came from the ranks of defense, either as players or assistants. Now that's been reversed, too. The genius offensive guy has become very attractive to NFL owners and GMs. Twenty NFL head coaches come from offensive backgrounds, six are from defense, and two worked equally with both. Offensive coaches have won the last four Super Bowls—Tom Flores twice, Joe Gibbs and Walsh.

"I'd hire an offensive coach," Gillman says. "Defensive coaches just play guessing games on Sunday. They guess what the offense is going to do and call a Cover-One defense, Cover-Two, whatever. But offensive coaches learn to make major decisions all day long, all week long, whether to run or pass, whether to use play action, when to go deep, where to attack, and a million other things. I'd want that kind of mind as a head coach."

But let's not be too hard on defensive coaches. Football is a cyclical game and I think we'll see the end of the offensive cycle and a return to defense, as we had in the seventies, unless the rulemakers start messing around again. I think that through necessity defensive genius will again emerge. Don't forget that for many years defensive concepts changed and evolved, while offenses stayed in the same basic Pro Set.

Remember when everybody said Dallas's defense was impossible to crack? Well, people figured out how. "In 1981 we audibled out of the Flex 67 percent of the time and into a pass-rush situation," former Cowboy safetyman Charlie Waters says, "because everybody was throwing on us on first down. Hell, that's been the book on Dallas since the days of Unitas and Starr. How had teams beaten us? By putting us in strange fronts and coverages we weren't familiar with."

Much of the great defensive brainwork of the eighties has gone into trying to figure out ways to control the San Diego Air Coryell show. In 1979 Houston did it in the playoffs by stealing the signals, and Vernon Perry, a rookie safety, picked off four Dan Fouts passes. "Actually we didn't steal signals as much as read Fouts's feet," inside linebacker Gregg Bingham said. "When they were together, as he waited for the snap, it was going to be a run. When one foot was back, a pass is coming. Simple, huh? But it worked."

In 1980, in a Monday night TV game, the Steelers opened up with six defensive backs. So the Chargers won by running the ball. In the playoffs that year the Bills came up with the idea of stacking 6'6" defensive end Sherm White behind the middle guard and blitzing him like a middle linebacker. "Gut pressure," Chuck Knox said. "We've got to bloody his nose." It worked for a while, but Fouts pulled the game out with a touchdown pass in the last two minutes.

When he was the Chiefs' defensive coach, Rod Rust had some pretty good days against Fouts, generally holding him to low numbers. His trick was to get his two inside linebackers into the passing lanes, to have them popping up in strange places.

"You want to get Fouts taking time, not throwing in rhythm, off that three- or five-step drop he takes," The Chiefs' All-Pro free safety Gary Barbaro said. "He'll look confused. When he holds the ball he'll start dancing back there. He'll look around in a panic, trying to find a receiver. Then you hope the rush gets to him. If it doesn't, you're in trouble."

In Kansas City in '81 the Chiefs had him on the ropes. Frank Manumaleuga, a 245-pound inside linebacker, picked off two of his six career interceptions that day. But the rush never arrived, and the Chargers won, going away, 42–31.

The big challenge these days is defending the proliferating one-back, two-tight-end offense. Coryell initiated it at St. Louis and perfected it at San Diego. It gave his former assistant, Joe Gibbs, a Super Bowl ring in Washington, and then it gave Atlanta coach Dan Henning, Gibbs's former offensive assistant, 5628 yards last year, 33 off the club record.

"We had trouble with Atlanta's one-back," said Rust, who moved to New England as defensive coach in '83. "I was very tempted, but I didn't have the guts, to line us up in an old-fashioned, wide-tackle, six-man line, an old 6-2 defense. It keeps going around and around in my head. You can do it with nickel people. The defensive ends are strong safeties, then you've got four linemen inside them, then the two inside linebackers are, well, inside linebackers. I still might do it. You might see a lot of people going back to old ideas next year."

One peculiar phenomenon of the 1983 season was the great explosion in defensive touchdowns. Forty-nine passes were run back for TDs, 29 fumbles were returned for scores, producing a grand total of 78. The previous NFL record was 52. What happened?

"The one-back offense has done it," Pittsburgh's defensive coach, Tony Dungy, says. "There used to be two backs in the backfield, and they'd make the tackle. Now there's one, and sometimes he's out in a pattern like everyone else. If you block the quarterback, there's no one left to tackle your guy, especially with the speed of the linebackers nowadays. We'd have had four more if the quarterback hadn't tackled our man. Sipe got Tony Woodruff one time, Archie Manning got Sam Washington. We have a standing joke . . . we tell our players, 'You've got to do a better job blocking the quarterback.'"

One final word on defense. Something I hear from coaches all the time bugs me. I can't understand it. What they say is, "Our offense has to control the ball, and keep our defense off the field." Why? Unless the defense is crippled through injuries or it tires easily, they're going to be on the field for the same number of series the other team's defense is out there, roughly 12 to 14 per game. The trick is to score more points on your 12 series than the other team does, not to score slowly. It's like if you're playing tennis and your opponent has a terrific serve and you say, "I've got to keep serving for a long time to keep him from serving to me."

I can't understand it. The idea is to break service, which is what defense is all about anyway. Break service, break concentration, play tough—and then all you've got to fear is the next round of rule changes.

CHAPTER SEVEN

The Front Four: Half-a-Ton of Defense

At halftime I told the coach my deepest secrets. I said I never wanted to be buried at sea, I never wanted to get hit in the mouth with a hockey puck, and I didn't want to go out and play that second half against Lee Roy Selmon.

—Ted Albrecht,
Chicago Bears Tackle

On the first day of rookie camp Floyd Peters came in and told the defensive linemen, "The number one rule is this— tackle the man with the ball." That immediately cleared things up.

—Bubba Baker

You build a defense with a foundation of ends and tackles and nose guards. You add the linebackers, and you top it off with cornerbacks and safeties. If the foundation cracks, the whole thing comes down, because the line is where it all starts.

A weak pass rush means terrible pressure on the defensive backs, which means that the linebackers have to help them, which means that the running defense is weakened. Weak front four against the run means that the linebackers have to stay in close and play mop-up all the time, which means that the defensive backs can count on no help on pass coverage, which turns them into psychos.

But stick a couple of real studs on that front four, and the whole operation takes on a different look. The quarterback will have to pass from positions he doesn't especially care for. The defensive backs will intercept, and so will the linebackers. The defense can indulge in

134

more trickery and artifice. More interceptions. Better field position for the offense. More points. More wins. More money.

As the game moved through the sixties and into the seventies, most of the league's powerhouses, the perennial playoff teams, were keyed around mighty front fours. They achieved a new identity; fans gave them catchy nicknames—the Dallas Doomsday Defense, L.A.'s Fearsome Foursome, the Minnesota Purple Gang, Pittsburgh's Steel Curtain.

A defensive lineman became the most prized collegiate commodity. From 1970 through 1977, 47 of them were drafted on the first round, the heaviest representation of any position. In 1975, 20 of them were chosen in the first three rounds, which meant that better than one out of every four players picked was a defensive lineman. Eight of them were drafted in the first round in 1977, five falling within the first nine picks. There were six defensive linemen selected before the first quarterback was chosen.

A new breed was developing: the greyhound defensive end, tall, lean, sprinter types who could get off the ball and get upfield on their pass rush before the blockers could set themselves—Cedric Hardman of the 49ers; Jack Youngblood of the Rams; Pittsburgh's L. C. Greenwood, who could run a 4.7 forty. The lasting tableau of the 1975 Super Bowl, Steelers against the Vikings, was of Fran Tarkenton running for his life, trying to get off a pass, and the 6'6" Greenwood slamming the ball back in his face.

In the draft next season Minnesota was late on one of its rounds.

"Minnesota passes," said the guy at the microphone.

"And L. C. Greenwood knocks it down," came a voice from the room.

The mean, tough guys always had been part of the defensive-line picture. Vince Lombardi used to say that usually he could look at a big lineman and tell whether he would play offense or defense. If his hair was combed and he said "yessir!" and "nosir" and "I'd really like to become an outstanding professional football player," he was an offensive man. But if he came in in an old leather jacket and a two-day growth of beard and spat on the floor and asked, "How much you paying me?" then he was defense all the way.

The pattern of offense was control, everything within its prescribed limits. Left foot here, right foot there; mustn't hold too much, mustn't forget the play. Of course defense had its mechanics, too, and its plays, but a lineman could just say the hell with it and start teeing off and smacking helmets and generally raising the kind of hell he did in the saloon back home, and he would be a success. Defensive line play was innovation. Offensive work was precision.

When the Lions' Roger Brown, a 300-pound tackle, was traded to the Rams, he was immediately rushed into action. He had only a vague notion of the Ram defensive signals.

"I didn't have much time to learn the plays," he said, "so I invented my own. It was called Number 12, which happened to be the jersey number of the quarterback we were playing. I just kept calling the Number 12 play all day."

The best locker-room quotes usually came from defensive linemen. Or if they were not from them, they were about them—the quarterback talking about the lick that so-and-so delivered, the offensive tackle talking about the blow that spun his helmet halfway around. When defensive linemen talked about a game, they got right to the point.

"We're like a bunch of animals kicking and clawing and scratching at each other," said the Rams' great defensive end Deacon Jones. "Going in, going into The Pit, I like to slap the guys' helmets. It shakes them up. When I get to the man with the ball, I hit him as hard as I can. If I can hit a man hard enough so he has to be carried off the field, I'll be glad to help him off."

"What I like to do," said Kansas City's 6′7″, 275-pound defensive tackle, Buck Buchanan, "is come down around the quarterback's head with the club—this [his forearm]—the club. You try to ring his bell. You just sort of shake it down around his head all the time. I very seldom tackle a quarterback around the body anywhere. I try to strip 'em through here—the head. You really crush him to the ground, and the next time he'll be looking for you."

It affected all of them, even the pensive and analytical Merlin Olsen, who played left tackle, next to Jones.

"Even if the quarterback is going to get the pass away," Olsen said, "you have to bloody him up a little, to remind him you were there. You have to punish him to discourage him. He begins to listen for your footsteps. He begins to hurry. As he loses his rhythm and timing, you've got him."

A quarterback's head, and an offensive lineman's, was fair game in those days.

"I've got a pretty good catalog of the way different tackles attack your head," veteran guard John Wilbur once said. "There's Alex

Karras of Detroit. His specialty is the karate chop. It can numb you for a second if you don't learn how to get out of the way of it. Olsen likes to keep banging his hands over the ear holes of your helmet. Both hands at the same time. It hurts like hell, from the pressure change or something. And the noise scares you. He knocked me flat out twice before I learned how to dodge it."

The head slap became a favorite technique. It doesn't sound like much, a slap on the side of a hard, plastic helmet. But a lineman's arm, taped from fingers to elbow and then soaked in water to harden, could come across like a club. "On a cold day," says former Bengal tight end Bob Trumpy, "it would take chips out of your helmet."

There were great head-slappers in the old days, but the best was Denver's left defensive end, Richie Jackson, nicknamed Tombstone. His greatness as a player will never be fully realized because his career was cut short by a knee injury, but during a brief period from the late 1960s to the early 1970s he dominated the game as much as any of them. He was great at playing the run; he was tall and quick, and he had any of a half-dozen pass-rushing techniques, and he came to the Broncos with a great hunger for the game.

At Oakland he'd been a nondescript linebacker and a part-time tight end. The Broncos got him as a throw-in in a five-player trade in 1967. Stan Jones, the defensive line coach, looked him over the night he arrived in camp.

"You seem a little big for a linebacker," Jones told him. "I think we'll try you at defensive end."

Jackson stared at him. He had fought his way through the minor leagues. He had been bounced around in the pros. He was 26, old for a second-year pro, and he had driven 24 hours straight, across the mountains, to get to the Broncos' camp.

"Mister," he said. "I'm gonna play somewhere. I've driven as far as I'm gonna drive. Here's where I make my stand."

"If a guy was Hollywooding you, you know, trying to show you up," says Raider defensive end Lyle Alzado, who was a young Bronco in Jackson's final years, "they'd move Richie over to him and he'd straighten the guy out. He was our Enforcer. When we played Oakland one time they built up this big match between Richie and Bob Brown, the Boomer, who was near the end of his career. Rich nearly killed him.

"I saw Rich knock guys to their knees with his head slap; I saw him knock people out. Jim Nicholson, the 6'6", 270-pound tackle for the

Chiefs . . . I saw Richie knock him off his feet and then go into Len Dawson and knock his helmet off. Bill Hayhoe, the Packers' 6'8" tackle, kept holding Richie one day. Richie knocked him to his knees and split his helmet wide open. Remember that famous picture of Y. A. Tittle on his knees, with blood dripping down his nose? That was Hayhoe. They had to help him off the field."

The head slap, the multiple head slap. . . . "You practiced it in the gym on the heavy bag and the light one," Youngblood recalls. "You came through the line of scrimmage like Rocky Marciano. Left, right, you hit anything that got in your way right in the helmet."

It was different in the old days, the 1940s and earlier, when players performed both offensively and defensively. The lineman you freely used your fists on this time would do the same to you on the next series, when the ball changed hands. You were careful about roughing up the enemy quarterback too much. Every team had its policeman, and if you got his team's quarterback he'd soon get yours. Revenge was very big in those days. By 1977, though, defense was ravaging the land, and the defensive tackles and ends were beating up on everybody, and offensive scoring and passing stats were being knocked back into the 1940s. So the league stepped in.

They'd already outlawed the multiple head slap. It slowed the rushers down but didn't really stop them. Then in 1977 they ruled out the head slap altogether. The statistics reflected this with a slight notation. Sacks, which had been at an all-time high in 1976 (9.98 per 100 passes thrown), took a slight dip to 9.76, the second highest ever. Speed rushers took the place of head crushers. Not as much fun but no problem, really.

Then in 1978 the NFL Competition Committee fed the defense a double-dipper. Passing lanes were opened up by the rule that allowed defenders only one bump, and that one within five yards of the line. And offensive linemen were given a license to hold when they were permitted to use open hands and extend their arms on their blocks.

This practically dictated their blocking style—the push block, the open-handed shove, on both running and passing plays, one of the uglier aspects of offensive line play. Not that the push block was a stranger to the NFL. Oakland's Gene Upshaw had been a master of it for 10 years, but he had to be sneaky about it in the past. Now everyone could do it.

"My whole game was ball anticipation, getting off on the split second," the 49ers' Cedric Hardman said. "Then I could use my moves. Today some of those big old lead-foots on the offensive line can still get off a step late and get a hand on you and push you off-stride.

"You're blessed with a God-given talent. You work a whole career to learn the skill to use it, to get it down. And then some rich guys who never played the game get together in Hawaii or someplace, over a cocktail, and take away what you've perfected."

"They want a circus out there—more throwing and scoring at the expense of those who rush," the Rams' Fred Dryer said. "We have become the scapegoats in the dilution of the great American game."

Holding, which always had been difficult to call, became even tougher. An offensive lineman could now get his hands on his man, and it was up to the officials to determine whether or not he closed his fingers, and if so, for how long, and with what effect. The foul had always been in one of those gray areas of the NFL, anyway. Each official had his own interpretation of it. I've always had the feeling that a lot of calls were dictated by compassion . . . poor devils, they have a rough enough time, let 'em hold a little . . . especially if the ref had once been an offensive lineman himself. Besides, how many times could you call it? There were the esthetics of the game to consider. "We could call holding on every play," is the referee's traditional claim, but could they really? How many people would watch a game like that? And the offensive lineman, knowing that holding had just been called on two straight plays, realized that it would take something really outrageous to draw a third one. So he grabbed on for dear life.

The first education a rookie defensive lineman always got in the NFL was about holding. "I never knew what holding was until I came into the pros," Gary Pettigrew, a defensive tackle for the Eagles, said after his first year in the league.

"The first time I played against the Browns I thought I was in against an octopus. They're the best holding team in the game. Dick Schafrath has more hands than a dirty old man."

Tom Landry used to get so outraged about all the uncalled holding fouls against his great All-Pro tackle, Bob Lilly, that he started sending game films to the NFL office, with special notations marked "Holding fouls against Bob Lilly."

For the offensive linemen, holding was a calculated risk. If the official caught him, it was 15 yards—10 yards now. But he wouldn't catch him that often. The defensive lineman could either inform the referee or umpire, which didn't amount to much, since every other play was always punctuated by shouts of, "Watch the damn holding!" or he could deal with the offender in his own way, which merely involved a step-up in the volume and intensity of what he'd been doing all afternoon anyway. So the offensive lineman figured it was worth it.

But to a pass rusher it was infuriating. So was the crackback block, or "hideout," or "bastard block," as Alzado called it, a technique so vicious that it's amazing that it took the NFL until 1974 to start acting against it. Simply stated, the bastard block was a technique designed to slow down an outside pass rusher. A running back would circle wide, draw a bead on a pass rusher's blind side, and drive down on his outside knee, low and hard. It ended many careers. The Jets saw their pass rush wiped out for the season on one afternoon in October of 1971, by one man, the Patriots' Carl Garrett, who blew out the knees of two All-Pro defensive linemen, Gerry Philbin and John Elliott. Some coaches simply refused to teach it. Chuck Noll said, "Even if I put it in, none of my guys would do it. Could you see a Franco Harris or Rocky Bleier doing that to someone?"

The league moved against the rule in mincing little steps, first designating a wide area where the block was illegal, then gradually moving it closer to the line. In June of 1979, when middle guards were suffering from a technique that Denver's Rubin Carter calls the Wham Block—one man stands you up, another chops you from the side—Pete Rozelle sent out a memo urging coaches not to teach it. Two years later the league ruled that a man could not chop block a defender from the side when he was in the grasp. But defensive linemen still got chopped plenty, by the tight ends from the outside, by the motion tight end in the one-back offense, veering into the line and chopping at someone's knees, often from the blind side.

"I'd put in a rule," says Pittsburgh Maulers coach Hank Bullough, "that says no chopping from the side, period. If you want to cut a guy, do it face-up. Clipping's illegal downfield. Why should it be permitted on the line?"

The league has been very careful, though, to crack down on the defensive linemen who rough up the quarterback. His head is now strictly off-limits. Put your arms up to deflect the pass, they say, but when you bring them down just make sure they don't come anywhere near the guy's helmet. The quotes of the old bell-ringers are now obsolete.

This has led to some very chintzy calls by the officials, often in crucial situations. After Jack Lambert got thrown out of the Cleveland game for tackling Brian Sipe too forcefully, a disgusted Chuck Noll said, "Ben Dreith's call. One of the real old ladies in the league. That's all he looks for."

The rule has served to intensify a built-in professional hatred that has always existed between defensive lineman and quarterback. The QB draws the big salary, the big press, the big cheers—and boos, too—and don't forget that booing can be a real spur to a defensive lineman. A QB can torment the defensive lineman in subtle ways. A quick-release quarterback can snap off his pass at the last second with a flick of the wrist, just as the lineman is zeroing in for the kill, leaving him only with the sound of the referee's "Leave him alone! Don't touch him!"

And a scrambler can run a poor tackle or end until his tongue hangs out, until his body is tired and spent and the injury factor becomes a real hazard. The reward is that clean blow that might come once a game, or every two games. And when people talk about making the game safer for the quarterbacks, the defensive ends and tackles pause from their mauling and hammering in The Pit and give one long, loud laugh.

"Sure I think quarterbacks should be given more protection," Alex Karras once said, "if they want to put on a ballerina outfit and slippers. Then we won't hurt them.

"As long as they put on a jock, shoulder pads, and a helmet, they should be just as easy to knock down as it is easy to block us on the defensive line. As long as they're getting paid to do what they do, they don't need any more protection and they shouldn't gripe."

So the quarterbacks get help and the defensive linemen get chopped.

No one suffers from those chop techniques as much as the middle guard, or nose guard, or nose tackle, a position re-created when the 3-4 defense came into vogue in the mid-to-late 1970s. Middle men always existed in football, from the days of the old 7-Diamond, to the 5-3 and the 5-2 Eagle Defense. But in the three-man line, with only one lineman outside him on each side, the nose guard is strictly a pigeon. He is routinely blocked by two men, and often three—center and both guards; center, guard and a motion H-back or second tight end; or center, guard and running back. Any combination is possible. It's a position that shouldn't exist in pro football. The Humane Society should step in and outlaw it. The very name itself, "nose guard," sounds like a piece of equipment, which in a sense he is.

"You're trying to make the tackle with your head and torso," former 49er Pete Kugler says. "The center grabs one hand, the guard grabs the other. It's like playing with no arms."

"If you don't mind my saying so, it's a hellhole," the ex-Raider Archie Reese says. "There's just instinct and reaction, no time to sort out or recognize."

"It helps," the Bengals' Jerry Boyarsky says, "if you don't have a brain. If you took all the nose guards in the league and put them on the field, half of them would probably be drunk and the other half lunatics. They tell you to play with 'reckless abandon' on the field. Two guys are coming down on you all the time . . . you just have to be a little bit crazy . . . but I love it! I love it!"

Bum Phillips once said about the 6'3", 290-pound Boyarsky, whom he had coached at New Orleans, "Jerry's the kind of kid you'd like anywhere on your team . . . well, maybe you wouldn't want him at cornerback. . . ."

Boyarsky's a little bigger than most of them, but he's contoured along the same lines, roughly those of a Frigidaire. The ideal NFL nose guard must be compact and tremendously strong through the legs. Last year, when he switched the Rams to a 3-4, John Robinson traded away a decent defensive tackle, Mike Fanning, because at 6'6" he was simply too tall to play the nose. Too much leg to shoot at. The average height and weight of the starting nose guards for the 21 NFL teams that used the 3-4 last year was 6'2¼", 261. Only five were taller than 6'3"—four at 6'4", and Miami's Bob Baumhower, the tallest of them all, at 6'5".

Baumhower, perhaps the best of the bunch, is also the strangest. At 265 he's fairly lean. When Baumhower came to camp as a rookie, Manny Fernandez, who was trying to make a comeback from five knee operations and one on his shoulder, took one look at him and told him, "Playing nose was my downfall. It could be yours, too."

What saves Baumhower, though, is the size of his legs. They're massive.

"He's the only guy on the team whose knee socks can't stretch around his calves," Dolphin linebacker Bob Brudzinski says. "If he had normal legs and a big upper body," Don Shula says, "he'd never play nose."

Not only does he play it, he plays it without relief . . . one of the few NFL nose tackles who's in on every down . . . and he plays it well enough to have made four out of the last five Pro Bowls.

The Baumhowers of the league are rare—defensive linemen who actually have an identity. How many fans can give you a list of the better-known players, once they get by the Cowboys' Too Tall Jones and Randy White, and the Jets' Mark Gastineau because of his now illegal sack dance, and the Raiders' Alzado? The glamour and notoriety have gone out of the position. In the 3-4 defense, fighting for survival against the stranglers on the offensive line, it's just too tough to play the game and make a name for yourself. Even the nicknames are disappearing. Defensive linemen have turned into sacrificial lambs, double-team absorbers, gap occupiers, freeing up the linebackers to make the big plays.

It's Monday night. We're watching the ABC-TV game with the sound turned off. They break for a commercial and all of a sudden my 11-year-old son is yelling, "Turn it on! That's L.C.!" Sure enough, it's L. C. Greenwood doing a commercial. My boy is a heavy Steelers' fan.

"Can you name the Steel Curtain defensive line?" I ask him.

"Sure," he says. "L.C. and Mean Joe and Mag Dog and, uh, and. . . ."

"C'mon now," I say, "all four."

Suddenly he shoots a fist into the air. "And Fats!" he yells. "Fats Holmes!"

"Right," I say. "Now name this year's defensive line."

He thinks. "Number 92," he says. "The guy who twisted Kenny Anderson's neck."

"Keith Gary," I say. "He's not a starter. I want the starters." He gives up. "Goodman, Dunn and Beasly," I say, and his look is as blank as if I'd said Rote, McKissack and Benners. I mean why should he know something no adult east or west of McKeesport would know?

Where have they gone? No more Steel Curtain or Purple People Eaters or Gold or Silver Rush, no more Mean Joe and Fats and Rosey and Deacon and Tombstone and Merlin the Magician. No more Doomsday Defense. No more nicknames. OK, you say, there's one—Miami's Killer Bees—but let's hear you name another, just one?

Instead we have situation substitutions, waves of people coming on and off the field, chess men. It's a space game, a game of speed, cerebral football played on synthetic grass. "On one series we can use up to 20 different people," former Steeler defensive coach Woody Widenhofer said in 1983. "We can use two different sets of defensive lines. It's more efficient than the old Steel Curtain defenses. Everybody makes a contribution."

I tell my son, Michael, what the coach has said. He snorts. "Makes a contribution," he says. "What is this, the March of Dimes?"

Actually situation substitutions have been going on along the defensive line for some time. Once a tackle in the 4-3 was pulled and replaced by a nickel back in what was the old 3-3-5 "prevent" defense, but then it dawned on the coaches that maybe the fans were right, that prevent defenses don't prevent a thing, except the two-play score, and you can't get any heat on the quarterback with only three men rushing, so the defense on passing downs became a 4-2-5, or a 4-1-6, or even a 4-7. The four stayed. Sometimes you'd pull your nose guard and replace him with a tackle. If your regular right defensive end was a strong run-stopper but only so-so against the pass, you might pull him in favor of a pure sacker. That was traditionally the sack side, the right side of the defensive line, because most of the time it would be the open side, away from the tight end (although that designation is disappearing, as teams load up with two tight ends). At Oakland, Al Davis even had people sitting on the bench who were designated right-side sackers, first Pat Toomay, then Willie Jones, then Greg Townsend. Stan Walters, the Eagles' left offensive tackle, said that he could spot real personality differences between the right ends he played against and the ones on the left side, who faced his teammate, Jerry Sisemore.

"I was talking about it with him once," Walters said. "I said, 'Size, how come you always get the nice, dedicated head butters, and I get all the loonies and whackos, like Coy Bacon and now the new one the Skins have, the guy with the arrow on his head, Dexter Manley? It's not fair.'"

The defense will do all it can to get a sack, which some coaches feel is the equivalent of a turnover, which often can affect a game almost as decisively as a touchdown pass or a blocked punt. A sack—it will bring a defensive lineman back from the depths of despair and get the adrenaline pumping again.

"I think I cried after my first NFL sack," says Bubba Baker, the

Cardinals' defensive end. "It was in our first preseason game, against Buffalo, when I was with Detroit. I gave the tackle a 360-degree move, a basketball move. I'd been waiting all during camp to try it out. He'd come out to block me aggressively and he never touched me, and I got to Joe Ferguson before he'd even set up. I couldn't believe it.

"I heard that roar from the 50,000 people in the stands. My God, I thought, every time I do this, are they going to do that? I've got to get me another one of those. I was crying. I got excited. I went crazy. Next play I jumped offside."

Sack. The term didn't catch on until the late 1960s. Some people think it originated in L.A., with the Rams' famous Deacon Jones–Merlin Olsen–Rosy Grier–Lamar Lundy Fearsome Foursome team. Until 1983 the NFL still didn't officially recognize the term. "Tackled, Attempting Passes," was the rather stuffy way the league described sacks in its record book.

Sack. A graphic description of a football play. Dallas calls it a trap, but that term hasn't caught on elsewhere. It sounds too sneaky. Drops? Nope, sounds too much like medicine. Dumps? Uhhh, no, for obvious reasons. *Webster's* unabridged, second edition, defines *sack*, from the Latin *saccus*, as "the pillaging or plundering of a captured town or city by its conquerors—often in phrases as 'to put to sack, to deliver up to sack'; hence, ruin through despoliation." For instance, the sacking of Rome, or Carthage, or Steve Bartkowski.

Until 21 years ago the league record keepers didn't know how to handle them. At first they weren't recognized at all. The losses were just lumped in with rushing yardage. Then in the early 1960s the yardage was recorded as "team yards lost passing," but the sack itself didn't show up anywhere on the stat sheets. "Total defensive plays" consisted of rushes, passes, punts and field-goal attempts, but a sack was a nothing, a bitter memory to be erased. When Oakland set its record in 1967, no big deal was made of it. "I knew we were getting a lot of sacks," defensive tackle Tom Keating says, "but no one talked of records or anything like that."

Sadly, no individual sack records were kept by the NFL before 1982, so the great pass rushers of the past, like Baltimore's Gino Marchetti, Green Bay's Willie Davis and Denver's Jackson, have left no statistical tracks by which they can be measured. Individual totals were compiled informally by most teams for 15 years or so. Coy

Bacon's 26 sacks for Cincinnati in 1976 is believed to be an NFL high for a season, but who knows? The Cowboys' Harvey Martin had 23 one year. So did Baker, who came into the NFL in 1978 and whose record of 89 sacks in 83 games ranks him as one of the best pure sackers in the game today.

In 1982 the league began keeping individual records after sending out detailed instructions to the clubs on how to determine them. Before that each team had its own system. Jets' (currently Atlanta's) defensive line coach Dan Sekanovich had a unique method of awarding half a sack for every two "spooks," a spook being "every time you spook the quarterback into someone else's tackle."

Some coaches give almost the same weight to a spook—or a "pressure" or a "hurry"—as they do to a sack. "Sacks are like garbage collection," says former Houston defensive line coach Joe Galat. "One guy does all the work and the other one gets the sack." Veteran defensive line coach Doc Urich says, "A pass rush is a pass rush, and a sack is a public relations thing." Weeb Ewbank used to talk about "inherited sacks."

Most players disagree. "Coaches always tell you how important hurries are," Baker says, "but the players don't believe it. There's nothing like seeing the quarterback go down with the ball. One year our left end, Dave Pureifory, and I came up with our own statistic. We figured 500 hurries equal one sack."

Some coaches feel that no other play in the game serves as such an exact barometer of success or failure. One doesn't have to look any further than the sack stats to understand how the New York Jets rejoined the ranks of the living in 1981. They had been notoriously weak pass rushers for almost a decade—their 16 sacks in 1976, when they finished 3–11, was one away from the all-time worst—but in '81 they erupted with a sacking frenzy, getting 66 of them. As a result, the Jets picked up their first playoff check in 12 years, and the front four of ends Joe Klecko and Mark Gastineau and tackles Marty Lyons and Abdul Salaam picked up a catchy nickname, the New York Sack Exchange.

The Pittsburgh Steelers' fall from greatness came when their sack total decreased from 49 in 1979 to 18 in 1980. When the Atlanta Falcons lost their sacking linebacker, Joel Williams, with an injury to his right knee in 1981, their sacks dropped from the 46 they had in '80 to 29, and their preseason Super Bowl hopes ended at 7–9. In 1981 each of the nine double-digit winners in the NFL finished in the top half of the league in team sacks. And in 1983 Seattle, which had never finished in the top half of the NFL in sacks, finally did so, and the Seahawks had their first playoff team in their eight-year history.

San Francisco coach Bill Walsh says, "A pass rush, late in the game, is the key to NFL football.

"Sometimes you see a boxing match where for seven or eight rounds the underdog holds on or even gets ahead. You think an upset is in the making, but then at the end the champion gets him; the champ has worn him down. The pass rush can be like that. Constant pressure by a whole group of superior athletes will wear a blocker down. He gets a little tired, and he isn't able to deal with it anymore. The odds have run out on him."

But not the league office. Their new rules have sent the offensive linemen stampeding into the weight room. Pump iron, pile on walls of muscles, especially in the upper body, the arms; and if the weights don't do enough, there are always anabolic steroids for that extra bulk—and strength. It was time to take the defensive linemen in hand—literally. The Redskins built a Super Bowl champion with an offensive line that averaged close to 280, tackle to tackle. When guard John Hannah joined the Patriots in 1973 he was the heaviest starter on the offensive line—at 270. Last year he was the lightest. The Godzilla Syndrome. Nineteen-inch arms that fire out like pistons. Quick defensive tackle, eh? Well, here's a push for you, *whump!*

"It's like every offensive tackle is rubber-stamped these days," Youngblood says. "They all come off the press at 6'6", 280."

Muscle begets muscle. Back to the weight room go the pass rushers, the sackers, all those huge but lean 4.7 sprinters who once dominated the game through speed and moves and guile.

"Pass rushers are having a terrible time now," said Chuck Studley, when he was the 49ers' defensive coach. "Lots of arms out there. To beat his man, individually, a rusher must have the physical assets; he must be able to butt, to shoulder-drive, to power over the top or to swing his man around. Pushing iron is a religion for pass rushers. They must have the upper body strength."

"I hate all that weightlifting," says Klecko, the leading sacker in the NFL in 1981, with 20½. "It's boring, it's sickening, but it has to be done. I'd like to send a directive to all the offensive and defensive linemen in the NFL. From now on, no more weight training. You'll just rely on natural strength. Put 'em on the honor system. But you know some guy would cheat and then the cycle would start all over again."

In the old days, many of the better defensive linemen, even those who relied on strength, would shun the weight room.

"Unnatural size is useless," the 6'5", 270-pound Olsen once said. "Some players pack on poundage until their legs cave in. I've never even lifted weights. My size came natural, as a result of the sort of work I always did when I was younger, hefting hod and bucking bales of hay. I also worked as a ranger in Yellowstone Park until visitors began mistaking me for a bear."

Olsen's style was the punishing, straight-ahead bull rush, not as a steady diet but as a convincer, just to show his man what he was capable of doing when he wanted to turn it on.

"So many moves you can make, so many stunts," he said, "but the best philosophy was simply to keep hitting them with your best lick."

People who remember Olsen toward the end of his career, when he had only so many rushes in him per game and the energy factor became a real consideration, when he became a stay-at-home and mop-up guy, a reader, a "piano player," forget what a devastating force he was in his early years.

Karras and Lilly, the other great dominating tackles of the sixties, were different types. Karras combined a tap-dancer's moves with a vicious hand-fighting technique, Lilly was a grabber and thrower, a style popularized by the Colts' fine defensive end, Gino Marchetti, in the fifties and a technique that would be very hard to practice today.

"The offensive linemen tailor their jerseys real tight, so you can't grab them," Baumhower says. "And they hang plates from the backs of their shoulder pads, so you can't get a grip on the pads, either."

Deacon Jones, who played end next to Olsen, and who I believe was the finest defensive lineman I've ever seen, had power, speed, and a superhuman ability to keep turning it on long after he should have given up.

"The main thing is to keep going," he once said. "If I get blocked, I claw my way in, even if I have to crawl."

The Steelers' Joe Greene, the best defensive tackle of the seventies, was the quickest off the ball, a flash of lightning from the inside.

"He was my idol, my teammate at North Texas State. He was the Dr. J of football," Hardman says. "No one guard could handle his quickness. Hands are what finished him. He'd still be playing today, still killing people, except for the offensive linemen's hands."

The Cowboys' White, currant king of the defensive linemen, combines the moves of a Karras with tremendous upper body strength.

"He rises up out of his stance and, I don't know, it seems to paralyze you," Philadelphia guard Petey Perot says. "He gives you a little shake, and you see his feet moving so fast, *pitty-pat, pitty-pat,* and you think you've got your arms up, but then you don't. He gives you maybe two moves, and an arm-over, and there he goes."

The arm-over is a move designed to break the enemy's hold. But White says, "None of your moves or strength are any good if you don't get off the ball and into your man before he's comfortably set up." But then the inside battle begins, the war against the hands.

"What they love to do," he says, "is get their hands in close, where the official can't see them, grab your shirt and just roll back, with you on top. It's a takedown, a wrestler's move, and it drives us crazy."

Since the new blocking rules came in, the Browns have paid extra attention to the length of the arms of the offensive linemen they are drafting. One style they've developed is the double fist to the throat, holding the enemy at bay, literally at arm's length. The way to combat that, according to Michigan State coach George Perles, who coached Pittsburgh's Steel Curtain defense, is something the Jets perfected in 1981, their 66-sack season. "Lockout technique," he says. "It was the key to their pass rush. The offensive lineman is bent at the hips, in hitting position, arms extended. You get two defensive ends with enormous strength like those two, Klecko and Gastineau, and they do the identical thing the offensive linemen do, only Klecko and Gastineau beat 'em to the punch. They get their hands inside and lock the offensive guys' elbows out and then run them over, drive them right over the quarterback or on their cans. In the old days we said you couldn't use brute strength to push offensive linemen around. You needed technique; the game was played with your legs. But all this bench-pressing in the weight room has changed that. The guy who has his hands inside is winning. He's got all the leverage on his side."

In 1982, though, Klecko went down with a knee injury. He came back in 1983, but that little edge of quickness was gone. So they moved him inside, to tackle, for the injured Abdul Salaam. Klecko still played well enough to make the Pro Bowl, but the fine mesh that had worked so well in '81 was missing, the sack total fell to a respectable but far from imposing 48, and the Jets finished at 7–9.

With old-timers, such as Alzado, there's a whole catalog of moves and techniques to fall back on: the spin; the hand slide; the knowledge that when an offensive tackle shows discoloration in his hand, when he's down in his stance, and there's more pressure on it, he's getting set to drive-block and a run is coming. Less pressure and discoloration means that he's getting set to pass-block. Old techniques, plus a few of his very own.

"When I was a rookie with Denver," Alzado says, "Rich Jackson and Paul Smith, the defensive tackle, showed me a move they invented called the Halo Spinner, a pass-rush technique. You rush upfield seven yards, dip your shoulder, throw your left arm around, if you're playing on the right side, and spin back underneath. It can break a guy's hold on your jersey; it's a devastating move if it's done right.

"Rich and Smitty were great to me when I was a young player. They'd say, 'You're our rookie. We're gonna take care of you.' So whatever they taught me I tried to pass along to our young guys here, to Howie Long, to Greg Townsend and Bill Pickel, who were rookies this year. The beat goes on."

Some of them are blessed with breathtaking speed. Gastineau ran a 4.56 forty when he weighed 270. But the 49ers' Fred Dean might be the fastest defensive lineman in history. He said he was clocked in 4.48 in 1974. At 227 he's probably the lightest defensive lineman in the last 25 years, but he gets his sacks through a combination of speed and strength, a strength built not from the weight room but from "heavy farm labor and good eating," and a strength that's always shocking to someone facing him for the first time.

"He's unique," Walsh says. "He's not a dominant type of player, like Lawrence Taylor. He's a cat-and-mouse player. He'll pass-rush at three-quarter speed five or six times in a row . . . he'll go upfield, and if anything goes wrong he'll make the play. But then all of a sudden he'll explode before anyone knows what's happened. He did that against Minnesota. I was watching him and I said, 'He's playing cat-and-mouse.' Then *whoom!* Here come the jets."

In '81 the 49ers used Dean as a situation player, a right-side sacker. Next year, though, opponents made sure he never got to play in space—they always put someone over him. The 49ers moved him around. They used him in run situations at times, and his body couldn't take it. He played hurt most of the season. After the Atlanta game on Monday night TV, when his mother watched him go down with a shoulder injury she called and told him to quit.

"You know, Momma," he said, "I ain't got no hair on my chest because hair don't grow on steel."

"Yeah," his mother said, "and grass don't grow on no dirt roads, neither."

A player like Dean could never stand up as an end in a base 3-4 defense. Youngblood, whose style was always the extra-wide split as the outside man in the 4-3, figured it was even money that he'd make it in Robinson's 3-4 last year.

"I just had to buckle up and start lifting more weights and playing the run tougher," he said. "I've just about given up on pure sacks. The only sacks I get are pursuit sacks."

The pressure of the constant double-team, as a 3-4 defensive end, has finally gotten to the Bucs' Leroy Selmon, who has been a terror for years. In 1983 he played hurt most of the way. But once every year he gets a taste of the old life, the good life, when he plays in the Pro Bowl, which has never gone out of the 4-3. Then he's the killer of old.

If the offense wants to, it can usually load up to stop one particularly ferocious sacker. When Taylor was terrorizing the league as a rookie in '81 the 49ers stopped him in the playoffs by pulling their left guard, John Ayers, and having him pick Taylor up. Everyone hailed it as a marvelous innovation, but actually it's an old technique—and I've seen it have disastrous results. The NFL record for sacks is 12, but 32 years ago, before sack statistics were kept, I sat in the Polo Grounds and saw the Eagles' Pete Pihos and Wildman Willey dump Giant quarterbacks Charley Conerly and Freddy "Needle" Benners 13 times for 118 yards. Defensive ends in those days played the old "box" technique, a run-contain style, but the Eagles had Willey and Pihos crashing that day. The Giants tried to pick them up with their guards, Ray Beck and George Kennard, but the angle was off . . . it just didn't work . . . and the Giants never changed their blocking scheme. It was horrible to watch . . . like seeing a guy getting run over by a truck. Maybe the answer is that Ayers, one of the 49ers' best pass blockers, was just nimbler than poor Beck and Kennard.

The NFL sack average, which hit that all-time high in '76, with '77 close behind, dropped to 7.2 per 100 passes in 1981, the lowest since the figures began to be kept. But in 1982, sacks were up, and in 1983 they were up again—to 8.66, the highest number since '77. Two reasons. Blitzing schemes were becoming more intricate, and everyone got in the act, nickel backs, safeties. Defensive linemen were having to share the wealth. There was no 20-sack player in the NFL. And number two, stunts, or "games," were becoming more complicated: end-tackle games, in which the end pinches in and tries to contain two men and the tackle loops around him; tackle-end games, which are the reverse; tackle-tackle games; and deep loops, in which a man might swoop in from two positions away . . . plus, of course, all manner of stunts involving the linebackers.

Miami was always a great stunting team, the ends, Doug Betters and Kim Bokamper, doing a fine job of containing everything inside, while applying pressure from their 3-4, or gaming with inside linebacker A. J. Duke, who, in the four-man pass-rush situation, became the down lineman he once was. But the coach who is probably the best at it is Floyd Peters, who built the Gold Rush at San Francisco and the Silver Rush at Detroit, and whose 1983 Cardinals led the NFL with 59 sacks.

"The obvious key to stunting is the ability of one man to tie up two," he says. "You can shift your defense and put three guys one-on-one against their man and eliminate the double-team. You have to figure different types of stunts for a quick rush or a rush on a long passer. Most of all you have to believe in what you're doing. I've had coaches say, 'I've tried all your friggin' games and they don't work.' They didn't believe in it.

"You've got three and a half seconds, tops, so you have to work your games to get something open quickly, like tackle-tackle games. Or you can fake it and then club with your front arm across the guy's shoulder. Against L.A. two or three years ago they'd form a five-man wall with their hands out. What to do? So we sent the end down hard to collect the tackle and looped the tackle around him. We got four sacks that way, but it took half a game to break it down.

"Fouts throws one-two-three on rhythm, so stunting's no good against him. Against a team like San Francisco you've got to take them one-on-one. They just pick up stunts too well. You've got to keep changing things, too. If you run a certain stunt three weeks in a row you're looking for trouble. They'll have you pegged by the third week. You'd better just file your scheme and change it. A good stunt will last about three games, on films."

Many of Gastineau's Jet teammates were annoyed about his sack dance, which they felt was unprofessional, but for a while in '82 they were even more furious because he wouldn't run his stunts.

"He didn't like it inside, where all that traffic is," one of them said last year. "We'd practically plead with him, 'C'mon Mark, we've got to loosen up the middle,' and he'd say, 'Leave me alone, I'm doing my own thing.' His own thing! Well, we finally got *that* sorted out this year."

Gastineau is a great pass rusher, but it took him three years to learn how to play the run, and even in '83, when he made a lot of big plays against enemy ballcarriers, he did it more on physical ability and hustle than on technique. Some people feel that great pass-rushing lines necessarily sacrifice something against the run, but it doesn't always follow.

The top three sacking teams in history, the '67 Raiders (67), the '81 Jets (66) and the '76 Forty-Niners (61), finished, respectively, first, seventh and fifth in the entire NFL in rushing defense.

"Detroit was good against the run in the Silver Rush days," Peters says. "So was the Gold Rush at San Francisco. You can survive against the run if you stack your linebackers, station them directly behind a defensive lineman. We'll attack and keep the two stacked backers. I'm in favor of an attacking type defense. Everybody knows that."

"No one ever understood defensive linemen the way Peters does," says Hardman, the star on Peters's 49ers' Gold Rush teams. "He turned us loose. 'Attack,' he said. 'Attack the passer, don't worry about the ballcarriers, you'll collect them on the move.'"

The exact opposite is the Dallas Flex system, which offsets two linemen, a device geared toward stopping the trap play. Basically the Flex is designed against the run, with everybody filling an assigned gap. No defensive lineman becomes a star in the Flex right away. Lilly was first tried out as a defensive end, where he was just so-so. Jethro Pugh, the left tackle on all the great Doomsday teams, worked as an offensive tackle at first, and he didn't start until his third year. White was a bust as a linebacker, until he was moved to tackle. Too Tall Jones was disappointing his first couple of years, Harvey Martin was almost cut in camp as a rookie, and before he became a starter he was a designated right-side sacker. He called himself Harvey Banks Martin in those days.

As difficult as it is to learn the Dallas system, it's almost as tough for a defensive lineman to learn to play against Tom Landry's offense, which is geared to misdirection and influence blocking.

"They don't come at you, they use you to take yourself out of the play," Washington tackle Dave Butz says. "It's just happened so many damn times. All your instincts, everything you've learned about playing the run, say fight the pressure. But Dallas will give you pressure, take it away and then ride you in the direction you're going, while Dorsett bends behind you. It's frustrating and it takes a while to get used to."

Some coaches say the love of the sack, the pass rush, has caused some defensive linemen to neglect their run-stopping techniques, and because of that you'll see a return to a heavier ground game in the next few years.

"Defensive linemen, psychologically, are geared to sacks," Walsh says. "That's what they talk about . . . sacks, big plays, ravaging the quarterback. Consequently their run techniques are eroding."

"Some stuff that's taught in the NFL is just downright silly," Baltimore coach Frank Kush says. "For instance, the defensive lineman's head-butt technique. We don't teach it. To me it's stupid. You're completely lost on the run when you do that. So many times you see a guy head-butting his way in there . . . his head is down . . . the ball-carrier goes right by him and he never sees him."

Every now and then you'll see a team load up with extra defensive linemen. Washington stunned Green Bay in the '72 playoffs with a five-man line, something that hadn't been seen since the fifties. Chicago will occasionally use it as a mixer.

"It's so apparent," Studley says. "It's like sending them a telegram: Sir, we're going to blitz."

I saw something even stranger in '83. Kansas City came in with an old six-man line against the Giants. That's not four linemen, plus two linebackers in a down position; every one of them was a lineman by trade, a guy with a 70- or a 90-something on his back. They tried it four times and they worked stunts off it. The first thing it got was a delay-of-game penalty on the Giants. Then when Scott Brunner came back he overthrew his receiver, with a Chief lineman in his face. This was on a third-and-four situation. Next time was on second-and-10 and the Giants ran a halfback delay and picked up six yards. Its third appearance was on second-and-10 and the Chiefs got a sack from it. At halftime the Giants went in and talked it over and decided to run trap plays against the thing. When the Chiefs tried it a fourth time the Giants picked up 10 yards on a second-and-10, and the Chiefs put the six-man line back on the shelf.

Maybe that's what the future holds, more six-man lines, more guys on the field who are paid to rush the passer, not little shrimps who do it for a lark. It would be a nice, nostalgic switch, like a reversion to black-and-white movies or tea dances. And the defensive linemen would cheer.

CHAPTER EIGHT

The Linebackers

The night I was inducted into the Hall of Fame they told me, "You're going in with the unskilled labor. I said, 'Do you know what a skill position means? It means run like a sonofabitch." To me, skill is us guys who run down those fast S.O.B.s.

—Sam Huff

THE man who invented football never figured there would be a position like linebacker.

You just couldn't walk up to Walter Camp and say, "Walter, old boy, someday there's going to be a chap who weighs 230 pounds, and he won't be just a big boy like Fat Tom over there; he's going to have to run downfield with the halfbacks, and then next play he's going to have to charge through the guards and tackles to get to the ballcarrier. He's going to have to be vicious, you see, because when the interference forms, he'll have to wade through it and knock it to pieces; but he can't just be a killer. He's going to have to be a genius, too, because we're going to give him a choice of, oh, maybe 50 different plays to call, so we want him to be able to figure out what the other team's going to do before they do it."

And, of course, Camp . . . or Stagg . . . or Rockne . . . or any of football's pioneers would have looked at you and said, "Please, we're busy. We're trying to coach a football team."

The truth is that nobody expects a man to really be able to play the position. If they did, the linebackers would be drawing $500,000 a season, instead of the $130,000 or so they're paid now, putting them right about in the middle of the wage scale—more than the offensive linemen, less than the offensive backs and receivers.

It's a position of compensations. "We know you're not really fast enough to cover Billy Sims, man-for-man, straight down the field," the coaches say, "but we'll write it into the playbook anyway. Don't

156

worry, he'll get bumped around a little coming out of the backfield, and if he does get loose and breaks downfield, just hang in there. Our line will pressure the quarterback so he won't have time to hit Sims deep. And if he does . . . well, every pass isn't thrown perfectly, and pass coverage isn't so bad, anyway, once you get the hang of it. Yes, we know it's almost impossible to stop a screen pass when a guard and a center are out there leading the play, but just for playbook's sake we'll write it in as your responsibility. Just get out there and be tricky . . . or if you can't fake 'em, take 'em on, and who knows, maybe someone will back you up and bail you out.

"What's that you say? You're supposed to drop back for pass coverage when the quarterback is cocking his arm, and you have to come back and fill in for the draw play at the same time? Well, buddy, that's your problem. We're not paying you to look pretty out there."

The schizophrenic world of the linebackers: come in, back up, go deep, stay tight, be fast, be big, be mean, be smart. Actually, be everything.

In 1981 two Texas A&M psychologists did a study on hostility and aggression, comparing 108 football players with 120 regular students. Their findings, which were published in *Psychology Today,* showed that the players generally were less hostile and aggressive than the nonathletes, and both groups showed the same level of tension—except for linebackers. Linebackers scored significantly higher than everyone else in "depression, anger, fatigue and confusion."

The 1978 no-bump-after-five-yards pass-defense rule probably contributed greatly to all four categories, and even more to a fifth—frustration. Tight ends, running backs, wide receivers—the whole caravan, in all shapes and sizes—could now run their crossing patterns and picks through the middle and the linebackers couldn't touch them. At one time, when the great middle linebackers roamed the center pastures, Butkus, Nitschke, Schmidt, Lanier, receivers took their lives in their hands crossing in front of them. It was part of the game; a guy invades your territory, you take his head off. Now it's strictly a no-no. In 1982, when the Jets' Stan Blinka snapped a forearm into the Packers' J. J. Jefferson as he was crossing over the middle, a practice once as routine as tying your shoelaces, sirens went off and alarm bells started clanging in the Commissioner's office. Blinka was fined $1000 and suspended for a game, and the incident was afforded the kind of publicity usually reserved for a multiple slaying.

The big, mean headhunters who patroled the middle, men whose names were as familiar as the game itself, were becoming obsolete. Two things did it, the new passing rules and the 3-4 defense, which provided two inside linebackers, instead of one, and cut down on the freedom of the position. Some of the old-timers just melted into oblivion. Others, such as the Steelers' Jack Lambert, the 49ers' Jack Reynolds and the Giants' Harry Carson, who had been great 4-3 middle men, adjusted to the new alignment, often with considerable grumbling.

"In 1982, when I was 30, they switched to a 3-4 and I became the weak-side inside backer, then the left-side inside man," Lambert says. "My first year I was unsure of the whole scheme and how I fit in. It was a change for me. Having to worry about cutbacks, well, it goes against my nature. I always want to go to the ball and pursue all over the field. This way is an efficient way to play the game, and I accept it—but that doesn't mean I like it."

Reynolds bristles at the idea of getting lifted on passing downs— "often as early as second-and-six," he says. "They say you can't cover passes, then they take you out on passing downs, and it becomes a self-fulfilling prophecy. I don't know, under these new rules, maybe they're right. I used to love to jam the receivers eight yards deep, just when it screws up the timing of a pass. I can run with anyone for eight yards. Now you can't touch them past five. We used to cut the receivers when they started their break. The Axe technique . . . the Rams and Bears were masters at it. Now we can't. They just don't let you play anymore."

In 1983 seven teams were still using the 4-3 as their base defense. Their middle linebackers were practically anonymous—Ken Fantetti of Detroit, Dave Ahrens of St. Louis, Neil Olkewicz of Washington, Fulton Kuykendall of Atlanta, Bob Breunig of Dallas, Mike Singletary of Chicago and Bob Crable of the New York Jets. Only Singletary made the Pro Bowl. Only Singletary and Crable remained on the field in passing situations. The others were 60 percent players. The average size of the seven pure middle linebackers was 6'2", 227. None of them weighed over 230. Ten years previously, when all 26 NFL teams used the 4-3 (the Patriots' Chuck Fairbanks initiated the 3-4 as his base defense in '74), the average size was 6'2", 232.

"You're seeing the end of the 230-pound linebacker," the Packers' Hall of Famer, Ray Nitschke, said to Sam Huff in 1982, when Huff was inducted to the Hall. "Dick Butkus, at 245, would have a tough time today."

"I'm not so sure," Huff said. "It's still a game of hitting. Do your job and stop the run and you're going to play . . . maybe not as many downs, but you'll play."

I'm not so sure, either. "Butkus would be a strong-side inside backer in a 3-4 today," the ex–Cincinnati defensive coach, Henry Bullough, says, "then a down lineman on passing downs. A great player like Butkus . . . you've got to find a place for him . . . I don't care where it is."

The strong-side inside linebacker (most coaches don't even use that terminology anymore; they simply call the inside men "pluggers") is one of the least glamorous positions on defense. His job is stopping the run, sticking his nose in where the guards and centers live, and on anything remotely resembling a passing down he's the first one to get the hook. Yet the cold-weather teams, the clubs that know the importance of building a running game—and a defense against same—as something to fall back on in November and December, when the air turns frigid and the hotshot passers come down to earth, understand the role of the strong-side plugger. One of the best, and most underrated, was Buffalo's Shane Nelson, the heart of their famous Bermuda Triangle defense of a few years ago. When he went down with a knee injury after nine games in 1981 the Bills were fifth in the NFL against the run. They finished the season 17th, and they haven't been in the top half of the league ever since. And their record, since that day they lost Nelson, is 16–16. The fiber of toughness was gone, and it hasn't been recaptured.

I've often wondered why the inside pluggers flop, strong side and weak side, when they play so close to each other anyway, and the outside linebackers don't.

"It's easier with the inside guys," Houston player personnel director Mike Holovak says. "They're only two steps away from each other. The outside people have farther to go, and the offense might catch them in the middle of a shift. Plus the offense is always changing its strong side and weak side anyway now, with all the motion they use."

"The responsibilities are different inside," Reynolds says. "Most teams will blitz their outside linebacker who's away from the tight end, the strong side, so the inside man next to him, the weak-side guy, takes on his outside responsibility. He'll have to cover a back flaring out. The strong-side guy inside has to be stiff against the run, but the weak-side plugger has to have movement outside and strength to play inside against the run, too. He's a cross between a middle and an outside linebacker."

Modern offenses are coming up with terrible things to disrupt the flow of the linebackers, motion and fake motion and reverse motion. San Diego runs one of the weirdest of all, a move in which tight end Kellen Winslow goes in motion, does a full 360-degree pirouette, and keeps going in the same direction. ("Don't ask me where that came from," says Washington's special-teams coach, Wayne Sevier, who used to work for Don Coryell with the Chargers. "Maybe Kellen just felt like doing it.") Redskin coach Joe Gibbs has had great success with a play in which two linemen pull out one way and another one pulls in the opposite direction. "A key-breaker," he calls it. "Sometimes you'll get the inside pluggers bumping into each other." And the one-back, two-tight-end formation poses another problem, because it's a balanced alignment, with no strong side. To simplify things, more defenses probably will follow Pittsburgh's idea and just line up the inside pluggers left and right, instead of strong and weak.

It's a scary place to play these days. "With all the stuff the offense is doing now, an inside plugger better have speed and intelligence," Bullough says. "The big, slow, dumb linebacker is obsolete. Better find a job somewhere else."

In a way it's a dilemma of their own creation. By the mid-1970s linebackers who could run 4.5 and 4.6 forties, playing behind 4.7 defensive ends, were controlling the game. As athletes they were just too good for the people trying to block them. Defense had taken over. So in 1978 the rule makers went to work, and in the wake of the new pass-coverage rules came true offensive innovation for the first time in decades.

The defense tries to survive. There are few superstar defensive linemen these days, and fewer yet of the great, dominating defensive backs there used to be. The rules are too tough. Anyone can be beaten deep. But like a desperate poker player pushing in his whole stack on trip-aces, the defense has sent it all in on their outside linebackers, and these are the true superstars of the 1980s. The reason is that they have to do an impossible job.

They do the bulk of the blitzing, a familiar skill since most of them were stand-up defensive ends in college, anyway. Often they have to clamp on a wide receiver in the short zone. They have to play the run and drop back deep into coverage—without being able to bump a receiver. Their game is strength and speed, and this combination has produced a collection of the most breathtaking athletes ever gathered in one position in the NFL.

November 1983, Giants versus Redskins. The Skins look every bit as tough as they did in the Super Bowl year of 1982. The Giants are going nowhere, but they are blessed with the best defensive player in a decade, their right linebacker, Lawrence Taylor. His season has been played in a gathering rage. He asked coach Bill Parcells to let him run downfield on special teams. Request granted. Then he asked him to let him play offense, too—tight end. Request denied. Now it's early in the second quarter and the Giants are already 10 points down and Joe Theismann is back to pass and Taylor is blitzing from the Giants' right side. Joe Jacoby, the 300-pound All-Pro tackle, slides over to block him. Teams have already learned that you don't let a Lawrence Taylor play in space. You don't try to pick him up with a back, as you would in the old days; you put a tackle or a tight end on him and hope to slow him down. Taylor graps Jacoby by the shoulder pads and throws him. He flushes Theismann out of the pocket, and Theismann's off and running. George Starke, the 260-pound right tackle, peels back to pick up Taylor, who knocks him to the ground without breaking stride. Taylor catches up with Theismann 15 yards downfield. That's 560 pounds of linemen he's disposed of, and a 4.6 quarterback he's run down. I think it's the best defensive play I've ever seen—and it's in a hopeless cause.

Around the league everyone likes to talk about Taylor. "He came on a blitz one time," Rams' tailback Eric Dickerson says, "and I was just trying to beat him to the handoff."

"Everyone knows he's coming," his former teammate, Beasley Reece, says. "It's like a cop putting sirens on his car."

St. Louis linebacker E. J. Junior remembers going bowling with Taylor at the East-West Shrine Game when they were college seniors.

"He got ready to bowl, and he picked up the ball and threw it," Junior says. "It didn't hit the lane until it was halfway down the alley. It knocked down all the pins—and the fiberglass backing behind the pins. You could see people walking around back there. It was a sheer act of brute strength. We kind of quietly backed away and left the alley. I'd never seen anything like that."

The only reason the defense survives at all nowadays is because of the emergence of the great outside linebackers, bigger for the most part than the inside pluggers (there aren't any inside people the size of the Giants' Brad Van Pelt and Minnesota's Matt Blair, 6'5", 235, or the Raiders' 6'7", 230-pound Ted Hendricks) and certainly faster. Almost every team has a person of All-Pro ability at the position— Keena Turner of the 49ers, Chip Banks of the Browns, the Jets' Lance Mehl, the Raiders' Rod Martin, the Falcons' Buddy Curry, E. J. Junior of the Cards, Mike Douglass of the Packers, Hugh Green of the Bucs, Blair, Hendricks, Ricky Jackson of the Saints—the array is dazzling, and endless.

"Yeah, there's a lot of great physical talent out there," the 36-year-old Reynolds says, "and some of them are so talented that they don't work much on techniques, on reading and recognition, and because of that their careers are going to be shorter. In the old days a guy could fall back on techniques, but some of these guys, well, when they start losing a step, or they're not as strong, they'll find themselves replaced by a new guy faster and stronger."

The most unusual linebacker in the NFL today is Hendricks, who has never missed a game through injury in 15 years, who made the Pro Bowl for the eighth time last season, at the age of 36, whose game is a combination of innovation and calculated hunch-playing, based on an almost photographic memory of enemy tendencies.

"At least once a game he'll do something that I didn't know how he did it," says former Raider defensive coach, Charley Sumner.

"We were playing Kansas City one year and we were in a goal-line defense," Hendricks says. "I just had a feeling where they were going to run, so I drifted over to the other side. A couple of our guys looked at me . . . 'What the hell are you doing over here?' The Chiefs had some young players; they didn't have a checkoff system. I was standing in the hole, but they ran the play anyway. Our coaches must have been tearing their hair out in the press box."

"A lot of guys might be able to guess where the play is going, but wouldn't have the nerve to do anything about it," Sumner says. "When he's right 98 percent of the time . . . what can you say?"

I used to get a tremendous kick out of watching Larry Grantham in his last days with the Jets, 6', barely 210 pounds, potbelly, funny little stiff-legged gait . . . toward the end of his career I saw him knife in on a Buffalo sweep one time and spill O. J. Simpson for an eight-yard loss before O.J. had even gotten the ball tucked away, and I saw

O.J.'s gaze follow Grantham all the way back to the defensive huddle. *He* did *that* to *me?* I'd seen Grantham make the same play so many times before. In the locker room I tried to find out how he did it.

"Well, there's something to this being old," Grantham said. "It's not all bad. I couldn't coach anybody to play linebacker like I do. But when you've been around for a while, there are just certain things you pick up. When a back leans forward, he's coming out on a pass or he's getting the handoff. When he leans back, he's setting himself to pass-block. The young ones tip it off most of the time. Sometimes the old ones do, too.

"We've got our keys to play, but if you start figuring them out you're dead. You've got to look for that first movement, and that's the time you react—not your brain, but your legs. Your brain catches on later. I look at one man, but I'm actually seeing about five. And there's absolutely no waiting involved."

"Reading your keys gets you into your area," said the old Packer linebacker, Dave Robinson, who was, at 6'4", 245, one of the first of the great speed-and-strength guys, "but then it's up to you. It's seek and destroy."

Some of them played with an almost sixth sense, and they made it look easy. A leg injury ended the career of the Steelers' Jack Ham, but for almost a decade he was the dominant outside linebacker in football.

"We were sitting on the bench during a game, and he was telling me about some stock deal he was interested in," said Andy Russell, the other outside linebacker on the Steelers' early Super Bowl teams. "Then we had to go out on defense. On the first play Jack read the pass and dropped into the zone, deflected the ball with one hand, caught it with the other, flipped it to the ref and overtook me on our way off the field. 'Like I was telling you, this stock's really a good deal,' he said, like nothing at all had happened."

People like Ham and Taylor seem to have been born for the position. With others it's a painstaking process, a learning of new skills.

"In college we were taught never to run around a block," Russell said. " 'Fight the pressure,' the coaches would tell you. But if the blocker was bigger and stronger than you, and most of them were, and you fought the pressure, you'd wind up making the tackle and giving up six or seven yards to do it. I used to watch Chuck Howley of the Cowboys. He was like a matador out there. He'd dart inside, actually running around the block, and he'd make the tackle for a three-yard loss. When I was a rookie I tried to play it honest and I'd get killed, so then I tried to develop some of those sneaky moves and they worked. But I'm sure it would have driven my college coach crazy. He'd have said, 'You've turned into a sloppy ball player.' "

"Playing against the tight end," Blair says, "it's a finesse game. These guys are masters of deception. They'll give you the okey-doke over their shoulder, like they're going out for a pass, then they'll jump around and screen you off from the sweep. They're cute. You have to be ready."

"A tight end couldn't just blow me off the line," Ham says. "He might knock me back two or three yards, but then his momentum disappeared, and I'd just slip off to make the tackle. And one thing I learned toward the end of my career was not to hit them with a forearm anymore. They'd just lock up your arm. They'd clamp on so tight you'd become part of the tight end. So the whole thing was more like basketball, relying on quickness and technique. The tight end was trying to get position on me . . . I couldn't let that happen."

A lot of the old technique linebackers would have trouble today, though, and the reason is speed. The field has been spread out . . . it's a space game . . . there's more territory to cover.

"Speed and height are what the computer looks for when you're drafting linebackers," New Jersey Generals coach Walt Michaels, an old linebacker himself, used to say when he was coaching the Jets. "Well, I'll take a guy an inch smaller and a step slower if he's got the brains. I want to know what he's thinking when he sees them breaking out of the huddle and lining up in front of him. As far as speed, what I want to know is how fast he drops back covering passes, not how fast he goes straight ahead for 40 yards."

"I can chase a back but I can't run a 40," Mehl says. "The 40 is so much start. I get down in a stance and I stand up before I start running. It's a matter of technique. When you read your keys you don't need that flat-out 'speed."

Unless you find yourself chasing a Sims or a Tony Dorsett 30 yards deep, but usually when you see a linebacker in a coverage like that there's been a mistake. Only a few defenses nowadays assign a linebacker one-on-one coverage on a fast back, all the way down the field. Generally, after a certain point, he'll pass him off to a safetyman, in the zone. And watching a back turn up and race 40 yards downfield tells you another thing . . . the defense's pass rush isn't much good. He should never have that much time to slip out and take off.

I used to wonder why so many times when an outside linebacker would blitz, instead of trying to avoid the setback he'd go right into him. The reason was, he'd have a double responsibility—contain the back and keep him from getting out cleanly, and then go for the quarterback.

The blitz has gone through an up-and-down existence in the NFL. In the old days they'd call them Red Dogs, shortened to Dogs, or Shoots or Stunts. The birthdate of the blitz is credited as Dec. 1, 1957, when the San Francisco 49ers (defensive coach, Phil Bengtson) beat the New York Giants (offensive coach, Vince Lombardi), 27–17, by sending their linebacking trio of Matt Hazeltine, Marv Matuszak and Karl Rubke pouring in on Charley Conerly. Charley fumbled five times that day, losing four of them, and the brand-new weapon called the blitz supposedly turned the trick. It might have been done before (I have an image of Huff swooping in on quarterbacks from his middle linebacker position in 1956), but the 1957 Giant-49er game is its acknowledged birthdate. And two years later, when Lombardi became head coach of the Packers, the first assistant he hired was Bengtson.

The early Lombardi-Bengtson Packers blitzed heavily, and they were masters at unhinging quarterbacks by this mass of unblocked linebacking fury pouring in. But just when the rest of the world had picked up the blitz and wielded it like a giant cudgel, the Packers started to taper off. The theory was that it left too many holes in the vacated areas, and a quarterback who kept his cool and didn't get rattled could pick it to pieces. The great Packer defenses of the mid-sixties blitzed very little, but when they did, they came like the hammers of hell.

"A blitz," Lombardi once said, "is used to cover a weakness." And so it followed that the blitzing teams were generally the teams that were fundamentally unsound, weaker. Offenses developed the "hot man" technique, dumping the ball off to a receiver, generally a tight end slipping over the middle. It was a quick and easy throw for the quarterback, one that he could get off in a hurry. Quick-release quarterbacks like Joe Namath, guys who weren't afraid to stand in and face the horns until the last possible moment, were death to blitzers.

So the nonblitz became a status symbol. Strong defensive teams like the Cowboys and Steelers disdained it. Teams with particularly

formidable front fours had the added luxury of being able to drop
their linebackers back into coverage more often. The have-nots
worked on their blitzing schemes, and a couple of them—the Patriots
and Falcons—developed the ultimate blitzing weapon, the Maniac
Blitz. All 11 men were up at the line. On the snap of the ball two
or three of them dropped back into shallow coverage. The rest of
them came. It was 50-50 whether the quarterback would have a ner-
vous breakdown or throw a touchdown, but those aren't the odds you
win with on defense, so the Maniac Blitz soon returned to the filing
cabinet.

The new, liberalized pass-blocking rules, which have produced a
race of stranglers along the offensive line, have made blitzing a necessity once again. The difference is that the great thundering hoof-
beats of a Butkus or a Nitschke coming up the middle is a sound from
the past. Inside linebackers don't blitz that much. It's too crowded in
there. Whatever action there is in the middle usually comes from safeties and nickel backs, skinny guys who can fit through small cracks.
Outside linebackers are the featured blitzers nowadays, often lining
up as down linemen, sometimes stunting with the end next to them,
always looking for an open side, where they can go against a setback.

Old-timers look at the new breed of linebackers, the blitzers and
greyhounds, and they're saddened.

"You watch them today and you know they're making more
money than you ever did and they're not playing the game as they
should be," Nitschke says. "They don't know how to tackle. All they
worry about is pass defense and blitzing and doing sneaky things."

"True linebackers are historical landmarks," Reynolds says.
"Pretty soon there won't be any linebackers as we know them.
They'll either be blitzers or safeties. With everybody passing so
much, defenses will use four rushers and seven pass defenders as a
base defense."

I think he overstates it. An alignment like that would be an invita-
tion to run the ball, as teams found out in 1983 when they went into
their nickel or dime defense too early. But the glamor of the linebacking corps has shifted from inside to outside, and in a way it's sad,
because the old 4-3 middle linebackers were a breed unto themselves, a mighty race.

The 1960s and early 1970s was the great era for middle linebackers, and we used to have spirited debates about which were the
best. Almost every team had a great one—Willie Lanier on the

Chiefs, Nitschke, Al Atkinson on the Jets, Joe Schmidt on the Lions, Mike Lucci on the Lions, the Dolphins' Nick Buoniconti, the Colts' Mike Curtis, the Eagles' Chuck Bednarik, the Falcons' Tommy Nobis, the Cowboys' Leroy Jordan, Huff, Reynolds, the Bengals' Bill Bergey—the list is endless. And standing like a tower in the middle of them all was Dick Butkus of the Bears. The mere mention of his name brings shudders to people who had to face him.

"I played against him toward the end of his career, when his leg was barely attached to his body," Miami guard Bob Kuechenberg recalls. "The word was to take Butkus low and you'd have an easy game. I said, 'No, it's a point of honor. I'll take him high.' That was a very bad decision on my part. He just about took my head off. I thought, 'Hmmm, as much as I respect him, maybe going low wouldn't be such a bad idea after all. . . .'

"Guys like that . . . they played the whole game in a sort of frenzy. It's like he was from another world, another planet. You know, a writer could do a tremendous article if he really got into his brain. Why was a Dick Butkus the way he was? I always wanted to sit down with guys like him and Nitschke and Jim Brown. What motivates them? What separates them from the rest of us? Maybe I'd find something I could use, a key. A guy like Bubba Smith could have been the greatest at his position. He had it all, physically, but he was not a great player. But Butkus . . . he didn't run a 4.6 forty, he wasn't a great weight lifter, but he just ate them alive, all those 4.6 sprinters and 500-pound bench-pressers."

"Every time I play a game," Butkus once said, "I want to play it like it was my last one. I could get hurt and that would be it for keeps. I wouldn't want my last game to be a lousy one.

"You know some people think I have to get down on all fours to eat my couple of pounds of raw meat a day. Others think that George Halas taught me to walk upright and I have to have an agent do my reading and writing for me. But people who really know me know that I can read a little. I move my lips sometimes, but I can read things on a second-grade level, like newspapers."

You might catch him on the TV commercials these days, but the last time I saw Butkus in the flesh was a few years ago in the Giants' training camp. He was there selling Nautilus equipment. He was bitter. He had just collected a six-figure injury grievance from the Bears, from those last few seasons when he played on a crippled knee, and he still didn't walk right. "I'll never be able to go 18 holes around a golf course," he said. Every now and then he'd sign an autograph. He didn't enjoy it very much. "They don't want to know anything about you, they just want your name on a little piece of paper," he said. Then two kids in high school football jerseys asked him for his signature. He signed without a word, and as he watched them walk away he noticed that one of them wore a knee brace and limped slightly. For the first time Butkus smiled.

"Another ex-linebacker," he said.

CHAPTER NINE

Last Line of Defense: The Secondary

Defensive backs. Nothing but reactions. You train 'em like seals.

—Sam Baker, ex-kicker

We're gonna use the Corner Freeze defense. Take the cornerbacks, dip 'em in water and stick 'em outside the Silverdome until they're frozen solid. Then use 'em as spears. Throw them at the wide receivers.

—Cincinnati safety Mike
Fuller before the 1982
Super Bowl in Detroit

THE Jets had been beaten, 27–14, by the Oakland Raiders toward the end of the 1969 season. It was three days later—press luncheon day—and the newspapermen headed down to the locker room to ask for the umpteenth time, "What's wrong with the Jets?"

Only this time they knew the answer. It was right cornerback Cornell Gordon, who had given up two touchdowns to the Raiders' Warren Wells and had allowed Wells three more catches—all for good yardage. A cornerback's lapses cannot be hidden. They are right out there in the open, out of the traffic. Just you and me—and 60,000 fans.

So Gordon sat up on a rubbing table while half-a-dozen writers asked him what was wrong in half-a-dozen ways.

"It was pretty brutal," John Dockery, the left cornerback, said later. "Sort of like the Grand Inquisition. I sure felt sorry for Cornell, but you know what I was thinking while all that was going on? I was thinking, Thank God it's not me up there on that table.

"Do you know how tough this position is—how unbelievably tough? You're standing there all by yourself, and you're looking at a guy like Wells who can fly, I mean really fly. One missed step, one stumble and that's it. Curtains. I wish everyone who sat there in the stands and booed Cornell Sunday would get a chance to see what it's like—just once."

The position demands a sprinter's speed, no nerves, and no memory. Brood about a mistake and you'll repeat it, the coaches say. In fact some scouts say that the one position where too much intelligence can be harmful is cornerback; too much introspection can hurt. They figure that once a man starts thinking deeply about how impossible the job is, he comes apart.

Which doesn't mean that cornerbacks are dummies. Dockery was a Greek and Latin major at Harvard and he did fine. What cornerbacks were, though, was underpaid, and most of them still are. Next to kickers, cornerbacks are the lowest-paid players on a football team. John Sample said he got canned in Washington because of a contract squabble with Otto Graham.

"I wanted to get paid the same as the men I was covering," he said. "It was logical to me. The job I had to do was just as tough as the job they did. Why shouldn't we have gotten paid the same?"

The answer is that cornerbacks don't draw fans and receivers do, and that's the traditional salary index, fair or unfair.

The one standard quote you get from cornerbacks concerns the basic toughness of the position—physical, mental, emotional. It's all part of the game. The Raiders' defensive back coach, Willie Brown, the best cornerman in the AFL in his day, wanted to hold a clinic every June for cornerbacks. He said he would run it, and it made no difference whether or not the men were from competing teams.

Cornerbacks of the world belong to a common fraternity, he reasoned. A fraternity of misery.

"Nobody has it any tougher than us," he said. "The game is usually won or lost depending on how well a cornerback stops his man. But we still aren't paid what ends get. The clinic I have in mind would be on how to play the different receivers in football. And to discuss money."

It was tough in those days, but it's tougher now. The new rules have left them with one bump and taken away everything else. The bump must come within the first five yards, and then the defender is on his own, with only a sturdy pass rush or the defensive coach's brilliance to help him.

"I think," says Raider All-Pro cornerback Lester Hayes, "the five-yard bump zone is detrimental to a defensive back's sanity."

Once upon a time cornerbacks such as Herb Adderley and Night Train Lane would go half a season without getting beaten deep. Now you just hope it doesn't happen too often. Last year I picked the Bengals' Ken Riley as one of the cornerbacks on my All-Pro team for *Sports Illustrated.*

"But he gets beaten deep," someone said. Hey, join the club. They *all* do, buddy. It's the nature of the game these days.

"We preach to our kids, don't worry about getting beat on a bomb," Jet defensive coach Joe Gardi says. "Offenses can put so many points on the board that 14 points aren't going to beat you. Two or three turnovers will make up for it. Ten years ago giving up the bomb was disastrous. Not now."

Cornerbacks can gamble more now because much of the time they're the front men in two-deep zones, with a safetyman backing them up and covering anything deep. And the five- and six-back alignments for passing downs are built for gambling. Cornerbacks are drafted for speed and coverage instincts, and their lack of size often reflects it. They're not built for stopping sweeps. The big, tough cornerbacks, such as the former Steeler Mel Blount, are becoming obsolete.

"We played more like outside linebackers in today's 3-4 defense," CBS announcer Tommy Brookshier, a cornerback for the Eagles in the 1950s and 1960s, says.

"We'd come up on the run a lot faster than they do now. We didn't gamble too much. If you got beat long back then, the crowd would come out of the stands after you. Now they expect it.

"We'd just hit the guy all the way down the field. I had such a reputation for that, guys would stop coming my way. They had families. But these cornerbacks today can't do that. I don't know how they cover people that run 4.3, 4.4 in the 40 and don't even leave any footprints. Now they're getting guys to play cornerback who won't run when the media comes blitzing them after the game.

"Cornerbacks like Ronnie Lott don't have a conscience. They'll gamble on everything. If I ever gambled on a sideline pass I'd make sure I had one hand around the receiver's throat and the other hand to go for the ball. If I missed it I'd strangle him."

The NFL interception record is 14, by Lane in 1952, but the most impressive year I've ever seen a cornerback have was Oakland's Lester Hayes's 1980 season. He's a sturdily built cornerback, playing as high as 210 at times, a natural for the old bump-'em-down-the-field style, but in 1980 the new rules were already in effect. He intercepted 13 passes in the regular season. Most of the time they'd leave him alone on a receiver and roll the zone or the double-team help the other way. By the end of the year he was playing, as he said, "in a kind of euphoria." People were describing him in mystic terms. "The Force," they'd say, "Lester has the Force with him."

He peaked in the playoffs—five interceptions in four games. And in the Pro Bowl, usually devoted to relaxing in the Hawaiian sunshine, he had an astounding day. The NFC quarterbacks, Ron Jaworski and Steve Bartkowski, threw 11 times into his coverage and completed one pass, a 15-yarder to Alfred Jenkins on third-and-22. Hayes had one interception. His total postseason stats read: nine of 35 passes completed into his coverage; no touchdowns; six interceptions, giving him 19 for the year, counting postseason. Some cornerbacks don't pick off that many in a career.

Hayes had been scouted personally by Al Davis, the Raiders' boss. "He had what I call power speed," Davis says. "He jams people with power, runs with 'em with power, he has an explosion to the ball. Some guys are quick with no explosion. Lester can be beaten, then *whoosh*, he'll explode to the ball. I saw him make one play in the Hula Bowl . . . it was an option play . . . he came up from free safety and killed someone. I saw the explosion and I wanted him.

"Mike Davis, our strong safety, is almost as fast. He's a big, rough tackler, but he hasn't Lester's explosion to the ball. Coverage can be taught, but the explosion is unique."

The great ones seem to have it, explosion to the ball, "ball reaction," the scouts call it, an instinct, a knack of throwing it into a higher gear and reaching the ball when they seem to be beaten. Redskins coach Joe Gibbs talks about the Cowboys' Everson Walls having "athletic arrogance," a feeling that the ball belongs to him.

The scouts don't seem to have it all together when it comes to cornerbacks. Walls was passed over in the draft. The Cowboys signed him as a free agent and he rewarded them by leading the league in interceptions his first two years and making the Pro Bowl, three out of three. Herb Adderley and Night Train Lane, considered by many to be the two greatest cornerbacks of all time, were switched over from offense. Burgess Owens, drafted in the first round by the Jets, and called "the finest pure cornerback I've ever seen" by Weeb Ewbank, was turned into a safetyman his first year. Somehow the stopwatches and computers don't seem to have the answers when it comes time to judge who will hold up under actual man-to-man conditions in the NFL.

Walls is not a physically intimidating cornerback, as Lott is, nor is he a burner, which is why the scouts might have been thrown off.

"He could break for the ball, and that's what we missed," Dallas personnel director Gil Brandt says. "We just went on whatever times he'd run, and we didn't find out all we could. But at least we offered him a free-agent contract."

"During my first year in the league, I didn't know what was going on," Tom Landry says. "I was a defensive back who didn't know if the guard was pulling or if the end was releasing. Most rookies are just blind when they're out there, but I have to admit that Walls sure did a lot with what he had."

At the other end of the scale is the 49ers' Lott, who might not have the great ball instincts Walls does, but who makes it on athletic ability—4.47 in the 40, plus a knack of timing his hits so that he electrocutes people. He gets a lot of interference penalties called because he likes to play the receivers close, but to tone down those instincts would be to take his game away.

Pure speed won't do it. Henry Carr, an Olympic 200-meter man, found that out in his few years as a defensive back with the Giants and Lions.

"Running backwards was the hardest thing I had to learn," he said. "My speed was actually a detriment at the start. I depended too much on my legs."

Bruce Maher, the Lions' old safetyman, once offered this cryptic capsule on what it was like to get beaten for a touchdown: "The first thing you see as you run toward the bench is all the big linemen going down for the extra point. Your own guys are looking at you like a worm, and the other team's linemen sort of have a half-grin on their faces, conspiratorial-like, like you conspired to fall down and let their guy score. You run toward the bench and you know you're going to get hell there. You can see the coaches, with their clipboards, watching you come."

And the defensive back has a nice long stretch on the bench to think about that touchdown and brood about it. The coaches say that the good ones wipe it out of their minds and bounce right back. I'm sure the psychiatrists would have an opinion about that.

"The thing to remember is that you're going to get beat," Adderley said. "If you don't, you should be coaching, not playing. The question is, when you get beat, can you recover? You never give up on it. So someone scored a TD on you? You should never think about the play that's past, except briefly, and then only how you're going to keep your man from doing that again."

Players sometimes find that the maneuvers that seem so simple when they were diagramed on the blackboard turn into nightmares on the field.

"The toughest thing for me," said the Jets' defensive backfield coach, Billy Baird, a former free safety, "was to pick up a loose receiver. My job was all angles. On a blackboard, you always made the angles intersect, but out there the chalk didn't always get there on time."

Sometimes it's hard to tell where a player's instincts really lie. Eddie Meador, the old Rams' free safety, used to say that almost every defensive back in the NFL could play offense, but it wouldn't work the other way around. I'm not so sure. Adderley was an offensive star at Michigan State. Lane had been a receiver. Before black quarterbacks were accepted in the NFL they were routinely converted into DBs . . . sometimes white quarterbacks, too, such as Rex Kern of Ohio State, Jack Mildren of Oklahoma, Nolan Cromwell of Kansas.

One of the few who made the defense-to-offense switch was the Cardinals' Roy Green, who was drafted as a kick returner and cornerback, where he played for his two NFL years. In 1981, though, they started using him as a wide receiver, as well as the regular nickel back on defense. He finished the season third on the club in both interceptions and passes caught, and he was first player to catch a touchdown pass and intercept one in the same game since Eddie Sutton did it for the Redskins in 1957. His average of 21.5 yards a catch convinced coach Jim Hanifan that his future lay in offense, and last season he led the NFL with 14 touchdown catches and led the NFC with 78 receptions.

"Playing both ways in '81, like I did, could be done by a lot of different guys," Green says, "when you consider the caliber of athlete in this league. I think maybe coaches just have been afraid of the risks involved in doing it. For me the only hard part was learning the offensive terminology."

Occasionally coaches will spot-play an offensive man, usually a wideout, in the secondary, in five- and six-back situations. The Packers' James Lofton went in as a sixth defensive back in one game. And two weeks after Green emerged as a two-way player, the Browns' Sam Rutigliano used his split end, Dave Logan, as a nickel back against Atlanta. On his first play he nearly intercepted a Steve Bartkowski pass. On the next play Bartkowski threw again, and this time Logan grabbed it. I'm surprised that more coaches don't use their third or fourth wide receiver in prevent situations more often. Probably the logistics of the meeting rooms are too tough to figure out.

Many players say that a defensive back and a receiver have entirely different personalities. After he had shut down the Jets' longball threat, Wesley Walker, in the '82 AFC Championship Game, Miami cornerback Gerald Small put it in perspective.

"It seemed that after a while Wesley didn't put that much into running his patterns. If receivers aren't catching the ball, they get frustrated very easily. That's the mentality of those guys. They're really the pretty boys of the sport. It's their image. They like to run down the field free as a bird and not get touched. They get paid all that money to catch the bomb and spike the ball in the end zone. When they don't, they get upset.

"A cornerback, on the other hand, is probably a half-crazy guy. He has to be a little masochistic to play a position like that."

Depending on the defense called, cornerbacks will play the receivers either tight on the line or four to seven yards deep. Sometimes they'll take up an intermediate position, three to five yards off, and sometimes they'll either "cheat up" or back on their own. When Walt Michaels coached the Jets he taught the "slide" technique, sliding the feet in the manner of a basketball player covering his man, as opposed to the backpedal, taught by the Raiders and others.

In the old AFL-NFL days the AFL was the bump-and-run league. AFL defenses attempted to combat the wide-open style with tight coverage, bumping the receivers all the way down the field. The NFL played the more-conservative seven-yards-off system, mixing in more zone defenses. When Joe Namath riddled the Colts' strong-side rotation zone in Super Bowl III, and then the Chiefs' Len Dawson did the same thing to Minnesota's conservative, layback defense a year later, the styles drew closer together, although the really fashionable NFL defense of the seventies was the zone.

When a defensive back gets his playbook in camp the pass defense section probably breaks down into the following coverage.

Basic Man-to-Man: This could further be broken down into bump-and-run or four-to-seven-yards-off or intermediate coverage. The purest form of man-to-man was the old "one free," or "coverage one," in which the free safety was a roving center fielder, or free-lancer. Everyone else had definite responsibilities—cornerbacks on wide receivers, strong safety on tight end, outside linebacker on backs flaring out of the backfield, middle linebacker on second back out or backs running a tighter, closer route, such as a circle-in. A team that had a gifted ballhawk at free safety, such as Dave Grayson on Oakland, Larry Wilson on St. Louis or the Packers' Willie Wood, might want to free him up to pursue the ball, but the weakness was that it would leave a linebacker on a back, all the way down the field, a situation no one was happy about—except the back, and the quarterback. More common was a man-to-man defense that assigned the free safety definite responsibility, such as double coverage on a particularly dangerous receiver or deep responsibility on a fast back. The linebacker would simply pass him off to the free safety after a certain point, or maybe he'd pass him off to the strong safety, and another linebacker would assume the strong safety's coverage responsibility on the tight end. The strong or free safety might also switch assignments with a linebacker, if a running back was considered a more dangerous receiver than the tight end. The linebacker would jam the tight end at the line and then run with him, and the safetyman would be responsible for a back.

Unless it has exceptional coverage people, a 4-3 team that sits in a man-to-man too long these days, under the new, freer passing rules, is a dead pigeon. The base 3-4, though, puts another linebacker into coverage. The inside linebacker on the weak side, for instance, might take the second back out of the backfield, on his side, or the first back, if the outside backer was blitzing—a tough coverage but not impossible, considering that the quarterback will be under pressure and shouldn't have much time to get the ball away. Usually, though, a realistic team bases its man-to-man coverage scheme on the particular abilities of its players—and the ones it's facing.

Zone Defenses: Strong- and weak-side rotations, double zones, half-zones. The varieties are endless. More about them later.

Blitz or Dog Coverage: Fans think of a blitz as any time a linebacker rushes the passer. The coaches call it a dog, short for the old term Red Dog. A blitz, to them, involves a defensive back rushing the passer. The traditional concept is that in blitz coverage everything reverts to man-to-man, but this isn't always true. If an offense always leaves one eligible receiver back to pick up the blitzers, you might wind up with six defenders covering four receivers, so double coverage is possible, even a minor zone adjustment. Particular attention is paid to the hot man, the receiver a quarterback seems to favor when he has to get the ball off in a hurry, in the teeth of the blitz. The defense has to get on him quickly, and tight . . . "clamp on him," the coaches say. Usually the hot man is a tight end or wide receiver breaking his pattern off short and heading toward the middle, since that's an easier throw for the quarterback, or it could be a back swinging out wide, as San Diego does. The latter is called a side adjustment. When a defensive coach studies an opponent's scheme against a blitz, the first thing he'll want to know is do they "go hot" (throw to a hot man) or pick it up (leave people in to block the blitzers and go for a big one downfield).

Nickel, Dime and Seven-Back Defenses: Extra secondary men replace linebackers or a down lineman. Offense usually has three or four wideouts in the game. All types of zones are possible. Man coverage occurs when one or two of the defensive backs blitz. The fifth, or nickel, back will usually take a man-to-man position on a particular receiver. Some nickel and dime defenses always keep man coverage on the designated MDR . . . most dangerous receiver.

Keys, Mixers, Combinations: Can be a half-zone, in which one side of the field will play zone and the other, man-to-man. Can be a combination of man coverage shallow and zone coverage deep. Or it can be a key defense, in which some defenders, by reading predesigned keys, will switch from zone to man. A switch can be a prearranged swap in assignments by two defenders.

A team's defensive philosophy is often keyed on the pass rush. A team with a weak rush might play the bend-but-don't-break style, shut off the deep stuff and keep everything underneath—hoping to jar the ball loose with a good hit, hoping that a new scheme or some particularly brilliant defensive switch will produce an interception, hoping that somewhere during the drive the quarterback will make a mistake and misread the coverage, hoping, hoping. But a solid pass rush means a bold secondary. They're not as terrified of the deep reception. They can play bump-and-run. The linebackers can try to shut off the short stuff. People can go for the big play.

"Give a team the short passing and they'll keep taking it all the way for a touchdown," says Baird, whose Jet defensive backs had the luxury of the New York Sack Exchange operating in front of them in '81. "Part of the way you stop this is confidence."

With Joe Klecko hurt in '82, though, the Jets' rush dwindled to a trickle, and the secondary became more deep-conscious. Going into the playoff game against Cincinnati, Baird knew that the bend-don't-break philosophy would be disastrous against Ken Anderson, master of the short pass, so he changed gears again and tightened up the coverage.

"We tried to take away his short stuff, get him choking on the ball," Baird said. "We wanted to get him scrambling, so the rush could get to him." The result was two touchdown passes for Anderson, but three interceptions and four sacks—and a 44–17 Jet win.

Aside from the new rules, the thing that makes defensive coaches old before their time is the pick. It's like a pick play in basketball . . . an offensive player runs his man into another offensive player who's standing there, setting a pick. The defender gets picked off. Only in football it's more of a crisscross action: two receivers crossing close to each other, hoping the defensive back gets hung up on one of them, freeing his man. There are picks and there are illegal picks, in which the receiver deliberately runs into a defender, but it's a fine shade of interpretation. And although picks happen all the time, a good picking team will have its timing down so precisely that it will seldom get called for it.

"The only way the officials call it is from intent, and it's never called," New England's defense coach, Red Rust, says. "You can see it on films; a guy positions himself and makes his body thick. But a ref on the field doesn't see how he can call it.

"So what do you do? You call a switch, just like basketball. And what does the offense do? They run a false pick. San Diego is very big on this, with Winslow and Joiner. We call it the clap-hands pick.

They go toward each other and then break outside without picking, trying to get your guys in the middle of a switch. It's all basketball . . . the roll and go."

Sometimes a veteran defender will see something like this and he'll pick up his own key and play his own hunch. It happens more than you think, instinct plus years of experience telling a guy he should react in a certain way, no matter what defense has been called. Coaches allow it, unless a man guesses wrong too often. Then there's a heart-to-heart talk.

Lott was a gambler from day one with the 49ers.

"All sports have a gambling side to them," he says. "I've watched them as I was growing up. You get to the point where you can sense when it's time to go for it, when you know they're going to attack you. You've got to watch the quarterback, his eyes, the way he looks at his receivers, the way they handle themselves with the coach on the sidelines.

"In my rookie year I could practically read the Rams' Billy Waddy telling Dan Pastorini, 'Look, I'm open,' after one particular curl pattern. So next time Pastorini went to him and I'm waiting for it and I cut in front of him for the interception. But then we played the Giants and I guessed against Earnest Gray. I cut in front of him and the ball went right past me for a 29-yard gain.

"A rookie mistake," added Lott, who happened to be a rookie at the time.

The Jets' John Sample used to keep a little black book, in which he graded all the receivers. So did the Cards' Larry Wilson. Lester Hayes says he has his own film archives on receivers that go back to his rookie year of 1977. He says every receiver has his own little idiosyncrasies that don't change through the years.

"I've also got a mental chart of every pass pattern I've been beaten on since I started playing in the NFL," he said one day in '81. "Go ahead, ask me about a game."

Broncos in Denver in 1978?

"A five-yard fade to Haven Moses," he said.

Eagles in Philly in '80?

"No completions in man-to-man coverage."

Jets in Shea in '77?

"That was my rookie year. I didn't start."

The offenses keep a file on the special traits of defensive men, too. When the offensive unit is given its game plan on Wednesday before

the following Sunday's battle, there's usually a one-paragraph capsule on each man who figures in the opponent's defensive scheme.
Here are excerpts of one team's report on some of Washington's defensive backs, from an early 1983 regular season game:

> LC, No. 28, Darrell Green, 5-8, 170, Rookie . . . First round draft
> this year. Return man with exceptional speed (4.34). Fastest cor-
> ner in the NFL. Quickness. Plays our right and flops to a slot.
> Plays a tight alignment, basically seven yards off. [*Ed. note:* How
> can he play a tight alignment and be seven yards off? Oh well, I
> didn't write the thing.] Rolls late on cover 2. Cheats inside on
> dog downs. Intercept for TD vs. Buffalo. Great ability, but still
> plays tentatively and can be beaten [Note: This changed dra-
> matically by the playoffs.] He is not physical and should be
> blocked on the runs [this changed, too].
>
> RC, No. 32, Vernon Dean, 5-11, 178, second year . . . Excel-
> lent rookie year in '82. Their best corner. Plays a lot of inside
> technique. Fairly tight playing seven yards off. Will roll late on
> cover 2 and play even farther inside than normal on dog downs.
> Stays in his backpedal a long time, but is tough to beat deep.
> Works hard vs. the run but is not real physical [most coaches
> disagreed].

Sometimes a player is so formidable that he merits a page all to himself. Herb Adderley would routinely get a one-page treatment, but
one thing the scouting report didn't mention was that Adderley
played as the back man on a pretty mean threesome down the left
side of the Packers' defense—All-Pro left end Willie Davis, and behind him All-Pro left linebacker Dave Robinson, and then Adderley,
the left cornerback. Davis was a supreme pass rusher, and so de-
pendable against the run that Robinson could drop his 6'4", 245-
pound frame back into the intermediate passing zones, which made
Adderley's job nicer. On the Raiders last year Hayes played behind
two Pro Bowlers, Howie Long and 6'7" Ted Hendricks. At the other
end is a cornerback who might wind up playing behind two stiffs.
Half the time he'll be fighting for his life.

Redskin defensive coach Richie Petitbon said that playing strong
safety on the Rams with the great Deacon Jones rushing the passer

"added three years to my career. Who throws to their tight ends against us? The tight ends are always busy helping the tackle block Deacon."

A forced interception is one in which the pass rush forces an errant throw. A coverage sack is the result of such good downfield coverage that the quarterback has to wait too long and the rush finally reaches him. The two things feed on each other.

"The receivers throw head fakes at you," Night Train Lane once said. "They throw body fakes. I can follow two fakes, but when they throw three at you . . . well, it means somebody isn't getting to the quarterback."

"When I've got Number 74 [Fred Dean] and Number 76 [Dwaine Board] coming off the ball," Lott says, "you know that quarterback's got to get rid of it. It's a whole different ball game. Just like with the Giants when Number 56 [Lawrence Taylor] is rushing the passer."

I'm sorry I never got to see Lott playing under the old bump-and-run rules, because if ever a cornerback was made for it, it was he. The Rams' director of operations, Jack Faulkner, says K. C. Jones, the great guard for the Boston Celtics, invented the style when he tried out for the Rams in 1958.

"I was the defensive backfield coach then," Faulkner says. "K.C. was the first guy I ever saw come right up to the line and play the man head-up. He did it because it was the way he covered people in basketball. He was terrific and he had our guys complaining like hell."

The emotional advantage of the bump-and-run style, or of man-to-man coverages in general, is that a player who responds to challenge will enjoy the idea of direct confrontation with the enemy, rather than the more nebulous zone theory. Bob Cousy once described the idea in basketball, when someone asked him why he taught man-to-man rather than zone defense when he was coaching at Boston college. The same applies to pass defense.

"When you give a young, competitive athlete a straightforward assignment, like a man to guard, and say, 'Here he is. He's yours. Go get him,'" Cousy said, "the guy will generally respond better than when you assign him a zone to cover. He gets up for the man. He says to himself, 'Dammit, I'm going to shut that guy out.' He'll be diligent when you give him a zone, and he'll want to help the team and all that, but the adrenaline just won't be flowing the same."

The Raiders probably play more man-to-man coverages than any other team in football these days, and more bump-and-run. It's a philosophy they've never changed, Al Davis's concept of total annihilation, of a defense that attacks . . . we go after you, not vice versa.

Willie Brown, the greatest attacker in the game while he played for the Raiders, says the secret is a good, firm jam on the line of scrimmage.

"Make the receiver feel it," he says, "when he takes that first step off the line. I didn't jam a man every time, but he wasn't going to know that. I wanted to have him looking for the hit that never comes."

Brown's protégé, Hayes, says his own trademark is the "Riddell technique. Plant that Riddell helmet squarely in the numbers."

"It sounds good," Rod Rust says, "but the offense has ways to counter that. You see, the bump is basically an inside-outside tactic . . . you can use the sidelines for help. But when the receivers run inward, either from motion or a set, you're getting a lot of outside-inside movement, and it's hard to get a good relationship. If he runs a crossing pattern and you bump him, you'd better have the foot speed to stay on his shoulder—and you should have deep help behind."

Nowhere in defense is such minute attention paid to technique as in the secondary, where a mistake can mean six points. One NFL playbook breaks down man-to-man coverage into eight technical areas. The section looks like this:

1. **ALIGNMENT:** Squared up on the receiver for bump-and-run; shade his outside shoulder in intermediate alignment; outside foot forward when playing 4–7 yards off. Use a basketball stance.
2. **KEY:** Determine whether you'll be in coverage or in force position for the sweep.
3. **CONCENTRATE:** This is the key to good man-to-man coverage. Concentrate on his numbers until he makes his final move.
4. **BACKPEDAL:** Backpedal straight back, on the balls of your feet, with good balance and shoulders parallel to the line.
5. **POSITION:** Get to a position one yard outside and two yards off the receiver as quickly as possible. Never let him get a head-up position with you. Make yourself strong on one or the other of his sides. Be conscious of the jam by the strongside linebacker.
6. **DRIVE:** Drive for the ball after the receiver's final break. Push yourself to get in stride with him. Position yourself so he has to

make contact with you to make a change. Gear yourself mentally to break for the ball on his final drive.

7. INSTRIDE: Look for the ball, through the receiver, once you are in stride with him.

8. THE BALL: When it's in the air always be in a position to break through the receiver or to step in front of him to take it at its highest point. On a deep pass, make sure you can feel him. Strip the ball. When you get only one hand on it, be sure to have the other hand in a position to grasp the receiver.

Under "Zone Coverages" are added the headings "DROP" and "FOCUS," with attention given to an area rather than a man, and under "Bump and Run" is the reminder to "discipline yourself to concentrate on your man's hip."

A player trained in man-to-man style might have trouble if he's traded to a zone team, as Adderley was when the Cowboys picked him up for their Super Bowl drive in 1970.

"It was a problem," he says. "I never felt comfortable playing in the Dallas-type defense. Even when I'd make a big play or an interception it seemed like I was out of position or something. I just never really got the feel for it. And I think Tom Landry recognized the difficulty I was having because sometimes he'd allow me to just go ahead and play man-to-man while we were actually supposed to be in something else."

Patriot All-Pro Mike Haynes was in the reverse situation when he was traded to the Raiders midway through the 1983 season. Hayes had an interesting theory about a zone coverage man making the switch to a man-to-man team.

"For seven years of Mike's life he's been frozen in carbonite," he said. "His legs are fresh from playing all those zone pass coverages. Mike's a 30-year-old with a 24-year-old's body. There's not that much wear and tear."

The basic theory behind a zone defense is to get every area, or zone, covered, and to create movement, so the quarterback and receivers are working against a constantly shifting spectrum. Coverage zones, or "pass recognition zones," as Rust likes to call them, are defined in a language that uses many terms different from those the offense would use.

Horizontally, there are three areas, short, intermediate and deep. Vertically it breaks down into seven recognition areas in the short zone, seven intermediate ones and three deep ones. Obviously a defense can't drop 17 men into coverage and man each of these areas, so the coach has to make a choice—how many can he reasonably cover with the seven or eight people he has available (less if someone is blitzing)?

He'll condense his seven short recognition areas into four or five short zones, and assign one defender to each of them. The intermediate and deep areas will be combined and then vertically split into either two or three zones, again with one defender to each. The five-short, two-deep zone is called just that. The four-short, three-deep zone is called a three-deep. In pure prevent situations, at the end of the game or when a team is in an extreme long-yardage situation, a defense might rush only three people and drop eight back into coverage. This could take the form of a five-short, three-deep zone or a "twin-safety" zone, which strings four people across the field in deep coverage.

"A three-man rush, prevent situation is all right," Rust says, "when you're 90 percent sure of where the offense will go and you can get your coverage people there, or when you have a guy under duress— when they're really working one guy over."

A double zone is basically a two-deep, in which the cornerbacks play the receivers short, and they're backed up by safetymen. The weakness is the deep middle, where there's a hole. A receiver who catches a ball there is said to have "split the zone." Another expression you hear is "stretching the zone," sending receivers in motion or widening the offensive alignment to create bigger coverage areas for the defense, bigger zones. Finding the "seams" of the zone means hitting a receiver in the dividing line between zones, between the coverage areas of different people.

Figure 7 shows a typical five-short, two-deep zone, with safeties fanning out to create a double zone. One linebacker is rushing. "Pass recognition" areas are also designated.

People talk about "rotations" in a zone. All this means is that a team "rotates" a defensive back forward, adding an extra man to the underneath coverage. If it is a strong-side rotation the cornerback on the tight end's side will rotate forward, the strong safety will rotate over to take the cornerback's place, the free safety will rotate over to the strong safety's side, etc. One of the calls the defense makes designates which member of the secondary rotates up. Strict rotations are not as common now as they were in the seventies. They're too easy to

FIGURE 8

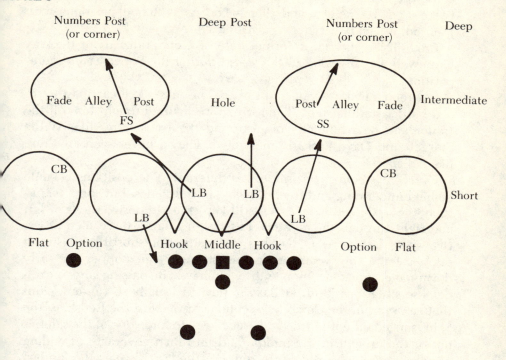

read. And the two-tight-end offense, plus all varieties of motion and switching sets, constantly changes strong-side and weak-side designations anyway. Sometimes there is none.

Once upon a time safetymen were cornerback flunkouts. Teams drafted at the corners and if the guy they picked didn't have the speed or the man-to-man coverage instincts he was turned into a safety, a strong safety if he was big, a free safety if he was smaller and quicker—or if he had a particular nose for the ball. Nowadays safetymen get picked—as safeties—in the first round. In 1977 the Rams drafted one of the country's better athletes, Nolan Cromwell, a 6'1", 200-pound Wishbone quarterback for Kansas, an accomplished decathlon man, and the Big Eight record holder in the intermediate hurdles. They plunked him at free safety right away, a position he'd played as a freshman and sophomore, and three years later they awarded a first-round pick to a strong safety, Johnnie Johnson, the consensus All-American from Texas. Cromwell made the Pro Bowl twice as a free safety, and then when he switched positions with Johnson, he made it twice as a strong safety.

Fred Dryer, the Rams' former defensive end, talks about the way Cromwell was revealed to the world during the Super Teams competition.

"At ten o'clock we put him to bed," he says. "We carried the social burden and he slept. Then, when we finally brought him off the trailer and he whinnied going around the track, guys like Willie Stargell and Dave Parker almost died. They'd never seen anything like Nolan."

Everyone's concept of safeties is different. The positions became defined into strong and free, or weak, in the sixties, but some teams, such as Seattle and Minnesota, still kept the old designations of left and right through the eighties. Pittsburgh rotated three men at the two spots last year. Dallas has been situation-substituting strong safeties for a few years, using one stronger run-stopper on early downs and replacing him with a ballhawk in passing and nickel-defense situations. Both Dallas safeties are usually so run-conscious that last year, in the Cowboys' second game against the Redskins, the Skins started off with three wide receivers, to force one of the safeties out of the crunch in the middle and into man coverage, providing more room for John Riggins to run. For the last 13 years the Raiders have liked the concept of the killer free safety, a wicked hitter who could draw a bead on someone from his deep position and shake him up—first Jack Tatum, then Burgess Owens and now Vann McElroy.

Last year Lott had the honor of playing three different backfield positions in three weeks: first cornerback, then strong safety, when Carlton Williamson got hurt, then free safety, when Dwight Hicks walked out of camp before the Rams' game.

"I enjoy the corner," Lott said on the eve of his free-safety debut. "It's more challenging. Strong safety's a corporate position. You just take care of business. If you get beat you might get away with it. But the thing that scares me about free safety is I have to make all the calls. At cornerback you're listening for the signals. Now I'm calling them."

The 49ers won the game, but Lott had a bit of trouble at the beginning.

"I had problems with my angle pursuits," he said. "The first four or five times guys came at me I was tripping, falling, getting knocked over. I wasn't used to people coming at me from all different directions. By the fourth quarter I started to see things more."

The safety blitz is a maneuver that was popularized by the Cards' Wilson in the early 1960s. Now everybody does it. It takes good acting ability . . . he comes swooping out of nowhere at the last minute to put a rush on the quarterback . . . but it also takes a good film study on the part of the defensive coach. He has to make sure the time is right, he has to make sure he'll get the crease in the middle, because that's the area that safeties usually attack. If he guesses wrong he might lose a safetyman to the padded forearm of a guard or center. Every team does it now—Dallas's Michael Downs probably has the highest success rate with it—but when Wilson first did it it seemed like the ultimate in deviltry, and insanity.

"I don't think I was the first to do it," says Wilson, the Cards' director of pro personnel these days. "Jerry Norton did it before me, but he did it on running downs. People just didn't expect to see somebody coming at 'em on passing downs from way back in the middle. We sent so many people there was nobody to block me.

"The first time I did it was against Charley Conerly of the Giants in 1960, my rookie year. At first teams didn't know how to handle it. Then they developed a scheme for picking it up. I had the freedom to take it off. There was a lot more freedom then, anyway. You were expected to have a feel for the game. Now there are so many coaches, defenses aren't geared for an individual's feel for what may happen."

He paused for a moment, remembering he was a club official. "But it's a better game now," he added.

Five- and six-, even seven-back prevent defenses aren't new in football, although George Allen would have you believe he invented them in the seventies. When the Giants went to their umbrella defense in 1950 they would sometimes change it to five defensive backs. When the Rams inundated the league with passes in the early fifties, teams would go to as many as six backs against them. They weren't called nickel and dime defenses then; those terms did originate with Allen. The Raiders used seven backs against Joe Namath in the 1960s. It's an extreme measure, and its weakness is that it's too easy to run against—big guys blocking little guys.

The Seattle Seahawks played a brilliant seven-back prevent when they beat the Dolphins in the 1983 playoffs, the backs doing a great job of letting the receivers catch the ball in front of them and then stripping it away. They also used eight backs on occasion. Why the

Dolphins didn't try to run against those defenses I'll never know. I've seen as many as nine men in coverage positions, an end joining the pass defense crew by dropping out to the flat in a "spy" position, and I also saw New Orleans use only two down linemen and nine defenders at the end of a game. No, they weren't all defensive backs. A team doesn't carry that many on its roster.

Sometimes in a five-back situation the nickel back will cover the third wide receiver, usually the slot man, one-on-one, usually with deep help. Or he could drop back and play center field. It depends on his individual talents. When the 49ers go nickel they like to play Tim Collier, their nickel back, at the left corner and drop Lott back deep.

"There are two types of nickel backs," 49er coach Bill Walsh says. "The first is the pure zone man who can't do much else but cover . . . he can't tackle but he can cover a lot of ground, a guy like Tony Dungy, who played for us and the Steelers . . . fine as a nickel man but not good as a regular. Then there's the big, strong-safety type. He can cover backs and tight ends from a close-in position. He's got the speed of a strong safety; he can be inserted for a linebacker. If you get a waify little type coming in against tight ends and running backs you're asking for trouble.

"You want your sixth defensive back to be smart and fast, a guy who can play three positions. A team with fast linebackers, though, isn't obliged to go to six DBs. Fast linebackers are OK for underneath coverage."

Occasionally in either a regular or a five- or six-back defense you'll see a team assign one particular cornerback to one receiver wherever he goes, all over the field. Rust says he did it with Raymond Clayborn last year; he would assign him to a team's most dangerous receiver in a particular game. He also did it with Gary Green at Kansas City "until the other cornerback, Eric Harris, proved he could cover well." Washington did it, too, in the '83 season. Against San Diego they assigned their nifty little rookie, Darrell Green, to Wes Chandler, wherever he played, but they kept him away from the Eagles' 6'8" Harold Carmichael.

"The Redskins have been doing that ever since Richie Petitbon started coaching their defenses in the George Allen days," the Giants' general manager, George Young, says. "A lot of times the matchups are based on pure speed, a lot of times they're on pure ability.

"A team that does that makes a scout's job easy. They're rating their own people for you . . . one-two-three-four-five, right down the line. You can get a reading on their relative speeds, provided you know the speed of the offensive people they're playing against."

Speed and ability—that's a pretty good capsule of pro football these days anyway, isn't it?

CHAPTER TEN

The Games Kickers Play

The first day at training camp it was 103 degrees and we were all dying out there, hitting, sweating, losing 15 pounds in a workout . . . we were at the absolute limit of our endurance. I looked over, and lying under the tower in the shade was John Smith, our kicker. He was lying on his back, using one of the light blocking dummies for a pillow, sucking on a popsicle, slowly raising his leg with a weight strapped to it. It's just the way they were in the NFL. We were preparing in our way, he was preparing in his way.

—Russ Francis

My parents sent me to Harvard to be a specialist. I don't think they were thinking of this.

—Pat McInally, Bengals punter

I was sitting around with the Steelers' personnel people at Yonkers Raceway one May after they had run about 100 kickers through a free-agent tryout. We were trying to think of the worst kicker we'd seen all day. I mentioned the guy who had actually punted a ball backward. Tom Moore, the backfield coach, said he favored the fellow with all the tattoos who kicked in combat boots. Then someone mentioned Mr. Brockhaus and the contest was over.

"Oh," said Dick Haley, the chief scout. "I didn't know we were allowed to count him."

Mr. Brockhaus was 62. He kicked in brown street shoes, and he'd taped them on the sides because he once saw someone do that on television. Except that he used scotch tape, which peeled as he kicked. He didn't get one off the ground. His longest grounder went about 20 yards. The Steelers said they'd let him know if they could use him.

Why do they do it? Why do they waste a whole afternoon looking at such strange specimens? Once I asked Jet coach Weeb Ewbank that question. He had just gotten through conducting a free-agent kickers' tryout at the Jets' Hofstra camp, a contest held late in the afternoon after the players had gone in.

"We don't let them try out while the whole squad is watching," George Sauer, the player personnel director, had said. "It's not good for morale."

A German kicker brought a little book of clippings with him. He had been the star of the New York German-American Soccer League, and around the Eintracht Oval people were whispering that he couldn't miss. He took the book with him when he left the Jets' camp 20 minutes later. The grass was too high, he said.

A 19-year-old high school graduate asked Ewbank, "Should I kick 'em left-footed or right-footed? I can do it either way."

"Just kick the damn ball," the coach said. The switch-kicker lasted about five minutes.

An Englishman planned to make it a big-money affair. He brought his agent with him, and they sat in the stands before practice, a sporty-looking young man and a little bald-headed gentleman of 50, with a potbelly. The bald-headed guy was the kicker. He had a unique style—grass skimmers. They never went a foot above the turf.

"Damn 10-percenters," Ewbank said. "Those agents ought to know better, pulling a stunt like that."

Anyway, that night I asked why Ewbank ran such a show when the chance of success was so minimal, and he said, "What am I supposed to do when these guys show up and tell me they can kick 10 out of 10 from the 50? Chase 'em away? Suppose one of them catches on with another team and does great? You guys would kill me in the papers."

It's probably the weirdest position in professional athletics—punter and kicker. You need absolutely no knowledge of the sport to be successful in it. With the old 33-man roster, places on the squad were too valuable to be squandered on a pure specialist, but the 49-man limit provides him with an entree. If he can do something else, too, if he can play a little and back up a position (punter Ray Guy is a Raider "disaster quarterback"), so much the better. Coaches and general managers are always looking for bargains. But such cases are rare, and an accurate foot will draw a professional football paycheck (granted, kickers and punters are the most poorly paid of any players) even if the player can barely walk or hobble onto the field.

Englishmen and Norwegians, Cypriots and Germans, anyone who has ever kicked a soccer ball will get a look. The Cowboys even tried to make a punter out of Colin Ridgeway, an Australian high jumper.

"I can't stand those little jerks," Detroit tackle Alex Karras said when soccer players first invaded the sport. "They come in singing their little song . . . 'I am go-eeng to keek a touchdown; I am go-eeng to keek a touchdown.' "

Denver coach Lou Saban, whose kicker was a tiny Englishman named Bobby Howfield, tells about the time his team came from behind to beat Cincinnati.

"When we scored the winning TD, Bobby was all over me yelling, 'Great chaps! Great chaps!' Then he took off for the end zone and started pounding the players and congratulating them. We had to chase after him all the way down to the end zone and tell him to get in there and kick the extra point."

The first time John Smith, an English bricklayer, ran on the field to kick an extra point for the Patriots the players had to remind him to put his helmet on.

"Oh," Smith said, "I've forgotten me bonnet."

It's the ultimate story. The game is getting more and more technical, but its outcome often is decided by only one man, a player with little awareness of what goes on between kicks, a player who's more removed from the game than anyone else on the team.

"I'm the hit man," the Vikings' Benny Ricardo said after his field goal beat the Packers in overtime last year. "Twenty-two guys out there can't settle this thing, so they have to call on me."

They're considered screwballs by the pro football establishment. On TV you might hear CBS's Pat Summerall say, in his low-key way, "Well, they *are* different."

Different from whom? Maybe from the hardnoses, the insiders who view anyone with distrust who's outside the club, but not so different from you and me. Many of them look at the game the same way a fan would, a guy who rides the train to work each morning. Taken not in the football context, but in the light of humanity in general, a lot of them are the most normal people in the sport. With exceptions, of course.

Jim Turner kicked for the Jets for seven years. He had his own way of doing things. He didn't want anyone bothering him during a game, talking to him.

"I stand in my own area at the end of the bench," he used to say. "People don't get too close to me. Sometimes the rookies will come over and say something at the beginning of the season, but they learn to leave me alone."

His contrariness puzzled Ewbank. He nicknamed him the Crab.

"Put him on the ground and he'll move sideways," Ewbank would say.

In 1971 the Jets traded him to the Broncos. Three years later the Jets were playing an exhibition game in Denver at the height of the players' strike. Turner led the Broncos' strike force. The night before the game he dropped over to the Jets' hotel and had a drink with his old coach.

"I can shut down the game if I want to," Turner said. "I've got the electricians with us. They could shut off the lights, pull the plug on the scoreboard, anything I want them to do."

"That's fine, Jimmy," Ewbank said. "You're doing a fine job."

When Turner left Ewbank's eyes followed him to the door. He shook his head.

"Was crazy," Weeb said. "Is crazy. Always will be crazy."

Lots of veterans dislike kickers—instinctively. In the locker room after the San Diego game last year, Pittsburgh's Jack Lambert was called on to present the game ball to kicker Gary Anderson. He started his speech with: "Much as I hate to do this. . . ." During his entire Steeler career, kicker Matt Bahr always called Lambert "Mr. Lambert."

They're players and yet they're not players. In 1979 Giant punter Dave Jennings competed in the Superstars competition, and he was sulking after he narrowly lost the rowing event to former Packer fullback Jim Taylor.

"That's OK," Ben Davidson, the old Raider defensive end, said to him. "At least you lost to another football player."

"I'm not a football player," Jennings said. "I'm a punter."

Sometimes kickers are thrown into a football uniform before they even know the English language, let alone the football language. The first time Austrian-born Toni Fritsch saw action for the Cowboys he was lining up for a 26-yard field goal, and from across the line St. Louis defensive captain Larry Stallings shouted, "Choke, you little kraut!" The Cowboys' Dave Edwards, who was blocking for Fritsch, shouted back, "Save your breath, Stallings! The guy doesn't speak English."

A few years later Fritsch was talking about his first year with Dallas, and how they assigned him an assistant coach who didn't really understand the soccer style.

"I tell him," Fritsch said, " 'Learn me the rules, learn me the English language, but don't learn me how to kick.' "

In 1981 Baltimore coach Mike McCormack picked up Mike Wood, an American-born kicker, and he said it made the players very happy.

"They like him," he said. "He's the first kicker we've had who speaks English and chews tobacco."

Sooner or later the NFL's week-to-week pressure cooker seems to get to them, though. Some coaches feel that in many ways the collegiate kickers who are drafted have a tougher adjustment than the foreign soccer players. Kickers are being drafted higher now than they ever were in the past, because they're kicking more field goals than anyone ever had in college before. But once they hit pro football it's a different world. Gone are their kicking tees that gave the ball an instant liftoff. Gone are the week-old practice balls they'd occasionally sneak into a game. Their target is now a set of goalposts 18½ feet wide, down five feet from the college width, and kickers and punters who might have spent a career booting the ball under balmy Southern California or Southwestern skies now have to do it in ice and wind and raw cold, against special teams that are relentlessly trained to stifle them. The anxiety factor becomes intense. Every day they read about another NFL team changing its kicker or punter. Do you wonder that sometimes they go a little flaky?

"We found kickers to be completely unique from other NFL players," Bruce Ogilvie, the sports psychologist from San Jose State said. "Incredibly exhibitionistic, much more independent, and having a strong need for external rewards. A quarterback can complete 55 percent and get accolades. But 70,000 people expect perfection on demand from their kicker. Often the torment of their teammates hurts them more than the fans' torment. As slight men in a world of giants, they are treated as childlike. They get put down with negative nicknames."

In 1980 the Saints' Russell Erxleben missed a 34-yard field goal in the last four seconds of a 26–23 loss to San Francisco in the season opener. Saints fans were mad at Erxleben anyway. He'd been the Number 1 draft in '79, a super–long ball punter and kicker at Texas, but they never forgave him for throwing an interception that cost the Saints a game in his rookie year, and now they were really on him.

"It was scary," Erxleben's new bride, Kari, said. "He came home and tortured himself with the TV set. He kept watching the sports news and clicking from channel to channel to see the miss, and hear the criticism, over and over. When I woke up next morning he was listening to some idiot disc jockey that would ask, 'What do you think of Erxleben's kicking?' and then squeeze one of those laughing bags."

A few weeks later Erxleben's sister, Cathy, made a surprise visit and found him asleep. She tried to wake him, and he spluttered in his sleep, "Go ahead, boo me, boo me, I don't care."

He went to a hypnotist, to a psychiatrist, to coach Dick Nolan. He said, "I'll punt but you have to bring someone else in to kick or I'm leaving."

"That one kick had ruined me," he said later. "My confidence was shattered in everything. Golf, checkers, jacks—anything I touched I felt I'd lose. I wished I'd never become a kicker. I didn't feel I was a good person."

Finally the Saints brought in another kicker and Erxleben was left to his punting duties.

"I don't even practice field goals anymore," he said. "I don't want to have anything to do with them."

There is no turning point in a kicker's career. It just keeps turning and turning. Mark Moseley was cut by Philadelphia and Houston. He spent a year building septic tanks in Texas. Then Washington picked him up and he became the NFL's best clutch kicker. Late in the 1982 season he set an NFL record by kicking 23 straight field goals. *The Sporting News* named him its Player of the Year. Then things went sour. He missed five out of his next nine; he went four-for-eight in the playoffs. In '83 he missed field goals that could have won the Dallas and Green Bay games, the Redskins' only two losses in the regular season. He missed four straight in the San Diego game, finally hitting on a 37-yarder that pulled the game out in the last four seconds.

"I feel like the whole world has been lifted off my shoulders," he said afterward. "I'm over the hump now. I hope they let me try one from 60 yards Sunday."

The clouds had parted, right? Well, not exactly. He went four-for-four two weeks later against the Giants. The Redskins coasted the rest of the way. But in the NFC title game against the 49ers, Moseley's foot went cold again. He blew his first four field goals, and then with 40 seconds left and the score tied, 21–21, he made his fifth one, a 25-yarder, to pull the game out.

"I knew he'd make it," free safety Mark Murphy said. "He's never missed one in the clutch."

"How about the Dallas game?" a writer asked. "How about Green Bay?"

"Don't ask," Murphy said.

Coaches usually don't have time to play psychiatrist. Sometimes they sound like they can use one themselves. Last December the Bucs' Bill Capece blew an extra point and a 35-yard field goal in a 12–9 overtime loss to Green Bay. Just before he picked up a Detroit castoff named Dave Warnke, a rookie free agent from Augsburg College, Tampa Bay coach John McKay made a solemn pronouncement: "Gentlemen, we will not kick a field goal next week if we are on the two-yard line, the one-yard line or none. There will be no more field goals kicked by the Bucs this year, no matter what the score is, no matter what the game is. It's over. I'm tired of being crucified. God bless you and Merry Christmas."

The next week, in a 23–20 loss to Detroit, Warnke missed an extra point, and the Bucs went for first downs on fourth-and-four from the Detroit 5 and fourth-and-one from the Detroit 12 . . . they missed both times. And did they try a field goal? Well, yes, a 29-yarder . . . missed, naturally.

Booth Lusteg, who toured the circuit in his 11 years as an AFL, NFL and WFL kicker, said that a field-goal attempt that takes off well but runs into disaster at the end is not a choke. A sudden breeze might come up and nudge the ball, the hold might be an inch or two off line . . . "Over 40 yards a hold that's an inch off line could mean a miss by a yard." A shank, a topped ball, a duckhook . . . those are chokes.

"Sometimes just one miscue is all it takes," he said. "One year, when I tried out for the Packers, another guy and I competed quite evenly on field goals, and I knew that kickoffs would make the difference.

"If I could only get coach Phil Bengtson to see my kickoffs, I'd be fine. I set everything up, waiting for him to walk onto the field. As soon as he came out, I was going to kick off . . . the way I felt, if I didn't get his attention, I might literally kick off. He came out all right, but he was with another guy, deep in conversation, and my kick went unnoticed. I started to panic. Other players were coming out. I kicked another one, but he didn't see it. He was still talking.

"Finally, I went up to him and interrupted the conversation. I knew I was forcing it, but I had to get his attention. I had trained three months to perform for three minutes. 'Do you have a minute, coach? I want you to see some kicks.'

" 'Yeah, go ahead,' he said, somewhat irritated. 'I can see you from here.' I went back and took one, but I hurried it and it didn't go. I screamed for the guy to throw me back the ball. I grabbed it hurriedly and set it up. Time was running out. In two or three minutes the whistle would blow for the start of practice. A terrible thought struck me . . . I could be cut before the whistle. Thank God I finally hit one right . . . and made the team . . . and lasted through the year."

Lusteg says that in his rookie year with Buffalo he thought the job was highly competitive because he had 12 other kickers to beat out. "In my last year, 1976, with Tampa Bay, 200 kickers and punters went through the turnstiles before they settled on one."

In 1982 Baltimore coach Frank Kush went through three regular kickers in 10 days. A year later he got lucky with Raul Allegre, who had come to the Dallas camp as a free agent solely for the purpose of getting the benefit of Ben Agajanian's tutelage, Agajanian being regarded as the foremost, and one of the few, real kicking coaches in the business. Agajanian worked the kinks out of the kid's style and then the Cowboys dealt him to the Colts for a ninth-round draft. That's quite a one-man farm system the Cowboys have doing for them . . . Agajanian, who turns free agents into draft choices.

They travel the circuit. When the Bills picked up Joe Danelo, who had been cut by the Giants, last year, it was the 10th regular kicker Buffalo had had since 1976 and the 20th in the club's 24 years. Moseley made 16 of 26 kicks with Houston, after he had been cut by Philly, and one of two in the first game of his second year. A day later he bumped into Oiler coach Bill Peterson in the parking lot.

"I had a dream that you were on waivers," Peterson told him. "So I waived you."

Last December I did a spot survey to see how many of the league's 28 kickers were with the teams that had originally drafted them or signed them as rookie free agents. The number was seven. The other 21 had been through 41 different camps before settling on their current clubs. Ricardo, for instance, had seen action for four other teams before Minnesota signed him in September.

"Ees a simple game, really," he said, slipping into a Spanish accent. "You keeck zee ball and zen you peeck up zee check."

Kick . . . punt . . . the words themselves are onomatopoetic, words used to describe the actual sound of the action. In the old days, when the ball was fatter, built for kicking rather than passing, those sounds had a more resonant tone to them, more of a "thump." But here's a funny thing about the old NFL kickers. They weren't very good.

I'm not talking about drop-kicking. That was an art form in itself. Half the stories you hear about the real old-timers, Jim Thorpe, George Gipp, etc., concern dropkicks from two area codes away. They could do it with the old, fat football, because it gave them a true bounce. It's impossible with the streamlined, pointy-ended ball of today. Sometimes they'd do it on the run. I read a story about Gipp faking a run in a punting situation and drop-kicking a 62-yarder. The technique he used was a side-foot, soccer-style kick, just like the kickers of today.

The straight-on kickers weren't very accurate. A kicker who made 50 percent of his field goals was something special. Until 1951 the overall league stats were under 50 percent every year, and for the next 15 years you'd only see it once every three years. (Last year only three NFL teams were under .500.) In the 1930s and 1940s the numbers were downright ridiculous.

The All-American Football Conference, with talented booters such as Agajanian and Lou "The Toe" Groza, was known as a kicker's league. Each AAFC team, during the league's four years of existence (1946–49) averaged only 5.2 field goals per season. That's for the whole team. But it was still better than the footless NFL, which in 1943 showed each team averaging two field goals out of 8.5 tries for the season. Don Hutson and Ward Cuff led the NFL in field goals with three apiece that year, which is one less than the 49ers' Ray Wersching kicked in the '82 Super Bowl. There were teams in the old Hutson-Cuff days that went 0-for-2 for the whole season.

So what was the matter with those old teams and their fat ball that should have been so ideal for kicking? Well, for one thing, field-goal kicking wasn't something a kid would practice in high school and college, knowing that if he got good enough he could make it into the pros on just his leg. The kickers had to be players, too, and a dedicated player just didn't have much time to bother with the boots.

"I tried only one field goal in high school and six in college," says Turner, who was Utah State's starting quarterback. "I just read an article about Allegre where he said he tried 50 at Texas. Erxleben kicked 49 of 78 in college. That many was unheard of in my day. I didn't have much real coaching, either. On the Jets, Weeb knew something about it because he'd been close to Groza at Cleveland, but now you've got kicking schools all over the place. You've got Agajanian at Dallas, and Aggie runs a kicking school in Long Beach. I've sent kids to him. I work with kids myself."

I asked Turner how a conventional, straight-ahead kicker like him could coach kids in the soccer style, how Agajanian can.

"The final approach is the same," he says. "People think that having the shoulders square is the most important thing. It's not. It's the hips. If you hips aren't turned you're not going to kick right . . . you'll hook it or punch it to the right. It's what happened to Moseley last year. You can't take too wide an approach, either, and sort of swoop in on the ball. Allegre was doing that before Agajanian straightened him out and got him to start his approach closer. The most important thing, though, is the plant of the left foot, just like in straight-ahead kicking. At the end your foot has to be pointed to the goal. Turn it and your hips will turn and you'll hook the ball."

The soccer-style kickers arrived in 1964—make that *kicker* arrived . . . the Bills' Pete Gogolak, who set a flame to the AFL-NFL war when the Giants grabbed him in 1966. By 1967 there were three regular side-footers in pro football. Ten years later there were 21. Last year the only straight-foot left was Moseley, after the Vikings' Rick Danmeier got hurt in preseason. Defenders of the old style say it's still better because the ball comes up more quickly, decreasing the chances of getting a kick blocked. Side-footers say they get them up just as quickly, and their distance is consistently better. Straight-foots point out that the NFL record of 63 yards was set by Tom Dempsey, one of their own, but the side-foots remind them that their style is built for consistency—and on that one they win the argument, because percentages never have been as good as they are now. In 1983, 10 NFL kickers made 80 percent or better of their kicks, statistics that are blazing new trails in field goal records.

How accurate is a kicker, really? How closely can he pinpoint a kick? Les Unger, sports director for the New Jersey Meadowlands and Giants Stadium, says that when he was sports publicity director at Rutgers they were filming a Wheaties commercial one day that involved Jan Stenerud, who was Kansas City's kicker in those days.

"He was supposed to hit one of the uprights and say, 'If only I had my Wheaties. . . .' We were out there for two hours. He was kicking from 25 yards out and he must have kicked 100 balls, and he couldn't hit it. Finally they filmed it with a cutaway. A guy threw the ball at a goal post and they showed the ball up close. They packed up all their gear, and Stenerud stayed out there, just screwing around. Damn if he didn't hit the goal post three times."

In the old days, if someone wanted to work on the booting phase of football, he worked on punting. Naturally they were players, too. All-NFL quarterbacks such as Sid Luckman, Ace Parker and Sammy Baugh were all good punters. The run from punt formation was a real threat. John Isenbarger, who played halfback for Indiana in the late 1960s and also punted (he was nicknamed "Punt, John, Punt") admitted that he had no idea what he was going to do once he lined up in punt formation. Kids who were good athletes just naturally slipped into punting.

It seems to me that punters these days just aren't as good as they used to be, that I've never seen so many bad ones at the professional level . . . consistent 36- and 37-yard punters . . . as I do now. But statistics don't bear that out. The overall averages are about the same as they were in the 1940s, but the return averages aren't as high. Punters try to keep the ball high nowadays to discourage runbacks. A lot of the good averages in the old days came from quick kicks. It was easier then because the single-wing tailback, the "triple-threat" man, was back there anyway. Baugh, who set the NFL record with a 51.3 average in 1940, got a lot of help from the roll on his quick kicks. And he only kicked on occasion. The Redskins punted 66 times that year, but only 35 of those punts were by Sammy.

It mystifies me why the quick kick has disappeared from football. How many times have you seen a team backed up, third-and-25, with the quarterback in shotgun formation, call a draw play or throw a little 5- or 10-yard pass, with no chance of gaining the first down? Why not call a quick kick, since you're just bailing out anyway? It would figure to be even more successful on the artificial turf, and you'd gain 20 or 30 yards in field position, which coaches always yack about.

The Jets' defensive coach, Joe Gardi, used to say that the quick kick would be a natural for them because their QB Richard Todd was a good punter, but he couldn't say why they never called one. Probably they were afraid of some of the fans booing. Former Bears general manager Jim Finks says teams don't call it "because they hate to give up the ball one down early, even when they're backed up." As I said, it mystifies me. It's probably a reflection of the "I don't want to be different" mentality that's gripped the NFL these days.

Another thing that bugs me is a punter who'll hit the middle of the end zone from the other team's 40—a booming punt that'll draw *oohs* and *aahs* from the TV announcers. "Wow, Ray Guy really hit that one," etc. It's not a good punt at all. It's a lousy punt, a 20-yard net. A shot at the corners, a punched ball, might not look as good, but it's a lot more effective.

When punters evaluate each other they always use the net yardage figure—length of punt minus distance on the return, or minus 20 yards if the ball goes into the end zone. It's not always fair—the skill of your punt coverage unit has something to do with it—but it's a much truer way to rate punters. Jennings wrote letters to the league office for years, urging them to list the net figures, before the league finally included them a few years ago.

Placing the ball on punt really seems to be a lost art. I remember standing on the practice field at Stanford after a spring workout one year, watching the 49ers' quarterback, and punter, Frankie Albert, put on a punting display. He was hitting, or at least coming near, towels he'd placed on the sidelines, getting the ball to roll right, roll left, forward, backward . . . he did tricks with the ball. Afterward someone mentioned that Frankie was punting in sweats, not pads, which makes a difference, but still . . . when there's only one return man in the middle of the field, why does a punter kick the ball right to him, instead of trying to place it *away* from him and count on the roll? It mystifies me.

For the last two years my All-Pro punter has been the Patriots' Rich Camarillo, who punts in consistently bad weather late in the season (domed-stadium punters and punters who perform in Denver's thin air have a decided advantage), who has never had one blocked or shanked one, and who works under a system that emphasizes placing the ball rather than booming it.

"We're taught to try to kick it away from the return man," he says. "If I would straighten 'em out and boom 'em I'd have 5 to 10 yards more on my gross average, I'm sure of it."

I asked him whether there wasn't a time in a game, maybe when they were way ahead or behind, when they'd just let him hit a few for the average?

"No," he said. "In our coverage scheme there's always a place they want me to go with the ball. Anyway, it probably helps my net, the fewer return yards."

I started keeping hang times for punts last year. I wish I would have years ago, because the Browns' Horace Gillom and the 49ers' Tommy Davis would have had phenomenal times. Davis was the best punter I've ever seen . . . make that the best clutch punter. I can still see him kicking 55-yarders into the wind when the 49ers were backed up late in the game and they really needed help.

I hear announcers say on TV, "This guy has a consistent five-second hang time, and sometimes he's up around six." Well, that's just nonsense. Most of the hang times are in the high threes, the good punts will get into the fours, and in 1983 I saw only three punts that had a 5.0 or better hang time . . . two 5.0s and a 5.1, all by the Dolphins' Reggie Roby.

The Jets used to have a punting machine at practice. They'd use it for the return men. They could set it at whatever height and distance they wanted. Once, after practice, we got the ball boy to set it at absolute maximum, to see how far and how high the thing could send the ball. It punted from end zone to end zone, 115 yards in the air. The hang time was 6.5 seconds. So much for your six-second hang times.

I had the good fortune to have been an eyewitness to the longest punt in history, the Jets' Steve O'Neal's 98-yarder in Denver in 1969. People say the record never will be broken, that that's the longest possible punt, from one-yard line to one-yard line. This is, of course, false. You could punt a 99-yarder, into the end zone. O'Neal punted with a wind at his back. The kick went about 60 yards from scrimmage. The Broncos' Billy Thompson circled under the ball and misjudged it. At the last minute it missed his outstretched hands, took a big bounce forward, and rolled to the one, where it was downed. If Thompson's arms had been an inch longer there would have been no record.

When Gardi was special teams coach of the Jets he had his optimum times for each phase of the punting game. He wanted the center to get his snap back in 0.7 seconds and the punter to get rid of the ball in 1.3 seconds. He wanted 4.0 or better hang time on the punt, which should go 40 yards or more, and he figured that if all the numbers fell into place the Jets could hold the returns down to three yards or less each time.

The Raiders allow 0.8 for the snap. They figure that if the snap and the punt take 1.8 seconds, the punt will never be blocked. They must be figuring right because Guy hasn't had a punt blocked in four years.

Their ideal kicking figures, incidentally, are broken down to 1.3 seconds for PATs and field goals, and they want a 4.0-second hang time on kickoffs.

The ultimate mess-up in the kicking game, the fumbled snap or the snap that goes awry, has occasionally produced unhoped-for dividends—a touchdown off a field goal play. It's rehearsed—the Fire play.

"I yell, 'Fire!' on a miscue," says Dallas holder Gary Hogeboom, who's also the backup quarterback. "Then I roll to my right and one guy goes out short and another deep. Then I have the option of throwing to either one or running myself. Randy White and Doug Cosbie are the most likely targets—or whoever is in the upback position.

"There's not much to holding, really. Just make sure you're seven yards and two feet behind the center. Normally you'd set the ball straight up, but if there's a crosswind, you want to tilt it just barely into the wind. And then there's the snapper, who's a big part of a good hold. If he puts the ball where it's supposed to be, it makes it a lot easier. And Tom Rafferty is the best in the league at that. He puts the laces right there. You don't have to turn the ball at all."

Turner used to buy his holder, Babe Parilli, and his center, John Schmitt, a box of cigars at the end of the year.

"A holder can kill you if he wants to," Turner said. "He can give you the white knuckle—hold the ball down real hard when you get your foot into it—or he can tilt it just half an inch one way or another. Then the whole equation goes *kaboom!*

"Laces are your worst enemy. A holder's got to spin the ball before you swing your leg, and he has to bring it down, all in the same movement—within a second. In two years with Parilli I saw laces only once, and that was on an extra point and it didn't matter."

Psychology plays a big part in the kicking game, especially with a man as jittery as Turner. Before the 1968 Oakland game, the Raiders' Al Davis made the officials examine Turner's kicking shoe, to see if it was legal.

"Sure it shook me up," Turner said. "Then after the game I asked Al why the hell he did it. He knew there was nothing wrong with my shoe. He said, 'Why Jim, you know I didn't do that.' Right to my face. He's amazing."

Kicking coaches at one time were regarded as a joke around the league. Once I heard the Redskins' combination kicker-punter, Sam Baker, talking to rookies, imitating the various coaches. "Bend the knee, lock the ankle; bend the knee, lock the ankle," he said, repeating the kickers' manifesto. And then the punting rules: "Get power from the knee and arch the instep." And then he mixed them up . . . "Lock the knee and arch the instep."

Nowadays, though, it's a serious business. This from Doc Storey, the punters' guru: "Lace your kicking shoe with the laces parallel to create a rifling effect. Tie your laces on the side or on the back to keep the knot from touching the ball. Wear low cleats to avoid catching the turf. Do the following at night before you go to bed: Sit down on the side of the bed and place the football on your ankle, then try to pass it to the wastepaper can. Do this 100 times or so."

Finks had an interesting analysis of the impact of the kicking game. "I always watch the kicker and holder to see emotion," he said. "I saw the Rams kick a field goal in '82 in a big game, and it was just like a practice or something. No emotion, no excitement; it was the first time I'd ever seen that. Right then I knew what was wrong with the Rams in '82."

Perhaps the most emotional play in a kicking situation is the successful onside kick.

"We plot it out," said the Vikings' kicker, Danmeier, after a successfully recovered onside kick led to Minnesota's 33–31 victory over San Diego in 1981.

"Bud Grant gives us a better than 50–50 shot at recovering it. You can't just kick it. You have to make the ball do something goofy. You have to make it bounce big and turn it into something like a jump ball in basketball—only your guys know where it's going to go and their guys don't. The high bounce is easier on artificial turf than on grass. You cut the very top of the ball, and as it comes off the tee it'll start to roll end-over-end. The third bounce is usually the high one."

Of course you also have to have someone with good hands leaping for the ball, and wideout Terry LeCount was the designated leaper. Randy Holloway, the 6'5" defensive lineman, was the man designated to bat the ball, and in the San Diego game he tipped it into LeCount's hands.

"We're four out of our last four," LeCount said, "and I've recovered all four."

"I was getting ready to catch the ball," the Chargers' 6'5" Kellen Winslow said, "and somebody jumped me."

One final word about kickers and punters—the barefoot booter, which is something of a new phenomenon. Former Eagle Tony Franklin says he's been asked about it on so many occasions that he makes up a new, and crazier, reason each time. "When I was a freshman at Texas A&M it rained so much I got tired of changing socks," was the last one I heard. "So I just kept them off and began kicking barefoot, and I've been doing it ever since."

But maybe it's not as crazy as it sounds. For one thing, a bare foot provides the same surface for the ball each time. No variables, unless the guy's foot gets swollen on a cold day, and then he'll probably have it wrapped in a special warm-up bootie between kicks anyway. And maybe, just maybe, these highly specialized sunbeams in the vast spectrum of pro football aren't as crazy as the world would have you believe.

CHAPTER ELEVEN

Sunday's Madmen: The Suicide Squad

Everyone has some fear. A man without fear belongs in a mental institution . . . or on special teams, either one.

—Walt Michaels

I've lost an eye, had a finger clipped, busted my back, paralyzed a vocal chord and had cancer of the colon. So I'm no Olympic athlete. So what? I hope you'll believe me . . . I find it very hard to convince other people. I don't mind dying and never have. Not that I want to die—I just don't give a damn.

—Moshe Dayan

A crazy man who can bench press four times his IQ lines up on the kickoff next to the kicker, collides head first 40 yards downfield at full speed with a 200-pound running back in an explosion of sound that brings oohs and aahs from 75,000 voices . . . Gordon Liddy would have been a coaches' dream as a special teams player.

—Mike Oriard, *The End of Autumn*

IT sounds innocent enough. It even has a scientific ring. "Special teams." Run down the field on kickoffs. Help block for the man returning those kicks. Punt and be punted to. Block for the placekicker, or try to block the other team's kicks. Not bad, right? But when I see those special-team specialists earning about a third of the paycheck of an average NFL starter, I start thinking about Henry Schmidt.

Schmidt was a reserve tackle on the 1966 Jets for a few weeks. His eight-year pro career had taken him in and out of four camps, and by the time he hit New York he was just about playing out the string. His salary was $15,000. I used to get a kick out of studying Henry Schmidt. His face was craggy and lined, and when he would get out of the team bus after a 15-minute airport trip, with his battered knees cramped and aching, he would hobble like a 60-year-old man.

When the Jets finally cut him, I was surprised to see that he was only 28. He looked like 40. And then I remembered who Henry Schmidt was. Schmidt was the greatest "hot man" I'd ever seen in my life.

The hot man is the wedge-buster on the kickoff teams, also called special teams . . . or speciality teams . . . or "money" teams (to be kind) . . . or simply "teams." The players call it the suicide squad, because the injury rate is so high. And hot man is the most suicidal of suicide squad positions, because the only requirements for the job are speed, size, and an absolute willingness to hurl oneself at the four big men that form the wedge in front of the kick returner.

A ballcarrier on the special teams takes his lumps, but he always has the option of downing the ball in the end zone or fair-catching a punt. A hot man has no options. He hits people every time, as hard as he can.

If he's extra good, he might wade through the wedge and somehow pressure the ballcarrier. If he's a superman, he might make a tackle. And those rare tackles are things you frame and nail to the wall, because the hot man is usually going at top speed, completely out of control. When a ballcarrier is hit by the hot man, he sails.

I saw Schmidt in his rookie year with San Francisco, in 1959, and if you can picture a guided missile, 6'4", 260 pounds, zeroing in on a target and totally destroying it, that was Henry. He'd split the wedge like kindling, and if he didn't smash into the ballcarrier himself, he'd fly by him at such speed that the poor guy would certainly remember Henry the Hot Man the next time he fielded a kick.

Seven years later I saw what all that wedge-busting had done to Schmidt, and the only miracle was how he had managed to survive as long as he did.

The special teams are the Lafayette Escadrille of pro football, the pilots in their white, silk scarves, raising one last glass before they have to go out and face the Red Baron.

"Lord, don't ever phone me the day after a game," said the Jets' kick and punt returner Mike Battle, nicknamed Punchy Mike or Joe Don Battle. "I'll either be still getting drunk or lookin' for bail. When you're on a suicide team like I am, you don't wait till next week to start living."

"Momentum. Momentum is what causes the greatest number of injuries in pro football," says the Jets' team physician, Dr. James Nicholas, who once figured out that the injury rate for a special teams player was eight times higher than the next most dangerous position.

"On special teams you're going at close to 20 miles an hour, often out of control."

Kansas City's Stone Johnson raced upfield on a kickoff play and threw a block against Houston in a 1963 exhibition game. The impact damaged Johnson's spinal cord and fractured a cervical vertebra in his neck. Eight days later he died.

Special teams claimed the Jets' number one draft of 1970, David Foley, a tackle, and the play didn't even involve contact. He was running downfield at top speed; he pivoted to make a cut, and his knee collapsed. He was operated on, lost for the season.

"It's especially dangerous for linemen," Dr. Nicholas said. "Backs are used to open-field running and cutting, but linemen aren't."

"Special teams will tell you one thing," Vince Lombardi once said, "who wants to hit and who doesn't. You find out right away."

After the Jets drafted Al Atkinson, a defensive tackle from Villanova, they toyed with the idea of making a linebacker out of him. And while they were experimenting, they gave him the job of hot man on the kickoff team. Midway in Al's rookie season, the Jets beat Denver, 45–10, which meant that the Jets kicked off eight times.

Atkinson made five unassisted tackles on those eight kickoffs, possibly the greatest day a hot man has ever had. Three games later he was the Jets' starting middle linebacker.

"We had to get him off those special teams before he killed himself," said Walt Michaels, the defensive coach. "Or killed someone else."

Cleveland coach Blanton Collier said he found out about Leroy Kelly, the Browns' perennial All-NFL fullback, through special teams.

"I could see he was a good runner," Collier said shortly after he moved Kelly in for the retired Jimmy Brown. "He was fast, with good balance. But what really struck me was his toughness on kick coverage. He was a vicious tackler. I knew then we had ourselves a good player."

Sometimes special teams can be used as a form of punishment.

When Packer All-Pro guard Jerry Kramer had trouble with his contract one year he suddenly found himself on the kicking team. He took out his frustrations on the Minnesota Vikings, made his point, and got his raise.

Sometimes the suicide squad can mark the sad end of a distinguished career. Matt Snell, the Jets' greatest fullback in their formative years, finished his days as a member of the wedge on kickoffs. The end came when he ruptured his spleen trying to throw a long body block.

"They get all they can out of you," said John Riggins, the fullback who replaced Snell, "and then when your can of gasoline is used up they throw you on the junk heap."

Hank Bauer busted wedges for six years on the Chargers. The San Diego fans loved him. There were Hank Bauer fan clubs, Hank Bauer posters. He was everything the Chargers weren't. He gave them that fiber of toughness they seemed to lack. Their image was the lightning bolt down the helmet, sleek, graceful athletes leaping high in the San Diego sunshine to make incredible catches. Hank Bauer was short, and blocky, and bald, a short-yardage fullback, a cannonball going downfield under kicks, a guy who spent six years doing the grubby little things that win football games.

Shortly after his 29th birthday the doctors told him he'd had it. Two vertebra were crushed in the back of his neck. There was nerve damage. Too many years of diving into the wedge, head first.

"I woke up one morning and I had no strength in my left arm," he says. "I tried to lift a frying pan and I couldn't. All those years busting wedges, I was never scared, but I got scared that morning."

The Chargers made him a special teams coach. Five months later he said that the strength was returning to his arm, but he still couldn't turn his head without turning half his body around.

A few years ago the league passed a rule outlawing cut-blocking on special teams. Steeler coach Chuck Noll thinks that increased the danger factor, switching the injury area from knee and leg to head and neck. Bauer agrees—sort of.

"In the old days it was like running through a mine field," he says. "When I first came in there were so many guys trying to cut you . . .

you really had to keep your head on a swivel, keep the searchlights going. But yeah, I guess it's more dangerous now. More neck and shoulder injuries."

"You'd never think about playing again, would you?" I asked him.

"Well, you never know," he said, smiling. "I'm only 29."

I always have to laugh when I read quotes from some backup quarterback pulling down his $200,000 a year and bitching about not playing. Well, there's not playing and not playing. How would they like to be not playing as a regular, but getting plenty of work running downfield on punts and kickoffs—at about one-third the salary? Teams always have little motivational hypes going, to keep their special teams people stoked up—and to make up for their low paycheck—weekly incentive awards posted in the locker rooms, special-team point totals, "lollipops," Walt Michaels used to call them. The Haggar Company runs a weekly Specialty Team Award in Dallas, $100 worth of clothes for the leading head-knocker.

Some teams have a Hit of the Week award. Some of the Buffalo special-team guys used to get together and give a Get Hit of the Week prize. Lou Piccone, who busted wedges at 5'9", 175, won it three straight weeks.

"I got rejected by the wedge," he said after one particularly terrifying hit. "After I got laid out on that play, Elijah Pitts, our special teams coach, implied that it hadn't really been that bad. Then he came up to me after he saw the film and said he was awfully sorry, that anybody who could take a lick like that and still play, well, my God. . . ."

When he was with the Jets, Piccone was the forerunner of a new breed, the mini–wedge-buster. Usually the job was reserved for bigger people, but the Jets' idea was to try it with little, fast guys, who could worm their way under the mass of blockers. Actually the Jets had a pair of them . . . L1 and R1, left of kicker and right of kicker, Piccone and Mike Adamle, a 5'9", 195-pound reserve fullback. Their performance was spectacular. The Shea Statium fans booed Joe Namath and his receivers but cheered Adamle and Piccone. They prepared for each game with a strange ritual—smearing shoe polish on each other's faces, standing face to face, staring into each other's eyes, and slowly slapping each other across the face.

One year I did a feature story on Piccone—the lowest-paid player in the NFL. His base salary had been $16,000 the year before, the league minimum. He held out for $30,000, a logical figure, since he had led the NFL in total kick returns and kick-return yardage, but Jets general manager Al Ward chopped his $16,000 salary 10 percent for playing out his option and tacked on a $1500 fine—$300 a day for the five days he'd stayed out of camp—making Piccone's net earnings for the 1975 season $12,900.

He came back before the St. Louis exhibition game, and retired from combat when he caught a shot in the groin. In the locker room he was handed his first paycheck of the season—$25.38.

"Twenty-five dollars and thirty-eight cents for the family jewels," Piccone said. "Not bad, huh?"

Each of them does it in his own particular way. The Giants' Larry Flowers, a ferocious little special teams man for the last few years, yelled, "Nobody can stop me!" when he ran down the field. Washington linebacker Pete Cronan, one of their more-effective special teams men, regarded his work as "an audition . . . every coach in the league is watching me, so when I go on waivers they'll want to pick me up."

On a team that's notoriously weak in blocking for kick and punt returns, the return men often have as hazardous a time of it as the guys trying to stop them. In the days of the smaller squads, some great running backs returned kickoffs . . . Marion Motley, Jim Brown, Gale Sayers . . . although punt returning was usually too refined an art. O. J. Simpson ran kicks back in his early years, then he refused. People such as Tony Dorsett and Billy Sims, who you'd figure would be good at returning kicks, have been spared the honors, although the Giants will occasionally use their starting halfback, Butch Woolfolk, for it.

"I can understand the coaches' position," Giants' fullback Rob Carpenter said. "When I was with Houston we used a bunch of rookies on special teams, then Bum Phillips decided to use his best people there, and we got to the playoffs three years in a row. But Earl Campbell never did kickoffs. They had enough trouble getting him to catch passes."

Not many people enjoy returning punts. "It's like embalming," Raider cornerback Ted Watts said, after he had taken his turn in 1981. "Nobody likes to but somebody has to."

I've always thought that punt returns would be harder than kickoff runbacks, since a punted ball often hooks or tails. But the Redskins' Mike Nelms, the premier punt and kick return man of the eighties ("they list me as a receiver, but I've got the heart of a return man"), says kickoffs are tougher for him.

"Bigger hits on kickoffs," he says. "You get hit unexpectedly, there are more of them and too many blind ones. On punt returns it's not too hard making the first man miss. He's coming straight on, you hope he's fast, and out of control. Then you just step one way or another and all he can do is stick an arm out."

Special teams often need special kinds of coaches, motivational specialists, guys who are often as fired up as their players. Fast becoming a legend is the Eagles' Frank Gansz, a 46-year-old military historian and former Air Force test pilot, a man fond of peppering his meetings with quotes from General George Patton, Stonewall Jackson and Lord Nelson. In Kansas City, his 1982 Chiefs blocked three field goals, three punts and an extra point.

"The first day they introduced Frank he gave the guys 100 years of military history," says Tom Condon, a guard on the Chiefs. "I remember what he said about Lord Nelson. He said, 'The guy had one eye and one arm. He had no business walking the streets, let alone walking the decks. But he got his troops so pumped up they would fight anything. They had bands playing; the men were chalking things on the side of their guns, like "Victory." It was a nasty place to make a buck, but not one of the ships in the French and Spanish fleets that Nelson defeated at Trafalgar ever sailed again.'

"By the third day, half the guys on the club were dropping into his special teams meetings, guy who didn't have to be there. The punt block was his specialty. He used to say, 'Men, mothers turn their kids' eyes away when we go in to block a punt.'"

Condon said Gansz had a couple of designated leapers as punt and kick blockers, 6'4" Dave Klug, a linebacker, and 6'5" Stan Rome, who'd tried out for the Cleveland Cavaliers in the NBA. "They always hurdled toward the kicker," Condon said. "And Stan would always land on his head or some place like that. You'd see kickers trying to angle their kicks because Stan leaped so high."

Some great kick blockers do it on natural leaping ability, such as ex-Packer 6'5" tight end, Gary Lewis. Some just seem to have the knack, e.g., the Raiders' 6'7" linebacker, Ted Hendricks, whose 26 blocks represent an NFL record.

"He has the knack of hitting and sliding his body sideways at the same time," the Raiders' former special teams coach, Joe Scannella, says. "Very few people can do that."

Some teams have the whole thing broken down into scientific operations with their own set of terms. The Vikings traditionally have been one of the NFL's most feared punt- and kick-blocking teams, and 6′5″ linebacker Matt Blair has accounted for 20 . . . "That's since the league started keeping the figures in 1976 . . . if they'd counted '74 and '75 I'd probably have more," he says.

"First of all," Blair says, "you have the Grubbers on our team, linemen mostly, Dave Huffman, Randy Holloway, Doug Martin, guys who are down on all fours. Then you have the Skinners, guys who lay out from the wings, defensive backs such as Keith Nord and John Turner. Fred McNeill, our right linebacker, is the Jumper; he's between the tight end and the wing. And then you've got the Leapers who go for the block, me and our 6′5″ tight end, Joe Senser, and Tim Baylor, a 6′5″ safety we used to have. You're surprised at all the regulars on that unit, aren't you? We have a tradition of using regulars on special teams. Maybe that's why we're successful.

"It's kind of a mental thing. It feeds on itself. It's all what you want to make it to be. If all 11 men on the unit think they can do it, your chances are greatly increased."

George Allen's Rams and Redskins won a lot of games with their special teams. He says the reason was simple—good special teams coaches.

"In 1969 we hired Dick Vermeil as our full-time special teams coach," Allen said. "A studious guy. He ran the projector, he was analytical. He wanted to know all the centers' snap times, the complete mechanism and timing of every center and kicker in the league. He studied the techniques of all of them, and how the blocking was set up for them. A full-time job. Then after Vermeil we hired Marv Levy.

"Very seldom in my career was a fake punt or kick not successful, because we were so well schooled. The other team couldn't cover it. We beat St. Louis one time throwing to John Pergine, a linebacker, on a fake punt. They asked Coryell about it afterward and he said, 'Gee, I never saw them do that before.'"

At the other end of the scale is Tampa Bay, whose special teams have been a disaster area for years. At USC, with squad sizes in triple figures, coach John McKay could always find enough eager people to play special teams, but at Tampa Bay he had a shortage of manpower. Phil Krueger, his assistant in charge of special teams, wasn't even a full-fledged coach; his main duty was contract negotiations. In 1981 McKay hired a special teams man, Howard Tippett from UCLA, who also coached the linebackers. The Bucs still blew a game

FIGURE 8   **Kick return ("L"-"R" designate kicker's side on which the cover man is lined up)**

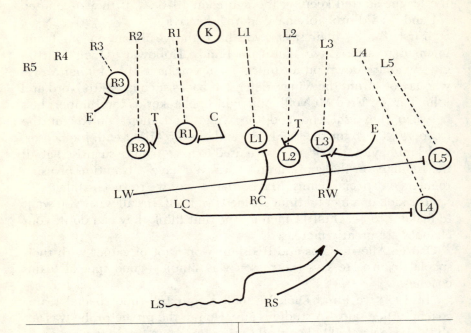

RETURN TEAM	COVERAGE TEAM

RETURN TEAM

1st Rank

E—ends   }   Must be able to block
T—Tackles   and run—linebackers
C—Center   and running backs are ideal

Wedge

W—Wings   (tight ends or full-backs)

C—Captains   (linemen who can run)

Note: On a middle return LW will pick off R1, a blind-side and high-injury rate block. Other blockers will peel back and block inside out, creating a lane in the middle

COVERAGE TEAM

5—Safeties ... def. backs or receivers—come down or feather out or play soft—you don't want to get them hurt

4—Contain men ... linebackers or safeties ... smart people

3—Can be anyone ... linebackers or running backs or tight ends

2—Speed and cover men ... linebackers, tight ends, running backs, fast linemen

1—Hot man, wedge breaker ... size and speed and courage ... can be anybody, from linemen to def. backs

Other 1—Second hot man or active cover man ... can be anyone ... can slip backs and take on wedge ... the best player.

FIGURE 9   Punt coverage

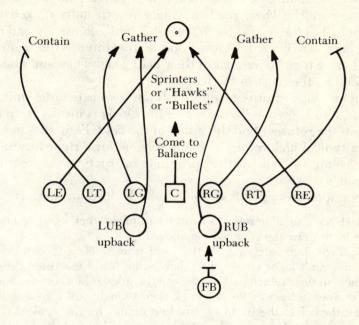

General Notes
1. If a return is successful at first, they'll keep trying.
2. If the first one or two are not returned, the effort will break down.

Coaching Points
1. Maintain lanes.
2. Never follow your same color.
3. Get an outside release.
4. As you approach within 5-6 yards of receiver, come under controlled speed and "break down," i.e., slow down, gaining your balance and getting into a hitting position.
5. Keep leverage and close in gradually.
6. Good footwork in coming under control and breaking down is the key to being a good tackler.
7. Fullback—you are *not* a safety . . . mirror the football initially. Read the return. Get upfield as fast as possible. Keep leverage.
8. Punter—you are the safety. Mirror the football.

solely on special teams . . . to Frank Gansz's screaming devils from Kansas City, naturally. Since then things haven't improved on the Bucs very much. Their punt- and kick-return units ranked in the bottom half of the league for '82 and '83, both offensively and defensively, and last year they were one of the three NFL teams that missed more than 50 percent of their field goals. They also missed six extra points, the most in the league.

Punt and kick returns generally fall into two categories, middle or sideline, also known as "wall," since the blockers ideally form a wall between the returner and the inside of the field. Figures 8 and 9 diagram a typical kick-return blocking scheme for a right return and a punt coverage scheme, with appropriate instructions, as described in one team's playbook.

Bauer adds these points to the regular kick-return pattern:

1. Even a sideline return should start upfield, then break to one side, to draw the coverage people over.
2. Two good safetymen is the ideal return. Then the kicking team can't favor one or the other. Some teams use three deep men on their return pattern, two on the sides as blockers and the returner in the middle. A good kicker, though, will consistently get the ball to the 10- to 12-yard line, aiming for the weakest return man of the three. Norm Johnson of the Seahawks is the best at getting the ball high and pinpointing an area and a receiver.
3. A return past the 25-yard line is considered successful, past the 30 is gravy, inside the 20 is terrible.
4. Down a kick in the end zone if you catch it three yards or more deep, if the hang time is good or if you catch it in awkward position. A line drive with poor hang time is a judgment play.

CHAPTER TWELVE

Football of the Eighties: Stagg Got There First

A touchdown wasn't some glop of red paint thrown in a spiral onto a crowded canvas. It was built with toothpicks of effort. It was put together with concentration and time, a fits-and-starts march down a field with a perfect ship inside a bottle as the prize at the end. Guys today score a touchdown every 30 seconds and don't even get dirty. The quarterbacks just hand the ball a boarding pass and lead it to the gate. Everything is in the air.

> —Leigh Montville, *Pro Magazine*,
> November 1981

What would happen if someone came out with a single-wing offense? It would embarrass the hell out of us.

> —Vince Lombardi

I am reading a couple of predictions on the future of pro football. Here's the first:

> The great quarterbacks in future years will have to run as well as pass to survive pro lines, which seem to get rougher and faster every season. . . . The pro ends of today are bigger than the guards and tackles were a decade ago. . . . The defense places greater emphasis on rushing the passer. . . . The new development in pro football, therefore, will have to be the running quarterback.

And here's the second:

When I started in this league everyone was using the same defense. Now there's a different defense for every play. The teams
themselves have improved tremendously over the past 10 years.
Personnel is now more evenly distributed than it was back when
I first got into this game. There are no soft touches around these
days. One big reason has been that the players coming out of
college now are better prepared to step into pro ball.

Pretty accurate, huh? Must have come a few years ago. The first one
anticipates the quarterback sprint-action of today, the roll and half-
roll and drop-and-roll, the bootleg pass, and a pair of twinkle-toed
Joes named Theismann and Montana. It came from an article by Paul
Brown called "I Watch the Quarterback," which appeared in *Collier's* magazine on Oct. 28, 1955.

The second one mentions the situation defense that changes every
snap and describes how parity has taken over. It was by Artie Donovan, the old Colts' defensive tackle, and it was printed in the official
program of the Giants-Colts NFL Championship Game of 1959.

What does this prove? Only that it's all been done before, said before, experted before. Maybe I'm getting old, but every time I see
one of those articles about the new formation that's going to revolutionize the game, the new this, the new that, I've got to laugh. Nothing is new. There are only new applications to old principles. The
writers who routinely crank out those pieces about some particular
fad that's taking the game by storm just haven't done enough historical research.

Remember Football of the Seventies? After Kansas City beat Minnesota, 23–7, in the 1970 Super Bowl, Hank Stram was the reigning
genius, and his Football of the Seventies concept, with its "moving
pocket," was going to stand the world on its ear. A new world of offensive football was dawning. Anyway, that's what you read in every
other off-season piece.

Well, eventually offenses did adopt some of that, sure, but the following season Hank's offense dropped to next to last in the AFC, and
in 1970 fewer points and yards were achieved than in any year since
1946, fewer offensive touchdowns since 1938. What caught on was
something hardly mentioned in those post–Super Bowl think pieces,
Hank's odd-front defenses, which gave rise to the return of the middle guard, who had been a staple commodity of the fifties, plus his
"stack," which hid the linebackers behind a lineman. Also, his soc-

cer-style kicker, Jan Stenerud. I remember one scouting report on him in those days . . . "Typical soccer-style, low-trajectory kicker. Will get a lot blocked." There were only a handful of them, but last year every team but one had one. And Jan was still booting 'em in Green Bay.

I've been hearing about new revolutionary formations ever since I was a youngster. I remember in 1953 reading through *Giant Touchdown,* a flyer mailed out to season ticket holders, my eyes opening wide as I learned how coach Steve Owen's new "Swing-T formation" would revolutionize the game.

> Owen's latest attacking masterpiece combines all the systems of the basic T. From play to play the Giants will be able to swing from T to single wing, or double wing or any variation of these, to select the most dangerous plays. The Swing-T achieves the all-time peak of offense, because it puts the ultimate pressure on the opposition. The Giants no longer may be "defensed," in advance of a game. Instead, defenses must realign for the play of the moment, in the few seconds from Giant line-up to snap of the ball.

The key man was supposed to be a 215-pound rookie named Butch Avinger, who was going to man the all-important quarterback-tailback spot. Well, the Giants finished with a 3–9 record in '53 and the offense scored 14.9 points a game, the fewest in the league. And Avinger was gone next year.

Remember the old story about how Notre Dame's famous passing offense of 1913, with Gus Dorais throwing to Knute Rockne, paralyzed the West Point Cadets, who supposedly had never seen such things? A *New York Times* report of the 1912 Army-Carlisle game casually dropped this line: "Both the Cadets and the Indians used the forward pass to great advantage."

Passing supposedly came about when President Teddy Roosevelt loosened up the game in 1906, but don't believe it.

Amos Alonzo Stagg, talking about his playing days at Yale in the late 1880s, mentioned that "we used to throw the ball around in practice, but coach Walter Camp wouldn't let us do it in a game because he thought it was too dangerous."

It was lateral passing, the watermelon-shaped ball held flat against the palm and sidearmed, or pitched with two hands, or thrown overhand, end over end, all of which became the early forward-passing styles. But even in those days, visionaries such as Stagg realized the advantages of the space game, of progress through the air.

Red Grange, in his book *Zuppke of Illinois,* mentions the old coach's reaction to the statement that the Dorais-to-Rockne game marked the beginning of the forward-passing era. . . . "That is perfectly true," Zuppke said, "except that 70,000 forward passes had already been completed by that time."

When the pass was legalized in 1906, Stagg's playbook contained 64 pass plays. In 1894 he first set his quarterback directly behind the center, to receive a between-the-legs snap. He used a man-in-motion out of the backfield in 1898, calling him a "flier," later changing the name to "Pedinger." He played the first indoor football game, in New York's Madison Square Garden, in 1890.

Is there a direct link between Stagg, who began his book *Touchdown* with the line, "When I was a boy in West Orange, New Jersey, in the years just following the Civil War. . . ." and the modern NFL? Most certainly. Eddie LeBaron, the Falcons' general manager, was Stagg's tailback at College of the Pacific in 1946. It's always fascinating to listen to Eddie, who later became an NFL quarterback, tell about his days of playing under the greatest innovative thinker the game had ever known.

"I was the tailback in a spread single-wing," Eddie says. "I ran and passed. We'd throw 25 to 26 passes a game. A lot of times our formation was like a shotgun, a lot of motion and movement. Stagg would call his motion men Pea Digger Left and Pea Digger Right. He had one formation where he'd set two wide receivers on one side, with one guy behind the other, and we'd throw a screen pass to the back guy—like Washington did in the '83 Super Bowl. He had a pass offense where anyone could throw.

"What he really knew was the kicking game. He'd been the first one to put in the spread punt formation. He'd cross the inside men on punt coverage. People averaged one to two yards on returns against us. I punted. He wanted 40 to 43 yards, no more, no less. He wanted a one-step approach, so the outside rushers couldn't get to me.

"He was 84, his wife was 82. He'd take the uniforms home with him and his wife would sew them. You'd go to his house and there were baseballs all over the place. He could have played for McGraw's Giants, but he didn't believe in professionalism. He didn't even know we were on scholarship. Once when we played in Chicago we rode to the game in a car and he had us all sing the school songs. I was 16. I loved it. But there were 23- and 24-year-old ex-Marines in the car, too. I don't know how they felt about it."

In searching around for ancestors of the modern flanker offense, you might try Carlisle of 1906, featuring Pop Warner's double-wing formation and a trio of great Indian backs, Joe Guyon, Pete Calac, and Jim Thorpe, who could all pass and run. And once I got a look at Weeb Ewbank's old playbooks from the 1930s, when he was coaching Oxford-McGuffey High School in Ohio. He had an entire passing series called the 50 Series in which all five eligible receivers got into the pattern. Can you imagine a high school safetyman of the thirties watching *that* come at him?

The "explode package" that the Redskins unveiled against Miami in the 1983 Super Bowl, a maneuver in which four people all jump to new positions before the snap, goes back more than 70 years, and after that it was popularized by Jess Harper and Rockne at Notre Dame. The backs jumped from a T to a "box" formation, but they'd run plays from either one.

Rockne even started the practice that's so lucrative to coaches these days, the motivational talks before business groups—"Let's get out there and sell those washing machines, men." In the 1920s the Studebaker Corp. hired Rockne to give inspirational talks to their marketing people. He got double his Notre Dame salary.

If there ever was a true innovator of the modern professional game it was Clark Shaughnessy, who was credited with renovating the Chicago Bears' old T formation to such an extent that the Bears beat the Washington Redskins, 73–0, for the 1940 NFL championship.

Shaughnessy was a compulsive tinkerer who was happiest when he was alone with an 11″ x 14″ sheet of graph paper, a set of freshly sharpened pencils, and six hours to kill.

"You're nuts," the Bears' Sid Luckman told Shaughnessy when Clark tried to convert Sid from a single-wing tailback into a T quarterback. "How can you send a halfback into the line alone, without a back to block for him. You'll get him killed."

"You worry about the signals," George Halas told him. "We'll worry about our halfbacks."

And when Shaughnessy was hired by Washington in 1944, for the express purpose of installing the T, the unhappiest man was Sammy Baugh, who had been a tailback for the Redskins for seven years and who was to become one of football's greatest T quarterbacks.

"I hated it at first," Baugh said. "Shaughnessy told me that Luckman actually cried over the thing when they started teaching it to him."

The Bears' modern, revitalized 1940 T formation, with its quick openers and man-in-motion, is treated by historians as the great offensive innovation of recent history. But on Nov. 17, 1940, the Redskins beat the Bears, T formation and all, 7–3, in a regular season game.

Washington, using the standard single wing, had a 7–1 record going into that November 17 game. Chicago's record was 6–2. The Washington offense averaged 27.3 points a game to the Bears' 19.6, and the Redskins' offense was gaining 58 more yards per game than Chicago's.

The legend is that Shaughnessy sent Halas some last-minute instructions for the title game (and it is a mystery how Shaughnessy could take time off from his job as the coach of Stanford's Rose Bowl team that year to worry about the Bears). The plan was to send halfback George McAfee in motion one way, and come back to the other side in what is now called a counter play. Hence the 73–0 whipping, instigated by Bill Osmanski's 68-yard run for the first touchdown—on a counter play.

"Our coaches had spent hundreds of hours studying game movies and charting every facet of the Washington defense," Halas said. "That off-tackle counter play was put in especially to capitalize on Osmanski's power and speed up the middle. But after all that scientific preparation, everything went wrong. Washington had the play jammed up on the inside, so Osmanski veered around end and we salvaged a 68-yard TD."

The answer to that 73–0 mystery is probably a lot more basic than the T formation and the counter plays off the man-in-motion and the hundreds of other playbook explanations that fans have been bored with for years. It comes down to personnel—and emotion.

The Bears of 1940 were a young team, the youngest ever to win a pro football title. They averaged 24.4 years per man, with 11 rookies on the 33-man squad and 9 second-year men. They were late in maturing, but by the championship game they had come of age, spurred on by the emotional incentive of their earlier loss to the Redskins and the reported quotes the Washington players had been tossing around.

But the talent on that Chicago team was awe-inspiring. Luckman, Osmanski, McAfee, end Ken Kavanaugh, tackle Joe Stydahar, guard

Danny Fortmann, center Bulldog Turner—all seven were chosen by the Pro Football Hall of Fame as the greatest players of the decade. And there was plenty of talent to back them up. Halas probably could have used Stagg's old ends-back formation and won the championship with that kind of material. The only sheer collection of talent to match it would be Vince Lombardi's mid-1960s Green Bay machine, which had 13 All-Decade selections (more players were picked in the two-platoon era).

The standard Pro Set has looked the same since the late 1950s—a 220- to 240-pound tight end set close to the tackle, with receivers flanked right and left and two running backs behind the quarterback. Shaughnessy introduced this alignment in 1949, when he was head coach of the Los Angeles Rams. The Rams won a Western Division title with it. Elroy Hirsch, whose history of concussions had changed him from a ballcarrier to a pure pass receiver during the 1949 season, was the wingman on one side. Tom Fears, a true end, was wide on the other side. The tight end was 225-pound Bob Shaw.

Stydahar replaced Shaughnessy as coach in 1950. He knew he had to keep the passing attack to accommodate the combined talents of his quarterbacks, Norm Van Brocklin and Bob Waterfield, probably the two finest passers ever to play regularly on one team (Waterfield and Van Brocklin finished first and second, respectively, in NFL passing in 1951). The ball itself had undergone a gradual slimming process since its watermelon days, and all the percentages pointed to a heavy passing game.

But Stydahar and his backfield coach, Hamp Pool, got out of the two-wide-men-with-a-tight-end approach in 1950 and 1951, using a succession of tiny halfbacks—Glenn Davis, Vitamin Smith, Tommy Kalmanir—as either runners or extra flankers, to team with Fears and Hirsch.

It was an explosive and devastating attack that produced total offense and passing and scoring records that lasted until the last few years. It gave the Rams a divisional championship and an NFL title, but it wasn't the offense of today. It had no tight end. When the defense countered with an overload of defensive backs (San Francisco used six of them in one game in 1951), Stydahar came back with his "Bull Elephant" backfield of Dan Towler, Tank Younger and Dick Hoerner, three men in the 220- to 230-pound range who destroyed the spacious defenses.

It was only when Fears began slowing down in the mid-fifties that he moved closer to the line, giving the offense a modern look, but Fears still didn't carry a true tight end's blocking responsibility.

The Chicago Bears effectively used what they called a "slot-back" in the late 1950s. This was a modern tight-end type of player who lined up in the slot between wide receiver and offensive tackle. He was set slightly behind the line of scrimmage, and Halas' slotbacks—Bill McColl, Bob Carey, Jack Hoffman—were all 225-pounders, capable of blocking a linebacker by themselves.

The Bears weren't alone in this alignment, which looked like offenses do now. But right up until the early 1960s, many teams were going with three runners in the backfield, or three pass receivers and no tight end. People were simply afraid to take a chance with something new.

The next great tinkerer, although his deeds will go largely unremembered because his teams met with little success, was Pop Ivy. He came down from Canada in 1958 with his head full of the spread offenses of the wide-open game up north. He got three or four receivers out wide with the old Cardinals for four years, he strung out three wideouts on one side with Houston for two years in the old AFL.

"We learned it all from him," Patriots vice-president Bucko Kilroy says, "but he never got the credit for it that he deserves. He never was very successful with it. His people weren't ready for it. He'd take full use of picks, which are the bases of today's successful passing games. He'd use formations we'd never seen before—one back and four receivers. He'd send a guy in full motion one way, with another guy going in back of the formation."

Perhaps this was the father of today's one-back, two-tight-end offense, the first really new offensive alignment to come along in two and a half decades. The idea of motioning a tight end from one side of the formation to the other started in 1963 with the San Diego Chargers, under Sid Gillman.

"It changed the defense's strong-side/weak-side alignments," he says, "and really screwed up their blitzes."

New England's defensive coach, Rod Rust, says he remembers Detroit using two tight ends, David Hill and Charlie Sanders, with Dexter Bussey as the lone setback, in the mid-1970s. In the same era Don Coryell in St. Louis used a pair of tight ends, Jackie Smith and the late J. V. Cain, much as he does Kellen Winslow and Eric Sievers at San Diego now, Smith playing in close and Cain playing the slot position. And occasionally the Cards would line up with only one back—either Jim Otis or Terry Metcalf.

Pittsburgh used the one-back alignment out of necessity in their AFC Championship game against Oakland at the end of the 1976 season. All their running backs were banged up, except for Reggie Harrison. So they replaced the second back position with Randy Grossman as a slot, or motion, tight end, and the alignment got stuffed. Grossman could never get his momentum going and turn up into the hole as a blocker. The real problem was that the Steelers only had a few days to practice it.

The one-back, two-tight-end formation came in as a base alignment at San Diego in 1980. Coryell had drafted Winslow in '79, and in the back of his mind was the idea of putting him in the old Cain slot position, but the experiment went on hold for a year when Winslow broke his leg. When the Chargers traded for Chuck Muncie in '80 and Sievers emerged as a strong, in-line blocker, the formation took shape in its current form. Joe Gibbs, who had been Coryell's offensive coach, took it with him to Washington. He went to it in 1981, after five straight losses. It had been primarily a passing formation, but in the Redskins' 1982 sweep of the playoff series and Super Bowl it became something else, an instrument of massed power. John Riggins had come on as a tireless, thundering runner. The emergence of two young linemen on the left side, Joe Jacoby and Russ Grimm, plus Jeff Bostic at center, gave Riggins a formidable well to run behind, the Hogs. The formation got the credit, but I've a feeling that with all the talent the Skins had they could have used any alignment and won with it.

Gibbs's backfield coach, Dan Henning, took the one-back with him to Atlanta last year. Larrye Weaver, who'd been on Coryell's staff, brought it to Cleveland as offensive coordinator.

"The one-back is still in its infancy stage," Weaver said last September. "But there's no end to where it can go. It's more than a current vogue. It's here to stay."

"All the wise ones are going to the one-back," Gillman said.

The advantages are obvious: another blocker set closer to the line; no weak side for a linebacker to blitz from, therefore the avoidance of the traditional running-back-picking-up-linebacker mismatch; a second tight end instead of a back to throw to, a guy who could get downfield quicker. A handful of teams adopted the one-back as their standard offense, a few more used it as a "mixer," but it didn't take over the NFL, as people were predicting in September 1983. Of the 10 teams that made the playoffs, only two were one-back teams, Washington and the Rams.

At his pre–Super Bowl press conference in 1984, Gibbs predicted, "You're seeing the end of the single, close-in tight end. They've taken him out of the offense." Someone mentioned that the Raiders' Todd Christensen had led the league with 92 catches.

"Yeah, but they flex him out a lot," Gibbs said.

"Like hell we flex him," Al Davis said.

The 49ers' Bill Walsh said he'd use a little one-back but he felt that two backs, one of them blocking in front of the ball carrier, was a sounder approach.

"The whole idea is to attack the motion tight end before he can position himself correctly," Walsh said. "It's the whole theory of defense—hit him before he's ready to block you.

"Actually," he added, "the tight end in motion is a refinement of single-wing football, with the blocking back trapping."

To me, that's one of the interesting trends I saw last season, the return of single-wing, power concepts, double-team principles. I saw that in the one-back. I saw it when Minnesota used two tight ends and three running backs against Detroit and the Eagles used three backs against Dallas, when Atlanta shifted to an old single-wing unbalanced line on occasion, pulling left tackle Mike Kenn over to the right side. And I saw some old defenses coming back, too . . . I saw Kansas City use a pure 6-2 against the Giants.

To someone who's never seen the single wing, believe me, it can be a thing of beauty, with its buck-laterals and reverses and spinners. In college it's been abandoned, and why I'll never know, because it seems that some of those nifty running quarterbacks would be just right for the run-and-pass tailback duties. In high school it's popped up here and there. Giles County High won the 1980 Virginia Class AA championship using a pure single-wing. The South Natchez Colonels took the 1981 Mississippi Class AA title using an old Notre Dame Box, which is very close to a single wing.

In the pros, its drawbacks are obvious. Your passer couldn't take the pounding.

"I've reflected on the single wing," Walsh says. "Those blocking schemes would just chew up NFL defenses. You could double-team every hole and trap at every hole. You'd have six men blocking three. Plus you'd have the power for the sweeps.

"Joe Montana might be able to play tailback, to run and pass, but you wouldn't let him do it unless you had another Joe Montana to spell him. The real key to a single wing, though, would be the snapper. You don't get them out of high school anymore. It's a lost skill, the pinpoint snap. It travels only four yards, but you have to hit a guy on the right knee, the left knee, the fullback's left hip. The shotgun snap's a looping type, the punt snap's a heave. Neither one's the rifle you need for the single wing. And even if you had a trained snapper, it would be very tough to train him to be an effective blocker after the snap.

"Two years ago, though, we looked very closely at the old 49er run-pass Shotgun. We were thinking very seriously about incorporating part of it. We'd just add the word 'gun' to anything we did."

So what have we got now in the eighties? Well, more passing, for one thing, and it'll probably increase for a while. The NFL set records for passing and total offense yardage last year, and scored the most points per game since 1965. And colleges are throwing the ball more, too. The old axiom, "When you put the ball in the air three things can happen and two of them are bad," has gone the way of the blacksmith.

"Somebody said that when the battleship was king of the fleet," Walsh says. "The more battlewagons you had, the better you dominated the sea."

Walsh with the 49ers and Coryell with the Chargers are the dominant passing coaches in the game today. The basis of Walsh's passing game is the Breakoff pattern, according to Bob Trumpy, who played tight end for him for eight years in Cincinnati.

"Everything is designed to break off, to go to the second plane," he says. He drew it up this way (see Fig. 10), showing designated routes and breakoff adjustments (dotted line).

Coryell's is harder to explain. The idea is to stretch the defense, moving people around until you create the matchup you want. The key is Dan Fouts's quick drop and delivery and the receivers' ability to make quick adjustments and to go a secondary plane. And in reserve is the quick screen to Muncie, who can make the first tackler miss all by himself . . . the "Waggle," as it's called. "The Waggle, the split end underneath, the slot tight end coming across, all of it from motion," Cleveland coach Sam Rutigliano says. "One thing evolves from another."

In 1983 Cleveland quarterback Brian Sipe learned the Coryell sys-

FIGURE 10   SF breakoff patterns

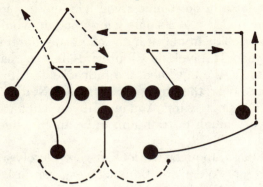

tem from Weaver. "Finesse movements, routes I never saw before, patterns I didn't think were possible," Sipe says. "Basically, timed routes for attacking the secondary, three of them to the tight end, for instance . . . one where he runs right at the linebacker and breaks to his right, another where he takes an outside release and crosses, another where he releases straight down the seam, runs right at the safety and you throw to his inside shoulder on rhythm. I didn't think it would work, but it does. San Diego's been getting away with it for years. You see it popping up around the league now. Green Bay did an espionage job on Coryell. They've got his whole playbook, the whole concept, the blocking scheme and everything."

Does all this passing mean greater happiness? I'm not so sure. I thought last season was a dull one. Teams lost their identity, except for a few. There was a great gray mass in the middle of the pack. Everybody threw like crazy, everybody substituted a million people on defense. Gone was the week-to-week excitement during the regular season. There used to be a big game every week . . . Green Bay–Chicago, Jets-Raiders, games that would make you tingle. In 1983 I counted three: the two Washington-Dallas battles at the beginning and end of the season and the Raiders-Dallas game in the middle.

"The playoffs were exciting," CBS's John Madden said, "but people didn't seem to take the same interest in the road to the playoffs."

Attendance was down from the all-time high of 1981. Pete Rozelle said, "Well, we still finished third, all-time, and that's pretty good." But larger stadiums and the population rise in general can account for that. TV ratings were down, especially on Monday night. Bad matchups, said the ABC people, but when unbeaten Miami played the unbeaten Raiders the game bombed out in the ratings. Why?

Maybe people are getting sated with all the scoring and passing. Maybe they'd like to see defense come back.

"What you have now is entertainment," the Lions' old middle linebacker Joe Schmidt said. "What we had was real football."

"I heard on TV, 'Well the defense is tired now. They've been on the field five minutes,'" former Lions' end Leon Hart said. Then he threw back his head and laughed. "Five minutes!"

The USFL has given us the phenomenon of year-round football. I don't know what the future will hold for the new league. I'm bad at league-predicting. I thought the AFL would fold and the WFL would make it. It depends on the USFL's staying power, if they can take their losses, now that their salary scale has jumped more than 200 percent, and come back for more, if they can make it if ABC cancels the contract. I don't like the concept of year-round football. Enough's enough already. Give us a rest. But I like the idea of more players and coaches getting work, and salaries finally getting near the levels of basketball and baseball, where they should be.

The higher salaries have produced a major problem, though, and that's cocaine. The NFL always has been a drug culture. Pop it, shoot it, swallow it . . . anything to get you through Sunday, plus the pain of postgame Monday. Team doctors and trainers made amphetamines available. They regularly shot up injuries to deaden the pain. They still do. The natural spin-off was coke, which until recently was too expensive to make the rounds.

"It's a 30-minute high," says one former player who used to dabble in it. "When it wears off, you need more. It gets expensive."

A young man with more money than he needs is tempted. The entertainment industry has been coke-ridden for years. At least two agents who deal with NFL players will make coke available, if they're trying to hook a client. It will destroy a player's ability to function, destroy a team, but it's a sweet lady. It feels good.

"With some players it's a macho thing," the Raiders' Lyle Alzado says. "They feel, 'We're so invincible we can do anything to our bodies.' You see it with the hard drinkers. Another guy has one drink, they'll have five."

The league office has a program for treatment for drug users who turn themselves in. Those who don't, and are caught, are suspended.

The treatment program involves 30 days at the Hazelden Foundation at Center City, Minn. Anyone who's ever done drug rehab work will tell you that's hardly enough, but the NFL is not in the drug treatment business. It's a problem the league is not equipped to cope with. Besides, the league has always been a step or two behind the pace.

On Nov. 28, 1983, Pete Rozelle sent out a letter to the clubs informing them that players' unauthorized use of anabolic steroids, the hormone that increases bulk and strength, would be dealt with by "disciplinary action." This comes, roughly, 20 years after the first time I heard of its wholesale use.

"The Chargers used to make us take steroids when I was with them in the early sixties," says former guard Sam DeLuca. "Every day you'd find one by your locker, a great big dyanabol pill. They'd watch you to make sure you took it. It scared the hell out of me. I'd wait till they left, then spit it out."

It's only taken the NFL 20 years to catch up to the fact that steroids are (1) harmful and (2) widely used among NFL linemen. All that bulk doesn't come from the weight room alone.

"In a matter of weeks you can increase your workout load by 20 to 30 percent," one lineman told me. "I take them because I can't keep up my same strength without them—and because the guys I'm playing against take them."

The joke is that the NFL, through one letter, thinks it can do what the International Olympic Federation hasn't yet been able to figure out—stay even with the steroid labs. For years the IOC has been playing a cat-and-mouse game with the medical center at Leipzig, which can beat each new rule as it comes up. But here comes the NFL, clumping along on leaden feet. One letter—that'll cure it, all right.

The NFL's blanket acceptance of artificial turf is another problem, as far as the players are concerned. In 23 years of covering pro football I've only talked to one player who liked it—Jet wide receiver Don Maynard. Do you remember the way this was first introduced? In the 1960s the Monsanto Corp., makers of Astroturf, would regularly take out ads in *The Sporting News*, ads that were designed to look like actual newspaper stories and which would claim that Astroturf would eliminate all knee injuries. When the players complained about the concretelike hardness, and some team doctors speculated that artificial turf actually might be increasing injuries,

Monsanto did a quick about-face and said a more complete study had to be made.

The only one to date is 10 years old. Stanford did one in 1974 and gave the NFL the results it wanted—the injury risk factor was no greater than on dirt fields. But since then independent researchers have indicated that, indeed, artificial turf is more dangerous than grass. John Tschirhart and Scott Atkinson of the University of Wyoming broke down 10 years worth of NFL injury reports and concluded that artificial turf produces 1.5 more knee injuries per game, one more head injury per four games and an additional shoulder injury per seven. The study was unofficial.

If you want my prediction on what Football of the Eighties—or what's left of them—will be like, I'll say that I think you'll see a rise in defense once again, even with these liberalized passing rules. Football is action and reaction, innovative thinking to combat a problem. And right now the big problem is freedom of the skies.

I think games will be longer. They'll probably bring in an extra TV time-out or two, an extra commercial spot to cover the heavier price. TV analysts will go more to chalkboard gimmicks, which delay the live action when you come out of the commercial break. You'll see more assistant coaches . . . the high number for a team was 11 last year . . . and the Rams were so specialized that they had an inside linebacker coach and an outside one.

"You'll see a continuing evolution of specialization," Walsh says. "The left guard might be a different type of athlete than the right guard. You'll see less of the great all-around players, the Dwight Clark types who can catch 80 balls a year."

It's coming. Colleges have long and short punters and kickers on their roster. Green Bay carried two kickers last year. There are designated pass-rush defensive linemen replacing designated run-stoppers, designated coverage linebackers replacing first-down linebackers, coverage safeties replacing run safeties. Washington even had one right guard to play against 4-3 defenses and another one for 3-4s at the end of the '82 season.

Former Chicago GM Jim Finks says you'll see less talent in front offices because so many individual franchise matters are now handled by the league.

"They've taken away the initiative," he says. "You have NFL

Films, NFL Charities, NFL Properties, the NFL handling drug matters. It's sort of like 'Big Brother will take care of everything.' "

The league was ridiculed for imposing a penalty on taunting . . . all that dancing and pirouetting and junk . . . but I've felt it was an artificial hype anyway. Tom Landry forbade it last year. Two Dallas players attacked the Washington Fun Bunch in the end zone. Anyway, nothing looks more professional than a player scoring a touchdown and then casually flipping the ball to the official.

In 1984, when Bronko Nagurski was interviewed during Super Bowl week, someone asked him if they had all that end-zone hoopla in his day.

"We were too tired," he said. "We had to play offense and defense."

Once I tried to do a story on the first time anyone ever did anything special after a TD.

"The first one I ever saw," said the late Giants' quarterback Paul Governali, "was in 1948, Emlen Tunnell's rookie year. He ran a punt back all the way, and as he crossed the goal line he twirled the ball on one finger and then tapped it back over his shoulder to the ref. I don't think these players would have the skill to do that."

CHAPTER THIRTEEN

The Coaches

At the top of the club you've got the owner. He doesn't have the knowledge he should have. He has a knowledge of business. He made it quickly. He wants things to be done quickly, without quite knowing how.

In the middle somewhere is the GM [general manager]. Nobody knows why he's gotten to that position. He's firmly within the owner's comfort zone. He demands quite a salary for doing very little.

Then there's a personnel man, often a frustrated player or coach. He justifies his position by sending the scouts out.

Then there's the coach. He's in there with his assistants at midnight, looking over the film again and again, trying to find out what's wrong. And while he's in there the owner and the GM and the personnel man are having dinner, and over martinis they're discussing the team. The GM says, "Look, we've got the best facilities and administration and exhibition schedule. We've set up every possibility to do a job." The personnel man says, "Well, we've certainly got the players. We had a great draft. I know because I read it in the papers. Look, everybody knows Smith is a guard, not a tackle. Everybody knows he should be playing instead of Jones. Everybody knows So-and-so should be the quarterback."

They put their heads together. What do we do? So they get a new coach, obviously in the GM's comfort zone but not too strong a threat. The personnel man's going to side with the GM on anything. He knows where he got his job. So the cycle starts over again.

Every seven or eight years a GM is spat out. And the situation continues to exist. Why? TV, the hype, NFL Films, NFL Properties. Well, it should get the hype. It's a great sport. But it's sure tough on coaches.

—Bill Walsh

BEFORE we begin our examination of the Lombardis and Shulas and Walshes, let me bring this down to its most elemental plane, my own relationship with coaches, based on roughly 10 years of competing at a more or less subsistence level.

One of the great myths of football, and I think anyone who has ever played the game will tell you this, is that coaches inspire and motivate players. They seldom do. You motivate yourself. Coaches teach you. They put you in the right formations and give you the right plays, and if you have confidence that they know what they're doing, then the motivation will come. Coaches scare you. Fear is a great spur. Nothing gets the adrenaline flowing faster. But as far as the real, teeth-gritting motivation? Uh-uh. You have to do it yourself. Of course you might get help from a teammate . . . I'm not talking about a quarterback, or someone like that . . . I mean the guy who's down there struggling the same way you are . . . and an opponent is always good for a quick motivational jolt if he gets you so mad you want to kill him. But the player who needs a coach to motivate him better pack it in.

I'm talking about over the long pull. Any coach can get you psyched for a play, or a series, or even the better part of a game. I remember hearing stories about the legendary Lou Little, for whom I played at Columbia, about the great upset of Stanford in the '34 Rose Bowl, and the upset of Red Blaik's Army team in '47, but that's all they were to me, stories. After the season was over I found out what kind of clout Mr. Little had when, with one phone call, he got me into journalism school after they had turned me down. But during the season he was just an old coach who'd yell at you and embarrass you if he caught you doing something naughty; the trick was not to get caught. Until one afternoon at training camp.

I was alternating at defensive tackle with Ben Hoffman, three plays apiece, and on my third play I got lucky and nailed my roommate, 155-pound Lenny Florentino, just right on a blindside hit, and the guys on the sideline went *oooh*, and I gave it the Hollywood bit, adjusting my pads, twitching my neck, etc., and I started to leave the field. All of a sudden Mr. Little was next to me.

"Where are you going?" he said.

"I'm alternating every three plays," I said.

"After a tackle like that you don't alternate," he said. "Get back in there!"

So for four or five more plays I was a psyched maniac—until I started getting tired.

The greatest inspirer of players is a coach who knows what he's doing, whether it's at the assistant or head coaching level, the guy who'll catch you every time you make a mistake, and correct it. That will get your concentration where it belongs, concentration being a necessary companion to motivation. You'd be surprised how many can't. I mean at the point when it happens . . . that's when coaching has its greatest impact. By the time you get to the film room it's too late. Films are always conducive to sleep, anyway.

The personality of the coach is mere window dressing, if the players suspect that underneath it all neither he nor his staff really know what they're doing. The words of inspiration and motivation, the screaming, the pleading, are mere blah-blah if he's screwed up and put them in the wrong formation or made some bad decisions. How many times have I seen a coach butcher the clock at the end of the first half, or make some obviously stupid call? Oh, only about every week. The players know it, and I wonder how they feel when he comes into the locker room and claps his hands and says, "OK, now we'll get 'em!" Hey, come off it, Jack.

"You always hear coaches say, 'You didn't run hard enough; you didn't block hard enough; you didn't want it bad enough; you made too many mistakes,'" Bill Walsh says. "You never hear, 'I didn't coach enough.'"

Nice guy or tyrant, disciplinarian or easy rider, the formula won't work if the players don't have confidence in a coach's intellect, if he doesn't have an eye for talent and drafting and trading and keeping the right people. A college coach must be a recruiter. A pro coach must be wired to the scouting department. Then comes the coaching. And far behind that, way down on the scale, comes his personality, although that's the aspect of it that gets written about the most.

I always have to laugh when I read players' quotes after a coach has been fired. You can chart them on a graph. A nice guy replaces a tough guy. ("He treats us like men. We were scared to death.") Then the nice guy gets fired and a tough guy comes in. ("It was like a country club around here. Thank God we've got some discipline now.") Then the tough guy gets fired and a nice guy comes in ("We were tired of being treated like high school kids. Now we'll be treated like men.") And on and on.

A nice guy who isn't a very smart coach will fail, unless . . . I've seen this happen a few times . . . there's a nucleus of really solid and hip old veterans who realize they'd better protect him because they're never going to find a nicer guy to work under. But a tyrant, a screamer who's also dumb, will fail the quickest because no one will protect him. A smart screamer, like Vince Lombardi, had no problems.

"The most sadistic are often the least intelligent," Walsh says. "That's the extent of their reasoning."

Some coaches motivate through money, and this can be very strong, if they've got older veterans who are toughing it out on pain-killing shots and greenies every week. George Allen coached the oldest team in football, the Redskins, and he had them playing in an emotional frenzy for years. It wasn't so much all the hand-clapping or the "Hip-Hip-Hooray for the Redskins" in the locker room. It's just that they knew that if you took care of George he'd pay you.

"It's not hard to figure out his formula," Tommy Prothro once said. "Just get a bunch of fat, indolent people and pay them too much."

Al Davis figured this out long ago. Of course his wallet was swelled by the $49.2 million he won from the league in the lawsuit, but he was never bashful about upgrading a veteran's salary, if the guy was putting out for him.

"No matter how long a contract you signed for," Gene Upshaw says, "it was always understood that it would be upgraded after two years if you were doing your job."

In 1982 the Raiders got Lyle Alzado from Cleveland. He would be Al's designated right-side sacker, but after four games it became obvious that Alzado was doing a great job against the run, too. He was good enough to play in the base defense, and play very well. So Al called him in and quietly upgraded his salary from $170,000 to $230,000.

"It shocked the hell out of me; I never expected it," said Alzado, who played most of the 1983 Super Bowl season with pain-killers in his right ankle.

Practically all coaches lie to some extent. They all play favorites. And on an organizational level, clubs are notorious for it. The more sophisticated players understand this. But they don't forget. Last year, though, with the USFL giving players a bargaining clout they hadn't had since the old AFL-NFL wars, the shoe was on the other foot and the players got a chance to wheel and deal—and lie.

"He just lied to my face, out and out lied about everything," the Giants' GM, George Young, said last spring about his dealings with one veteran. George has never been called a liar. He's got Old World values. But his remarks drew a smile from O. J. Simpson.

"The phrase that clubs have always used, with the utmost hypocrisy," O.J. said, "is, 'There's a principle involved.' A principle that only goes one way, the club's way. When players get together everyone has some story about how he's been lied to by his organization."

"Ironically, NFL players learn that playing well actually is more important than winning," former Kansas City center Mike Oriard wrote in *The End of Autumn.* "Playing well in the NFL is important not for the personal satisfaction it brings but for survival. Winning is the only thing that matters to *coaches.* But the situation of the players is different. Their value to the team is measured not by victories but by individual performance. The difference in primary goals between players and coaches can lead to an uneasy relationship."

Don Shula has never been called a hypocrite. He doesn't lie to his players. They're fairly well paid. He's demanding on the practice field, but he's straight with them. As his former middle linebacker, Nick Buoniconti, said, "If you've put out for Shoes, he'll never stiff you." Plus, they've got the security of knowing they're with a solid organization. The staff is well organized. They know what they're doing, which can be a great spur to mental stability.

Players who have pride and sense know that getting with the right organization is a dream not many realize during a career. It's worth taking a lower salary for. How many paychecks would Archie Manning have given up to have landed with a decent club? Often agents know it, too.

I remember sitting in the L.A. office of John Dutton's agent, Howard Slusher, in 1979, when Dutton was trying to leave the Colts, and the trading deadline was one day away. Every time the phone rang Slusher said, "That might be the Cowboys now." The price he was willing to accept from Dallas was lower than what the Colts had offered. I asked him why.

"Because it's the right team for John," he said. "I can just see him in that Dallas uniform with the star on the helmet, 6'7" tall, standing at attention while they play the National Anthem."

He had a dreamy, glazed look in his eyes. He was supposed to be one of the tough-guy agents. I started laughing.

"Howard," I said. "Get yourself a pompom, for Christ's sake."

"I'm not kidding," he said. "It's right for him."

Vince Lombardi never paid his Packers very well. He terrorized them. But underneath was the secure feeling that they were with the right organization, that Lombardi would bring out every bit of potential they had and they'd never play better anywhere else. His was the all-seeing eye. He knew talent, he had the right people in the right places. His concepts were sound, and a few of them were very advanced and sophisticated, such as his system of optional reads on pass patterns. From preparation to execution, everything was consistent. The rest of it, the hollering and crying and emotion, the great "family feel" the Packers had, sure, that was fine, but it would have been just so much air if the basics weren't already there.

Dick Vermeil was a very emotional coach with the Eagles, also a very loyal one. Stan Walters, the veteran tackle, told me that the thing they all loved about him was that when he came in he didn't start cleaning house. He said, "I'll win with what I've got," and then he gradually added to it. But in '82 they died on him. The fires that had burned brightly every week, spurred by Vermeil's driving intensity, became embers. The inspiration was gone.

"Some guys had started turning Dick off," quarterback Ron Jaworski said. "He'd get emotional, and it was, 'Here we go again.' The bang effect was gone."

I've played for two really emotional coaches in my life. One was Charley Avedisian, my high school coach who'd played guard for the Giants for three years. One day, after I'd screwed up, he got me after practice and set me in a stance and went one-on-one with me, right up and down the field. When it was over he told me, "You're never gonna play against anyone tougher in your whole life. It's all gonna be downhill from now on."

OK, that kind of inspiration will work in high school. You're dealing with babies, with embryos. And actually Charley scared the hell out of me more than anything else. The fear of having to go through it again motivated me. Finney Cox was different.

He was an assistant line coach at Stanford, working under the cool and remote Phil Bengtson, who later became Lombardi's assistant on the Packers, and then their head coach. Phil didn't even know our names. But Finney blazed hot. He was a fiery redhead with a crew cut and a thick, sunburned neck that was so powerful he could toss a blocking dummy with it. A great teacher. He taught me a block once, a pin block on the line where you lock your elbow into a man and turn him with your neck, that I loved so much I'd practice it in my room at night. I taught it to my 12-year-old son last season and he terrorized the Pee Wee league with it. I still show it to people; I was showing it to someone in the press lounge at the last Super Bowl, and as I demonstrated it I ripped my pants.

Assistant coaches can fill that role. They're motivators—of learning—which, in turn, is the basis of actual game motivation, which is your own. But while an assistant coach can get close to his players, and be one of the boys, a head coach cannot . . . "The loneliness of command" is the way George Young once put it . . . which is why an assistant is seldom successful when he assumes command in the same organization. He's been too close to his players. He's been their confidant, their confessor. Now he has to turn around and be the tough guy. Often he can't. He remains close to some of them. That element of fear is missing, and even though they think they're busting their hump for him, they're not.

Many general managers don't understand this. A day after Bud Grant quit in January, 1984, GM Mike Lynn rushed to hire the Viking receivers coach, Les Steckel, to succeed him, a classic failure formula. I'm not talking about a guy brought in after he was an assistant with another team; I mean promoting one of your own. In 1983 four assistants assumed command. None of them had a winning record . . . Kay Stephenson was 8–8 with the Bills, Joe Walton 7–9 with the Jets, Marion Campbell 5–11 with the Eagles and Bill Parcells 3–12–1 with the Giants. I researched it, going back 15 years. Not counting interim coaches, guys who were sentenced to finishing out a year, the record for assistants hired to take over the same team is as follows.

From 1969 through 1983, 29 were hired. Twenty-two had losing records in their total tenure with the club. Seven had winning records—Charlie Waller with San Diego, Don McCafferty with Baltimore, John Madden and Tom Flores with the Raiders, Bum Phillips with Houston, Nick Skorich with Cleveland and Ray Malavasi with the Rams. Of those seven, five were fired. The only ones that escaped firing were Madden and Flores, and the Raiders' system is different. A head coach can get closer to his players there. He doesn't have to be a fear figure. They've got Al Davis for that. The rest of that roster of unlucky coaches is dotted with some of the real disaster records in recent NFL history, i.e., J. D. Roberts's 7–25–3 at New Orleans, Jim Ringo's 3–20 at Buffalo, Ed Biles's 8–23 at Houston.

"An assistant can talk to you differently," says Beasley Reece, who went from the Giants to Tampa Bay last year. "As a head coach he has to be more political. He's the one who has to tell you, 'You're not producing. You're cut.' "

Here are some more formulas about the business. The average term for an NFL coach, since the dawn of history, has been 3.2 years. The average age for a Super Bowl coach is 46.3 years, and for a winning Super Bowl coach slightly higher—46.8—both slightly under the 1983 overall NFL average of 47.5. I don't mean his actual age when the game is played, I mean his age during the bulk of that season, when the hard work is done. Only one man under 40 has ever coached a team in the Super Bowl, Don Shula in '69, and he went against the only man over 60 ever to have a team in it, Weeb Ewbank. Ewbank won. Seven times a man in his fifties has coached a Super Bowl team; a man in his forties has done it 27 times. The numbers for Super Bowl winners break down the same way—3 fifties against 14 forties.

"This year I'm a 10 percent better coach than I was last year," says Walsh, who was 52 last November. "The finer points, the details . . . I'm finally getting 'em together. I'm a better teacher at 52 than I was at 42; I've a better grasp. Some people might think they're excellent coaches at 32. I don't think so. I think you're best as time passes. You're willing to have some others do the teaching you've developed. At one point in my career I was in the huddle calling every play in practice. Now it's simplified for the game; the first 20 plays I'll call, no matter where we are.

"At 60 you begin to slow, physically, especially in the Midwest, where there's a tough climate. It's not as bad out here on the West Coast. The key to professional growth is a natural inquisitiveness. When you lose that you're not going to grow at all.

"The energy is the critical area. This job or any other can become a bore if it's the same basic life routine. First you get rather bored with practice, with the film breakdowns, everything but the game itself. Before long you're not a detail man; you're just waiting for the game. And some of them are not even game coaches."

More formulas. Football is not like baseball, in which a manager makes the rounds until he hits it lucky. The verdict is in pretty quickly. I could come up with only two coaches in history who were losers one place and then went somewhere else and won—Forrest Gregg from Cleveland to Cincinnati and Lou Saban from Boston to Buffalo in the old AFL. In Saban's case it was iffy, because in the AFL's infant years success was determined by who you could sign, not how well you coached.

Here's a tougher one to pin down. Some systems seem to produce lots of head coaches, many of them very successful, and some simply don't. Paul Brown turned out more famous head coaches than you could count. Landry's system has produced a few, and the jury is still out on them—Dan Reeves, John Mackovic, Mike Ditka and Ron Meyer, who was a scout for Landry for two years. The Sid Gillman system produced Al Davis, Chuck Noll, Bum Phillips, Dan Henning and Kay Stephenson. Walsh, who worked with Gillman briefly, said he was the "best offensive mind [he'd] ever seen." In his six years at San Diego Don Coryell has already turned out one head coach who reached the playoffs, Jim Hanifan, and one who won the Super Bowl, Joe Gibbs. Chuck Noll's system has produced very few—Woody Widenhofer and Rollie Dotsch in the USFL and George Perles at Michigan State. Perhaps the strangest case of all is that of Lombardi at Green Bay.

People rushed to hire Lombardi products, and the results were usually a succession of losing records—Norb Hecker, Tom Fears, Bengtson, Bill Austin, Bart Starr, Willie Wood in Canada, Bill Curry at Georgia Tech. The only one who reversed the trend was Gregg.

I've heard lots of explanations for this—Lombardi did almost everything himself, he didn't allow his coaches much initiative, former coaches and players of his tried to copy his personality and failed, etc. There have certainly been very few like him.

Two years after his Block of Granite days at Fordham, Vince Lombardi moved to Englewood, N.J., for eight seasons as coach of St. Cecilia's High School, "The Saints," as they were known in Jersey. Lombardi, his ears still ringing with those old Jock Sutherland, "Sweet Jesus, here they come again" single-wing power plays and sweeps he faced as a lineman at Fordham, gave the Saints an attack as basic and brutal as Sutherland's had been at Pitt.

From St. Cecilia's he went to West Point as Red Blaik's assistant, and the rough edges were rounded off; he learned refinements and finesse, plus the idea of total discipline. From there he went to the

Giants, where he coached across the hall from Landry and put in his Run to Daylight concept, which revolutionized both running and blocking, and from there he went to Green Bay.

There have been at least a dozen books written about Lombardi. A year after he died the NFL put out a 204-page book that consisted of nothing but quoted tributes—from 116 different sources. I never really saw a good, solid, critical book written about him . . . Jerry Kramer's *Instant Replay* was closest, but Jerry was family.

Lombardi was a hard man to figure. Even his most famous quote, "Winning isn't everything, it's the only thing," was recorded wrong. I was at the dinner at which he said it. The original quote, which makes sense, was, "Winning isn't the most important thing, it's the only thing." And when he used it, he was himself quoting another coach—Fielding Yost, I think. But the way it's been handed down, it makes no sense. You could turn it around and it would have the same impact: "Winning isn't the only thing, it's everything."

He was complex and at times inspired. He drew his Packers into a tight little unit; often he treated them as a father would. Marvin Fleming, the tight end, was only 21 when he joined the Packers. He tells a story about sitting by his locker one day and Lombardi kept passing him by and staring at him.

"Finally," he says, "coach Lombardi came over to me and said, 'Marvin, your eyes look dull. Have you been abusing yourself?'"

No one denied his coaching genius, but at times the yelling and driving turned some of them off.

"He coached through fear," said Curry, his former center. "Most of the Packers were afraid of him, of his scoldings and his sarcasm. It's a form of motivation that works for some people. But it didn't work for me."

Gregg admitted that Lombardi was the finest coach he'd ever been around, but he added that there was a constant air of tension in Green Bay that he never felt in the year he played for the Cowboys.

"In Green Bay we planned both babies for the off-season," Barbara Gregg says. "Lombardi wouldn't have liked it during the season. We never thought about it—it was just the way it should be."

When I was a young writer, Lombardi terrified me. I would have given my right arm to have played for him, but the stories about how he browbeat the press were legendary. I remember covering a Packer game against the Bears in 1966. Green Bay had held Gale Sayers to 29 yards, and that was going to be my story. I looked for

Lombardi in the Packers' cramped Wrigley Field dressing room after the game, and he was sitting next to the cage where they handed out the equipment, surrounded by writers in overcoats and hats. It had been a cold day, and steam was rising from the gathering. It looked like they were cooking him.

I finally got my question through: "What was your theory on defensing Sayers?"

"Get him back into the flow of traffic, cut off his pursuit, it's a theory as old as football itself," Lombardi said. Fine, I had my Lombardi quote and I headed into the adjoining players' room.

"What was your theory on defensing Sayers?" I asked linebacker Dave Robinson, and before he could answer, Lombardi had popped up from that mass of steaming overcoats 30 feet away.

"Wait a minute, wait a minute," he said. "You just asked me that same question." A hush fell on the group. I don't know how the hell he heard me. Everyone stared at me. I wanted to die. Robinson laughed and motioned me farther down the room. As we moved on, I heard Lombardi telling the writers, "The same question, the very same question. First he asks me, then he asks him, the very same thing."

A few years later I was talking to a psychiatrist and I told him the story. "One of the earmarks of genius," he said, "is absolute control of your surroundings." I wasn't so sure. Maybe it was just a case of rabbit ears. At any rate I never forgot it.

Nor do I forget the last time I ever interviewed Lombardi, probably one of the last times anyone did. It was in the spring of 1970, a few months before he died. The NFL was having its meetings in New York and they provided the press with an afternoon session with all the league coaches. Lombardi had coached the Redskins the previous year. He looked tired and drawn. The cancer that was to kill him was already raging in his system.

I asked him about the unrest that had marked the young people in the late sixties, the feeling of turbulence in our society. I expected him to say something about people who were too lazy to go out and get a job, or something like that, but he didn't.

"All the things going on in this country, all the things I'm so far removed from," he said. "You live in such a narrow world as a coach. My kids come home and tell me stuff, and I don't even know what they're talking about. I've got to change that. I've got to take more of an interest in these things, learn more about them. There's so much I don't understand."

It makes me very sad when I think about it now. I wish I'd gotten to know him better. I wish I could have known him as a young coach with the Giants. Lombardi and Landry on the same staff . . . that really must have been something.

"One day I was walking down the hall," Kyle Rote says, "and I looked on one side and there was Lombardi, looking at films. I looked on the other side and there was Landry, looking at films. I continued on down the hall and saw Jim Lee Howell, the head coach, reading a newspaper."

Landry's first love was defense, and it was Lombardi who actually inspired his Flex, in which two linemen are offset. The Flex was designed to counter Lombardi's Run to Daylight offense, to shut down all the gaps and close off that daylight, to protect against the trap plays. When Landry got to Dallas in 1960 he also put in the offense, an offense that became forerunner of modern concepts. The Cowboys were an expansion team with little talent, so Landry had to do it with formations, with motion and shifts and sets that destroyed recognition.

"Tom once told me," Gregg says, "that if he had come to Dallas with the same material Vince had when he went to Green Bay, he'd probably have run the same type of offense he ran."

It was a triumph of the cerebral. How many coaches take charge of the offense and defense both, as Landry still does? After a year he had given the Cowboys, with their castoff players, an offense that ranked in the top half of the league, that finished less than 17 yards a game behind the champion Packers. A remarkable coaching achievement.

When they changed the rules in 1978 and opened up the passing lanes Landry was a dissident, even though the Cowboys' president, Tex Schramm, was one of the heavies on the Competition Committee who had helped push them through. The rule makers had accomplished, with one swoop of their pen, something that should have been the job of the coaches; and Landry, who always enjoyed the challenges of the game plan and chart book, didn't think it was right.

History will evaluate Landry as the captain of the smoothest ship in the game for many, many years. Ask him what his trademarks are and he'll say, "Consistency, proper organization, proper preparation." A lot of people get a lot of credit within the organization, but, as former Bear GM Jim Finks said, "It's that bald-headed guy who runs the show."

But, and here's the big *but*, a cycle has repeated itself, and once again the Cowboys are being referred to in terms they haven't heard for 13 years—a team that can't win the big one. Remember when that was everybody's popular description of Dallas, back around 1971 or so? It's surfaced again, after they've lost out in their final game for six straight years, or ever since the first year of the new rules. You hear a lot of reasons, most of them psychological (how the analysts love to go to work on this team), the idea that their approach is so cerebral, with their "influence" blocking and finesse on the line, and their gap defense, that the emotion is lost. I've heard this since the late 1960s . . . "We're going to start giving that final, killing lick" (middle linebacker Lee Roy Jordan), or "From now on I'm going to make the guy opposite me worry about just surviving the game" (defensive tackle Bob Lilly). Funny that no one worried about it when the Cowboys won the '72 and '78 Super Bowls.

They turned the emotional burners way up high when they met the Rams in the playoffs last year, or at least they gave the outward appearances of it. They came out of the tunnel in a full sprint, with their fists thrust in the air, and on TV John Madden and Pat Summerall were remarking how unlike the Cowboys this was. And then the Rams took the opening kickoff and drove the length of the field for a score.

Strategists have said that Landry's defense became Old World, that the 4-3 Flex was too geared toward stopping the run in an era of the pass. Veteran defensive backs such as Cliff Harris and Charlie Waters hinted to Landry that perhaps he ought to get his linebackers off the trolley tracks and go into a 3-4 as everybody else was doing. "He looked at me like I was a traitor," Waters said. Personnel men said that the once great Doomsday Defense had sprung leaks, that recent draft choices hadn't worked out and no longer was there an All-Pro or a near All-Pro at every position.

I have my own theory on what happened to the Cowboys last year. I think they got old. Age has never been as important as it is now, in the era of the 16-game season, and last year the Cowboys were the second oldest team in football. The oldest? The Raiders, but they do things differently. They baby their older veterans. "When you're banged up," Alzado says, "you don't have to go to practice and stand around in 40-below weather all afternoon. They give you a couple of days off. And they'll give you an early hook in a game or two. They'll sacrifice a game, if they have to, if it means getting you ready for the long pull at the end."

Age ended the dynasties in Green Bay and Pittsburgh. Lombardi's old-timers just couldn't get it up for Bengtson when Vince quit as coach. Noll was loyal to his old vets and perhaps he held onto them just a year or two too long, a tribute to him as a human being but not as a member of the corporate world of coaching. The Cowboys never had those problems. They were the epitome of the hi-tech, corporate club. A part starts wearing out, you think about replacing it.

"Just when you got on top," Calvin Hill once said, "when you were a star, that's when you felt you were standing on the banana peel, that the organization was thinking about your replacement."

But maybe as he gets older Landry is mellowing and he feels closer to his older people. Maybe it's just that he didn't have much confidence in his backups. But last year the Cowboys were a very old team at the end of the season, and they played like it. OK, you say, if Gary Allen didn't fumble the punt against the Rams, if the receivers hadn't dropped so many balls, things would have been different. I disagree. What beat the Cowboys was young legs. Reggie Doss, Greg Meisner, Mel Owens, Jim Collins, Carl Ekern, George Andrews . . . the Cowboys couldn't keep them out of there. Old legs blocking young.

Landry, incidentally, is my mother's favorite coach. She loves watching him on the sidelines. "Such dignity," she says. "The way he carries himself . . . he's a real man."

One final note: The year he won his first Super Bowl they threw a banquet for the team, and on the dais Landry drank Dr. Pepper, and then the band played his favorite hymn, "How Great Thou Art." Sam Huff came up to him afterward.

"Hey Tom," he said. "This is carrying things too far."

The only NFL coach who played for both Landry and Lombardi was Gregg. When he took over the Bengals and brought them to the Super Bowl, the media buzzword that week was Discipline. There always is one, every Super Bowl. In 1983 it was Intimidation. The year before, Hogs. With Gregg it was Discipline, and I'm sure some of the writers expected him to come out for his first press conference with a whip and chair. Actually Gregg, in person, is a very nice guy, with a finely tuned sense of humor ("I'm from Texas but I outgrew that a long time ago"), but the writers, reasoning that he came from the Lombardi system and turned a lax club into a winner, figured he must have done it with barbed wire.

The keynote quote, from the Bengals I talked to earlier that season, came from punter Pat McInally. "I think he's starting to like us now," he said. Usually you hear it the other way around. I asked McInally what first impressed him about Gregg when he faced the team for his first meeting, his size, his Super Bowl rings, what?

"The size of his feet," he said. "I thought, 'Man, what a pair of hooves on him.'"

I asked another Bengal what Gregg had done to turn things around so dramatically.

"Cleared out the old Paul Brown gang," he said. "Got the cronies away from the team, got Brown away from the team."

In 1983 the Brown influence was felt once again. The club wouldn't spend money. Stars slipped off to the USFL. So did the offensive coordinator. And Gregg moved on to Green Bay. "You can't win if you can't sign your players," he said.

Brown's new coach was Sam Wyche. When Brown introduced him at his first press conference he said Sam would have a free rein in hiring assistants, and then announced the first three that the club— i.e., Paul Brown—had decided to retain. Total control. It's been Brown's trademark ever since he first brought a collection of Ohio State undergrads with him to the Cleveland Browns (named after guess who) and ran off four straight All-American Football Conference titles, and then, when they challenged him to do it in the big leagues, either won the title outright or reached the championship game for six straight seasons.

He started most of the modern innovations in pro football. For years he had one of the youngest teams in the game. When a guy got a little old he was gone. He was the first to time people in the 40. "Write this in your notebooks: Youth and Speed. You Can't Lick Speed."

He started psychological testing: "If you do not like food or service you get at a restaurant do you protest to the waiter_____NEVER _____SOMETIMES_____OFTEN_____ALWAYS?" People laughed at it, then copied it.

He started IQ tests. "I don't know how important that test was," said Pete Perreault, an early Bengal guard under Brown, "but we took it in camp the first day, and next day four guys were gone. If that doesn't put the fear of God into you. . . ."

Fear. A Paul Brown trademark. He started calling plays for his quarterback in 1946. Everybody blasted him for it. Now everyone does it. "My quarterbacks have leeway to call audibles," he said, but in Cincinnati, when John Stofa and Dewey Warrent were his QBs, all the audibles were dummy audibles.

"When the man who's called the play is not only the head coach but GM and president of the team," Stofa said, "you've got to think twice about changing it."

He was unforgiving. Jim Brown, his great fullback, ripped him once. Paul Brown never forgot it. When the team went to a movie the night before a game there were three rules: no X-rated, no R-rated and no Jim Brown.

"I can remember all of us sitting through *101 Dalmatians*," former Bengal tight end Bob Trumpy says, "because the only other movie in the area was *Ice Station Zebra* with Jim Brown."

In the area of technical football, though, Brown delegated authority, and Walsh, for one, was very grateful. Brown burned him deeply when he passed over him for the head coaching job in 1976, after he'd been running the Bengal offenses for eight years. But looking back on it now, Walsh realizes he'd been given a rare opportunity to develop his own style of football.

"I had the advantage of longevity in a given system," Walsh says. "I had eight years to develop and mature and refine my own philosophy. Paul would say general things, like when he wanted more motion he'd say, 'I want more of that swishing and swaying offense.'"

So the Bengals went with motion, and one Monday night in 1975 Walsh put everybody in motion in a game against Buffalo, tight end, backs, receivers, and Ken Anderson threw for 447 yards, a very high number in that era. Against the Steelers one year Walsh got three wideouts into the game, and Andy Russell, a linebacker, wound up covering flanker Isaac Curtis, who promptly beat him for a long TD.

"What happened?" they asked Russell when he came out.

"What happened," he said, "is that I can't run a 9.3 hundred."

When you ask Walsh about the influences in his life the first man he names is Bob Bronzan, his coach at San Jose State.

"He coached and developed Dick Vermeil, too," Walsh says. "He was a man ahead of his time, a great theorist, a highly detailed coach. He coached it as a science, a skilled sport. He gave us vistas.

"Going to the Oakland Raiders in '66, though, was the biggest event of my life. I learned the Al Davis–Sid Gillman system, a completely extensive offensive system, the most advanced since Clark Shaughnessy, except maybe for Don Coryell at San Diego. It was a complete pass offense in its detail, its variety and ability to attack from anywhere; far more so than anyone else's. That single experience gave me the real jump in my career.

"Then I went to Paul Brown and the atmosphere was completely different. Paul was more disciplined in the areas outside technical football; Al was technique, Paul was the psychologist. He dealt with emotion, with character and related areas, with organization. He offered you the opportunity to almost clinically coach a football team. You knew you had the players' attention. You knew you'd get results from them or they wouldn't be with you. Paul delegated authority, never publicly but you had the job."

With Walsh you're always aware of a mind at work, churning, clicking, recording and discarding information. People who worked with him in 1962, when he was a defensive assistant on Marv Levy's staff at California, remember him as a man whose ideas would pile up so fast he could barely get them out in time.

"We ran our coaches' meetings in a room with three blackboards," one of them said. "Walsh would scribble a play, but before he'd finish his mind would shift to another one. He'd move to the second board and begin writing while he was still talking about the first one. Levy would follow him around with an eraser and rub out the play because the other coaches were getting confused."

He likes to talk football in terms of boxing, and tennis, which he plays. "Shock the defense, put 'em in a shock, a quick striking offense, beat 'em to the punch." The lightning volley at the net before the opponent is set, the quick crosscourt slash. When he talked about his 49ers in the NFC title game against the heavier Redskins in 1984 it sounded like Dempsey against Firpo.

In 1981 the Giants scouted him before their playoff game. They studied three games and threw up their hands. He'd called 52 different plays on first-and-10. His first year at San Francisco was marked by great offensive innovation but few players. The season ended at 2–14.

"Watching him before and after that season," guard Randy Cross said, "was like watching Jimmy Carter's presidency. The smiling face in '76, and all of a sudden three years later here's the sagging face and the wrinkles and gray hair. 'Hey, I can't take this anymore.'"

Walsh never hired an offensive coordinator. "That's step four," he said. "Step five is toward the exit."

Before the '82 Super Bowl they started calling him a genius. Walsh's genius versus Gregg's discipline. That would be the keynote of Super Bowl XVI. The coaching fraternity sneered. The labels bothered Walsh.

"Is discipline like slapping a child in the rear end or performing like a great Russian ballet dancer?" he said. "Such a wide spectrum in semantics. We play as controlled as any team in the NFL. That's how we interpret discipline. This isn't just a wild, ravaged game, you know, with players slashing through each other.

"As for genius . . . usually that's associated with a certain figment of crackpot."

The absentminded professor. Walsh is fond of making fun of himself in that area.

"I'll be with my wife, Geri, and I'll have my arm around her back," he says. "It's an affectionate gesture, but I'll be going like this . . ." and his fingers punch out a pass pattern.

"What will Geri do?" someone asked him.

"She'll say, 'Did it work?'"

"Here's one for you," he adds. "I've been out in a parking lot at 2:00 A.M. looking for a rental car with absolutely no memory of what it looks like or where I'd left my luggage. How's this . . . I stop at a coffee shop an hour before I have to be at a banquet. I tell myself, 'Now don't lock the keys in the car,' and as I'm saying it I'm doing it. *Slam!* I have to call the police . . . call the banquet . . . 'Sorry, but I'm going to be late. . . .'"

The organization that seems to have continually bucked the system with the greatest success is the Raiders. They've got a reputation as a wild, maverick outfit and this goes back to their old AFC days, when Al Davis would do outlandish things to get a competitive edge. Rival coaches would accuse him of bugging their dressing rooms.

"Well, I don't know about that," Lee Grosscup, his old PR man said, "but you can bet that every room in the Raiders' office building is bugged—or at least I think so."

Al Davis. "Bummy," Jim Finks called him, in honor of the late

Brooklyn welterweight, Bummy Davis. The Jet's trips to Bummy's turf were like troop movements to Vietnam. There was the time the workmen tried to unroll their tarps and throw the Jets off the practice field; the time Al planted one of his cronies, Morris Schleicher, on a Jet team bus; the trip to New York for the '67 AFL Championship when Al smuggled workmen into Shea Stadium the night before the game and constructed a whole heating apparatus behind the Raider bench. Even the Jet-Raider playoff game after the 1982 season brought back memories ... the way the Jets' security guards went crazy looking for Davis spies the week before the contest, the phone call to the Jets' locker room at halftime and Walt Michaels' fierce denunciations of Davis for pulling a stunt like that. (It turned out to be a Queens bartender.)

It was always "us against them," on Bummy's club, but it's been a tight, fierce organization with remarkable success through the years. In 1983 seven ex-Raiders worked for the team. No other organization has maintained such loyalty. Al scouts players himself, a holdover from the old AFL days when it was absolutely essential to grab the right people. The Raiders belong to no scouting combines. Secrecy is the key. When one piece of the puzzle was missing in '83 they signed cornerback Mike Haynes. Never mind that it cost them $400,000 a year and a first- and a second-round draft choice. Hey, the guy would get us to the Super Bowl.

John Madden and Tom Flores coached the Raiders to Super Bowl triumphs, effective, low-key "players" coaches, reared in the Raider system. But the overall direction of a system that's been consistent since the sixties, with its one-free, bump-and-run defense and standard-set offense, belongs to Davis. Oh yes, and the quarterback calls his own plays.

"They wanted to get rid of me after the '79 season," linebacker Ted Hendricks says. "The vote was 9–2 that I go. One of the two was Charlie Sumner, the defensive coach, and the other one was Al, and you know what kind of weight his vote carries. He said, 'Uh uh, he's my puppy.'"

There's one word that Davis always uses to describe his organization, though, and it's the one thing they've never had, and that's *class.* Class is something you don't talk about. It's either there or it's not. The organization that never mentions it at all, and yet has more of it than any other, is the Steelers. Part of it comes from the Rooney family, part of it from Chuck Noll.

Once I devised a nifty idea for a column. I'd ask every NFL coach to capsule himself in one paragraph, how he'd like to be remembered, and then I'd print the results. The idea died after three responses, but they're worth repeating. Shula, Allen and Noll. Each gave the matter considerable thought.

"Always fair," Shula said. "Never screwed anybody. His team traveled first class."

"I want to be remembered," Allen said, "as a guy who wanted to win so badly that he'd give a year of his life to be a winner."

"Just put down that I was a teacher," Noll said. "Don't ever call me a winner. Players win, coaches teach. I was a teacher."

I remember the game in which the Pittsburgh four–Super Bowl dynasty officially ended, a 6–0 loss to Houston on a Thursday nighter in the AstroDome in 1980. I was standing outside the Steelers' locker room as the players walked down the concrete stairway leading from the field. The Houston fans, all those raucous, nasty, Luv Ya Blue maniacs, leaned over the railings and screamed abuse at the Steelers and laughed at them. Not one player turned around. Not one of them looked up. Eyes straight ahead, heads high, they walked to their dressing room in silence. They looked like kings abdicating the throne. I almost broke down, watching that sight. The only sign of emotion I saw was from linebacker Dennis Winston, who was unwinding the tape from his wrist. When the jeering got loudest he balled it up tightly and casually tossed it over his shoulder.

There are so many more coaches I haven't talked about, so many of the game's true innovators, such as Don Coryell, who has been typecast as a pure passing theorist but is really much, much more. In 1955 he used a Power-I formation at Wenatchee Valley JC in Washington when the world hadn't yet heard of it. A year later he brought a Fort Ord team into the L.A. Coliseum and held the Ram rookies to a 14–14 tie, mostly with a power running game. He had the nation's second leading rusher at Whittier, Maxie Fields, and it was only when he went to San Diego State and material was thin that he started building his great passing attacks, through necessity.

The one-back, two-tight-end offense did not begin with his Charger teams of the late seventies . . . he'd done it half-a-decade earlier in St. Louis, with Jackie Smith as his set tight end and the late J. V. Cain as his slot man. He took advantage of the new rules and brought the passing game to an absolute frenzy in the modern era, but I've got a theory on Coryell's operation. He likes to run in Monday night games—Steelers in '80, Cleveland in '81, Kansas City in '83. Maybe it's just to show the world at large he really can run the ball, but check it out when the Chargers play on Monday night.

From the Coryell system came Joe Gibbs, who added the hammer to the one-back offense at Washington, winning a Super Bowl by using his passing game to tire out the rushers on the defensive line, and then coming back to hammer them with the Hogs and John Riggins.

They're all a bit quirky, a bit strange at times. The job does that to them. An assistant tells about the time Shula ran on the field and screamed at the referee, "You're ruining my life! You're ruining my life!" It was in an exhibition game.

Most coaches get fired, a few go somewhere else, some, like Vermeil, are victims of burnout. I have a list in front of me of one wire service's Coach of the Year choices for the last 10 years ... 1974, Coryell at St. Louis—fired; 1975, Ted Marchibroda at Baltimore—fired; 1976, Gregg at Cleveland; 1977, Red Miller at Denver; 1978, Jack Patera at Seattle; 1979, Jack Pardee at Washington—fired, fired, all fired; 1980, Chuck Knox at Buffalo—quit; 1981, Walsh in San Francisco—admittedly exhausted a year later, almost quit; 1982 and 1983, Gibbs at Washington—we'll see.

"At first we were mad because it's our life," Phyllis Pardee said when her husband was fired by the Redskins. "Jack Kent Cooke's a millionaire and football's his toy. It happens that his toy is our life."

In January 1983, I sat in a Los Angeles coffee shop with Jet receivers coach Pete McCully as he read aloud the story about the firing of Atlanta coach Leeman Bennett.

" 'At the press conference Bennett was teary-eyed as he sat next to Falcons owner Rankin Smith,' " McCully read. Then he paused for a moment.

"Can you imagine what that press conference must have been like for him?" he said. He stared into his coffee cup for a while. He mumbled something I couldn't hear.

"What did you say?" I asked him.

"I just said," he repeated, "no damn owner is ever going to make me cry."

CHAPTER FOURTEEN

Game Plans . . . and Other Deep Thoughts

When Weeb first came to New York, he gave us a playbook; we'd been without one for three years. It's a sensible sort of thing for a professional football player to have.

—Larry Grantham

The idea is to have a plan and still allow for the unforesee-able. I've been reading about Nelson's battle with the Franco-Spanish fleet at Trafalgar in 1805. He had 25 days to make his plan. He was outnumbered, but his plan worked. He had steps prepared for the contingencies, and the plan left a certain flexibility in the choices of his captains. That is the basis of football.

The goal is to attack the other side with clean, sharp blows while you're moving faster than the opposition. That was Wellington. That was Von Clausewitz. I don't relate football to warfare other than in those dynamics, but the military axioms of Von Clausewitz about people under stress, about the individual soldier, make the best book on football.

—Bill Walsh

"WHY we have a playbook."

"The proper execution of a push-up."

"Dealing with newspapermen; learn who you can trust."

It's all part of a playbook, that mysterious thing that can cost a player $500 to $1000 if it's lost—or swiped. The basic offense and defense and diagrams are only part of the whole picture. Club rules, even rules of life (depending on the moral nature of the head coach),

254

timely hints for behavior—they're all there. It's the philosophy of a professional football club; it's like a newspaperman's style guide; or the Eleven General Orders for a soldier on guard duty.

"The plays and diagrams and things like that, the players write that down themselves in the book," Weeb Ewbank used to say. "We lecture and they write. They learn it better that way. We used to have them write down the other stuff, too, the club rules, but it just took too much time."

That's the old Paul Brown method, but it's generally been discarded now. The theory is that you can read something or write something, but you can only learn it when you walk it through, on the practice field.

"There's an old Chuck Knox saying," Jack Reynolds says. " 'Perfect practice prevents blank, blank, blank.' "

The offense gets one playbook, the defense gets another. The books usually run upward of 200 pages. An economical one can go 150 or so. But this isn't as tiresome as it sounds. Diagrams are deliberately large, to ease comprehension, and a few of them can eat up a whole page.

The book usually starts with "League Rules," such as the NFL's drug enforcement and gambling policies, and goes on to "Club Rules," subtitled "Basic Information": fines, player rating systems, dealing with the press, basic stances, how to use the machines, how to wear your equipment, how to run, how to exercise, mental attitude, etc. This is included in all books, and through the years the section has become more basic as the college backgrounds of the new talent have become more diverse. And by now the coaches probably realize that many of the rookies come to camp with very little in their heads—except possibly the knowledge of how to get an agent.

The offensive book's next part is a basic information section: quarterback calls; the huddle; the terminology; the play numbering system; the numbering of the backs; formations, both offensive and defensive (the offensive players must learn to recognize defenses); the two-minute drill; the "automatic" or checkoff system at the line; where to sit on the bench; the pregame warm-up; the means of calling signals.

Signals, surprisingly, can be called in hundreds of different ways. The quarterback can say "hut, hut, hut," without breaking his rhythm. He can say "hut-hut, hut-hut"; or he can get tricky with broken cadences, which are supposed to throw the defense off, but can foul up a rookie on his own team, too. It's generally expected that when the snap count is, say, the second "hut," the player is supposed to be off a split-second earlier and into his man by the time the actual "hut" comes around.

Then the book devotes itself to diagrams, broken up by frequency charts for formations ("On first and 10 we were in a flank-right 61 times last season; on second and seven, 43 times; 28 times in a slot-left," etc.) and then actual plays from those formations.

The more basic coaches might have 60 to 75 running plays in their books and the same number of passes. Multiple-offense teams, such as Dallas and Denver and San Francisco, have more. People like George Halas, who used to say that his men had to learn 500 plays, didn't really use 500 different plays. They were just switching terminology and calling each variation of a play a new play. It added to the mystique. Actually there are only so many plays possible, and the number is a lot less than 500.

A defensive playbook usually contains an early section on "Defensive Philosophy," which starts with the number one philosophic imperative—Prevent Scoring. Then come things like Theory of Pass Defense, which concerns zone or man-to-man preference; Theory of Blitzing ("We blitz to create confusion and sow destruction," etc.); and standards of achievement.

Both the offense and the defense have standards, e.g., hold the other team to 250 total yards in a game, sack the quarterback four times, complete 60 percent of your own passes. There are generally between 15 and 20, and they'll be repeated on a giant board, if the locker room is spacious enough. And from game to game the figures actually achieved will be entered next to the ideal, so the players can see if they were good boys or bad boys.

Rookies are expected to read their playbooks diligently. Veterans often put them on the shelf, where they'll remain for the whole season. Things don't change much from year to year.

"I had to collect the playbooks at the end of the season," says Mike Ornstein of the Raiders. "The players would wrinkle them up, so it looked like they used them. What's a book gonna tell Gene Upshaw about playing guard?"

A layman opening a playbook at random wouldn't understand much. It's written in a mysterious language.

"When Howie first joined the Raiders," says Diane Long, the wife of defensive end Howie Long, "he'd say stuff like, 'Well, the linebacker moves here and the tackle moves here.' Now I hear him on the phone and he's talking about 'easy-over and orange-two.' It sounds like he's working in a diner or something."

When Lyle Alzado came to the Raiders he was surprised to hear a lot of the same terminology he had heard on the Broncos, his first team—stuff like Cloud and Sky. Finally he realized it was old Chicago Bear language. Defensive line coaches Earl Leggett of the Raiders and Stan Jones of the Broncos had both played for the Bears. They were still using the terms they grew up with.

A fan might be surprised to learn that there are no *X*s and *O*s. Make that no *X*s. Offensive players are indicated on the diagram by an *O*. Defensive players are *V*s or triangles. When abbreviations are used you never see "LB" for linebacker. It's either "P" for plugger, or "W" or "S" for weak side or strong side. Receivers are either *X* (split end), *Z* (flanker), *Y* (tight end) or *U* (second tight end).

Bill Walsh says the terms date back to Clark Shaughnessy and the 1930s.

"*ABC* motion, *XYZ* receivers, they're all Shaughnessy terms," he says. "He had a term for every conceivable thing that could happen in football—Red Right, Two Left Double, like that. He really put football into an ordered system. Instead of saying, 'Move a little to the left,' he'd say, 'Move to the *A* position.'"

When a rookie first gets his playbook he worries about learning his own assignments. After a while he sees the sense in memorizing the whole scheme.

"When I was a rookie I knew my own routes, but never the whole play," Dallas wide receiver Tony Hill says. "Then I started learning secondary adjustments, what you do when the primary receiver is covered, and finally I got the big picture."

Assume that everyone has worked hard in camp and everyone knows his playbook. Now it's September and the season is about to start. The scouting reports on the first game or two are brief. They're based on the tendency charts and frequency patterns and film reports from exhibition games and last year's action. As the season goes on, the reports become more complete. And the coach's life takes on another aspect—the movie projector.

Teams film their own games and practices. The films are ready a few hours later, instantly if videotape is used. Dallas uses three different cameras for a variety of angles and views. The Cowboys have their own film processing lab; they duplicate every opponent's film and store it in their files. They estimate that in the course of a season they process over 1.2 million feet of film, 227 miles.

As part of the NFL's film exchange requirements, an opponent's last two games must be received on the Wednesday 11 days before you play the team, so that when you're getting ready to meet, say, Pittsburgh that weekend, you're actually starting your work on next week's Buffalo game. The following Monday, six days before the game, the most recent Buffalo film will be in. A favorite trick of George Halas's was to tamper with the film he was sending out, and every time the Bears had a long gainer the film would become strangely blurred or smudged. Now the league requires play-by-play sheets to be sent along with the film.

Monday and Tuesday are a race against time, as the coaches look at the final film and perform the tedious, nonthinking, mechanical task of "breaking it down," so the game plan will be ready for the players on Wednesday. It is during this period that coaches go buggy, or get "square eyeballs," as New Orleans line coach Joe Spencer likes to say.

The Jets were once playing in San Diego, and Weeb Ewbank and Sonny Werblin and a couple of writers spent an evening in Tijuana, right across the border. They were taking a stroll down the main drag when a little guy holding something that looked like two cans of film approached the group.

"Movies?" he said. "Feelthy movies?"

"Christ no," Ewbank said without breaking stride. "I've been looking at movies all week."

Under the old method, two offensive assistants would get the other team's defensive film, and two defensive men, the offense. They would set up their projectors in two rooms, and one coach would call out formations while the other one would write. The writer would go through a whole session without ever seeing the movie.

"Once we tried a computer," said the late Clive Rush, when he was coaching the Patriots. "But it was faster just to write everything down on a big, yellow, legal-size pad. You have to feed stuff into the computer, and by the time we set up the feeding system, we could break down one whole quarter."

Nowadays, though, everyone admits that computers speed up the work—and free a couple of assistants during each breakdown. Dallas has lived by the computer for almost two decades. Their Diable 1620 coughs out more than 300 pages of raw data on each weekly opponent. The Cowboys are developing a "formation analysis," in which the computer will detect weaknesses in enemy formations, based on a player's position, his physical strength, speed, reaction time, etc., all learned through films.

Teams always have more films broken down on an opponent than the required three. If you're playing both teams on the same game film, for instance, one immediately and one two months later, you'll break them both down. Horse trading with friends on the other clubs will fill in the gaps and give you a complete film record of a team.

"Anytime I can latch onto a film," Walt Michaels said when he was a Jet assistant, "I'll grab it and break it down."

With some coaches, it's almost a waste of time, looking at their more recent game films.

"If you have the last three games on Walsh's 49ers," Reynolds said when he was a Ram linebacker, "you might as well throw them away. He's not going to repeat those plays. If you have six games, look at the oldest one. That might be what you'll see. There's no pattern to it."

There are many tales of the film room. The Jets tell the story about the day one of their assistant coaches got mesmerized while the projector was running backward, and the players sat there for 10 minutes, watching themselves jump back out of their stance and retreat to the huddle, until Winston Hill gently tapped the guy on the shoulder and informed him: "Coach, the film's backwards."

At UCLA Dick Vermeil and his staff were peering at a film of their game against Oregon State the previous year when all of a sudden Vermeil punched a button, froze the picture and blurted, "My God!" The assistants leaned forward, but all they could see was a sideline shot of Vermeil's second-oldest son, David. "God," he said, "has David ever grown a lot in a year!"

Once, in San Diego, Sid Gillman called in his defensive assistant, Bum Phillips, to watch a particularly meaningful piece of footage. He ran it over countless times, while Bum yawned.

"Bum," he finally said, "this is better than making love."

"Either I don't know how to watch film," Phillips said, "or you don't know how to make love."

Mike Adamle was a Bear fullback when Gillman arrived as offensive coordinator in 1977. "Sid ran one Hadl-to-Alworth pass play 71 times by actual count," Adamle says, "but the problem was that just before the ball reached Alworth's fingertips Sid would reverse the film and run it back. It was like a Chinese Communist torture, a sensory deprivation experiment. Guys were squirming in their seats. They were screaming, 'Let him catch it!' We never did see that pass completed."

What have the coaches really got, once they're through breaking down all those miles of film, once the computer has finally gone to bed? Tendencies mainly, frequencies, formations, statistical probabilities . . . they've been in Brown Right 13 times on second-and-eight this year, and eight times they ran the 35-Lead play, and four times it picked up three yards or less, etc. The unimaginative coach bases his game plan on the probability of what's likely to work against what the other team has shown so far, and how he can best anticipate what the other team will do to him in each situation. The creative, or innovative, coach uses that as a mere starting point. He'll expand on it; he'll anticipate the unexpected, because maybe five years previously he'd worked with their offensive coordinator in college, and like a poker player, he has a pretty good line on his thinking. Player evaluation will enter into it, intangibles . . . their fullback's coming off a knee injury, the long-range weather forecast says snow, they've played three weeks on artificial turf and their legs have got to be tired.

And then on Wednesday the players get their game plans. These can run up to 40 or 50 pages, most of them diagrams. The offensive game plan is a distillation of the 70 or 80 most favored plays in given situations, with variations, of course. On defense it's a list of the most favored fronts and stunts and coverages, when to use the WHAM blitz, WHAM meaning "W," meaning weak-side linebacker; when to use the SLAM—strong-side plugger. Statistical breakdowns are included, often in diagram form, with each hole and position illustrated and accompanied, underneath, by the frequency with which the enemy has run that hole and the results. Lineups are listed, words of inspiration ("WE HAVE WORKED AND SWEATED FOR THIS EVERY DAY SINCE JULY 19th. WE HAVE PAID A BIG ENOUGH PRICE. NOW IT'S UP TO YOU," etc.). Opposing players are scouted in capsule form, a lineman's setup, his stance, his first move and his favorite one: e.g., Steeler center Mike Webster: "Can jack up nose guard, wrestle and move feet to position-block. Likes to area-joker or scoop. Will use scramble block as change-up. Short sets—area. Can square up rusher. . . ."

It's a condensed guide, to supplement the players' midweek film study, but Dallas also gives its troops the pages and pages of raw computer data, a mind-boggling list of each individual play, thousands of them.

"Why the raw data?" Tony Hill says. "Because this is the Dallas Cowboys. If someone else has 10 pages, we have to have 100."

"Sometimes you might want to check a tendency, but I can't think of a guy who'll read everything," Randy White says. "Wait a minute, there's one. Bob Breunig. That's why he's been Tom Landry's middle linebacker all these years."

Coaches tinker and mess with their game plans right up to Sunday. Don't believe it when they tell you they don't.

"The worst statement you can make is, 'The hay is in the barn,'" Joe Gibbs says. "You keep changing things right up to kickoff. You stay awake at night dreaming up things."

Walsh kept putting in things right up to his Super Bowl game against the Bengals. On Saturday he put in an unbalanced line formation, "to give them something else to think about." On Sunday morning the 49ers' team bus was held up in traffic for 20 minutes on its way to the Silverdome. "Here comes a new play," Joe Montana said.

Walsh scripts his offense on Saturday night; he draws up a list of the first 20 plays the team will use, to keep the enemy from reading tendencies. When he scouted the 49ers for the '84 NFC Championship game, Gibbs said, "They have 150 formations. That's more than I've seen since I've been here."

"They use a formation once and they never come back to it," Redskins' linebacker Mel Kaufman said.

"In 1980 he had 100 passes for our game plan against Buffalo," Montana said. "Then it poured down rain. He might change everything from week to week. You get the game plan, and everything is changed, and you say, 'God there just can't be any more. There are only so many plays possible.' But he always finds something. I've wondered what would happen if he just ran out of plays, but he'd probably go back to stuff he used in junior high and start all over again."

Russ Francis, the tight end, calls Walsh's game plans "exciting," because they're not based so much on tendencies as they are on people.

"It's all keyed to screw up one player," he says. "Say a cornerback has trouble with his backpedal. Walsh will run three different things at him to screw him up in his backpedal, something he's been doing for three weeks, uncorrected."

Films can only show you so much, which is why teams send out pro personnel people to scout opponents in the flesh. The movies can't show the intensity of the hitting or the action on the sidelines or how a team goes through its pregame drills.

"They won't show you if a guy's playing hurt," Pittsburgh Maulers' coach Henry Bullough says. "You can't get the snap count from films, whether a team likes to go on a long or short count; you can't tell how long they like to stay in the huddle."

"Watch the head coach on the sidelines," Walsh says. "Does he have the headphones on? Is he in touch with his assistants in the press box, or is he ranting and raving, with the players avoiding him? Does he interfere with the normal flow or does he contribute to it?"

Once the Colts sent Dick Bielski out to scout the Lombardi Packers. He had an unproductive day. "Nothing fancy," he said when they asked him for his evaluation. "How do you scout blocking and tackling by experts?"

I enjoy sitting next to scouts in the press box. Some of them are remarkably astute, all-seeing eyes . . . "Watch this guy when he comes off the field . . . none of his teammates will go near him." Some of them seem to be doing idiot's work. I sat next to one guy who spent his whole afternoon listing formations, every one of them—nothing else, not how many yards the play gained or what particular talents any players were showing, just the formations. He'd made the whole, long trip just to give the film breakdown guys an hour's jump on their work. I sat next to another man who scribbled like a maniac all day, barely having time to glance up at what was going on. Finally I looked at what he was writing. He was listing all 11 names in the lineup, each play.

Finally I said to him, "Why don't you just list the changes? It'll save a lot of writing."

"Coach wants it this way," he mumbled.

Some organizations have a spy at enemy practices. I remember one player showing me the scouting report on an opposing lineman and saying, "The only way we could have found this out was to have someone at their practice."

Two years ago, before a Redskins game, someone asked Landry, "Do you miss George Allen?"

"Not particularly," he said. "At least this week we don't have to buy out all the rooms in the motel behind our practice field."

Game plans will take you to the point of the game, but once the actual battle starts adjustments must be made; sometimes you have to play hunches.

"There are great practice coaches and great game-day coaches," said tight end Todd Christensen, who's been with both the Cowboys and Raiders. "Tom Landry is the greatest practice coach I've ever seen, the best at putting a team in the right stuff for a game. Tom Flores is a great game coach, great for adjustments and a feel for the flow of a game.

"Don't believe it when they tell you there aren't times when they go into a game and right away they can see they've given the team the wrong game plan. Sometimes you can tell after the first series or two that you're in the wrong offense. The question is: How long does it take for you to just junk what you've been working on all week and get out of it and go to something else?"

"We say to the other team, 'Don't show us what you can do by design, by formation,' " Al Davis says. "You've got to show us by doing it. If you stop us we'll go to something else, but not because of your concept or formation."

When the Jets played in Buffalo in 1983, the Bills had a terrific stunt cooked up, a lightning-fast formation shift modeled after the "explode package" the Redskins had used in the previous Super Bowl. Before the snap, four receivers all jumped into new positions, *boom*, like a jack-in-the-box. It was a great idea, except that on the right side of the line, Tim Volger, replacing the injured Joe Borchardt, couldn't handle Joe Klecko, and next to him Justin Cross couldn't control Mark Gastineau, and these two guys had a field day in the Bills' backfield, disrupting any kinds of packages.

I saw Tampa Bay play the Jets in Shea in 1982 and the Bucs ran the ball 10 straight times on first down, for a net gain of 10 yards, and during this span the Jets were building a 16–3 lead. Afterward John McKay blamed the loss on his kick return unit.

If I'd have to point to the one area of greatest coaching screw-ups it would be the management of the clock. Some of them don't seem to understand the most basic clock fact, that when you're behind and you're fighting the clock, you call time-outs on the other team's plays, not your own. Three running plays can eat up two minutes.

But call time after each one and you've only lost 20 to 30 seconds.

"I've seen teams call time and line up for a field goal with 10 seconds left, when they could have run another play," Davis says. "If I'm on the other guy's two-yard line with five seconds to go, I can throw a pass in four seconds and still get my field goal team on the field, if the pass is incomplete. A quarterback can complete a 10- to 15-yard pass, turn to the official and call time-out, and only six seconds will have run off. A 30-yard completion downfield takes 10 seconds, and if you've called two plays in the huddle it'll take another seven to 10 seconds to put the ball in play again. If you complete that pass and call a time-out, it's another 10 seconds, but you can run up and throw the ball away and the whole thing has only taken 12 seconds and you've saved a time-out. Those are things a quarterback and a coach have to know, but you'd be surprised how many of them don't."

"In college, so few coaches get to know the clock," Walsh says. "You can hear it at the clinics. They always want to talk about some drill they run, not about how to work the clock."

I once saw a 49er practice at which Walsh and Montana worked for half an hour on the deliberate incomplete to stop the clock . . . throw the ball on the ground, don't sail it out of bounds because it takes the official five seconds longer to get the clock stopped when he's watching the flight of the ball. But then in the '84 NFC championship game against the Redskins the 49ers butchered the clock at the end, losing 15 vital seconds before they called time-out with 54 seconds to play. It happens to everyone.

With the Raiders, Ken Stabler was a terrific two-minute quarterback, but in New Orleans those skills seem to have eroded. Last year against the Jets the Saints got the ball on their 20, trailing by three points, with 2:05 and all three time-outs left, plus the two-minute warning. They lah-de-dahed out of their huddle, they called time-outs late (they blew 19 seconds on one of them alone), they took 1:46 to run off eight plays to reach the Jets' 34, where they called their final time-out and sent in kicker Morten Andersen to try a 51-yard field goal, which he missed. His longest all year had been 50 yards. They had 19 seconds left, time to call two more plays and get closer.

Not to be outdone, the Jets had butchered the clock at the end of the first half. This is where most clock butcheries take place, and largely go unreported, because the sense of urgency isn't as great. The Jets could have had the ball with a minute and a half left, but they let the clock run and got it on their own 20 with 23 seconds to go, whereupon they ran the clock out and trooped into the locker room, to await words of wisdom.

I'm depressed about the whole lack of originality in the NFL. In college you see some wild, daring stuff; the rugby play that Cal used to beat Stanford in '82; Tom Osborne's Fumblerooskie, in which right guard Dean Steinkuhler ran for a TD against Miami last year; the deliberate bounce pass backward, whereupon the intended receiver scoops up the live ball and throws the long pass downfield. But in pro football there's only standard trickery—the flea-flicker, the fake punt, an occasional pass to a quarterback, the end-around. We need more and better junk.

Every time I've seen the old Buck and Wing play it's worked. That's the one where you pass to a wide receiver and he laterals to a trailer. Why not work something off that, such as a double lateral, or a fake lateral outside and then one *inside*? Why not use it at the end of the game, when there's nothing to lose anyway, instead of that tired old stuff like the three-wide-receiver, Big Ben play?

"Because people want to play it safe," Walsh says. "The conservative approach won't cost anyone his job."

"I saw a lot of it up in Canada," Frank Kush says, "but coaches here get so stereotyped, so concerned about their image. It sure spices up your practices, though."

"The good players I've been around don't want to win a game with tricks," New England defensive coach Rod Rust says. "They don't want you to do it for them. They just want you to put them in the right formation and give them a 50–50 chance to compete."

I still don't buy it. One year I went around asking coaches why they don't try a pass off the clock-killing quarterback kneel, the ugliest play in football? You'd do it at the end of the first half, when you're backed up deep.

"Because next time they faced that quarterback they'd kill him," Roger Staubach said.

"Do it with your second-string quarterback," said another ex-QB, Len Dawson.

"Uh-uh, it's a no-no," Francis says. "There's a gentleman's agreement out there when you're killing the clock. The other team asks you, 'You going to run a play?' and if you say no, you'd better not run one."

Nevertheless Walsh did it against St. Louis in '82. It came at the end of the game, which makes absolutely no sense at all. The pass was overthrown.

"I had a set of maniacs on my hands," Cardinal coach Jim Hanifan said. "They were all yelling, 'That dirty S.O.B.' I'm trying to calm them down but I'm just as mad as they are. Bill came over to me afterward and said, 'Couldn't help it. It was sent down from the press box. They felt it would help the point differential.'"

"I don't know what I was thinking at the time," Walsh admits. "It was a bad decision—but that doesn't mean it's in mothballs."

I see some things that coaches do that continue to amaze me. Why do they run a draw play on third-and-25, or call a swing pass, to buy a few yards, when they could quick-kick and gain 30? Why do they call time-outs at the end of a game they're losing by 30 points? When they get a 15-yard roughness penalty on an extra point or field goal, and they're kicking off from midfield, why don't they onside kick— every time? An onside kick's supposed to be 40 or 50 percent effective anyway. The downside risk is a loss of 15 yards of field position. The upside potential is the ball. When the other team's punting from your 35 and trying to pin you in the corner, and it stays in the huddle and takes the deliberate delay-of-game penalty to give the punter a better angle, why not refuse the penalty? Few do it.

Worst of all, with a first-and-goal on the seven- or eight-yard line, why do teams always do the same thing—a power run? The results are always the same, a two-yard gain. Why not throw the ball, or call a bootleg, or pull out your gimmick play on first down? A few coaches do it, Walsh, Sam Rutigliano at Cleveland, but not many more. I've got a theory about this. I think that subconsciously they're afraid of losing an image of toughness . . . by God, we'll ram it in there. I remember when Minnesota played Pittsburgh in the '75 Super Bowl, and the Vikings were held to only 17 yards rushing all day, they got down to the Steeler six and brought in two tight ends and tried to punch it in. Their longest running play up till then had been two yards, but they were going to do it like men or die trying. Naturally they got stuffed.

Finally—the two-minute offense is so exciting at the end, a defense that might have been dominating all day is suddenly playing on its heels; why not run a hurry-up, no-huddle offense early in the game, and keep coming back to it from time to time? At least you'll keep the defense from making situation substitutions and you'll be going against the people you want to go against. I've seen teams fool around with this, but never come back to it.

Pittsburgh backfield coach Tom Moore says that when he was the offensive coordinator at the University of Minnesota and Tony Dungy was the quarterback they ran a no-huddle offense for a whole game against Iowa "and we killed 'em. They couldn't get their defensive calls right." OK, so why not do it in the NFL?

"An offense can run itself out of steam in a hurry that way," former K.C. coach Marv Levy says. "You can't really duplicate a two-minute situation in the middle of a game."

OK, I know all the logic, but sometimes when you're a heavy underdog and there's nothing to lose, maybe it's time to stop being so logical.

I thought of all this strategic devilment during the strike of '82 when I, and the whole NFL fraternity at large, had unheard-of time on our hands. Some coaches went fishing. Others reported to work and mechanically drew up game plans they'd never use.

"This is what hell is going to be like," Forrest Gregg said. "This is what's going to happen to coaches, if they go down below. They'll go to their offices, work up game plans and never play the games."

CHAPTER FIFTEEN

Training Camp Days

Training camp is like kissing an ugly girl. At first there's a fear of the unknown, but once you get started it's not so bad.

—Dave Casper

THERE are many eyes that see a training camp. The coaches see it through eyes that are filled with hours and minutes and unreasonably tight schedules: "By Aug. 16 your roster must be down to 60 players; by Aug. 23, 50," etc. They think in terms of cramming the most learning into the least time and forcefeeding their playbooks into the brains of the rookies.

Camp is a giant warehouse of talent, and the coaches must evaluate, decide, and make quick judgments. And at night they spend many hours scanning the waiver list to see if they can latch onto some bargains that were cut from other clubs.

For the writers covering the club, camp is a picnic. The reporters who so desire can have their own rooms on the campsite, and if there isn't a refrigerator stocked with cold beer in their room, there's one down the hall. It's a time for getting to know the coaches and their assistants in the informal chitchat of the dining hall or the tavern. It's a breeze because there is usually very little "hard copy" that comes out of camp. The season hasn't started, so the reporters don't have to crank out stories that start: "What's wrong with the Colts?" Or the Rams or the Dolphins.

They write features and mood pieces and close-ups of rookies, relaxed in the knowledge that this kind of story usually reads just as well as the exposés, and is infinitely more fun to write.

The veterans who are secure in their jobs see camp through eyes that have seen it all. They run and sweat and curse the heat, but it's still low-key for them because the pressure hasn't really started yet.

The ones with a thirst try to figure out a way of beating the curfew, and this is fun, too, because they know that most coaches accept the late-hour sneak-outs and the fines as part of the game. After all, the season hasn't started yet, and thirsty veterans often make the best players.

Sometimes a different kind of problem comes up on clubs that have a closely knit veterans group: the problem of saving a buddy his job when a rookie threatens to take it away from him. It can be brutal on the rookie, especially if he comes to camp with a big reputation and an even bigger contract. And many a sensitive youngster never makes it because the veterans ride him off the team—in subtle ways, such as a steady hammering on the field, even in dummy scrimmages, and the silent treatment when practice is over. For the veterans, though, it's a matter of relative morality. What's more important, saving your best friend's job or worrying about a rich rookie's tender sensibilities?

Unless a regular is trying to work on a particular technique, he won't kill himself in the exhibition season.

"I probably wouldn't have made the club, based on my preseason play of the last nine years," Franco Harris said last season.

"Exhibition games are crap . . . I mean who cares?" says Lyle Alzado, a 13-year veteran. "It means nothing. The veterans don't even want to go on the field. One year at Denver we were 4–9–1, but in the exhibition season we went out and beat the hell out of Minnesota, which had the best record in the NFL the year before. Who remembered?"

For the borderline veteran, camp is a horror, and he views every wind sprint, every set of calisthenics, as an excuse for the coach to unload him if he doesn't perform well enough. The man who has a working knowledge of his body knows that once he gets to a certain age, sprinting and exercising in 90-degree heat will take that much more away from the energy he is desperately trying to hoard for the contact scrimmages, which he knows are the real tests of who stays and who goes.

Minicamps before the start of regular training camp usually can weed out the absolute undesirables; they can give the coach an update on conditioning progress; and they can provide an unexpected boost to the free-agent rookie. Often it's a place where a coach will make the final decision on a marginal vet who's nearing the end of the line. Weeb Ewbank used to say that the worst mistake a coach can make is to bring an old veteran whose days are numbered into the July camp.

"What if he beats out people?" he said. "Then you're stuck."

The high-draft rookie knows that he's almost assured of a spot on the roster, since (1) he probably has a guaranteed contract, and even if the club cuts him it must still pay him his full salary, which will usually swing the economy-minded coaches over to his side; and (2) cutting a high draft choice right away lays the coach's original judgment wide open to assaults from the press and the owners. The rookie should be responsible enough to want to absorb the system as quickly and as thoroughly as he can. And the high-priced youngster must be careful that he doesn't rub any of the veterans the wrong way, since they can make his life intolerable on the field. He knows he can expect little help from the coaches in this area. Their primary interest is seeing how well he takes the pressure. "Intestinal fortitude" is their name for it.

"I used to practice by myself that first year in camp," says former Ram quarterback Roman Gabriel, who was a first-round draft choice in 1962. "I'd throw the ball, and then run and pick it up, and throw it back. That was my practice."

Camp is usually a nightmare for a low-draft rookie, but the pressure he faces isn't as severe as that of a marginal vet. The low-draft or free agent knows his status pretty well before he even gets to camp. Unless he's very naive, he realizes that he won't get as long a look as the rookie who represents a sizable investment by the club, and he knows that, statistically, the chances of his making the squad are slim. Sometimes that can be an even greater incentive.

The inequalities of the system often strike me. Everybody makes excuses for the high draft choice. If he's asked to switch from left tackle to right, for instance, the coaches give him time to pick up the different nuances of the position. The free agent has no such luxury. He's expected to jump in and perform right away, to fill in at guard or center or anywhere else, or he's gone. Beat writers covering the Patriots said that, based on his play in camp in 1982, defensive end Kenneth Sims would have been cut if he were a low draft or a free agent. But as the number-one pick in the whole NFL, there was no way he was going.

Once, when a Jet coach was fired during the season, I asked Randy Rasmussen, the veteran guard, if he felt bad about it.

"No worse than when John Bush was cut," he said. Bush was a

free-agent defensive back from Delaware. Not enough size, not enough speed, ran kind of funny. All he did was knock down passes and tackle anyone who came near him. He didn't get much of a look. The old WFL, and now the USFL, have proved that a lot of decent players filter through the NFL camps, unnoticed.

Veterans who survive a change in regimes look back at the early days of a new coach, the waves of recruits who come in and out of camp, and scratch their heads.

"It's like you lose part of your family every day and then gain some more," says veteran tackle Jeff Hart, who survived the Frank Kush changeover at Baltimore.

"It's like an orphanage. People leave, people get adopted."

"It's crazy, really," kicker Jan Stenerud says. "One hundred and fifty free agents come in. Within a week 75 are gone. They run them out by the busload. Where do they all go? What are their lives like after they've been cut?"

A rookie who gets decent treatment by veterans often remembers it through his whole career.

"When I first joined the Colts in '69 they were an old team, very set in their ways," Ted Hendricks says. "But my first day there as a rookie all the vets came over and shook my hand and said, 'Glad to have you with us.' Even John Unitas came over. I found out later that Unitas was glad to see me because I was the only guy on the team with skinnier legs than him."

One year, the Jets drafted Tom Myslinski, a square-jawed offensive guard from Maryland. His cut personally pained Ewbank, who got more sensitive about the job of cutting as he got older.

"You'll never see a better attitude on a kid," Ewbank said that night at dinner.

"The tears were streaming down his face when I told him he was cut. 'It's my pass blocking, isn't it?' he said. I told him it was.

" 'I know it,' he said. 'I just can't keep those guys out of there.' "

The year Joe Namath announced his retirement—and then came back—the Jets brought an extra quarterback to camp, Harold Olson, a free agent from Illinois State. The day Namath reported, Olson was cut. The two quarterbacks took part in one practice session together.

"At least I had that," Olson said. "I can say I met him. That's all the people back home will ask me about—Joe Namath. I wonder if he'll remember my name."

When he was the Giants' defensive backfield coach, the late

Emlen Tunnell used to have a special place in his heart for low-draft rookies, especially the ones from the poorer homes. Not all assistants were so concerned.

"Do me a favor, will you?" he once asked a writer. "Go over to some of these guys with your notebook and pencil and pretend you're interviewing them, even though you don't really intend to write anything. It'll mean a lot to them. It'll give them something to remember."

The actual cutting is handled by the coach, but the most feared man in camp is the ball boy or assistant equipment man or assistant PR director, the one who has the unenviable job of knocking on the player's door and delivering his dreadful message—"Coach wants to see you." He is called the Turk, a reference to the traditional vision of a scimitar-wielding Turk. The big cut night (which usually precedes the day in which rosters have to be trimmed to conform to league standards) is called the Night of the Turk.

"Turking" is a job no one wants. Stu Kirkpatrick, an assistant supervisor of officiating in the league office, remembers handling the assignment as a 17-year-old ball boy with the Giants in 1967.

"Jimmy Ryan was the Turk, but he lateraled the job to me," Kirkpatrick says. "All the other kids in camp were coaches' sons or whatever, and none of them would do it. I'd get the cut list from the coach in the evening, and I'd have trouble sleeping that night. The nightmare would always be two men with the same name, or my reading the handwriting wrong. I was so scared I'd go check with an assistant coach and say, 'Is this the guy?'

"One morning I was walking after a player on the list. The faster I walked, the faster he walked. I could see him around the corner, going into his room. I knocked on his door. No answer. I could feel him on the other side of the door. I called his name. No answer.

"Then I passed a note halfway under the door. I could see it disappear. Fifteen seconds later the note came out again. I said, 'Listen, if you don't come out, I'll be in the same boat as you.' I think that got to him because he came out. They understand that you can't shoot the messenger.

"Sometimes guys who were marginal would come up to me and ask, 'Am I OK?' and if the cuts were over I'd say, 'It's all over for the day.'"

The Jets' director of operations, Tim Davey, turked when he was an assistant trainer.

"One kid said to me, 'Thank God I've got my degree,' " Davey says. "When I first started, I'd tell them on the chow line. Then I realized it was embarrassing to them, to be told in front of the other players, so I started going to the rooms at 6:30 A.M."

Davey said that in all his turking days there was only one player he couldn't tell, Louie Giammona, who'd become a friend. He had a coach do it.

"I remember when Lou Holtz cut guys," he says, "they were singing in the van on the way to the airport. One guy said to me, 'I can't thank you enough.' "

One summer Abe Gibron, the Tampa Bay defensive line coach, didn't think a certain player was paying much attention to his playbook. So he slipped a $100 bill between two pages of required reading for defensive linemen. A week or so later the player was told to report to Gibron, who opened the playbook. The bill tumbled out.

"That's why you're cut," Abe said.

Often the bad news is handled by phone. Rookies are notorious for leaving it unanswered.

"You just sit up in your room and concentrate on making the phone not ring," a Dallas rookie linebacker named Charlie Collins once told sportswriter Steve Perkins.

"One morning the phone rang at nine o'clock. My roommate said, 'It's for you.' It was the girl on the switchboard. My head was buzzing so bad I could hardly make out what she said—'Coach Myers wants to see you.' By this time there's a big crowd of rookies at the door. They said, 'Did they get you, Charlie?' I said, 'Yeah, they got me.'

"I bounced from wall to wall going down the hall. The one thing that kept going through my mind was, 'But I'm not ready to stop playing football.' I asked the girl where coach Myers's room was and she said, 'Not coach Myers—Curt Mosher, the PR man, is the one who wants to see you.' I could have kissed her. Mosher had a Dallas radio station on the line that wanted to interview me."

One year Atlanta cut veteran wide receiver Billy Ryckman because of lack of speed.

"What the hell," he said, "I'll do 70 going home."

Bob Kuechenberg, who in 1983 finished his 14th year as a guard for the Dolphins, never forgot being cut by the Eagles and then the Falcons.

"When Atlanta picked me up," he says, "they told me, 'We like you. We're gonna put you on the cab squad. Go home to Chicago, get your wife and come back here and settle down. I did. Then Norm Van Brocklin cut me and six other guys. He didn't have the decency to tell me himself. I never talked to him.

"But I'll tell you what was one of my great accomplishments in my professional football career. I helped get Van Brocklin fired. We beat them, 42–7, in 1974. I wanted to run a sweep to their bench so I could put my cleat marks on his neck. Anyway, he got fired the next day. It's one of the top 10 highlights of my career."

The seventh and eighth floors of the Jets' Hofstra University dorm traditionally are filled with free agents. As camp progresses the rooms empty.

"It's a weird feeling up there," Mike Augustyniak, a free-agent fullback from Purdue who eventually made the club, said in his rookie year. "It's dead quiet. I'm just glad I'm one of the guys left. I went downstairs to the fourth floor the other night, where the veterans were, and it was all noise and music. That's where I want to be next year."

For an old veteran who sees his comrades leave, one by one, camp can be just as lonely. In 1973 tackle Winston Hill was the last of the old Jets.

"You know what I did my first night in camp?" he said. "I went down to Matt Snell's old room, 903, just out of habit, and I pounded on the door. I started hollering, 'Matt, where are you?'

"Rich Caster and Gee Barkum were standing in the hall and they laughed at me. They said, 'What's the matter with you, man? Matt's gone. John Ebersole lives there now.' "

Sometimes the older vets help each other out in camp. "Verlon Biggs lined up across from me in the scrimmages, and we worked together so much that it got so that if Verlon would have a good year, so would I," Hill said.

"When he'd get tired at the end of a scrimmage I'd help him a little. Like if it was, say, a sweep to the other side I'd unfasten my chin strap when I came up the line. That would let him know the play was going the other way. But if I was going to block him, or if it was a pass play, I'd fasten my chin strap, then we'd go all out."

The thing the veterans remember most about training camp is the conditioning, the sheer physical drudgery, the two-a-day workouts that keep them in a constant state of rubber-legged exhaustion. In the old days some coaches would keep the two-a-days going right through the exhibition season, and the injury rate would mount as players' resistance got lower. Now, except in very rare instances, two-a-days stop in early August, when the exhibition games begin.

Practically every team starts training camp with a distance run— to see what kind of shape the veterans are in. At Dallas Tom Landry used to have everyone run a mile in camp, and he made his players do it until they ran it within a specified time—six minutes for backs and ends, seven minutes for linemen, etc. He did it until his tight end, Pettis Norman, collapsed one day during the fourth lap and needed emergency treatment from a heart specialist. Then he cut back on the program.

The Jets used to have a 12-minute run. The players were judged on how many laps they ran. One year the beat writers put up a dollar a man to see who could pick the last-place finisher. Dropouts didn't count. The run started and Ewbank noticed a flurry of activity among the writers. He wanted to know what we were doing and we told him.

"Too late for me to get in?" he said, and we told him it wasn't.

"How much?"

"One buck."

"I'll take Randy Rasmussen," he said, which seemed surprising. Starting players are seldom picked. You concentrate on free-agent linemen. Randy had come back heavy at 267, but a starting guard's a starting guard.

"Randy's just not built for this," Ewbank explained.

After a couple of laps it became obvious that the coach had backed a definite contender. Head down, eyes staring blankly at the ground, Rasmussen trudged along, mechanically lifting and dropping his massive legs.

"Take it easy, Randy boy!" Ewbank would yell as Rasmussen went by. "Slow down! We're not trying to make a miler out of you."

Ewbank didn't collect the money. That honor went to Vinny Di-Trani of the Bergen (N.J.) *Record,* who backed Jim Nance, the full-back. But Rasmussen had finished next to last, which shows that some coaches can read their distance runners as well as their linemen.

Some coaches run a fairly brutal camp. In Mike Ditka's first year with the Bears he had his players in full pads, full contact, twice a day from the opening whistle. "I have to find out quickly," he said. Others, such as Minnesota's Bud Grant, let the squad work into things gradually. The 49ers' Bill Walsh thought he ran a fairly normal camp until one day in 1982 when Russian track coach Valentin Petrovsky visited the facility and called the entire practice "dogmatic, barbaric and old-fashioned." Next year Walsh cut back, with no more than two consecutive two-a-day workouts.

Every coach has his idea of what the training camp setting should be like, and most of them agree on one thing—it shouldn't be near the temptations of a big city. So most clubs take their players to college campuses that are remote.

Before the 1968 season the Jets switched to the campus of Hofstra University in Hempstead, Long Island, about 30 miles from Manhattan. The first thing the players noticed were coeds, lovely ones in all shapes and sizes. Hostra's summer school was in full session.

"Weeb—the players—they're all going up to the girls' rooms," John Free, the road secretary, gasped one night.

"Well, that's one good thing about this place," Ewbank said. "If they want it, it's right here on campus. They don't have to go driving into New York at all hours for it. And you know the ones that are going to get it are going to get it somehow."

The Jets' old camp was at Peekskill Military Academy. The bedsprings were ancient and they would collapse under too much stress. The field was uneven. The food was terrible. Players called the hamburgers "sinkers." But even Peekskill was better than the Titans' old training base—East Stroudsburg, Pa.

"Not once during that hot, dry summer of 1962 had anyone watered the field," said Alex Kroll, an offensive tackle on the '62 Titans. "Don Maynard's legs took six weeks to loosen up after sprinting on the concrete-hard surface."

The Dallas Cowboys now train in Thousand Oaks, California. Their initial season of 1960 was spent at St. John's Academy in Wisconsin.

"The place was like a medieval castle," recalled Jerry Tubbs, a linebacker on the early Cowboy teams. "All it needed was a moat."

The buildings were old and dark, and the players dressed in a basement that was so murky that they named it the Dungeon.

"It was so damp in that basement," said Jack Eskridge, the equipment manager, "that a player could leave his shoes overnight and find them covered with mold in the morning."

The players roomed two to a cubicle, with a bare light bulb in the center of the room. Every night, when the lights went out, the dorm would be filled with hooting and groaning, and somewhere a player would invariably yell, "Quiet down there! This is the warden." At breakfast one morning one player asked another, "Was that you rattling your cup against the bars last night?" The camp's biggest hero that year was defensive tackle Ed Hussman, who killed a bat on the second floor of the players' dorm one evening.

The club moved to St. Olaf College in Northfield, Minn., next year, and the players used to dress in a converted cow barn. Next year the site was Northern Michigan College in Marquette, near the Canadian border. The pipes used to freeze at night, the temperature rarely got above 50 degrees and the trainer reported a record number of knee injuries. "They just can't get loose," he said. "It's not warm enough." Thousand Oaks, though, with its hot days and breezy nights, proved to be the answer.

"I'll never forget my first camp, Atlanta in '66," said linebacker Ralph Heck. "Black Mountain, North Carolina. A little YMCA retreat 25 miles from Asheville. They just hacked a practice field out of the woods, where no air could get in. They held their first practice at 10:00 A.M. The first rookie passed out at 10:16."

Sometimes a club's choice of practice venue is dictated by finances—or lack of them. The Miami Dolphins' first camp was in St. Petersburg, Fla. There had been an offer from Suncoast Sports, Inc., to underwrite the camp cost of $70,000, but when the club arrived, it found no Suncoast Sports, Inc., only John Burroughs, whose son was a linebacker candidate. The field was a thin layer of sod over seashells that Burroughs Sr. used to go over with a roller every day. When the son was cut, the father, and roller, vanished, and the team practiced on just seashells.

Players dressed in their hotel rooms, which were decorated by socks and jocks and pads hung up to dry, which gave an interesting smell to their living quarters. The hotel dining room served so much Chinese food that middle linebacker Wahoo McDaniel once remarked, "From now on they'll have to carry me to practice in a ricksha."

Coaches are not always the best judges of the training camp attitude of their squad. Two days before the 1957 season, Buddy Parker quit as Detroit coach.

"This is the worst team I've ever seen in training camp," he said. "They have no life, no go; they're just a completely dead team. I know the situation. I don't want to get into the middle of another losing season."

So Buddy went to Pittsburgh, where he had a 6–6 record, and George Wilson took over at Detroit. Three months later, after Detroit beat Cleveland, 59–14, to win the NFL championship, Wilson said, "These are the fightingest damn bunch of guys I've ever seen."

Curfew is normally at 11:00 P.M., but almost every veteran has ridden the midnight express. Jack Youngblood of the Rams says the key is having a room on the ground floor. "The guys on the second floor always have been handicapped," he says.

"I've seen them use ladders, bedsheets, all sorts of things to get out. I remember one time seeing a guy jump. He suffered a severe sprain and was reserved-injured the next day."

He says the biggest problem with coaches Chuck Knox and Ray Malavasi was in keeping from running into them in the same bars. And he adds that Tommy Prothro was the easiest coach because he didn't have a curfew.

"He felt we were grown men, mature enough to take care of ourselves," Youngblood says. "Well, he was wrong. Not having a curfew is like pulling the guards at Fort Knox. You know you're asking for trouble."

Tommy Brookshier, who played defensive back for the Eagles, says that when Buck Shaw came in as coach, his first rule was no rule whatsoever regarding curfew. He told the Eagles he trusted them.

"Two weeks later our team is going straight downhill," Brookshier said. "Some of the guys were playing drums and dancing at night as far away as Pittsburgh."

One year, when the Raiders' Pete Banaszak was a rookie, they roomed him with a veteran, Ken Herock. Herock skipped out one night, laid the floor lamp on his bed, put a blanket over it and told the rookie to cover for him. Shortly thereafter came the knock on the door.

"Banaszak!"

"Here, coach."

"Herock!" No answer.

"I think he's asleep, coach," Banaszak offered.

The coach opened the door, flipped on the wall switch, and watched Herock's bed light up.

Bert Rechichar was a training-camp legend in Baltimore. The old Colts talk about the day he dumped two bottles of vodka in the players' lemonade. Old Raiders recall Ben Davidson and the way he'd collect husks of discarded tape after every workout and mash them into a ball. By the end of camp it got so large that to get it out of the locker room the equipment manager had to cut it up with a saw.

Almost every veteran admits that the food at camp is better now than it was in the old days.

"We used to eat family-style meals," Brookshier says. "In my rookie year I sat between Mike Jarmoluk, one of those 290-pound guys with a 57-long jacket, and Chuck Bednarik. The steaks would come around and Jarmoluk would take five and Bednarik got four, and I'd be sitting there looking at the juice. That was the year my weight went down to 170 before the season started.

"The only time we'd really eat was on the train, when they'd let us have some greasy lamb chops or something. Fact is, I don't remember seeing a good meal at all, in those early years. But what the hell. Our wives probably weren't cooking very well then, either."

Reaching for the Stars: The Art of Scouting

If you'd ask me, what's the common religion among scouts, I'd have to say Hindu. They all believe in reincarnation. You're always hearing, "This guy's another Dick Butkus, this guy's another Willie Brown."

—George Young

I didn't know what free agent meant until I saw my first paycheck.

—Pete Gent

THEY'RE there every year, the free agents and low draft choices who have made it big, a constant embarrassment and reminder that the computers and their science can only take you so far.

The Packers' All-Pro free safety Willie Wood wasn't drafted at all. They noticed him when he jumped up and touched a goalpost. The Vikings grabbed Super Bowl middle linebacker Lonnie Warwick off an Arizona railroad gang. The 49ers' Bill Walsh went to Clemson to look at quarterback Steve Fuller and he wound up taking the guy who was catching all his passes that day, Dwight Clark—in the 10th round. Cowboy All-Pro cornerback Everson Walls was a free agent. His test scores weren't good, they said.

"It was the weirdest thing," Walls says. "First they put me on a mat and said, 'Jump,' and I jumped. Then lights and buzzers went off. I thought I was being electrocuted. I guess I'm just not a computer player."

Washington's Bobby Beathard talks about scouting All-Pro tackle Joe Jacoby in the early 1980s.

"I saw him at Louisville," Beathard says. "He was a big guy, couldn't move. His own coaches didn't like him. He didn't impress you. Charley Casserly, our scout, said, 'Well, we ought to sign him as a free agent.' No one disagreed. We sent Joe Bugel, our line coach, to work him out. He wasn't excited. But the kid was real intelligent, dedicated to learn.

"In the spring he came into our complex to sign, along with a dozen other free agents. I'm running around, trying to figure out how much money to give him. His next stop's Dallas. I said, 'Hey, Joe, they sign 150 free agents there. They'll change you around, you'll play different positions.' Finally he signed with us.

"One of our biggest needs was defensive linemen, but we wound up drafting offensive linemen that year. Joe Gibbs went in to meet with the kids. He told Jacoby, 'Hey, we didn't draft any defensive linemen. It's a great shot for you.' He thought he was a defensive player.

"Later I asked Joe, 'What did you think of that big kid?' and he said, 'Well, he's not very impressive on film,' and I said, 'Well, Bugel will work with him.'

"He said, 'Bugel? I thought the kid played defense. Cripes, we've got 13 offensive linemen. Bugel can't sign every guy you look at. Is it too late to let him go?'

" 'Too late,' I said."

The last two Redskin Super Bowl teams were loaded with free agents—24 of them were on the squad last year. "We were an old, slow team without any draft choices," Beathard said. "We had to go after free agents. We didn't have any choice."

Free agents. Computer rejects. The very term makes some people cringe. Lou Piccone, a 5'8" wideout and return man, came into the league as a free agent, after interning with the Youngstown Hard Hats and the Bridgeport Jets. He'd gone to West Liberty State— "Somewhere in West Virginia," he says. He had a highly productive nine-year career in the NFL.

"I saw so many guys who could play, but they were just lost in the free-agent shuffle," he says. "Wrong height, wrong image, wrong this, wrong that. Nobody's baby. Nobody'll take the responsibility. 'I don't want him.' The image stays with you. I've played for six head coaches. They come in and the first thing they want to do is clean house. They look around, see me, and figure, 'We gotta get rid of *this* guy.' They run me through the computer and I come out in the trash can. So each time I have to re-prove myself. And I've done it—for nine years."

The most unfair thing about the NFL system is the salary structure. It's based on a man's original contract, which is based on his drafting position, or how he performed in his last two years in college. It follows him through his career. Often a free agent or low draft will never catch up to a Number one, no matter how productive he becomes.

A few years ago I was talking to some college players going into their senior year. They were part of that NCAA-ABC preseason tour. I asked each of them if he realized that he was about to enter the most important earning year of his life—his senior year in college. Most of them looked at me blankly. Only one tuned in—Terry Miller, the halfback from Oklahoma State. Later I asked him what he did in the summer.

"I work as a banker," he said.

The unfairness of the system bothers me, but many of the hard-nosed teams are starting to get their comeuppance. It's called the USFL. There's nothing like competition for setting a true value on contracts.

In 1981 Jet middle linebacker Stan Blinka staged a miniprotest. He'd been a fifth-round draft in 1979 and he'd signed a five-year contract, without an agent. In 1981, after leading the team in tackles for two straight years, he was making $40,000, a $3000 raise from '80. Jets president Jim Kensil took a hard line. "Last season we had a 4–12 record," he said. But in that same 1980 season he'd signed Lam Jones, a minimally productive wide receiver, to a $2 million package. Jones had been a number one draft, naturally.

"Stan did more for the Jets last year than Jones did," said Randy Hendricks, who was hired to negotiate for Blinka, "but he's still got that '5' for the fifth round branded on him like a scarlet letter."

"I like signing low-round drafts and free agents to a two-year contract . . . actually I'd prefer only one year," Beathard says. "The worst thing you can do is sign them to a five-year and then hold them to it. All you create is an unhappy ballplayer."

Beathard feels that the low-round choices are "just as exciting for us as the high rounds . . . more of a challenge." Some teams disagree. New Orleans, for instance, traded away its ninth through 12th choices in both the '82 and '83 drafts.

"Every year before the draft I hear, 'From the fourth round on you're just throwing darts,' " Beathard says. "I like to hear trash like that. It makes it easier for us."

Eight starters in the last Super Bowl, incidentally, were drafted in the ninth through 12th rounds.

Naturally, your higher rounds produce a greater success formula. In 1983 no first-round rookie was cut, and only one second-rounder and one third-rounder. They get a longer look. No one wants to admit he's made a big mistake at the high-money level. Besides, more rookies in general stayed with NFL teams than ever before, probably in an attempt to keep the young talent away from the USFL.

The Cowboys have a curious drafting history. The heart of their team has always been their defensive line, and their front four last year showed three first-round choices, each of whom had been one of the first five players taken overall—Too Tall Jones (first player picked), Randy White (second) and John Dutton (fifth . . . by Baltimore . . . the Cowboys traded a number one and a number two to get him). The fourth man, Harvey Martin, was a third-round draft. But for some reason the jinx round for the Cowboys has been the second. In the last 10 years they've gotten only one eventual starter from the second round, Burton Lawless, a guard, and he was a part-timer. But look at all the Cowboy free agents who have gone to the Pro Bowl: Walls, Drew Pearson, Rafael Septien, Cornell Green, and one of the great free safeties in history, Cliff Harris.

I've never been able to figure out what it means when a free agent makes it big with your club. Are you smart because you signed him, or dumb because you didn't draft him in the first place? With the Cowboys it's largely a law-of-averages thing. They simply bring in a lot more of them than anyone else does. Of course, once they get there, there's the matter of developing them, and Tom Landry and his staff know what that's all about. Landry, incidentally, has the final say on all Cowboy draft choices.

I've tried to work up a chart showing comparative drafting records for the 28 NFL teams in rounds 1–5, the "money rounds," over the last 11 years. Why 11? Because when I sent out survey sheets I wanted the study to reflect a decade's worth of drafting, so I put down 1973–83, forgetting that it represents 11 years, not 10. So you'll just have to accept 11. I fiddled with it and amended some of the original data, too. A lot of it's subjective. I mean, how do you determine whether a guy became a starter or a reserve when he started for half a year after spending a year and a half on the bench? I just had to

284 The New Thinking Man's Guide to PRO FOOTBALL

use my judgment. "Nonproducers" is another tricky category. This includes people who were cut in camp, signed with another league, got hurt and never played more than a few games or so, never reported, etc. Nonproducers would be guys who never really did much of anything—for example, a quarterback who spent a year on the sidelines, carrying the clipboard and never getting into a game and was then gone—as opposed to a player who spent a year on special teams, who'd be classed as a "Reserve." Pro Bowl selections are only for a player's original team. "Eventually Traded" is another tough category. Everyone has his own idea of what constitutes a trade. I think a significant category is "On Roster, Spring 1984," since that shows how many of a team's high drafts were still around. But I added another one, "On Roster up to 1983," because teams such as Houston showed artificially inflated total numbers; 10 of Houston's high-draft rookies made the squad last year.

You might notice some surprising things, such as total choices. Washington, with only 19 high selections in 11 years, made the Super Bowl for the last two, whereas Cincinnati and the Rams and Buffalo, with 76, 75 and 71, respectively, did not. Teams that have gone through periodic house-cleanings, such as New England and Baltimore, will show a great number of "Starters." But many of them were only for a year or so, then they were gone. They still must be classed as starters. Old, established teams such as Dallas and, until last year, the Rams, show a lot of flunkouts, but it's tougher to break in with a club like that. I think it's significant that the Rams and Patriots show so many Pro Bowl selections. It might reflect the presence of Dick Steinberg, an influential figure in the scouting operations of both teams in this period.

Drafting's an inexact science, but so is medicine. The cure for cancer is just over the horizon, or so we're told, but the common cold still haunts us. And the drafting of quarterbacks is perhaps the most inexact science of all.

Of the 28 quarterbacks who started most of the time for their NFL clubs last year, only five were first-round picks, and two of those were from a different team. Not one of the 10 playoff teams had its own number-one draft playing quarterback. "In scouting quarterbacks," Walsh says, "less emphasis should be put on strength of arm and more in the ability to retain poise in the face of adversity. But how do you scout that?"

In 1980 David Woodley was the Dolphins' eighth-round draft

DRAFT CHOICES, ROUNDS 1–3, 1973–83

Team	Total Selections	Pro Bowl	Starters	Reserves	Nonproductive	Eventually Traded	On Roster, Spring 1984	On Roster up to 1983
Atlanta	55	6	19	23	13	+	22	20
Baltimore	56	4	34	12	10	10	17	14
Buffalo	71	4	23	29	19	6	27	25
Chicago	44	5	20	17	7	5	19	19
Cincinnati	76	6	27	35	14	7	24	22
Cleveland	52	4	23	16	13	11	17	18
Dallas	66	11	20	25	21	8	23	27
Denver	46	5	21	13	12	5	17	18
Detroit	62	5	31	22	9	12	26	22
Green Bay	43	4	23	14	6	6	20	20
Houston	46	3	25	14	7	10	24	17
Kansas City	58	5	23	22	13	6	19	19
L.A. Raiders	53	8	17	24	12	7	24	21
L.A. Rams	75	11	29	20	26	17	21	16
Miami	61	8	27	22	12	7	24	24
Minnesota	55	3	25	16	14	+	28	27
New England	64	10	34	22	8	9	28	26
New Orleans	59	4	28	24	7	10	25	21
N.Y. Giants	48	4	21	18	9	8	17	14
N.Y. Jets	54	4	19	18	17	9	19	21
Philadelphia	37	8	16	15	6	+	21	16
Pittsburgh	65	3	28	24	13	19	24	21
St. Louis	61	3	27	19	15	15	22	17
San Diego	46	6	24	15	7	10	14	12
San Francisco	55	5	27	22	6	5	17	15
Seattle°	44	2	17	16	11	16	16	15
Tampa Bay°	38	3	24	8	6	7	17	15
Washington	19	2	10	3	6	1	11	9

° 1976–83 + Data incomplete

choice. He was the fourth-string quarterback in camp, behind Bob Griese, Don Strock and Guy Benjamin. One paper called him "the Dolphins' latest sacrificial lamb." Woodley's bio file in the *Miami Herald* library was labeled "Sacrificial Lamb," even after he became the starter.

Most of the better GMs in the league got their early NFL training as scouts. I mean, what's more important than knowing how to pick players? Many great coaches also have a unique ability to assess talent. It's a knack. Weeb Ewbank, who put together a Super Bowl team on the Jets with free agents and castoffs, was one of the best at it.

"Weeb's amazing," his old flanker on the Colts, Jimmy Orr, once said. "He could put 15 guys in a room and have them jump over a Ping-Pong table and then tell you which ones are the ballplayers."

I love to hear old scouts when they get together and tell stories about beating the bushes. When George Sauer, Sr., was head of the Jets' personnel department he used to get out and look at kids himself.

"One year I drove down to Delaware with my wife to scout the Delaware-Buffalo game," Sauer said. "I was interested in John Stofa, the Buffalo quarterback, and a Delaware back—I think his name was Brown. It was a cold, miserable, rainy day, and, as usual, I was roaming up and down the sidelines without a coat.

"Well, Stofa didn't look like he had a strong enough arm, and the other kid didn't show me much, but every time Delaware had the ball and they ran it near one Buffalo kid, there would be this tremendous crash of bodies. I checked the program and the boy's name was Gerry Philbin, a defensive tackle. I wrote that name down.

"When I got back to the car, my wife was already inside, warming up the motor. I sat there shivering for half an hour before I could drive.

" 'No player is worth this,' she said.

" 'This one is,' I told her."

Philbin eventually became All-Pro defensive end.

Beathard talks about meeting with one particularly arrogant player personnel director, who leaned back in his chair, lit up a cigar and bragged: "I don't have to go out on the road. That's what I pay scouts for."

"I felt great," Beathard says. "I love to hear that. Once you start drafting players you haven't seen . . . once you get too big for the job

. . . you're worthless. I'm against those big scouting combines, too. It defeats the purpose. I liked it when every team was on its own."

Last year the Dolphins' pro personnel director, Charley Winner, scouted the Steelers at Baltimore. On Saturday he went out to watch C. W. Post at nearby Towson State.

"I figured I was in town so I'd might as well look at a game," Winner says. "When I got in the stands, who do I see but Bobby Beathard. He said to me, 'What are you doing here? There's nothing here.' I said, 'So what are you doing here?' He said, 'My son plays here.'"

Film can only tell you so much. UCLA and North Carolina, with their pale numbers on pale blue jerseys, make it tough to identify players. Before the Giants drafted North Carolina's Lawrence Taylor, George Young remembers getting eyestrain trying to pick his Number 98 out of the lineup.

"Only one thing made it easier," he says. "Every time there was a huge pileup at the line or behind it, you could be sure Number 98 was at the bottom."

And do player personnel directors ever look at a whole film before they realize they're scouting the wrong number player? More often than they'd like to admit.

"Once I spent a whole afternoon looking at a quarterback," the Steelers' Art Rooney, Jr., says. "He wasn't bad. Just to be safe I checked his number again. Was it Number 15 or 16? It turned out I was looking at the wrong guy. It's scary. You get shaky when something like that happens. We could have drafted the wrong kid. Anyway, the other guy's actually a prospect now. He's on our list."

What surprises me sometimes is when a guy is drafted high but he's got a severe problem, such as drugs. His college coach knows it, the scouts who have done their homework know it, the guys in the bars in his hometown know it. But the team commits a lot of money anyway.

"That happens in a system where the coach has no respect for his scouting department," Beathard says. "Maybe he's looked at a little film. He knows all."

Scouting has come a long way since the dark ages, though, when people used to show up at the draft meetings with copies of *Street & Smith's Football Yearbook* in their pockets.

"In 1936, the first year they had the draft," George Halas said, "all the names were put on a blackboard. If a man's name wasn't on that blackboard, you couldn't pick him. So there was always a big scramble for free agents. We came into the session with about 14 names, and when we got down to our last selection there were two names left on the board. One of them was Danny Fortmann, a guard from Colgate.

"I said to myself, 'Fortmann, that sounds like a nice name, and Colgate is certainly a fine school. I'll take him.' He became a Hall of Famer."

Halas also remembered signing George Musso, another Hall of Fame guard for the Bears, and showing Red Grange a picture of Musso with a full mustache, in a Milliken basketball uniform.

"He'll never make it," Grange said. "He looks like a walrus."

Bronko Nagurski, the greatest Bear fullback in history and an All-American at Minnesota, says, "I heard the Giants were interested in me in college, but no other teams contacted me but the Giants and Bears."

In the days of the AFL-NFL war, drafting and signing was a high-espionage business. The AFL would hold a secret draft a few weeks before the NFL's and immediately send people out to sign the players. The NFL would get wind of it and send out "baby-sitters" to keep them on ice.

"Around the fourth round of the AFL draft," the Jets' PR man, Frank Ramos, recalls, "the room would be just about empty. Everybody was out looking for the guys they had drafted. So they'd have to adjourn the meeting and hold it over until the next day."

The AFL's Lamar Hunt once placed a long-distance call to first-round draft choice Roman Gabriel. The Rams' Elroy Hirsch, who was camped in Gabriel's room as a baby-sitter, got the call instead, imitated Gabriel's voice, heard the whole AFL pitch, and finally signed off with, "Yes, Mr. Hunt, I'll certainly consider your offer."

Oakland superspy Lee Grosscup once rerouted an NFL sleuth by imitating the voice of the guy's general manager.

"I told him to get his ass over to Seattle in a hurry because the AFL was steeling his player," Grosscup said. "There was a blizzard out there, and he got locked in. It took him out of commission for three days."

One year, when Don Klosterman was the Dallas Texans' general manager, he tried to keep first-round pick Buck Buchanan, a 6'7", 287-pounder, hidden in the Klosterman household.

"How do you propose keeping this one a secret?" his wife asked him one day. "I've just given him 30 pancakes, 12 eggs and a loaf of bread I had to borrow from a neighbor whose husband is sports editor of a Dallas paper."

"Maybe we can stick some acorns in his hair," Don said.

I expected the AFL-USFL war to heat up at the drafting level in 1984. The USFL, with its January draft, had a three-month jump on the senior league, and I thought the NFL would draft at least the first two rounds in secret, so their people could be busy locking up the top guys, to shortstop the USFL, but it didn't happen. The NFL has adopted a "wait and see" attitude, and sporadic attempts to get the draft moved up were voted down. But the NFL sent a horde of coaches, scouts and executives to the East-West Shrine Game in San Francisco to make a recruiting pitch to the college seniors.

"We're not fooling around anymore," said Patriots vice-president Bucko Kilroy. "We're fighting back."

The way they fought back was to show the collegians a one-hour NFL Films production called *The NFL and You*. The USFL got a good laugh out of that. The NFL's feeling was that if the NFL draft were held at the same time as the USFL's there would be a frantic rush for talent, which would bring the price up. And a team would run the risk of losing draft choices. Wait until May, let the USFL skim some of the cream from the top, and at least you'd have a better shot at signing the guy you'd drafted. It's an old boy mentality that cost the NFL some talent. In 1984 the USFL picked off at least 30 players who would have been in the top 100 of the NFL draft.

"Our player personnel people didn't want the draft moved up," Pete Rozelle said. "They didn't want to have to rush their decisions. They wanted more time to study the prospects."

"The hell we did," Beathard says. "I'd love to go head to head against the USFL."

All-Star games such as the Blue-Gray Game in Montgomery, Ala., and the Senior Bowl in Mobile seem like gigantic Oriental bazaars. The town comes alive with scouts, club execs and agents. These days everyone's an agent; everyone's trying to cash in on a piece of the big money.

"When you'd go to the Blue-Gray Game in other years," the Patriots' Steinberg said last year, "you'd find a handful of agents, second-line guys mostly, trying to hustle for clients. This year there had to be 200 of them, all promising stuff they couldn't deliver."

The Senior Bowl is the biggest show, because everyone goes there. Club presidents and even owners want to inspect the merchandise firsthand.

"Ralph Goldston, the Seattle scout, would read off a player's height, weight and agent," the Giants' George Young says, "and then the guy would walk across the room. An owner who'd never seen him before would say, 'Take off your pants,' and the kid would say, 'But I'm not wearing anything underneath,' and the owner would say, 'OK, then, roll 'em up. I want to look at your legs.' It was embarrassing. It was like a livestock show."

"You're in a big room," says the Eagles' Dean Miraldi, who went through it three years ago. "They call your name. They weigh you here, measure you there. I thought they were going to check my teeth and stamp me USDA Choice."

True heights and weights are recorded and carefully annotated many times during the season—by syndicate scouts, club scouts, and then maybe by the player personnel director himself. Nobody believes anybody. It's all fed into the computer. Big money's involved. A player who's hip enough to keep the tape on his ankles when he's measured, and slide some strips of metal or wooden wedges under the tape, can pick up an inch in height—and maybe an extra $50,000 in his first contract. Former Colt linebacker Stan White used to do it, and he'd always measure out at 6'1" instead of his normal 6'0". The old Colts center Buzz Nutter would be weighed wearing a T-shirt, and he'd have lead weights under each arm.

"When I was weighed I used to put two 5-pound weights in the waistband of my jock," former Dallas guard Mike Connelly says. "The needle would hit 240 and Jim Myers, the Cowboys' line coach, would say, 'You don't look that heavy. I guess you've just got a real solid build.' "

Everything's tested—reactions, vertical jump, speed, strength. Bengal tackle Anthony Munoz's stock went way up after he'd gone through a session on the Cybex machine, measuring leg strength. "He put the thing off the chart," a scout said, "and that's after three knee operations."

There are some little axioms known to scouts who have been around for a while. Measure a man in the morning and he could be an inch taller than at the end of the day. "Gravity pulls 'em tighter," was an old saying of Charley Mackey's, a West Coast scout for the

BLESTO-V syndicate. They know that big guys mature slower and need more time to develop. Patience must be shown.

"In the ninth grade I was the first one on the football signup sheet and the first one cut," Rams Hall of Fame defensive tackle Merlin Olsen says. "My coach told me, 'Merlin, why are you doing this to yourself? Why don't you apply this energy somewhere else, like the school paper?' "

And then there are tests that measure the intangibles, like intelligence and personality.

"Dallas says they invented those psychological tests," Ewbank says. "Hell, 35 years ago Paul Brown used tests like that in Cleveland. Bill Willis didn't test out aggressive, but he's in the Hall of Fame now. Stormy Bidwell, the owner in St. Louis, made Charley Winner give them to his players. The tests didn't know who the hell they were testing. Larry Wilson graded out bad and he was All-Pro every year. Then Stormy decided to give his coaches psychological tests. He needed one himself; he's the guy who needed it."

IQ testing is more widely accepted now. The idea that a guy can be dumb off the field but a genius once he puts on pads and cleats, that he can have "football smarts" as opposed to real smarts, is pretty well discredited.

"Check the punt returner who catches the ball on the one-yard line or the guy who blows an audible at a key moment," one scout says. "Ten more points on the IQ and he probably wouldn't have made the mistake."

Sam Baker, the widely traveled kicker, tells about the first time his club sat him down and tested him, to see if his 142 IQ was for real.

"The team psychologist gave it to me, and then afterward he had a private talk to explain how I did. The first thing he said was, 'You know, you're not a genius. You know it, don't you? You know it! You know it!' I figured he was sore because I had a higher IQ than he did."

The standard quickie, or short-form, test most scouts give is a 50-question affair put out by E. F. Wonderlic of Northfield, Ill. It's a 12-minute test. I've included it here, so you can test yourself to see how you stack up with prospective NFL draftees (answers are at the end of the chapter). One personnel man says that he gives 200 of them a year, and over a five-year period offensive tackles grade out the highest. The averages . . . tackles, 26 right out of 50; centers, 25;

quarterbacks, 24; guards, 23; tight ends, 22; safeties and middle line-backers, 21; defensive linemen and outside linebackers, 19; corner-backs, 18; wide receivers and fullbacks, 17; and halfbacks, 16. As far as kickers and punters are concerned . . . "Who cares?" he says.

"I took it and my wife took it," Rooney says. "I realized that after 20 years of marriage my wife was smarter than me. She's a graduate mathematician. She scored 47 in 11 minutes. The last minute was spent yelling at me, 'This is ridiculous!' "

Steinberg recalls giving it to Patriots All-Pro guard John Hannah.

"It was in the lobby of the Hilton in Honolulu," he says. "John was down there for the Hula Bowl. He'd just finished a workout and he was still sweating when I gave it to him. And guys kept coming by interrupting him. He still scored the highest of any lineman I tested that year. That means something, in circumstances like that."

"If a guy's Wonderlic is low I give him a verbal test," Young says. "I just want to make sure it's not reading skills that are involved. I give an abstract reasoning test, the California Mental Maturity Test that's half-verbal, half-nonverbal . . . Wechsler-Belleview blocks, spatial relations things."

"I don't care about that stuff," Al Davis says. "If a kid is street smart, that's enough. Our coaches' job is to make a kid smarter. I just wonder if they checked some of the coaches' IQs around the league, how high they'd score."

John Madden says that a team's system and the conditions it plays under often influence its choice of players to draft. The Steelers, for instance, play on artificial turf in Three Rivers Stadium. They have a toss-and-trap offense, and they want their linemen to be nifty and mobile, and they don't mind if they're smaller. His own Raiders, though, worked on the heavy sod in Oakland, so he wanted big drive-blockers and pass-protectors.

"No one would ever mistake Art Shell or Gene Upshaw or Mickey Marvin for finesse football players," he says.

There's one test that's taken more seriously than any other, though, and that's speed. The standard timing distance is 40 yards, and qualifications have improved considerably since the game became wide open. The Cowboys' Gil Brandt says his club started it in 1961. Sid Gillman says he can remember timing guys in the 40 back in college in the mid-1940s.

"We used to run them at 50 yards, but someone decided they'll hardly ever run 50 in a game, so they cut it down to 40," Gillman

FIGURE 12
WONDERLIC

PERSONNEL TEST

FORM B

NAME...Date.............................
(Please Print)

READ THIS PAGE CAREFULLY. DO EXACTLY AS YOU ARE TOLD.
DO NOT TURN OVER THIS PAGE UNTIL YOU ARE
INSTRUCTED TO DO SO.

This is a test of problem solving ability. It contains various types of questions. Below is a sample question correctly filled in:

REAP is the opposite of

    1 obtain,   2 cheer,   3 continue,   4 exist,   5 sow .... [_5_]

The correct answer is "sow." (It is helpful to underline the correct word.) The correct word is numbered 5. Then write the figure 5 in the brackets at the end of the line.

Answer the next sample question yourself.

Gasoline sells for 23 cents per gallon. What will 4 gallons cost? .... [___]

The correct answer is 92¢. There is nothing to underline so just place "92¢" in the brackets.

Here is another example:

MINER   MINOR — Do these words have

    1 similar meaning,   2 contradictory,   3 mean neither same nor opposite? .... [___]

The correct answer is "mean neither same nor opposite" which is number 3 so all you have to do is place a figure "3" in the brackets at the end of the line.

When the answer to a question is a letter or a number, put the letter or number in the brackets. All letters should be printed.

This test contains 50 questions. It is unlikely that you will finish all of them, but do your best. After the examiner tells you to begin, you will be given exactly 12 minutes to work as many as you can. Do not go so fast that you make mistakes since you must try to get as many right as possible. The questions become increasingly difficult, so do not skip about. Do not spend too much time on any one problem. The examiner will not answer any questions after the test begins.

Now, lay down your pencil and wait for the examiner to tell you to begin!

Do not turn the page until you are told to do so.

Copyright 1942 by E. F. Wonderlic©

1. PAIN is the opposite of
   1 poison,   2 torment,   3 agony,   4 comfort,   5 punish .... [___]
2. One number in the following series is omitted. What should that number be?
   100   97   94   ?   88   85   82 .... [___]
3. GENEROUS is the opposite of
   1 noble,   2 popular,   3 moody,   4 neighborly,   5 stingy .... [___]
4. LUXURY is the opposite of
   1 plenty,   2 rapture,   3 poverty,   4 devotion,   5 failure .... [___]
5. In the following set of words, which word is different from the others?
   1 Methodist,   2 Easter,   3 Lutheran,   4 Catholic,   5 Quaker .... [___]
6. LINGER is the opposite of
   1 maintain,   2 hasten,   3 require,   4 remain,   5 tarry .... [___]
7. Assume the first two statements are true. Is the final one: 1 true,   2 false,   3 not certain? The violin is in tune with the piano. The piano is in tune with the harp. The harp is in tune with the violin. .... [___]
8. Suppose you arrange the following words so that they make a complete sentence. If it is a true statement, mark (T) in the brackets; if false, put an (F) in the brackets.
   fuel   wood   are   Coal   and   for   used .... [___]
9. FURTHER   FARTHER—Do these words have
   1 similar meaning,   2 contradictory,   3 mean neither same nor opposite? .... [___]
10. A man's car traveled 16 miles in 30 minutes. How many miles an hour was it traveling? ...... [___]
11. Are the meanings of the following sentences: 1 similar,   2 contradictory,   3 neither similar nor contradictory?
    A faithful friend is a strong defense. They never taste who always drink. .... [___]
12. A dealer bought some cars for $2,000. He sold them for $2,400, making $50 on each car. How many cars were involved? .... [___]
13. How many of the six pairs of items listed below are exact duplicates? .... [___]

3421	1243
21212	21212
558956	558956
10120210	10120210
612986896	612986896
356471201	356571201

14. A boy is 6 years old and his sister is twice as old. When the boy is 10 years old, what will be the age of his sister? .... [___]
15. In the following set of words, which word is different from the others?
    1 armada,   2 band,   3 brood,   4 boy,   5 crowd .... [___]
16. Suppose you arranged the following words so that they make a true statement. Then print the last letter in the last word as the answer to this problem.
    is   world   The   round .... [___]
17. VOCATION   WORK—Do these words have
    1 similar meaning,   2 contradictory,   3 neither same nor opposite? .... [___]
18. Look at the row of numbers below. What number should come next?
    81   27   9   3   1   ⅓   ? .... [___]
19. This geometric figure can be divided by a straight line into two parts which will fit together in a certain way to make a perfect square. Draw such a line by joining two of the numbers. Then write the numbers as the answer .... [___]

20. How many of the five items listed below are exact duplicates of each other? .... [___]

Patterson, A. J.	Patterson, A. J.
Smith, A. O.	Smith, O. A.
Bleed, O. M.	Bleed, O. M.
Petersen, O. W.	Peterson, O. W.
Cash, I. O.	Cash, I. O.

21. Suppose you arrange the following words so that they make a complete sentence. If it is a true statement, mark (T) in the brackets; if false, put an (F) in the brackets.
    all   are   Americans   countries   of   citizens .... [___]
22. Assume that the first 2 statements are true. Is the final statement:
    1 true,   2 false,   3 not certain?
    All red-headed boys are mischievous. Charles is red-headed. He is mischievous. .... [___]
23. Two of the following proverbs have similar meanings. Which ones are they? .... [___]
    1. A friend in need is a friend in deed.
    2. Fields have eyes and woods have ears.
    3. A fox is not caught twice in a snare.
    4. A setting hen never gets fat.
    5. A rolling stone gathers no moss.
24. A rectangular bin completely filled, holds 900 cubic feet of lime. If the bin is 10 feet long and 10 feet wide, how deep is it? .... [___]

25. A watch lost 1 minute and 12 seconds in 24 days. How many seconds did it lose per day? .... [___]
26. Assume that the first 2 statements are true. Is the final statement: 1 true,   2 false, 3 not certain?   Most business men are progressive.   Most business men are Republicans.   Some progressive people are Republicans. .... [___]
27. Gasoline is 15 cents a gallon. How many gallons can you buy for a dollar? .... [___]
28. Are the meanings of the following sentences: 1 similar,   2 contradictory,   3 neither similar nor contradictory?   Every pumpkin is known by its stem.   Like father, like son. .... [___]
29. If 2½ tons of coal cost $20, what will 3½ tons cost? .... [___]
30. How many of the five pairs of items listed below are exact duplicates? .... [___]

Silverstein, M. O.	Silverstien, M. O.
Harrisberg, L. W.	Harrisberg, L. M.
Seirs, J. C.	Sears, J. C.
Wood, A. B.	Woods, A. B.
Johnson, M. D.	Johnson, M. D.

31. Two men caught 75 fish. A caught four times as many as B. How many fish did B catch? .... [___]
32. In the following set of words, which word is different from the others?
    1 faculty,   2 fleet,   3 flock,   4 friend,   5 force .... [___]
33. Assume the first 2 statements are true. Is the final one: 1 true,   2 false,   3 not certain? Bert greeted Alice. Alice greeted Lou. Bert did not greet Lou. .... [___]
34. Which number in the following group of numbers represents the smallest amount?
    2   1   .9   .999   .88 .... [___]
35. A side of beef weighs 250 lbs. The average daily beef consumption of a family is 1⅔ lbs. How long will this beef last them? .... [___]
36. Are the meanings of the following sentences: 1 similar,   2 contradictory,   3 neither similar nor contradictory?
    Friends agree best at a distance. Friends are one soul in two bodies. .... [___]
37. How many square yards are there in a floor which is 9 feet long by 21 feet wide? .... [___]
38. One number in the following series does not fit in with the pattern set by the others. What should that number be?   8   9   12   13   16   17   18 .... [___]
39. Three of the following 5 parts can be fitted together in such a way to make a triangle. Which 3 are they? .... [___]

40. A soldier shooting at a target hits it 40% of the time. How many times must he shoot in order to register 100 hits? .... [___]
41. Which number in the following series represents the smallest amount?
    2   1   .8   .888   .99 .... [___]
42. CENSOR   CENSURE—Do these words have
    1 similar meaning,   2 contradictory,   3 mean neither same nor opposite? .... [___]
43. Are the meanings of the following sentences: 1 similar,   2 contradictory,   3 neither similar nor contradictory?   A chip off the old block. A beggar's son struts like a peer. ...... [___]
44. A clock was exactly on time at noon on Monday. At 8 P.M. on Tuesday it was 32 seconds slow. At that same rate, how much did it lose in ½ hour? .... [___]
45. Are the meanings of the following sentences: 1 similar,   2 contradictory,   3 neither similar nor contradictory?   He who demands, does not command. He that complies against his will is of his own opinion still. .... [___]
46. For $2.40 a grocer buys a case of oranges which contains 12 dozen. He knows that two dozen will spoil before he sells them. At what price per dozen must he sell the good ones to gain ⅓ of the whole cost? .... [___]
47. Are the meanings of the following sentences: 1 similar,   2 contradictory,   3 neither similar nor contradictory?
    Where there's a will there is a way. The gods sell everything for labor. .... [___]
48. The hours of daylight and darkness are nearest equal in
    1 June,   2 September,   3 May,   4 December .... [___]
49. This geometric figure can be divided by a straight line into two parts which will fit together in a certain way to make a perfect square. Draw such a line by joining 2 of the numbers. Then write these numbers as the answer. .... [___]

50. Three men form a partnership and agree to divide the profits equally. X invests $5500, Y invests $3500, and Z invests $1000. If the profits are $3000, how much less does X receive than if the profits were divided in proportion to the amount invested? .... [___]

says. "Then we'd put two watches on them, one to get them at 20 to check the burst, and then at 40 to see how they did over the long haul."

The Cowboys now have a 20-yard Jingle Jangle for running backs . . . they run five yards to a line, then turn around and run 10, then run five back again. They say their time should be close to their clocking in the 40. If it's much slower they know they have a player with decent straight-ahead speed but not the quick burst.

Beathard says the 40 time is only important for wideouts, defensive backs and tight ends. For linemen, it's quickness, not speed, that counts. Their 20-yard time is more important.

Legend has it that Olympic 100-meter champ Bob Hayes ran a 4.1 for the Cowboy scouts, but it hasn't been verified. The Generals' Herschel Walker, a world-class sprinter, says the fastest clocking he ever ran for a scout was 4.28, and if it's true, it's the best I've ever heard of. When Hayes made it big as a Cowboy receiver the door was open for all varieties of flyers in track suits. Frank Budd, Henry Carr, Tommie Smith, John Carlos . . . all manner of World's Fastest Humans came and went, some of them pretty quickly.

"There are a thousand sprinters who try out for football teams and 999 go home," Dan Fouts says. "It's not a damned track meet. It's a football game."

Hand clocking doesn't give a true measurement of speed, anyway. That was proved when they used to run a Football 40 in the old professional indoor track meets, featuring some of the game's fastest players. The race was electronically timed and the winner usually came in with a 4.6 or so true reading.

"All those 4.35s and 4.4s you read about . . . they're a myth," Frank Kush says. "When I was coaching at Arizona State . . . well, you remember all those fast guys we had there . . . we'd never get anyone faster than 4.5 or 4.6, with legitimate timing. And we only had maybe three of four who ran that, in the whole time I was there."

"Guys who have been around know how to cheat when they run their 40s," Rooney says. "Traditionally, you start your watch when you see the guy's hand move, so you get guys who try to take off and drag their hand. Frenchy Fuqua was the best in the world at that. Beforehand you'd tell them to pause before they took off, but Frenchy would walk over, put his hand down, and all at once he was off and running. You couldn't get him. We call guys like that scout-killers. If they're 4.7s, they'll clock out in 4.6. Rocky Bleier was pretty good at it, too, toward the end of his career. They'll cheat up on the line, and you can't see it from 40 yards away, so you need a guy at the start, too. Walter Abercrombie tries, but he's an amateur compared to Frenchy and Rocky."

San Francisco tight end Russ Francis tells about Steinberg coming to his college campus to time him.

"I was in jeans, barefoot," Francis says. "He said, 'Do you want to change?' and I said, 'No, I don't care.' He said, 'Do you want to warm up?' and I said, 'Nope.' Then I ran a 4.6 for him. He said, 'This can't be right,' so I did it again. Another 4.6. He said, 'You'd better do it one more time,' and I said, 'No, that's enough,' so he went back to Boston telling them about this kid who ran a 4.6 barefoot, in jeans.

"Little did he know that I'd been warming up for an hour and a half before he came, and training for a month. Going barefoot was no problem because I'm from Hawaii. It's more natural for me. The only variable was the jeans. I didn't know how that would work, but it worked out OK."

Every team except the Raiders and 49ers belongs to one of the three scouting combines—BLESTO, United and Quadra. The 49ers agreed to drop out during the 1984 league meetings because owner Eddie De Bartolo, Jr.'s father owns the USFL Pittsburgh Maulers. The Raiders don't believe in syndicate scouting. They don't want to share any secrets. You'd wonder why a club such as Dallas, with its vast scouting machinery and its famous Book Room that contains the records of thousands of college players, from freshman to senior year, filed in different colored portfolios, would want to hook up with a group. The reason is that the club can use syndicate people to perform the menial tasks of checking out the hundreds of rumors that come in each year.

"Say we hear of a 6'5", 250-pound tackle from Whitworth College in Washington," Brandt says. "We get hold of the combine people, and they check him out and report he's 6'2", 220. So we haven't tied up one of our own scouts for a day on a wasted trip. Syndicate scouting eliminates a lot of wasted hours for your own men."

The Cowboys' computer has been around for 20 years. Statistics on the 1000 or so prospects tracked every year are fed into it to determine how they measure up to current Cowboy players. The system even evaluates Dallas scouts, to see how their assessments compare with actual player performance. The club's empire is vast. Many high school and college coaches around the country are on the Cowboy payroll as part-timers.

Stanford coach Jack Elway, father of Bronco quarterback John Elway, once did some free-lance work for Dallas, grading prospects in the Washington State area. One night he was filling out forms on players and just for the heck of it he decided to fill one out on his son, who was 12 at the time.

"I wrote down, 'Great arm, good speed, 6'2", 185, outstanding student, knows the game,'" he says. "But then I had to indicate he had an 'attitude problem,' because he hadn't taken the trash out that week, like he was supposed to."

The opponents of computerized scouting and organized syndicate testing and measuring say that it gets you into a whole bunch of fringe areas of athletic ability and away from the basics—how a guy does on the field.

"We're getting away from drafting guys who look good in their underwear," Rooney said a couple of years ago. "I want football players. The late draft now, all these workouts and tests that show you who the great athletes are . . . well, you can go to the Olympic Games and get all the great athletes you want, and half of them will be girls and the other half won't play football."

"One year all our scouts had those Reid-Johnson portable computers to file their reports on," Beathard says. "They were 28 inches high, too big to fit under the seat in a plane. They'd spend 45 minutes typing their report into the computer, and all they were doing was worrying about their punctuation and grammar. They couldn't even tell you if a guy could play. Then they were too busy grading the reports when they came in."

"You let the computer draft for you," said Davis, who's the only owner who personally scouts college practices, "and you'll always fall back on it."

"What you wonder about," Walsh says, "is whether a scout's going to put himself on the line for a player, or if he's going to recite some numbers. It's so much easier to say, 'He's only a 4.7, only 6'1⅛", only 202½ . . . I measured him myself . . . wait I'll measure him again.' But can he play? What can he do? I like the Al Davis theory . . . look for the best players. That's the thing that's hurt the scouts, the computers. Sometimes you look for the intangibles: desire, if he's coming from a big winner in college. But, of course, if his legs are too short, all it means is he'll chase a guy over the goal line."

Jack Lambert, the Steelers' middle linebacker, puts it a little more basically: "I'll take 22 guys with heart over 22 guys with great athletic ability any day. If I were a scout, the first thing I'd look for is heart."

At the end of April or the beginning of May the NFL draft is held in a hotel in downtown New York. Fans line the streets for hours to get a seat in the gallery to watch the action. It's also the occasion for the great gathering of Draftniks, guys who make their living experting the draft, like handicapping a horse race. Joel Buchsbaum, Mel Kiper, Palmer Hughes, Joe Stein . . . it's a breed that's sprung up in the last few years, but many of them run a thriving business, writing for football publications, putting out their own sheets evaluating hundreds of seniors. Often their data is surprisingly accurate, which annoys many personnel directors, who don't like the idea of scouts handing out free information.

Each team has a table, manned by some local contact in the area, and the two phones at each table are hooked up to the drafting room in the home club's personnel office, the War Room, San Diego calls it. That's where the real action takes place, the intramural battles over a player that can go right down to the wire.

"In 1967 Al Davis and I were having a big fight over our number one pick," says the Raiders' player personnel director, Ron Wolf. "He wanted Gene Upshaw, I wanted a halfback from Arkansas named Harry Jones. We were battling right up until it was time to

FIG. 13 ANSWERS TO I.Q. TEST, PAGE 294 AND 295

Question No.				
1. 4	14. 16	27. 6⅔	40. 250
2. 91	15. 4	28. 1	41. .8
3. 5	16. D	29. $28	42. 3
4. 3	17. 1	30. 1	43. 2
5. 2	18. ⅑	31. 15	44. ½
6. 2	19. 5–11	32. 4	sec.
7. 1 or T	20. 2	33. 3	45. 3
8. T	21. F	34. .88	46. 32¢
9. 1	22. 1 or T	35. 150 days	47. 1
10. 32	23. 4–5	36. 2	48. 2
11. 3	24. 9 ft.	37. 21	49. 9–13
12. 8	25. 3	38. 20	50. $650
13. 4	26. 1 or T	39. 1,3,4	

make our choice. We had a loudspeaker hookup from the draft room in New York. Finally Al threw up his hands and said, 'You win. Go out in the hall and use the pay phone and call up Jones and alert him.'

"So I went out in the hall, and as I was dialing I heard over the loudspeaker: 'In the first round the Oakland Raiders select Eugene Upshaw, guard, Texas A&I.' "

Finally there's the first minicamp, the first look at the merchandise you've chosen. It can be a great joy or a tremendous disappointment. In 1975 the Jets took a center from Widener College named Joe Fields in the 13th round. They needed a long snapper. When he reported to the first minicamp the field was muddy, so they asked him to snap the ball in the hallway of their training complex.

"It was kind of funny to be snapping in a back hallway," says Fields, who's been the Jets' center ever since. "I remember I knocked a picture off the wall. Weeb Ewbank came out of his office and said, 'That's enough. We know he can snap.' "

CHAPTER SEVENTEEN

The Armament Factory

I played football before they had headgear, and that's how I lost my mind.

—Casey Stengel

Three hundred pounds of player and 34 pounds of equipment just teeing off.

—Dave Butz

THERE exist great love affairs in football—a man and his helmet, or maybe his shoes, or perhaps a pair of worn-out shoulder pads that he filched from a high school locker but he knows fit just right.

A player will sit by, stony-faced, while his best friend is cut from the team, but let them put his headgear on waivers and he'll break down and cry.

Lester Hayes, the Raiders' cornerback, wears the same chin strap he wore as a senior at Wheatley High in Houston, a replica of the one worn by his idol, Zeke Moore of the Oilers.

"Some friends of mine in Houston visited this sporting goods store one night and managed to procure some intangibles," Hayes says. "They ended up holding a big garage sale. I bought the chin strap for a dollar."

Ram tailback Eric Dickerson fumbled six times in the first three games last year, and he was slipping a lot. Finally someone took a look at his shoes. They were $8 specials, the same kind he'd worn since junior high, with short cleats. After much coaxing they persuaded him to give them up.

Players of old were fond of tinkering with their equipment.

"I kept adding features to my helmet," said defensive end Bob Dee, an original Boston Patriot who finally retired in 1967.

301

"I started out with a double face bar, then added a third bar because I was getting cut on the chin. I also added a horseshoe bar at the top of the helmet to protect myself from getting a forearm in the eye or the nose.

"I also had it repaired every year until my last season. I didn't let 'em paint it that last year because it was getting worn and I was afraid they might take it away from me. I didn't want to lose it.

"I cracked it near one of the ear holes in practice. I don't know how. It was just a plain old dummy scrimmage. Just hit it right, I guess. Anyway, the crack got worse. The helmet was pretty well battered out of shape, too. The edge of the top kept digging into my skin, and I'd come out of every game with a bloody forehead. But I wouldn't let 'em get rid of that old baby of mine."

Pads were smaller and less ferocious in the old days. The Packers' famous pass catcher Don Hutson probably set the record for stinginess.

"I remember the first time I saw Hutson," said ex-tackle Bruiser Kinard. "He had on a little-bitty ole pair of shoulder pads he bought in Woolworth's or maybe his wife made them."

"I'll tell you why," Hutson said. "We had to buy our own."

They love those old pads and helmets, but there's one set of equipage that has drawn evil looks ever since the dawn of football, and that's the family of dummies. Blocking dummies, tackling dummies, sleds, reaction testers—the business has come a long way since the days when Illinois coach Bob Zuppke said, "I keep dummies on the field to make the alumni happy."

The early dummies fell into two classes. There was the single dummy that one player would hold and another one would block, and old Giants talk about the way coach Steve Owen's craggy Oklahoma face would light up as he'd yell, "Git it! Go git it!" to his linemen. Then there was the two-man sled that's still in use: two dummies mounted on metal runners and attached to a base, upon which a coach stands and yells, "Drive! Drive it now!" until the blockers' legs start quivering. And there are also seven-man sleds, which allow a tired veteran to fake it every now and then, provided the six other pushers are doing their jobs.

The Edison of the dummy business was a Connecticut squire named Marty Gilman. His first breakthrough in the field was the Springback, which would bounce off the grass by itself, ready to be knocked down again.

"I got the idea," Gilman said, "when Lone Star Dietz of the Carlisle Indians said he'd like a dummy that picks itself up like a spittoon in a saloon."

Then came the Fightback, the Tackleback, the Chargeback, the Runback, the Breakthrough and the Big John, a huge, inflated parody of a defensive lineman, with arms upraised. Big John's role was to give quarterbacks the idea of passing under pressure.

The Giants under Allie Sherman were very big on Gilman dummies, which came in all colors. A visitor to the Giants' Fairfield, Conn., camp took a look at the rainbow collection on the field and dubbed the place "The Lollipop Farm."

Vintage Giants remember the two weeks that Joe Don Looney was in camp as a rookie in '64. Looney, king of modern flakes, took an instant dislike to one of Gilman's monsters, whose forte was striking back at tacklers after they hit it.

"Joe Don sidled up to it and gave it a lick, and the thing knocked him on his ass," a veteran Giant recalls. "So Joe Don went berserk and attacked the dummy and punched it with his fists and kicked it and screamed at it.

"I don't want to say who won that fight, but the dummy is still here, and who knows where Joe Don is right now."

Gilman's masterpiece, though, was a special contraption called the Ramback. The Giants tried it out in 1966, and Vince Lombardi also gave it a look, but the world wasn't really ready for it. The Ramback worked this way:

A great foam-rubber dummy swiveled back and forth, capable of striking out with 1200 pounds of thrust. Stationed at either end were transparent helmets with red spotlights inside them. A coach would mount an elevated platform and sit in front of a control panel. A lineman would take a stance in front of the dummy. The coach chose a button from rows of red, yellow and blue knobs. He pushed it and a helmet lit up. That was the "get ready" signal. Then he pushed another button, the other helmet lit up, and *bam!* the dummy shot out at the lineman, who was expected to meet the machine's thrust with that of his own. A gauge measured the player's reaction time, another his thrust power. The team physician stood by, just in case.

None of the Giants volunteered to test out the Ramback, so Allie Sherman grabbed Willie Young, a 270-pound rookie tackle. Willie stopped the Ramback's charge, teetered a little, and then, dazed, staggered off to rejoin the rest of the linemen. "He's amazing," said

Shaeffer Smith, the electrician who had installed the machine. He pointed to Young, who was still walking in circles. "He actually stopped the machine's thrust. And his reaction time was 30-hundredths of a second. Amazing."

The Ramback claimed no victims for a couple of days, and then one afternoon Sherman happened to be walking by. He looked around to make sure no one was watching. Then he decided to see if it was as tough as its reputation.

"I was all set to give it one of my patented shoulder blocks," the coach said, "when it struck out at me. I just escaped. It must have been around feeding time."

The Giants finally decided the Ramback was too tough for human consumption and they got rid of it late in the training season.

"They hitched it up to a truck—with chains—and dragged it off the field," said Don Smith, the Giants' publicist. "It reminded me of the bullfights, when they hitch the bull up to a team of horses and drag him out after he's been killed."

The Jets' killer dummy was called Big Bertha, sometimes just the Killer . . . one huge blocking or tackling dummy, attached to a lever by a set of coiled springs. The tension—and the force of the dummy's power—could be increased by adding more springs. One spring was for backs, two for linemen, and then there was a third spring. They tried the third spring only once, on a 6'6", 230-pound tackle named Steve Chomyszak, who was considered the strongest man in football at the time. It rendered him unconscious. They found out what they wanted to know. The third spring was removed.

The world of the personal equipment isn't so ferocious now, but in the old days, players would tape pieces of fibreboard and plaster—even sheet metal—to their arms to increase the power of the blow. When officials began to scrutinize the armaments more closely before each game, the illegal weaponry decreased. The old padding was of the heavy leather and fiberboard variety, and a full set of equipment could weigh up to 35 pounds, even more on a wet and muddy day. A big man could carry a heavy load.

"One day when we were at Utah State," said former kicker Jim Turner, a college teammate of the Rams' 270-pound Merlin Olsen, "we were messing around with some of Merlin's equipment, sort of trying it on. The weight of it almost brought me to the ground. That helmet—my God, it weighed about as much as all my equipment combined."

When football became a speed game, lightweight plastic and foam rubber replaced the cumbersome equipment of the past. "You know the hitting's good," Miami line coach John Sandusky says, "when you can hear the leather pop . . . make that the *plastic* pop."

Lightweight plastic can be just as effective as the old heavy armament, because the speed of the blow will add greater force to it.

"Once, when I was with Baltimore and we played Green Bay," Raider linebacker Ted Hendricks says, "Jim Grabowski was coming through the line and Mike Curtis gave him a good old-fashioned clothesline shot. He hit him so hard it popped his helmet off. Grabbo got up wobbly. One of our guys handed him his helmet. He started heading toward our bench. I tapped him on the shoulder and turned him around and said, 'Yours is on the other side, Jim.' Then I looked at Curtis. I figured his arm had to be broken from a shot like that. No problem, he was wearing those plastic pads on the inside of his arm. Next week I started wearing 'em, and I've worn 'em ever since."

Players were forever trimming their equipment down, discarding pads, lightening it, in the old leather and fibreboard days. The new plastic and foam rubber, plus innovations such as girdle pads, which fit neatly into shorts with pockets in them, have made the practice almost unnecessary, but there are guys who still like to fiddle with their gear, particularly the jerseys.

Most jerseys are made by Sand-Knit of Berlin, Wisc. Receivers' sleeves and shoulders are looser, making it easier for them to catch passes. Linemen's jerseys are tighter, to prevent an opponent from grabbing on. But many receivers make slits in the armpits of their shirts, to provide even freer arm movement, creating a flapping effect that the league, in its uniform code of equipment, frowns upon. Flappers don't look good on television. And linemen, particularly on offense, are contouring their jerseys so that they're practically skin-tight.

"For a while everyone was greasing up with slick substances, such as silicone and Vaseline, but the officials are watching for that now," says Dave Lapham, a guard for the New Jersey Generals and a Bengal for 10 years. "I've seen the umpire come up and feel the jerseys of all the linemen on the field. So everyone's tightening up his jersey. They're stuffing knee pads into the gaps created by the shoulder pads to smooth those areas over. Some guys are punching holes in their sleeves and putting in laces, and then lacing them up tight.

"At Cincinnati we went to a velour-type jersey in '81. It's hot as hell, but it's a slicker material. They're form-fitting, too . . . picture French-cut football jerseys. We had to go and get them fitted. It's gotten to the point where you have to put on your shoulder pads and jersey as a single unit now. And you have to be a contortionist to get the stuff on. You practically choke yourself."

Some linemen have gotten rounded shoulder pads—nothing to grab onto. Forty-Niner offensive tackle Keith Fahnhorst tapes his jersey down.

"I tried that at the University of Hawaii, where I coach," says John Wilbur, a long-time NFL lineman, "but the mesh in the jersey is too big. Also you can't get the tape to stick in Hawaii. I think it's the humidity there. But I'll tell you one thing . . . I was the first offensive lineman to use thread and junk on his shirt.

"I'd get upholstery thread and sew my jersey tight, especially in the hanging places, like under the armpits. The other guys used to laugh at me . . . 'There's Wilbur doing his sewing' . . . but pretty soon they started doing it, too. I'd have trouble getting into my jersey; someone would have to help me, like a matador getting into his costume.

"Then I'd put Vaseline on it and silicone spray on top of the Vaseline . . . Len Rohde, the old 49ers' tackle, taught me about silicone . . . and water on top of that. The defensive lineman would go to grab on and he'd leave his armpit exposed, and I'd punch him in the armpit. That would bring his hands down. One game against the Giants the defense was all complaining, and the ref made me change jerseys. I had to leave the game. My parents were watching it. They thought I was hurt or something."

All the stitching and greasing used to drive the Steelers' old defensive line coach George Perles crazy. He figured the defense had to do some stitching of its own.

"I tell my people," he said, " 'Take your jersey home. Have your tailor sew it. Have your wife sew it. Get involved.' "

Often the very design or color of the team uniforms can impart a psychological edge. The Chargers, with their lightning bolts down the helmets and sleeves, truly might feel like flashes from the sky. The Oilers, with their drilling rig above the ear holes of their helmets, look like they need a radio tower for messages. Rod Martin, the Raiders' linebacker, says, "We seem to draw something from our black jerseys, some inner strength. Teams try to get us out of them."

"They felt mean in their black jerseys," Mike Oriard, a former

Kansas City center, wrote in his book, *The End of Autumn,* when he described the first time the Chiefs had to wear their new red shoes. "But it was difficult to look or feel ferocious in red shoes. The first time we put them on for a game, George Daney, a guard, said, 'You go out there first and see if they laugh.' "

Last year, when the NFL suggested that visiting teams wear white jerseys, I heard a way-out theory of handicapping games. The idea was that in September, when the temperatures are high, the road teams had an edge.

"It's 10 to 15 degrees cooler in white jerseys," Denver coach Dan Reeves said, "and that can mean a lot. It was very hot in Pittsburgh and Baltimore for our first two games. Those teams wore black and blue jerseys, and we were a lot stronger in the fourth quarter and we beat both of them."

Sure enough, not counting night games or domed stadium affairs, the visitors won 24 and lost 18 in September of 1983. In October, when there's still considerable heat in some places, road teams went 24–22. But in November, when the weather turns cool, the home teams went 21–12, not counting warm-weather sites such as Miami or L.A. And in December the home teams in cold sites went 14–8. That's straight up—without the point spread. Maybe there's something to the theory after all.

When Seattle played its 1983 opener in Kansas City 100-degree heat was predicted, so the Seahawks' trainer, Jim Whitesel, got 900 pounds of block ice, stationed the blocks behind the bench and put three big fans behind them, creating a cool zone. It was an 1890s type of air conditioning, but Seattle lost anyway, 17–13.

You see all sorts of innovations. Shoe companies are fighting to invent lighter footwear with better traction, to make the swift swifter. Dolphins reserve fullback Woody Bennett has marketed a special girdle that stretches from crotch to shoulders, a washable garment that weighs 18 ounces and contains polyurethane closed-cell foam padding to protect five key areas—hips, ribs, spine, tailbone and shoulders.

Gloves have long been in existence for linemen, but now many receivers use them, presumably for cold weather. Bengal receivers use them everywhere.

"We went into the Silverdome before the '82 Super Bowl," former Bengal coach Forrest Gregg says, "and our wide receivers took their gloves off and they could hardly catch the ball; they were so used to them. Isaac Curtis had to put 'em back on. M. L. Harris had gloves so thick that I don't see how he could catch anything."

I even saw a quarterback wearing gloves on one snowy day in December 1982, when the Jets' Richard Todd completed 17 of 29 passes for 189 yards and a touchdown in the 32–17 win over Tampa Bay— wearing gloves.

"I never wore them before," Todd said. "I never even heard of a quarterback wearing gloves, and I hadn't tried them in practice. But on a day like that I was worried about numbness . . . the ball gets cold and slick and heavy. It doesn't feel right with your naked hand. So I wore lightweight golf gloves and I had a better grip."

Byron Donzis of Houston made a name for himself in 1978 when he invented a flak jacket to protect the ribs of Oiler quarterback Dan Pastorini, later expanding it to protect other areas as well. Donzis got a $190,000 grant from the NFL and a flood of orders for two of his companies, which began to thrive. The custom-made jacket cost $310, but some players complained of the bulkiness—also of leaks in the air inflation—and he had to change the formula and lighten it up. Jet fullback Mike Augustyniak switched from a Donzis flak jacket to a Casco rib guard against the Patriots in 1981, and suffered two broken ribs when the strap broke.

"I didn't wear the flak jacket because it was bulky and I was worried about fumbles," he said, "but I'm going back to it now."

Helmets always have been subject to the most careful scrutiny. Just as man once searched for a way to fly, doctors always have felt that the helmet which absolutely eliminates concussions is right around the corner, waiting to be discovered. So far no one has.

In 1982 Chris Thompson, a Seattle high school student, was awarded $6.3 million for a paralyzing injury he suffered in 1975. The suit was against the West Seattle High School District, and his contention in court was that he had not been instructed by coaches to avoid running with his head lowered. He had already settled out of court for $98,000 with Riddell, Inc., which manufactured the helmet he was wearing. Between 1980 and March of 1982, 11 lawsuits involving brain injury or paralysis from neck injuries were tried against equipment firms, with another 75 pending. Some $25 million in damages had been paid.

"Football is being litigated into extinction," said Richard Black, a Phoenix lawyer who worked as a consultant to helmet manufacturers. "It won't be here two years from now, at this financial pace." In 1982 there were seven companies making helmets; a decade before that there were twice as many.

Helmets now contain careful warnings and instructions on the inside bands, plus cautions against head tackling, which everybody does anyway. Their design is more sophisticated. There are suspension types, with inflatable pads to cushion the shock. There are special mushroom-shaped helmets for players with a history of head injuries. But I can't help feeling that the safest helmets of all were the old small, leather ones, with no face bars. No one felt his head or his face was invincible in those days, so the players were protected by basic instinct, i.e., don't hit someone head-first . . . or face-first.

"In the old days," the Colts' trainer, John Lopez, says, "before face masks, you used to get shoulder and arm injuries. The pads weren't designed right. Then they made them better, and they also brought in the face mask. People started tackling with their heads, so you got more head and neck injuries."

I've often wondered what would happen if helmets would be cushioned by a layer of foam rubber—on the *outside*. You certainly couldn't use them as a weapon. Forrest Gregg says it wouldn't work.

"Ohio State tried that once," he says. "Rawlings made them, a strip of sponge with leather over it and rubber on top. The problem is that it'll grip, it'll stick. You hit somebody with that and you'll break your neck. Plastic helmets will slide."

Donzis says, "You need to make a helmet that will move. Essentially it's an extension of the head now. They emphasize the fit. We might be traveling in the wrong direction. I think the ideal helmet someday will be a motorcycle-type, with a glass shield instead of a face mask. The face mask as it exists now is a natural handle for people to grab."

Early face-mask–era quarterbacks had one bar across, but after Joe Namath's cheekbone was broken by the Raiders' Ben Davidson in 1967 he requested an additional bar.

"I once asked for it before," he said, "and they talked me out of it. They said it would cut down on my vision. Vision, hell. This beak of mine is too big a target for some of those guys."

Bobby Layne held out against face bars of any kind until he retired in 1962, long after face bars became mandatory. He was football's Ted Williams, who always refused to wear a plastic batting helmet.

And the last of the original barless hardnoses was Boston defensive tackle Jess Richardson, who played naked-faced until his retirement in 1964.

Wilbur says he used to turn his face mask into a weapon.

"We'd remove the rubber from the bars," he says, "and then file the metal until it was razor sharp. Head slappers would wind up with a lacerated pair of hands."

Austrian-born kicker Toni Fritsch's first reaction to American football centered around the helmet.

"I don't like that hat I have to wear," he said. "It makes me feel like my head is in a fishbowl."

But often the helmet can set the whole tone for a uniform. Paul Brown says the flashy new Bengal helmets, and uniforms, were the first step in the push toward the Super Bowl in '81. The helmet has six tiger stripes of uneven width running vertically . . . "When do the batteries run out of those?" Chicago defensive end Dan Hampton asked quarterback Jack Thompson after an exhibition game. There are curving stripes down the legs and wide bands around the shoulder pads. "The team looks like it's just been run over by a Goodyear radial," Ron Martz wrote in the *Atlanta Journal.*

"I remember when Los Angeles came out with their new ram-horn helmets in 1948," Brown said. "People were rolling off their chairs laughing. Today everybody would like that helmet. What we did was set ourselves on the helmet first and then coordinated the rest of the uniform to go with it."

Someone asked punter Pat McInally how he liked the new helmet.

"Well," he said, "it's too early to say. Last night was the first time I'd slept in mine."

Shoes always have been a subject of concern, ever since Tom Dempsey kicked his record 63-yard field goal and the Cowboys' Tex Schramm, showing a notable lack of class, demanded that Dempsey's kicking shoe be outlawed. Dempsey was born with only half a foot, and the extra leather in his shoe had been surveyed by the league and found acceptable.

"It's funny," New Orleans GM Vic Schwenk said, "that nobody said anything about it when Tom was five for 15."

Another great toeless kicker, Ben Agajanian, also wore a special shoe. Once a high school kicker asked him how he could get one like it.

"Well," Agajanian said, "first you get yourself a hatchet."

Dallas equipment manager Buck Buchanan keeps an inventory of 350 to 400 pairs of shoes. He says that prior to artificial turf a player could get by on one pair plus a couple of different sets of cleats. He said that a player's position often determines the type of shoes he selects.

"Your defensive backs look for something that offers the best grip and is also light," Buchanan says, "while offensive linemen, with bigger and wider feet, can sacrifice a little of the grip for stability's sake."

Some 15 to 20 Cowboys have contracts with companies that supply them with free shoes. Offensive tackle Pat Donovan chooses them from a catalog in 10 to 12 different varieties. Defensive backs, receivers and running backs change their shoes almost compulsively, Buchanan says. "If they slip one time and lose their confidence in that shoe, they just feel they need another one. Linemen wear them longer. They average two pair a season, although Donovan wears out shoes every four to five weeks. The heat of the artificial turf does it. Benny Barnes used to wear them until they fell off."

A fairly new trend is to wrap tape around the shoes to keep them from slipping, especially on artificial turf . . . the heel slips up and down . . . although some players do it for looks, creating a kind of spats effect.

When George Allen took his Rams to play in Minnesota for the 1969 NFL Western Division championship, he took along four different kinds of shoes—regular cleats, the longer mud cleats, ripple soles for a frozen field, and Canadian broomball shoes for a field covered with ice.

"Yes, we have them, too," former Viking coach Bud Grant said. "I brought them down from Canada three years ago. The shoes have 19 suction cups on the bottom. They're for running on ice. Broomball is a game like hockey. You play it with a broom handle and a soccer ball. Except that you don't wear skates; you wear broomball shoes."

The broomball shoes reappeared last season when the Redskins met the Rams in the playoffs. Joe Gibbs bought 37 pair from a company in Winnipeg, at a cost of $2000, in anticipation of icy conditions on the practice field, although he said he wouldn't use them in the game itself.

Cold-weather gear has been a constant concern of equipment men, ever since the horror stories emerged after the Green Bay–Dallas Ice Bowl championship in 1967. Packer quarterback Bart Starr, for instance, had three fingers frostbitten that day in Green Bay. When the weather turns cold, the fingers still turn white.

"I never did have the feeling in my fingers I would have liked after that game," he said.

The contest left the fingers of Dallas tackle Jethro Pugh permanently discolored, and Cowboy halfback Dan Reeves remembers his face mask being smashed in a collision that left a tooth protruding through his lip.

"My face was so numb I didn't feel it," he says. "It didn't even start bleeding until they put heat on it."

When Gregg, who played right offensive tackle for the Packers that day, coached the Bengals in their AFC Championship Game against San Diego in frigid Cincinnati 14 years later, he was prepared. He equipped his troops with scuba gloves, thermal underwear and a plastic bench in which hot air circulated. He also coated himself and his players with Vaseline.

"We used chemical hand warmers at that game," Charger quarterback Dan Fouts said the following spring. "We'd been told they would last three hours. They froze up in 10 minutes. On the sideline, I wore electric gloves and put frostbite cream on my face. My fingertips and toetips were frostbitten, and my fingertips still hurt when I touch anything hot or cold."

"We wore so much cold weather gear," San Diego guard Ed White says, "that we got a tight, stuffed feeling. We couldn't move, and so we got colder. Any movement would have been better. I had a gladiator feel that day; I felt like Frankenstein."

When the Chargers played the Steelers in the '83 playoffs in Pittsburgh, their equipment man, Sid Brooks, who had once lived in Anchorage, Alaska, cut down on the quantity of gear but increased the sophistication.

"We have a couple of items that haven't been used in football yet," he said. "We have specially made jerseys that are eight ounces heavier than regular. They're 100 percent nylon, with reverse weave and pockets sewn on. We have regular gloves and scuba gloves, special Poly Pro quarterback jerseys that are worn by mountain climbers and skiers. They don't freeze up when you sweat. We have new socks for liners, to be used the same as glove liners. We're ready this time."

The NFL, whose needling insistence that uniforms must conform to a prescribed standard, seems to relax a bit where cold-weather gear is concerned. The rest of the time, such things as improper stocking height will draw a stern letter.

"They're pretty much a joke," 49er guard Randy Cross says. "For a while they got on me because of the way I was folding my socks back. Then the letters just stopped."

The Patriots were warned that players may be fined if they continue to pull their socks up too high. Singled out were running backs Tony Collins and George Peoples.

"They said I wasn't showing enough red on the tops of my socks," Collins said with a straight face. "I didn't mean to do it—honest."

Peoples, a third-string fullback, mentioned that he was amazed that the league noticed his socks. "I usually have my legs curled under the bench," he said.

The league has shown a resolute vigilance in matters of stocking height, but when a real crisis occurs in terms of equipment or playing conditions it is often a step or two late.

Patriot coach Ron Meyer managed to finesse a snowplow onto the field in the 3–0 win over Miami in 1982. Officials at the game stood around scratching their heads, and then three months later the league passed a rule against it. In the AFC Championship Game in the Orange Bowl that season the league officials supervising playing conditions at the scene remained silent while the field was left uncovered during a midweek rainstorm. No tarp had been provided. The suction pumps which were supposed to drain the field malfunctioned. The game was played in a quagmire, and the only official response was a memo handed out in the press box, detailing the ideal workings of the drainage system.

One of the Players' Association demands in contract negotiations in '82 concerned elimination of artificial turf, which is universally disliked by anyone who has to play on it, but it was one of the first giveback items when the talks got serious.

"The Players' Association really should have done something in their last contract," 49er coach Bill Walsh says. "They should have insisted on an inspection and evaluation when a carpet gets five years old, an evaluation by an outside, third party. Carpets are better now than when they first came in. There's a thicker pile, plus a cushion. But the problem is that after a while it wears down and gets hard, and then it becomes a financial thing—when do you replace it?"

Oriard, in *The End of Autumn*, describes playing on the Houston

Astrodome's artificial turf for the first time: "The surface felt hard, with none of the springiness of dirt and grass, and it had seams that separated, leaving two and three-inch gaps, and others that had overlapped, forming ridges high enough to trip over. I was surrounded by synthetic grass, synthetic air, synthetic light, synthetic sky—all dead."

CHAPTER EIGHTEEN

Keepers of the Faith: The Officials

We are under a constitution, but the Constitution is what the judges say it is.

—Charles Evans Hughes, 1907

FIRST there were three officials, then four. Then in 1947 there were five, six in 1965 and seven in 1978 (plus two rodmen, a boxman and an alternate on the sidelines). In 1980 they talked about making it eight, but vetoed the idea. Someday they may decide to platoon the officials like football players.

But some things never change. Officials will always catch hell from the players and coaches and sportswriters and fans. Maybe even from their wives.

Off the field the officials might look like anyone else, except for a few tired lines around the eyes. On the field they line up as shown in Fig. 14.

Officials hunt in packs, or crews. A crew stays together for the season, and there are 15 of them, one for every game, plus an alternate team, plus two alternate officials—107 total. Pay is figured according to length of service, not official duties, so a back judge can earn as much as a referee, if he's been around as long. But a referee gets to click on his little box and make the announcements, and back home his wife and kiddies will see his face on TV—and wave at the set.

The scale is $400 for a preseason game for an official with 1–10 years experience, $500 for 11 or more years. It starts at $450 per regular season game for a first- or second-year man, and goes up to $1200 for a veteran with 15 or more years of service. Everyone gets $3000 for a playoff or championship game, $5000 for the Super Bowl and $2000, plus a trip to Hawaii, for the Pro Bowl. So a rookie offi-

FIGURE 14   NFL officials: Primary duties and coverage areas

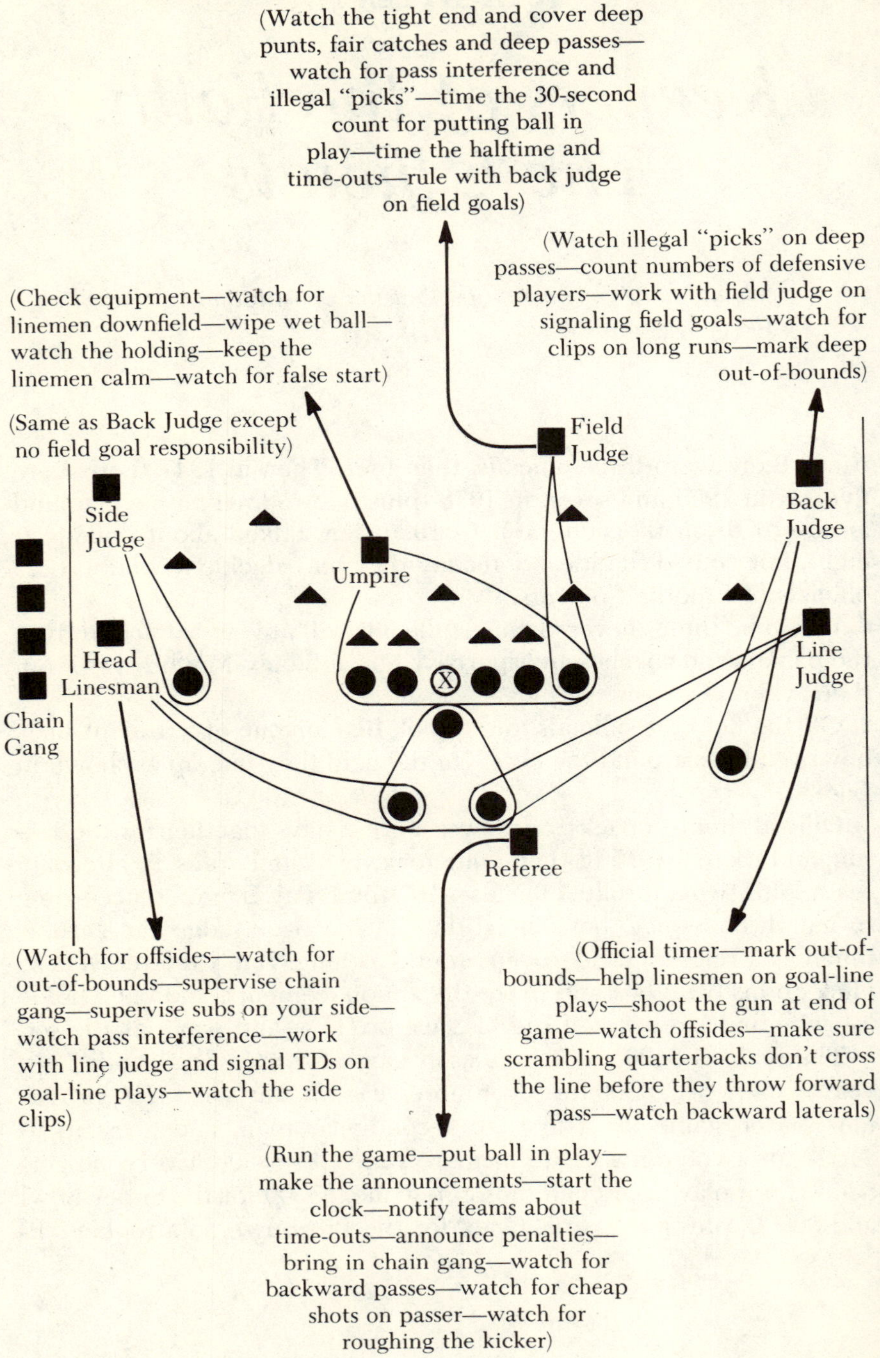

(Watch the tight end and cover deep
punts, fair catches and deep passes—
watch for pass interference and
illegal "picks"—time the 30-second
count for putting ball in
play—time the halftime and
time-outs—rule with back judge
on field goals)

(Watch illegal "picks" on deep
passes—count numbers of defensive
players—work with field judge on
signaling field goals—watch for
clips on long runs—mark deep
out-of-bounds)

(Check equipment—watch for
linemen downfield—wipe wet ball—
watch the holding—keep the
linemen calm—watch for false start)

(Same as Back Judge except
no field goal responsibility)

Side
Judge

Field
Judge

Back
Judge

Umpire

Head
Linesman

Line
Judge

Chain
Gang

Referee

(Watch for offsides—watch for
out-of-bounds—supervise chain
gang—supervise subs on your side—
watch pass interference—work
with line judge and signal TDs on
goal-line plays—watch the side
clips)

(Official timer—mark out-of-
bounds—help linesmen on goal-line
plays—shoot the gun at end of
game—watch offsides—make sure
scrambling quarterbacks don't cross
the line before they throw forward
pass—watch backward laterals)

(Run the game—put ball in play—
make the announcements—start the
clock—notify teams about
time-outs—announce penalties—
bring in chain gang—watch for
backward passes—watch for cheap
shots on passer—watch for
roughing the kicker)

cial could make as little as $8350 for a season, if he doesn't work any postseason action, whereas an old-timer could make $28,000 if he goes the full route (Super Bowl officials don't work the Pro Bowl). This is a much lower scale than those of baseball, basketball or hockey, but there are a lot more NFL officials and they work many fewer games—plus they're weekend warriors. In the other sports, officiating is a full-time job.

The crew is expected to check into the hotel in the city it's working 24 hours before game time. On Saturday night the referee gives his colleagues a quickie rules quiz, then he opens up the film of last week's game, spreads out the rating sheets by the two coaches involved (if they have bothered to fill them out), reads the report and comment from the league office, hands out play-by-play sheets. Then the group watches itself on film.

On Sunday morning there's a quick rule check, and the trip to the stadium. The officials are expected to get there no later than two hours before kickoff time. They check with the TV people, the chain crew, and the home team, to make sure the required 24 new footballs are on hand—plus a hand pump on the sideline.

From the time an official leaves his home for the game until after the game he is not permitted to drink alcoholic beverages. Once the league would hand out a printed list of off-limits bars or restaurants, such as Jilly's in New York and the LaCosta Country Club outside San Diego, but the establishments complained and the practice was discontinued.

Overseeing everything from the league office in New York is 59-year-old Art McNally, the NFL's supervisor of officials. His background includes baseball and basketball coaching at the high school and college levels and college basketball refereeing. He was an NFL ref for nine years. His supporters say he's fiercely loyal to his officials and to the league, which must perform the dual functions of maintaining quality and protecting the image. McNally shields his officials from the coaches, the players and the press. Popes and presidents can be interviewed but NFL officials cannot. His detractors say he is a stonewaller, a company man who won't make waves. Some are ex-officials; the current ones cannot be quoted by name, because they're not allowed to talk. Neither can coaches or players—to pop off means a fine, although some of them do anyway. In the heat of the moment it's occasionally overlooked. Cold-blooded criticism, especially when films are produced for evidence, is a fining offense. For officials themselves it can be worse. Cross McNally, they say, and you get the freeze.

The most vocal ex-official is Fred Swearingen, who had 21 years of experience. He said his problems with McNally started in 1972, when he was the referee in the Pittsburgh-Oakland Immaculate Reception game. He said the problems reached a climax in the 1979 Dallas-Pittsburgh Super Bowl. He was the field judge who ruled that Cowboy cornerback Benny Barnes had interfered with Lynn Swann at a crucial time in the game. He said that the Cowboys' president, Tex Schramm, had vowed to get him and he was so powerful in league circles that he could do it. He was finally fired after the 1980 season.

Both Schramm and McNally call the charges nonsense. Officials are graded on a 1–7 basis by a three-pronged system—coaches' reports, the report of the NFL observer at the game, and the weekly film study at league headquarters (see figs. 15 and 16), and when a man's ratings fall too low he's gone. No outsider has enough clout to get an official fired, McNally says.

"My ratings were consistently high," Swearingen says. "All of a sudden, after I made that call Tex didn't like, they dropped. Isn't that strange?"

An officiating source said that Swearingen was a competent official on his own calls, but sometimes he'd leave a crew member hanging without backing him up, and that was the problem. It's still a very sensitive issue.

So is the one involving umpire Tony Sacco and field judge Frank Kirkland, men of 17 and 12 years experience, respectively, who were fired after the 1974 season. They had complained about their postseason assignments. Ditto the one involving Jack Steffen, who worked as a line judge and back judge before he was fired after the 1977 season. There had been a newspaper article in which he was critical of the NFL's administration officials.

It's a tight ship, and at the league level the scrutiny is pretty complete. If a coach has a beef he can get it off his chest in his weekly report, although McNally says that after they've had a chance to look at films most of them calm down. If the coach is right he'll get a letter from the league office telling him yes, you were correct . . . sorry. In 1980 a Monday night TV audience saw Don Shula, whose Dolphins have been the least-penalized team in football for the last eight years, screaming that a Philly lineman was downfield on a punt. The

FIGURE 15

NFL Scouting Report of Officials

_____ ( ) _____ ( ) Date_____
　　Visiting Team　　　　　　　Home Team

Type of Game:　Routine_____ Difficult_____ Observer_____

Rating Scale:

		R	U	HL	LJ	FJ	BJ
Excellent	—7						
Very Good	—6						
Good	—5						
Satisfactory	—4						
Fair	—3						
Poor	—2						
Unsatisfactory	—1						

	R	U	HL	LJ	FJ	BJ
1. Appearance						
2. Judgment						
3. Game Control						
4. Position and Coverage						
5. Reaction Under Pressure						
6. Decisiveness						
Total						
Average						

Comments:

FIGURE 16

Coaches Report

Date:_____ Game:_____ ( ) vs. _____( )
                              Visiting Team   Home Team

Game No._____

Position	Referee	Umpire	Linesman	Line Judge	Back Judge	Side Judge	Field Judge
Number Name							

In our opinion crew performance was:
Please check one.

Above Average (   ) Average (   ) Below Average (   )

If you felt crew or individual performance was below average please indicate why.

General Comments:

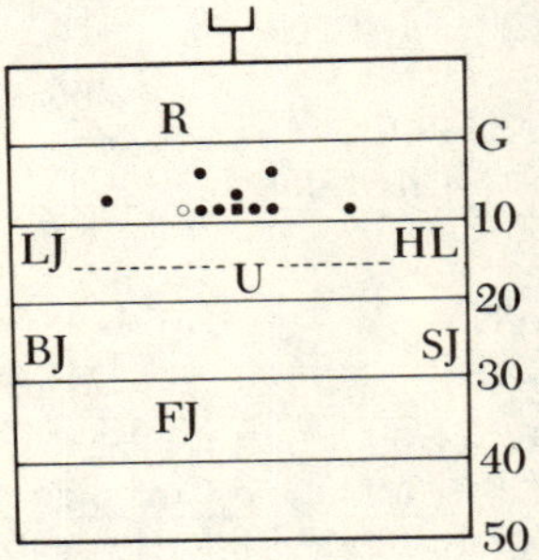

```
                              ⊥
         ┌─────────────────────────┐
         │          R              │G
         │       • °•:•• •          │10
       LJ│- - - - - - U - - - - - HL│20
       BJ│                       SJ │30
         │          FJ             │40
         └─────────────────────────┘50
```

_____
                        Signature

league office agreed with him upon reviewing the film, but he was still fined $1000 for stepping out on the field.

Shula and Tom Landry have a reputation for being pretty consciencious in filing their reports. Another coach I talked to says, "I don't even bother. What good does it do? It won't change anything."

In 1982 the *Philadelphia Inquirer* did a comprehensive survey on NFL officiating. Among the major complaints of coaches they found the following:

- Inconsistency of officiating among different crews. Certain crews might be tough on holding, for instance, and lax on other things. Players are informed accordingly, and one coach even has an elaborate scouting system on officials.

- League policy allowing officials' physical exams to be given by their own personal doctors, leading to what one coach calls "a lot of doddering old men out there."

- The part-time nature of the job. Coaches and players are full-timers, they say, so why shouldn't the officials be? They feel that one day of film preparation isn't enough. "We're a multi-million-dollar business being run by amateurs on Sunday afternoon," Bud Grant said. To which John Madden added: "They do a good job under the circumstances, but the circumstances should be changed. Anyone who's part-time just isn't as good." To this the league answers that there really isn't that much more that the officials could do during the week, and both their performance and their preparation is fine. The real reason is that the price would go way up. A survey taken after the 1977 season showed that more than half the NFL officials would quit rather than give up their regular jobs. The NFL would have to make it worthwhile.

- A really big game, such as the Super Bowl, will have a different standard of officiating. Fewer holding calls will be made, for instance, because they'd lengthen the contest for the millions of televiewers.

This leads to another complaint I've heard among coaches ever since the Houston-Pittsburgh AFC Championship Game after the '79 season—all-star crews, instead of the regular ones. It happened after side judge Don Orr had called no-possession—juggling—on Oiler flanker Mike Renfro, nullifying a touchdown. He had hesitated on the call, looked around for help, and gotten none.

"The big problem is that officials who work the playoffs have no experience working together as a crew," Houston coach Bum Phillips said. "I've been telling them all year that one complete team should be chosen to work a playoff game, then one guy will be used to covering for another, and they won't have problems like this. But instead, individual officials are picked, and each one feels, 'Well, if I keep my nose clean and don't make a mistake, then I'm still a good official.' No one helps the other guy. It's like a football team making the playoffs, and then when they get there, an all-star team goes out on the field."

"If you sent complete officiating teams into the playoffs," McNally says, "then some good officials might not make it. This system rewards our better officials."

Separate officials work each of the eight playoff and championship games. There are no repeaters, which means that slightly more than half of all officials got a crack at the $3000 postseason money. Then an all-star selection, chosen from those 56 playoff officials, gets to work the Super Bowl.

"The answer," one official says, "is to make one or two substitutions per team, giving the good guys work but still keeping your crew basically intact. It would be a lot more efficient. After working together for a year you have certain signals with the other guys . . . watch this guy on a pick, be careful of this guy downfield."

Tough-guy officials often have their own set of standards. Joe Muha, the old Eagles' fullback, and an NFL umpire for many years, used to tell the linemen, "Don't cry to me. Work it out yourselves." You know what that means.

"I was popping Bob Baumhower as he was sliding off the center," one AFC lineman told me. "It was a clean shot; I was taking away a side, and Pat Harder, the umpire, came over to me at halftime and said, 'That's a chickenshit way to block.' I said, 'What's wrong with it?' and he said, 'It's just chicken. I'm keeping my eye on you.' It affects the way you play, you know."

Old AFL fans knew that if you wanted to see a fight, you went to a game Bob Finley was refereeing. Trouble followed this fiery Texan like a shadow. He refereed both the '67 and '68 Jet-Raider bloodbaths on the Coast. After a particularly rough Jet-Broncos game in Denver, New York defensive end Gerry Philbin said, "He was laughing at us and taunting us and challenging us to do anything to him." He worked the 1970 Kansas City–Oakland battle, in which a big brawl broke out after Ben Davidson speared Len Dawson on the ground, and in the hallway after the game Finley challenged

Chiefs' coach Hank Stram to a fistfight. The following season Finley's name was quietly removed from the roster of officials.

"You can't let the officials intimidate you, keeping your players from giving a good shot," Chuck Noll says. "The league has a rule, but we have a rule about officials intimidating us."

Umpires call most holding, consequently they get the most heat from the defensive linemen.

"I made a statement before the Super Bowl," one coach said last year, "that the key to it is who's umpiring the game. The Raiders get away with murder. I said if they're not called, they'll win big. How many holdings did they draw, one?"

"If you're a second- or third-year player you don't have a chance," one defensive lineman says. "You get no recognition from the officials at all. The umpire's standing right behind you and a guy grabs your face mask and pulls you down, and you scream to the official, 'What are you looking at?' and he says, 'Get back to your huddle.' When a 15-year vet like Ted Hendricks talks to him, he'll listen."

John Brodie says that 49er fullback Ken Willard always used to head for the umpire when he got through the line. "Best blocker I have," Willard would say.

Are officials sensitive about what's said about them on television? I think so. Last year CBS's John Madden was making fun of offsetting foul calls, in which nobody's really penalized. So the following week, when Bob McElwee's crew worked the game between the Bills and the Raiders, who finished one–two in most penalties, four players were thrown out. Mickey Marvin and Eugene Marve got the heave for a fight, Chris Keating and Cleo Montgomery got it for a routine bumping match on a punt.

There have been some famous bad calls in history. Jim Tunney, the NFL's showpiece ref these days, made the call that gave Green Bay a divisional victory over Baltimore, in overtime, in 1965. He ruled Don Chandler's winning field goal good. Films showed Chandler kicking the turf in disgust after his miss. Now there are two officials, one stationed behind each goal post, to call field goals.

The most famous call was in the three-downs game—Bears against Rams in 1968. It cost the Rams a shot at the Western Division title. Norm Schachter's crew blew it when they allowed the Rams only three downs on one crucial series, after a holding call had nullified a play. The press never caught it, neither did the Ram coaches upstairs, nor Pete Rozelle, watching the game on TV. It was a case of mass hypnosis, but Schachter, one of the league's most able referees, was punished by being taken off the playoffs.

There were a couple of bad ones in the regular season last year, one of which was noticed—the errant signaling of Billy Johnson's game-winning touchdown on the final play of the 49er game—and one of which was not, or at least it didn't get any publicity. This was in Dallas's sudden-death victory over Tampa Bay. The play that sent the game into overtime, a 52-yard touchdown by the Cowboys' Timmy Newsome, should have been whistled dead. His left foot split the sideline marker.

But whenever you feel in an overly critical mood about NFL officiating, watch the USFL. Those guys make the NFL officials look like supermen. Last year Arizona guard Frank Kalil felt like he was getting a reputation as a holder, and officials were watching for that. So he switched jerseys for a game against L.A., from 67 to 75. He wasn't called once. Afterward he said one official asked him where Number 67 was. "I told him he was waived," Kalil said.

When the Generals played in Chicago, though, on Monday night, April 25, 1983, I saw something I've never seen in 40 years of watching pro football. I saw a referee blow the coin toss. It happened just before the overtime period started. Referee Bill White was meeting with New Jersey captain Keith Moody and Chicago captains Stan White, Greg Landry and Eddie Brown. At our house we run the tape over to entertain guests. Here's the actual dialogue. Moody is calling the toss.

Ref:	Heads he calls.
White	(as coin is in the air): He called tails.
Ref:	Heads it is.
White:	He called tails, ref.
Landry:	He called tails! He called tails!
White:	What'd you call, Keith? Tell him what you called.
Moody:	We'll take the ball.
White:	Ah, you cheat! You're a Christian cheat!
Ref:	Which way do you want to kick the ball?
Landry:	He said tails! He said tails!
White:	He called tails!
Ref:	Which way do you want to kick?
Brown:	That way.

LANDRY:	You just blew it, ref.
JIM SIMPSON:	(announcing for ESPN): I can't believe what I've just seen and heard.

Don't get upset. The Blitz won it in overtime, anyway. And the next year the USFL fired 12 of its 36 officials. Bill White was not around in 1984.

Players who do something particularly nasty are called in to the league and fined. They can also be suspended. In 1968 Randy Beverly of the Jets clotheslined Buffalo flanker Haven Moses. The officials missed it but the league office caught it in the films and they stepped off their own penalty on Beverly—a $100 fine.

"I just bumped him," Beverly said.

"Bumped him?" a league official said. "You might as well have hit him with an axe. He was out a minute."

"That's what we call bumping."

In 1982 the NFL office took an interest in anatomy. One November weekend Jets middle linebacker Stan Blinka clotheslined the Packers' J. J. Jefferson as he was coming across the middle. Jefferson left the field and came back one play later. Blinka was fined $1000 and suspended for a game. On the same weekend, though, the Lions' Leonard Thompson had taken a full run at the Giants' Leon Bright, who was waiting to return a punt, hit him early and stretched him for 10 minutes. They took him off on a stretcher. Thompson drew the same fine as Blinka did, but no suspension. How come? "Blinka's blow was to the head, Thompson's to the chest and neck area," was the explanation, which makes as much sense to you as it does to me.

The worst cheap shots, though, are not to the head or neck. They're to the knees, and they're seldom detected. I watched an exhibition game on TV between the Oilers and Cowboys. On one play Too Tall Jones, normally a mild player, shoved Houston's rookie guard, Bruce Matthews, after the whistle and drew a 15-yard penalty for it. Jones was noticeably upset. They ran the play back on TV and it showed Jones picking himself up off the ground and going after Matthews.

"Must be an awfully brave rookie to take on Too Tall," Pat Summerall said. At halftime I ran the tape back to see what had really started the argument. After the play had gone by, Matthews had circled around Jones' blind side, drawn a bead and launched his 276 pounds at his outside knee, a vicious, nasty piece of work. If Jones hadn't seen him coming at the last minute and turned slightly, his career might have been finished. I called the league office a few weeks later to ask if any fines had been handed out on the play.

"On Jones? No. It was just a routine penalty," the guy told me.

From a writer's standpoint, the thing that bugs me most is the way we're kept away from officials. If there's a controversial call in a game the official may be questioned by a designated pool reporter, but only if he goes through the chain of command—home team PR man, league rep, referee, then the official in question. Often, in the postgame mayhem, things foul up. Thus it was that none of the officials were questioned about the controversial interference calls at the end of the 49er-Redskin NFC title game in 1983. The Redskins' PR man and the NFL guy couldn't get the message down to the officials before those gentlemen left the scene of the . . . well, the game. In the 1983 L.A.-Atlanta contest the pool reporter was denied access to the officials because he got the visiting PR man when he couldn't find the home guy.

I remember a game in Shea Stadium some years ago when an official had blown a big call at the end of the game, and we sent our pool reporter down to get the scoop. The pool reporter was a Jersey writer named Bob Kurland, a very mild-mannered chap. Two league people with tape recorders met him downstairs. Pat Hagerty, the referee, stopped him outside the door. He had his own tape recorder. The KGB would have been proud. Hagerty kept him away from the official in question; he gave him some blah-blah about it being a "judgment call," everything was recorded, and then the two league guys led poor Bob back to the press box. He was white-faced and shaken when he arrived.

I was still steaming about it in my office that night, so I looked up the official in my league press book, got his home town, called information and got his number. I called him and told him I was from the league office, and we'd better go over his story, in case we got calls. So he spilled it all, how scared he was as a first-year official, how a guy didn't cover for him, the works. I didn't use the stuff because it would have been a cheap shot, but I called McNally the next day and told him how easy it was for a writer to get the stuff he wanted if he really went after it . . . so how about letting us interview officials, huh?

And what was the reaction? Shortly thereafter officials' home towns were removed from the press book.

"I think if you asked most of the league officials they'd have nothing against a 10-minute press conference after the game, so we could give our side of it to the writers," one official told me. "But there's a muzzle in the NFL, a gag rule. You're not supposed to say a word to a writer during the season, even socially. As an official, I don't feel the need to run and hide."

The Professional Football Writers for years has been trying to crack this gag rule, with no luck. Even the inadequate pool reporter system was considered a huge breakthrough.

"You'll never get it done while McNally's there," Swearingen says. "He's paranoid about publicity."

Recent publicity has dealt with the possible use of TV's instant replay as an aid to officiating. On the surface it sounds good, but so far no one's figured out a way it would be practical. How would you keep from slowing down the games by an hour? How do you decide when to use it, and how many times a game? And even the replay camera doesn't reveal all, if the shot's taken from the wrong angle.

"Five or six years ago we made a study, and monitored a game using it," Pete Rozelle says. "On some plays the camera caught blatant holding that wasn't called, so that would change everything, dual fouls on the same play. You'd have a game filled with offsetting penalties. Plus a huge delay."

As I watch more games every year, some questions seem to come up all the time. In capsule form, here are a few of them, plus the answers:

Q: Why is "illegal block from the back" called on so many punt and kick returns? Last year Madden called it the "House Special . . . just like every time you go into a restaurant the House Special is red snapper."

A: I'll let Swearingen answer that one. "No one ever saw it until recently," he says. "The problem is that you can't block a guy below the waist, you can't hit him in the head or neck. So that leaves a little square that's legal . . . in the chest area . . . and when a guy's got both arms in front of him there's no way he can be blocked there. So every little nudge that's outside the square is called an illegal block from the back. In the old days, if there was a little contact from the side we'd let it go." Personally, the infraction I see all the time is never called . . . like steps in basketball . . . and that's offside on the kickoff by the kicking team. Just watch it sometime.

Q: Did Eric Wright of the 49ers really interfere with Art Monk of the Redskins at the end of the NFC Championship game?

A: League films show that Wright got a hand on him, and they say that despite Bill Walsh's contention to the contrary, the ball *was* catchable. So they say Tom Kelleher's call was correct. A few officials I talked to in the off-season (sorry, can't use names . . . I don't want to get anybody fired) said that in order for interference to be called three questions must be answered positively: (1) Was contact made? (2) Was the ball catchable? (3) Did the defender materially affect the pass route or hinder the progression of receiver to the ball? They said the answer to the first two was yes (although Wright lightly putting a hand on Monk's side was hardly contact), but the answer to the last was no. Therefore it was, at best, a very chintzy call at such a crucial time in the game.

Q: What's a pick? When you read that a team runs a "pick passing offense," isn't that illegal?

A: A pick is when two receivers cross close to each other in an attempt to "pick off" a defender, or get two of them bumping into each other. "For a pick to be illegal you've got to have contact," Hagerty says. "In other words, the receiver actually has to run into the defender, and it has to have a bearing on the play. Going close is OK." "If a coach has complaints," says the NFL's assistant supervisor of officials, Nick Skorich, "we tell him, 'Review the rules relative to holding or offensive pass interference.' Usually it's one or the other."

Q: Who are the best refs?

A: Tunney's number one, said the guys I talked to. Ben Dreith's a stubborn Dutchman who won't be shoved around. Very solid, although Chuck Noll calls him an "old lady," because he protects the quarterback so much. Gene Barth is a comer, although he always looks worried. Personally I like Chuck Heberling, plus a pair of Jerrys . . . Seeman and Markbreit.

Q: When there's a fumble and a big pileup, how do they really figure out whose ball it is?

A: "There's really no way to tell," Swearingen says. "Just unstack the pile, and the one who hands you the ball, he gets it. In Super Bowl XIII Dallas fumbled a kickoff return. When I blew the whistle and started sorting through the pile, Number 53 of Pittsburgh, Dennis Winston, was standing alongside me. Finally, when it was all over, do you know who handed the ball to the official? Number 53. He'd found it somehow. So it was Pittsburgh's ball."

Q: Do officials favor some teams, or coaches?

A: They might lean a little toward the "legendary" coaches, such as Shula or Landry, but I don't think it's a conscious thing. The Raiders' Al Locasale tells a story about when he was scouting a Georgia Tech game, and before the game, there was Tech coach Bobby Dodd, with his arms around the officials, chit-chatting. "Another scout said to me," Locasale says, " 'There's Bobby . . . putting in his goal-line defense.' "

CHAPTER NINETEEN

A Gallery of Ruffians, Flakes and Oddballs

Joe Don Looney: Never was a man more aptly named.

—George Sauer, Jr.

BEST of all, I like the flakes, the loonies, the zanies . . . the throwbacks to a simpler era.

I felt very bad when Jack Rudnay retired after the 1982 season. Rudnay was Old World. He played center for the Chiefs for 13 years. He played with broken fingers and chipped vertebrae and torn muscles. He didn't have much use for people who hadn't paid their dues. Tom Keating, the Raiders' defensive tackle, finished his career with K.C. and he tells this story about Rudnay.

"It was 1974, the strike year. Rudnay was the leader of the strike faction, the pickets. The rookies were working out in camp. One day we read a quote by David Jaynes, the rookie quarterback, the number three draft. He said, 'I can lead this team to victory.' Rudnay just smiled. 'We'll see about that,' he said.

"Now the strike is over, we're back in for our first workout. Rudnay's the center, Jaynes has been the quarterback in camp so he's the first one to take snaps. Hank Stram's up in the tower. In the locker room Rudnay had taken a scissors and cut the crotch out of his football pants. Everything hangs out.

"Rudnay's over the ball. Jaynes looks left, looks right, just like he's been taught. He calls his signals . . . 'Brown right, X left, ready, set . . .' and he reaches down for the ball . . . whooo! The ball goes flying.

"Stram yells, 'What's going on down there?'

" 'He won't take the snap, coach,' Rudnay says.

" 'Let's get another quarterback in there,' says Hank, and that's the beginning of the end for David Jaynes."

330

Bill Bain is a mournful looking 300-pound tackle for the Rams. He'd bounced around the league for five years before L.A. picked him up, cut him once and then re-signed him.

"I love training camp," he once said, "because that's the only time of the season I get to play."

Last year Irv Pankey, the regular left tackle, tore an Achilles tendon and was through for the season, and Bain was the starter.

"All this means," he said, "is that I make the cut next week. Look, I know they like Irv more than me. I like Irv more than me, too."

One year in camp he decided life wasn't worth living. "Honestly, if I could get a $2 million life insurance policy, I'd hire a hit man to do away with me. We all have to die sometime. I've always loved to sleep, anyway. Why live all your life?"

Special teams is as good a breeding ground as any for flakes. If they didn't start that way, a career of wedge-busting will turn them a bit goofy.

It's October 1982. The NFL players are on strike. Redskin fullback John Riggins has just played two games in two days, the NFLPA All-Star games, and now it was late, and as the car carrying him back to his hotel after game number two was creeping through the deserted streets of Los Angeles, Riggins was suddenly aware that a very small and very crazy person sitting next to him in the back seat was digging him in the ribs with his elbow.

"Shot for shot, waddya say?" said 5'9" Louie Giammona, who'd spent eight years on the Jets' and Eagles' special teams.

"What?" Riggins said.

"I'll trade you shot for shot, you hit me, I hit you, waddya say?"

"Louie," Riggins said, "this is not the way to win my friendship."

"OK, then you hit me, hit me!" Louie said, bouncing up and down in the seat. "I don't mind. I love it."

"Well, Louie, I'll tell you what we'll do," Riggins said, brushing away the sleep for a moment. "When we get back to the hotel room, we'll tape your ankles together, and hang you from the ceiling upside down. Then we'll take turns using you for a heavy bag—if that's what you really want."

Riggins was the leader of an active little band of zanies on the Jets, before he went to Washington. There was Steve Tannen, the cornerback who wrote poetry, and Lou Piccone, the lowest-paid player in football one year, and Mike Adamle, who'd stand in the locker room slapping Piccone in the face—and vice-versa—before they took the field for special teams duty. When Adamle was traded to Chicago he said, "Football's like that. It's like *Let's Make a Deal*, the idiot's game. Pete Rozelle is Monty Hall, a guy comes in dressed like a radish and a deal is made."

But Riggins was the king. I remember phoning him at his home in Centralia, Kan., the day he was drafted in 1971. "What was your number one sports thrill?" I asked. It was late in the day and I was tired.

"Watching the neighbor's pigs being born," he said.

Two years later he was a holdout in camp. He grew a Mohawk haircut. He finally signed his contract four days before the season opener.

"Damnedest sight you ever saw," Weeb Ewbank said. "He signed that contract sitting at the desk in my office. He had that Mohawk haircut, and he was stripped to the waist and he was wearing leather pants and a derby hat with a feather in it. It must have been what the sale of Manhattan Island looked like."

"Sports to me," Riggins says, "was always fun. The real me was kind of a jerk . . . kick the basketball around, run around the court trying to pull a guy's pants down, throw the ball at a guy's head and yell 'Catch!,' hang around the back of the huddle and chitchat, cause distractions, get my share of belly laughs . . . I'm still that way.

"Don't forget that I'm from Kansas, and Kansas has a rich tradition of outlaws . . . the Younger Brothers, Quantrill's Raiders, Bonnie and Clyde. Meade, Kansas, was the Dalton Gang's hideout, and there are still a lot of flourishing Jesse James fan clubs in the state. I went out for athletics because in Centralia there were three types of kids: the big, fat sissies, the guys with the ducktail haircuts and black leather jackets, and the athletes. My hair was too curly for a ducktail, so I had to go with sports. If I'd had straight hair I might be in prison today."

Tannen is an actor in L.A. now.

"You know what killed me?" he said the day after Riggins was named MVP for Super Bowl XVII. "Watching Mike Adamle interviewing Jack Kent Cooke on TV after the game and asking him, 'Is Riggins as crazy now as he was then?' Crazy? With the Jets Adamle used to take off all his clothes on flights back from games and sit there in his underwear. 'Why, Mike?' I'd ask him. 'More comfortable,' he'd say.

The old AFL had more than its share of characters, but one of the most memorable was Larry Eisenhauer, the defensive end for the Patriots. Larry's father, old Dutch, a crew-cut 275-pounder who once upon a time raised hell for the Long Island Aggies in Farmingdale, used to accompany the Patriots on their trips. When the Patriots played San Diego they'd stay at a place called the Stardust Motel. The big feature of the Stardust was the Mermaid Bar, where you'd sip your drink and watch four young water ballerinas performing in front of you in a glass pool. One hot night Larry's dad felt like a swim.

"Where's the pool, Larry?" old Dutch said, and of course Larry steered him over to the Mermaid.

"Never saw anything like it," a writer said. "I was having a drink and all of a sudden this goddam whale in a blue woolen swim suit was swimming right at me."

"How was your swim, dad?" Eisenhauer wanted to know after Dutch got through with his show.

"OK, Larry, but I had this strange feeling that there were a whole lot of eyes on me."

One afternoon a Charger PR man stopped by and handed the Boston players a bunch of Charley Charger coloring books. The Patriots took them over to poolside, and the rumor that night was that Eisenhauer had spent the rest of his day coloring his Charley Charger book.

"It's a goddam lie," he said later. "I wasn't coloring the thing. I was just reading it."

Before games Eisenhauer was one of the noted dressing room maniacs. He'd attack walls, lockers, anything that got in his way. On the field he played with a wild intensity seldom seen today. Boston used to have a daytime kiddie show in those days called *Boom Town,* featuring Rex Trailer and his sidekick, Pablo. One day they decided to film a show at Fenway Park, and the action would center around the Patriots football team. Pablo would grab the ball and run for a TD, with all the Patriots chasing him. Eisenhauer was picked to be one of the chasers.

Once the action started, though, a hidden bell clanged and all the 6'5", 250-pounder saw was an enemy player running for a touchdown, a guy who had to be stopped. So he stopped him.

"I'm kind of ashamed of it now," he said later. "Pablo was only about 5'3", and he was slow, so it wasn't any trick catching him. I didn't really hurt him. I just sort of jumped on his back. But what the hell? Why give the guy a free touchdown?"

Not that the AFL had a monopoly on characters. The NFL in those days had people like Alex Karras and Artie Donovan and Alex Hawkins, who used to tell people, "I went to high school in Charlestown, West Virginia, and I'd get myself ready for the big game by playing solitaire, having a chew of tobacco and listening to Webb Pierce sing, 'I'm in the jailhouse now.' "

And, of course, there was Joe Don Looney.

By the time Joe Don got to the University of Oklahoma he had logged time at Texas, TCU, and Cameron JC in Lawton, Okla. He had been kicked off the team at Oklahoma for slugging a student assistant coach, and then came the pinball trip through the pros—New York to Baltimore to Detroit to Washington to the Army to New Orleans, all within six years.

Before his senior year at Oklahoma, he had spent a summer in a Baton Rouge, La., health studio. He was 6'1", 224, when he left. He could run the hundred in 9.8, lift 290 pounds in a military press, 450 in a squat. He drank a gallon of milk a day and swallowed 20 different kinds of protein pills.

"Have you considered his attitude?" someone asked Wellington Mara after the Giants drafted him number one in December 1963. "I have considered those shoulders, those legs, and those 224 pounds," Mara said.

He lasted with the Giants for 28 days. People remember him punching and flailing at Allie Sherman's recoil-blocking dummies. Trainer Sid Morett remembers that Looney wouldn't throw his used socks and jock into a bin so marked because "no damn sign is going to tell me what to do." He wouldn't talk to reporters because "they just get things fouled up," and when publicist Don Smith pushed a note under his door, Looney pushed it back out. "And don't you bother me either," he said.

Practices bored him and he preferred playing catch with a nine-year-old boy on the sidelines. In scrimmages he ran the seven-hole when he was supposed to run the five-hole. "Anyone can run where the holes are," he said. "A good football player makes his own holes."

In August he was traded to Baltimore, and after a few workouts the Colt coaches said his attitude was 100 percent improved. He scored a touchdown on a 58-yard run against the Bears and came off the field in tears. Joe Don was ready to blossom.

Then in November he broke down a door and slugged the male member of one of two young married couples cowering in the hallway. It was all a big mix-up, he said at the trial. He and his buddy were looking for the apartment of some nurses, and besides that, he was pretty upset because Barry Goldwater had gotten beaten so badly in the presidential election.

And when Looney's lawyer, William D. MacMillan, suggested probation before the verdict, he gave the world a definitive appraisal of his man: "This verdict would keep the one couple from having a feeling that Looney might develop a 'persecution complex' over the matter, and the other couple would not have a future fear of Looney retaliating against them."

A week later Looney jumped into the ring during a tag-team wrestling bout involving Red Berry and Bruno Sammartino in the Civic Center and helped quell what he figured was a riot. Promoter Phil Zacko thanked Joe Don for protecting his wrestlers. "He should be commended," the promoter said.

Baltimore coach Don Shula couldn't see it that way, and before the next camp opened, Looney was gone—traded to Detroit for Dennis Gaubatz. And while the Lions' coach, Harry Gilmer, was explaining, "I believe that with his rookie year behind him, things will straighten out. I don't believe he will be a problem," the Colts were relating a few Looney stories they had held back until then.

There was, for instance, the time he cut out of a party carrying a blanket. "Where are you going?" someone asked him. "I'm going to sleep in the cemetery," he said. "It's nice and peaceful there."

Next morning a teammate asked him how it was. "I had a good talk with a guy about death down there," Joe Don said.

There were the stories that John Unitas told—about the time Joe Don asked someone to "watch my cheeseburger for me," while a team meeting was going on; about the time the team was gathered in the locker room for the pregame prayer, and someone heard a noise in the equipment room, and there was Looney, listening to the radio and doing the Mashed Potato all by himself; and the night Shula dispatched his troubleshooter on the team, Hawkins, to baby-sit Joe Don.

"I watched him pace up and down the apartment," Hawkins said.

"I listened to him rant and rave. I heard of his grand scheme to buy an island near New Guinea, buy a boat, get some girls and some Texas buddies and go down there and breed a new race. Joe eventually went to sleep. I didn't dare close my eyes."

When Joe Don got to Detroit, Gilmer rubbed his hands and said that the Lions' running attack would center around Looney. The Detroit publicity department predicted that Joe Don could be the first 1000-yard runner in the team's history. But Looney's first real headlines in Detroit involved a fight in the parking lot of the Golden Griddle Pancake House in Royal Oak. There was something about a tab for $3.28 and a misunderstanding over who should pay it, and the scene finally ended with Looney trying to smash a beer bottle and use the jagged end, just like people did in the movies, only the bottle wouldn't break.

Then there were problems with his back, and finally, in one September game in 1966, Gilmer told Looney to carry a message in to quarterback Milt Plum. "If you want a messenger," Joe Don told the coach, "call Western Union." That ended his career in Detroit. Next stop, the Redskins.

"We're walking down Washington Boulevard in Detroit the day after Joe Don got traded by the Lions," said Bob Tate, a Detroit bartender and a friend of Looney's, "and Joe looks up and says, 'You know, Tate, I sure am glad I'm not a building.'

" 'Yeah, Joe,' I said, 'it would be awful hard on you moving from town to town.' "

In Washington he achieved instant stature. He scored a touchdown in his first game ("it was a twin-two-sweep-trap . . . that means as much to me as it does to you"), Coach Otto Graham said he was finally shaping up, the headlines involved the "new" Looney, and the honeymoon lasted right up until he announced he was playing out his option because of a salary squabble.

He wound up in the army for a year, and finally New Orleans picked him up as a free agent. He packed up his mastiff hound, which he had loaded down with barbells ("to build up the dog's leg muscles") and almost converted into a health food addict with a sunflower seed and wheat germ oil diet, and headed south. The last report on the dog was that he had made a raid on a nearby henhouse.

"I might have known," sighed Doug Atkins, the Saints' giant defensive end. "The minute the kid straightens out, the dog goes bad."

He lasted a year with the Saints. He traveled around the world:

Hawaii, Hong Kong, Peru. He became a hippie ... "Long hair, beard, sandals, beads, the whole nine yards," Hawkins says. He met a guru, Swami Muktananda, Baba to his friends, followed him to India, trimmed his weight to 150 pounds, and worked as a common laborer and keeper of the swami's elephant. He shoveled elephant droppings, "Chief of Compost" was the way he described his job. He wrote to a friend and said he had set a world record in the shoveling event, 12 wheelbarrow loads in one hour and 10 minutes, bettering the old mark by two minutes. When Baba died in November 1982, Joe Don came back to Texas and joined Baba's successors, a brother-sister team.

"I might add," Hawkins says, "the sister is not short on looks."

In a story syndicated by News Group Publications, Inc., last year, Hawkins wrote that at last sight, Joe Don, 40 years old now and 195 pounds, had found inner peace through Siddha Meditation and Siddha Yoga. "He has found the answers, he says," Hawkins wrote. "I hope he has, because if he hasn't, you ain't heard the last of Joe Don Looney yet."

In pro football's infant days there were plenty of gamblers and drinkers and roughnecks, but these were mostly poor men, and if not for football they'd be loading trucks and hauling freight and plowing rocky little patches of ground in country towns.

"Jug Earp, Mike Michalske, Cal Hubbard," the Green Bay druggist, John Holzer, once said. "They played their hearts out for $35 or $50 a game. They had a fierce desire, an almost animal desire for contact."

"I remember one time when Bronko Nagurski was horsing around in a second-floor hotel room with a teammate," old referee Ronnie Gibbs said, "and Bronko fell out of the window. A crowd gathered and a policeman came up and said, 'What happened?'

" 'I don't know,' said Nagurski. 'I just got here myself.' "

George Halas used to tell the story about a 1933 Bear game in which Nagurski knocked out Philly linebacker John Bull Lipski.

"Bull had great recuperative powers, and he came back in the game and tried to tackle Bronko again, and he was rendered unconscious again. Two of the Philadelphia substitutes came off the bench and started to drag Bull off the field. Bull came to near the sidelines and started muttering something about getting back in there.

"But play had already resumed, and the Bears were headed in his direction on a sweep with Nagurski leading the interference.

Bronko overtook Lipski and the two subs about five yards from the sidelines, and *WHAM*, he threw a block that sent all three of them flying into the Eagles' bench.

"Poor Lipski was knocked out for the third time, a record that should stand until another Nagurski comes along, if one ever does."

When some of these old-timers became coaches, they evaluated their talent in an elemental way. They set their linemen on each other, one-on-one. The guy who survived was the first stringer. The Giants' old coach Steve Owen was saved from the Oklahoma dust bowl by football and he never forgot it. He lived by two mottos: "Football is a game played down in the dirt and always will be" and "Football was invented by a mean son of a bitch, and that's the way the game's supposed to be played."

In 1924, Steve tried out for the Kansas City Cowboys in old Blues Park, along with a character named Milt Rhenquist of Bethany, Kan.

"The Swede was dressed in overalls and work shoes," Owen wrote in *My Kind of Football*. "He weighed about 240 and had heavily calloused hands. The Swede in scrimmage battered one-half of our regular line. He wasn't scientific, just effective."

They used to say that the Steelers' Ernie Stautner, who played defensive tackle at 230 pounds, could have been transported 40 years back into time, pound by pound, and he would have fit right in with the leather-helmet boys. Ernie knew one move, the straight all-out shot, dead on his man, with every sinew and nerve dedicated to that one killing charge.

Once in camp a rookie lineman challenged him to a fight, so Ernie, a trifle mystified, but no less vicious, beat hell out of the youngster.

"Some damn fool college coach told that kid," Ernie said, "that the best way to make a pro team was to lick the toughest veteran they had. He got some bad information there."

The ruffians of football came in all packages, from the wildly flamboyant Eisenhauer to the cold, tight-lipped Dan Birdwell, ex-defensive tackle of the Oakland Raiders.

"I've got bruises all over my body from bumping into Dan around the kitchen," his wife, Diane, said. "Or taking a gouge from him while he's asleep. He won't even play with our three children for fear of injuring them."

The toughest running back in those old AFL days was Buffalo's 250-pound Cookie Gilchrist.

"The oddest thing about him," said Jet linebacker Larry

Grantham, who'd been his teammate in the AFL All-Star game, "was that he would strip and shower at halftime."

"How did he get his pads back on in time for the second half?" someone asked Grantham.

"Pads? Cookie didn't need pads. Just a helmet and enough bennies to fill the palm of one hand."

Collectively the biggest group of flakes ever piled into one roster belonged to the Oakland Raiders. In their old AFL days they had some mean dudes but they weren't the real bullyboys of the league. That honor belonged to Kansas City, with a lineup of towering monsters who liked to grind people into the dust. The Raiders had their share of roughnecks, though—Ben Davidson, Birdwell and Ike Lassiter along the defensive line; and at fullback, Hewritt Dixon, Hughie the Freight, whose running style was to bludgeon prospective tacklers with a forearm. In 1971 they drafted a safetyman from Ohio State, Jack Tatum, reputed to be the hardest hitter in college football, and teamed him with George Atkinson, who'd been converted from a fairly mild-mannered cornerback into a vicious little strong safety.

Raider history is a dark tableau of violence—Davidson breaking Joe Namath's cheekbone with a roundhouse right that began somewhere between Hayward and Alameda, Atkinson clubbing Lynn Swann unconscious with a blow to the back of the head, the collision between Tatum and Darryl Stingley that left Stingley paralyzed for life, an incident underscored by the fact that Tatum showed absolutely no remorse thereafter.

"They're not really bad fellas," Kansas City coach Paul Wiggin said. "They're just trained to kill."

When they made it to the '77 Super Bowl, though, and came under scrutiny of the press, another element surfaced. Mixed in with the hard guys were some genuine eccentrics, some characters Damon Runyan would be proud of . . . Blinky and Tooz and Matzoh Ball and the Commissioner and the Scientist and Kick 'em in the Head Ted.

The Scientist was George Buehler, the 270-pound right guard. His specialty was electronic gadgetry. He had a little remote-controlled tank that would pick up his mail for him in camp. One day in practice he was flying his remote-controlled model plane around the field and it crashed into the goal post.

"I lost radio contact," he explained.

Training camp was in Santa Rosa, the only camp that players actually enjoyed going to. John Madden ran a loose ship. One day 16 of them walked off in the middle of practice. They had a golf tournament to go to. Another afternoon a rookie spotted all the defensive backs heading for the sidelines.

"Where are you going?" he asked.

"On our field trip," one of them said, and they walked through the gate and lay down in an adjoining field.

Blinky was flanker Fred Biletnikoff. On the road he roomed with Pete Banaszak, a halfback.

"Before every game," Banaszak said, "Blinky'd say he had to visit his friend Earl in the bathroom. Earl was the sound of Freddy throwing up."

Once, during a game, the referee called time out and walked Henry Lawrence, the offensive tackle, off the field.

"Why'd you do that?" Madden asked.

"Because he's goofy," the ref said.

"I know that," Madden said. "So what?"

One year the Raiders drafted a 6'9" defensive end named Charlie Philyaw because he'd looked good in the Senior Bowl practices. I remember interviewing Charlie in Mobile before that game.

"I'm glad they picked me to play here," he said. "I've never played in this game before."

Sometimes in camp Charlie would drift into the wrong meeting room. Once he sat in the offensive room for 15 minutes before someone told him he was in the wrong place. Meanwhile the defensive line coach, Tom Dahms, was carrying on quite well without him.

"Charlie's missing," someone told him.

"Good," said Dahms.

"All my life," said Pat Toomay, the defensive end who bounced around from Dallas to New England to Tampa Bay before Oakland picked him up, "I knew that somewhere in the league there must be a club like this. I just didn't know where it was."

The Raiders became a haven for outcasts. Having trouble? See Al Davis. They picked up Ted Hendricks from Green Bay in '75, Kick 'em in the Head Ted. He fit right in. One day in camp Madden called, "OK, everybody up," and Hendricks came charging onto the field on a horse, in full uniform, with a traffic cone for a lance. Once, on Halloween, he showed up with a hollowed-out pumpkin for a helmet. When everybody started lifting weights he made his own barbell, two empty drums attached to a bar, great mass but no weight. He called it the Hurricane Machine.

"How can you stand it?" Madden asked Hendricks's wife, Jane, one day.

"I'm into bird watching," she said.

Then the Raiders picked up John Matuszak, and that made the act complete. The 6'8" defensive end had been with three NFL teams and one in the WFL, briefly. A court order kept him out of the WFL after he jumped—and played in one game. At the hearing the Houston Oilers' lawyer, Bill Eckhardt, asked him if he could have signed with the Canadian League, rather than the Oilers, when he was drafted.

"No," Matuszak said.

"Why?"

"Because it's not my country. I love my country, as the land of the free and the home of the brave."

Before camp opened in '74, Tooz invited linebacker Steve Kiner to his apartment for dinner. Talk soon turned to the players' strike.

"I'm staying out," Matuszak said. "You're with us, aren't you?"

Kiner stopped between bites to answer, "No, I'm going to report."

With that Tooz reached across the table and picked up Kiner's plate. End of dinner.

He was violent and erratic and subject to abrupt mood switches. The only one who could control him was his wife, Yvette, who was as tightly wired as he was. When he joined the Chiefs in '74 Tooz snuck Yvette into the dorm at training camp. That was their honeymoon.

"You'd go down to the bathroom in the morning," Rudnay said, "and there were three commodes. In the outer two you'd see football players' feet, big, flat calloused feet. In the middle one there would be this pair of little, dainty feet in sandals. And outside the door Toozie would be standing guard.

"One night Toozie and I were walking back from the dining hall and he said, 'Better be careful. Yvette's on the warpath tonight.' No sooner has he said it but this car comes roaring up, with the headlights blinding us. Toozie yells, 'Run for it!' and we take off across a field, and she pulls off the road, and she's bearing down on us, and he says, 'This way . . . the cemetery.' So we make it to the cemetery, and she's madder than hell because she can't follow us, through all the tombstones, and she leans out the window and yells at him, 'You big pussy!' and he's laughing like hell and giving her the finger, and she's giving him the finger back. . . ."

"The last time I saw Yvette," Jane Hendricks says, "she was going down Union Street in San Francisco on roller skates, in a miniskirt, waving to all the people she passed."

In '76 the George Allen Redskins picked up Matuszak and then cut him in camp. It was unusual for George to cut a veteran defensive lineman. The writers asked him why. "Vodka and Valium," he said. "The breakfast of champions."

So the Raiders picked him up. Before they did Al Davis asked Hendricks if it was worth the gamble.

"Al," Hendricks said, "what difference will one more make?"

Since then the Raiders have added new ones, of course. In 1980 they drafted a 255-pound tackle named Matt Millen and made him an inside linebacker. When Millen was in high school he was troubled by calcium deposits in his right elbow that bent his arm into an **L** shape. He and his buddy went down to the metal shop and put his elbow in a vice and tried to straighten it.

"Ed grabbed my shoulder and pulled," Millen says. "It was straight out of the Three Stooges . . . Drs. Fine and Howard. But it only traumatized my elbow worse."

In '82 they traded for Lyle Alzado, the flamboyant defensive end who once spent a summer working as a garbage collector in Long Island.

"What was your major in college?" a writer asked him at a pre–Super Bowl press conference when he was with the Broncos.

"Garbiology," Alzado said. "I was a garbiologist."

"Oh, you worked out of the science building," the guy said.

"Yeah," said Alzado. "Inwood Sanitation."

Writers once asked him about his school song. He'd gone to Yankton College in South Dakota. What did he do, for instance, when he was a rookie with the Broncos and they made him stand up in the dining hall and sing the Yankton song? Once, when track man John Carlos was a rookie with the Eagles, they got him up to sing his school song, and he sang "Jingle Bells." A few veterans said that's when he first got in bad with the club—for not showing proper spirit. How about Alzado?

"I'll give you 10 bucks if you can sing one line of the Yankton song, if anyone can," he said. "Listen to this:

Hail Yankton College,
Center of the continent and yoooooon-i-verse,
We're the Black and the Gold, fight! fight! fight!
Fight for the Black and Gold. . . .

"Pretty good, huh? I made it up myself, but the guys in the dining room didn't know that. They'd listen for a while, and then they'd throw rolls and tell me to sit down."

When the Raiders met the Cowboys in their 1983 big midseason battle, everyone saw it as a clear clash of ideologies.

"I like our image much better than the Dallas Cowboys' image," Millen said, "because ours is much more appealing to the general public—especially the degenerates."

"It's really a fork in the road," the Cowboys' Drew Pearson said. "You go one way or the other way. There's absolutely no middle ground between these two teams."

Oh, the Cowboys have had their share of flakes through the years. There was Larry Cole and the Zero Club, a group devoted to total inactivity of mind and body. Once, when the Cowboys were playing in St. Louis, Cole's teammates and fellow Zero Club members, Toomay and guard Blaine Nye, decided to drag him down to Harold's Tattoo Parlor and get him tattooed with a plow inscribed with the motto "Born to Raise Wheat," a tribute to his home town of Granite Falls, Minn. The only problem was they couldn't get him out of the bathroom, where he'd fallen asleep. And of course there was Pete Gent, the free-agent wide receiver who wound up writing novels, such as *North Dallas Forty*. Gent enjoyed tweaking Tom Landry.

On one return flight from a game Landry came over to Gent on the plane and said, "Pete, Bob Hayes is hurt; you'll be moving to the other side next week. So be ready."

"You mean," Gent said, "that I'm going to play for Philadelphia?"

Defensive players always have seemed the flakiest. Alex Karras parlayed an NFL career devoted to concerted zaniness into a lucrative acting profession. The story I enjoy hearing him tell the most is the one about his participation in the 1957 Balkan Games in Athens.

"It was open to anyone of Greek or Slavic ancestry, so I signed up and got a free trip out of it," Karras said. "I told them I threw the shot and discus, even though I never tried it in my life. On the boat going over, our coach told me there was no place to throw, but I could practice my form.

"He watched me and then he said, 'Your style is pretty unorthodox. What kind do you use?' I told him, 'Step-over.' I finished last in the shot put with a 32-footer."

Kickers have always been a fine collector's item for flake hunters. One year Garo Yepremian, the little bald-headed kicker, turned down a $10,000 hair transplant offer. "There are already too many Elvis Presley lookalikes," he said.

A writer once asked him where he'd gone to college.

"Bald State," said his New Orleans teammate Barry Bennett.

Once, in Buffalo, Booth Lusteg blew a late field goal that cost the Bills the game. Two fans waited for him in the parking lot and assaulted him. Later the police asked him if he wanted to file a complaint.

"No," Lusteg said. "I deserved it."

Dallas writers were very saddened when Danny Villanueva, the Cowboys' Mexican-American kicker, left after the 1967 season. When he first came to the Cowboys in 1965, he took the regular team psychological exam, and the psychologist reported to club officials that he shouldn't be called Taco, the nickname the Rams had given him. "It saps his confidence," the psychologist explained.

"How about calling him Toro?" said a sportswriter.

"Great," said the psychologist.

Then Villanueva walked over to meet the press.

"Call me Taco," he said.

In 1966 he ran a fake punt 23 yards against the Cards, which started people speculating that perhaps he had been a halfback in college.

"I was a Mexican then, too," said Danny.

When George Blanda set the NFL kicking record, his younger brother, Paul, couldn't understand what all the excitement was about.

"I don't know why everybody's fussing over the records George set," he said. "I've had five fathers-in-law."

Sometimes the coach sets the tone. The old Colts were an incongruous bunch, but as long as they kept winning, Weeb Ewbank let them go their own way. The country boys used to like to play tricks on their Irish tackle from the Bronx, Artie Donovan. One night at training camp some of them found a dead groundhog, skinned it and buried it under his bed sheets.

"You hillbillies ought to have your mind on football," Artie said when he found it. "Just look at that poor dead fish."

And there was the time the late Gene "Big Daddy" Lipscomb, the Colts' other All-Pro tackle, made his off-season wrestling debut. He scored a pin with his secret hold, a "hammer slam." What, his teammates wanted to know later, was a hammer slam?

"Just squeezin', I guess," said Big Daddy.

"One year Jim Parker had a job selling cemetery lots," Ewbank says. "He kept pestering Big Daddy about them, and finally Big Daddy couldn't stand it any more.

" 'OK,' he said, 'gimme two in the shade.' "

"Old players just seemed to look different," Donovan says. "The Bears especially. Like John Kreamcheck, their defensive tackle. He had hair coming out of his nose, wild, bushy hair coming down over his face, he always needed a shave. Once when we came into Wrigley Field we saw him outside the stadium warming his hands over a garbage can. Weeb said, 'Why, he doesn't look like anything more than a damn derelict. I don't think he looks tough at all.' George Preas, our left guard, said, 'Oh yeah, then you go and play against him.' "

Coaches. The late Norm Van Brocklin once was asked in a magazine interview, "What's your favorite play?"

Our Town," he said, "by Thornton Wilder."

There have been mean players through the years, of course, ferocious hitters. Along with Tatum I'd rate Hardy Brown, a sandy-haired 196-pound linebacker, as the hardest hitter I've ever seen. He had no outstanding attributes as a player except for a knack of popping his right shoulder with killing force and velocity.

"When he hit a guy," said 49er teammate Ed Henke, "it sounded like a rifle going off in the stadium. He missed a lot of tackles, but he just killed 'em when he hit 'em. There were no face guards in those days, and Hardy had a shoulder block that could numb a gorilla. It was a skill nobody could duplicate."

"One year we played against him, when he was with Chicago in the old AAFC," Y. A. Tittle recalls. "We ran a play against him and one of our guys was lying on the ground. Then we ran another play and Hardy stretched another guy. So I called the Bootsie Play—everybody get Hardy Brown. When it was over there were two of our guys lying on the ground. There was a lot of grumbling in our next huddle.

" 'The hell with this,' one guy said. 'Let's go back to the old way. He was only picking us off one at a time then.' "

Sometimes it's just sheer animal instinct that drives them. Mike Curtis, the old Colts' linebacker, was nicknamed the Animal. Even the home fans booed him. Hendricks says he was once standing next to Curtis as they were coming onto the field in Buffalo's old War Memorial Stadium and "a hot dog came out of the stands and hit Mike right on the head, *bonk!* I mean I'd never seen that before. I learned not to stand next to him."

In a game against the Dolphins in Baltimore in 1971 a fan came on the field and grabbed the football as the Dolphins were about to run a play. He had come down from Rochester on a bus and he'd been drinking all the way. Before anyone knew what had happened Curtis was on the guy and had popped him with a forearm that sent him flying one way, the ball the other, and that completely unzipped his jacket.

"Did you see that, did you see those instincts?" Colt center Bill Curry said afterward. "Everybody else was just standing around but Mike reacted purely on instinct. I felt like telling that fan, 'That's what I have to face in practice every day.' "

I remember the week leading up to the 1980 Super Bowl. The Steelers were in a nasty mood. They'd been practicing on a soggy field. Their legs felt sore. One day after practice their middle linebacker, Jack Lambert, sat in the hotel bar, staring darkly into his beer. The teeny-boppers spotted him. They ran over to get his autograph.

"Are you into astrology, Jack?" one of them said.

"Yeah," he grunted.

"What's your sign?"

"Feces," he said.

CHAPTER TWENTY

We Never Lose a Game in the Press Box

A sportswriter looks up in the sky and then asks you: "Is the sun shining?"

—Sonny Liston

Goodbye reporters, so long cameramen. I'm going to miss you. In the past 14 months I've tripped over wires, been denied bathroom privileges in my house because you weren't through with the shots.

I drank three cups of sugared coffee or one black and cold that I poured for myself in the confusion.

You've been served pie or had the door slammed in your face, depending on my mood shifts during this time of frustration.

You're mad or hurt because you came at the wrong time.

You're nice enough guys. There have been Jacks, Jims, Jeffs, Johns, Joes and Steves and frankly, I'm getting so run down, you all look alike.

I can't remember if you were here before or if you're new from Canada.

I realize you're just trying to do your jobs, but I do have a breaking point. I'm only human.

Some of you, I'll cherish the memory of our brief encounter for a lifetime. Others I'll try to forget as quickly as possible.

Bye now. I'll miss you—like a cold.

—Dorothy Hall, mother of freed American hostage in Iran Joseph Hall, letter to the press, January 23, 1981.

347

It took a newspaper strike, a long one, to convince me that I really liked my job as a sportswriter.

The first clue came during one of those depressing interviews that was supposed to land me a job until the strike was settled.

"Well, you report in at nine and you leave at five," the guy said, and I got my hat. Nine to five? I'd forgotten that kind of world existed. My time schedule was measured by the pro football schedule—kickoff was 1:00 P.M. Sunday, press luncheons at 12 noon on Monday and 11:30 A.M. on Wednesday. In between, I was on the phone; I made the practices in the afternoon; I talked to people; I hustled up stories. The sheer volume of work was greater than the average 40-hour week, but no one told me that my day started when I came into the office at nine and ended when I left at five.

I used to laugh at the guys who said, "What a racket you sportswriters have. All you do is get paid to watch games." I laughed because it was the thing to do, and what did they know about all the slammed doors and "no comment" statements and people who yelled that you misquoted them, to save their own necks?

But I had been jolted by that nine-to-fiver. I really did like being a sportswriter. In fact I liked it better than almost anything I could think of, except maybe being a movie star or a restaurant reviewer for the *Michelin Guide*.

I was a beat writer in those days. I didn't like TV or radio guys, with their hand-held mikes and idiot questions. I didn't like the magazine writers and the free-lancers. We were the foot soldiers, the infantry. The magazine writers were the guerrilla fighters, the hit-and-run guys who could come in, do a quick hatchet job and never return, leaving a group of very angry ball players, or perhaps just one, who would vow, "Never again will I trust those newspaper bastards." So we were left to clean up the wreckage and try to smooth things over.

Well, I still don't like the radio and TV guys with the hand-held mikes. But the magazine writers? Well, I'm one of them now. Except that pro football is my beat. I don't cover anything else, so I don't really class myself as one of those guerrilla fighters I hated in the old days. Other people aren't so sure.

In August 1979, when I had been with *Sports Illustrated* for less than two days, I was sent out to L.A. to do a piece on the Rams. I was standing around with a few of the writers at practice, chit-chatting, and one of them said, "Well, the thing you magazine writers don't understand. . . ."

I looked at the guy. He was about 23 but he looked 19. I felt like telling him, "Hey wait a minute; I was a newspaper man for 20 years and a magazine writer for less than 48 hours," but what the hell. I probably would have felt the same way if I were him.

It's different now. The stories are longer. You put more air in them. When you're doing a feature you spend a week with a guy instead of an hour. You find out his favorite flower. In the off-season they'll give you a month to do an investigative piece that my old paper, the *New York Post*, would have expected me to have done in two days.

The mechanics are different, too. I used to get gray hair watching Western Union telegraphers mangle my copy when they retyped it for transmission, substituting "played like hell" for "played very well," or "388 yards rushing" for "88." Now I feed my typed copy into a telecopier, and an exact reproduction is received in the office six minutes later. Even that is an anachronism. People now use VDTs, video display terminals, computerlike things with screens that transmit instantly. I don't understand them. They scare me. I've seen them eat up whole stories, and never give anything back. I don't like the idea of typing into a computer. I like to see a piece of paper in front of me and hear the click of the typewriter. People laugh at me. They call me a relic. I don't care.

Some things haven't changed—for instance, the way I work a game. Every reporter has his own method of watching a game and scoring it. Most of them use a longhand system that duplicates the mimeographed play-by-play sheets that are handed out in the press box after every quarter. Some of them use a chart book filled with sheets that represent the field and the yard markers. That's always been my system. You use different colored pencils for the two teams, and you detail their progress up and down the field, using symbols for different types of plays; e.g., straight line for a run, wiggly line for a pass, dotted line for a kick, snapped pencil and perhaps a drop of blood for a play you miss, etc. I also include the numbers of players who figure in the play, good blocks on the line, good defensive plays, giving the force equal weight to the tackle.

By the second half, the morning-paper writers with early deadlines are usually deep in their typewriters or VDTs, sending "running" accounts of the game. Some of them can only glance up to catch a play here or there, so every long pass or dramatic run is followed by a chorus of "What happened?" in the press box.

In addition to my play-by-play I keep two other charts. One is a running statistical breakdown, up-to-date yardage figures for each player involved. I do this because I trust very few of the official statisticians—there are usually one or two mistakes per game—and I like to have before me each player's progress report. The third chart is one of my own invention. It lists each team's five eligible pass receivers on offense and seven possible pass defenders on defense, and each time a pass is thrown I make the appropriate notation in the offensive and defensive player or players' columns. I never knew this kind of chart had a name until one day in 1968 Clive Rush, the Jets' offensive coordinator, happened to glance at it and said, "Oh, you keep a field chart." So I guess it's called a field chart.

With about three or four minutes to go, whether the game is a runaway or a cliff-hanger, there's usually an exodus from the press box, as the writers start heading for the dressing room. This is a part of the job I hate, because I like to watch the game until the very end. It's not always possible. In a stadium with a direct elevator from the press box to the locker room, you can wait until the final whistle and then race out like a madman, knock over a few fans, hop the elevator, and arrive at the locker before the door is opened. But in a place like the Sugar Bowl (1970 Super Bowl), with a system so archaic that a guide had to lead the press to the dressing rooms, you had to leave early or you were dead.

Late arrival outside the Kansas City dressing room, even though its door stayed locked for 15 minutes after the game, meant that you would lose your chance for a ringside seat for the number one postgame story—Len Dawson. You wouldn't be anywhere near his phone conversation with the president; you wouldn't be able to fit in the trainer's room where Dawson answered questions for a dozen or so writers—while 60 or so milled around outside. Through judicious trading of quotes after the game, you might have come up with the same basic quotes as anyone else, but you would have had that left-out feeling, which unhinges so many of us.

Well do I remember that trainer's room in the '70 Super Bowl. Pete Brewster, the Chiefs' end coach, sat on a chair near the door, his long legs sprawled halfway across the room, snarling at the writers who tripped over him.

"Who's Dawson talking to?" a writer asked from outside.

"President Hoover," I said, trying to inject a tired note of humor into a grim situation.

"Not Hoover, dummy!" Brewster said. "Nixon!"

Oh, uh, right, Pete.

The Super Bowl is handled more institutionally now. With eight minutes to go, whether the game is a tight one or a blowout, you're led to a mass interview area near one of the dressing rooms. Unless you're in a stadium with a convenient getaway route, such as the Rose Bowl, you've got to head downstairs with the mob or you'll be trapped in the press box like a pea in a pod. The press elevator can only handle a few people; the aisles of the stands are jammed after a game. So I always root for a game that won't be close at the end. If it is close I hang in until the end and then hope that I won't miss too much of the early stuff downstairs.

The whole hype surrounding Super Bowl week . . . "the international quote-lifting championships" is what former fullback Mike Adamle calls it . . . is a study in mass hysteria, a look at the press at its very worst. The reason is that it's orchestrated not by the beat guys, the regular pro football writers, but by the desk, the editors back home, the men who have less of a feel for the pulse of the readers than the reporters on assignment have. More . . . give them more . . . more analyses, features, statistical breakdowns, predictions from any political or show biz figures who are reachable by telephone. Keep the hype going, because, God forbid, if you don't, the rival paper in town might print more inches of copy one day. The result is great masses of type, great walls of verbiage that are practically unreadable. And while the reporters on the scene shake their heads at the overkill, the desk calls for more every year, so for each Super Bowl the hype starts earlier.

I often wonder how the readers really feel about this. Can they actually wade through two weeks of Super Bowl stuff? I wish someone would do a readership survey and perhaps take a bold step and cut back a little. Feature angles that were alive in September and October are revived. The paper on Sunday a week before the game, with its great analytical pieces, looks very much like the stuff you read on Super Bowl Sunday itself. In between you seldom have much hard news . . . stories about when the wives will come down, and if they're staying with the players or not, or when curfew will be imposed, etc., are very big during Super Bowl week. You get acquainted with every Super Bowl cliché of past years, the favorite one being "Nobody expected us to be here," which is written about any team that wasn't a preseason Super Bowl choice. (A dozen teams that didn't make the playoffs in the previous year have reached the Super Bowl; you'd think the angle would be exhausted by now.) You get the most outlandish reaches. My favorite was a story UPI did before Super Bowl IV, the first one in New Orleans. They sent Milt Richman out to a nearby leper colony to get the lepers' angle on the Super Bowl. Joe Carnicelli of the UPI went along to keep him company.

"I don't know what they wanted me for," he said. "Maybe to carry the bell."

A favorite question of idiot-interviewers, usually the guys with the tape recorders and hand-held mikes, is "What do you think of us? What do you think of the media, all the attention?" This seldom gets aired or printed, but some guys simply love to ask it, year after year.

"What do you think of us?"

"We think you're ridiculous."

"Yes, but aside from that, how do you view the media."

"You're a pain in the ass."

"Yes, but really, you like all this, don't you."

"No, we don't."

And on and on.

Picture day, 1982: The 49ers' Randy Cross is asked, "What question has been asked the most?"

"This one," he says.

Picture day, 1984: The Raiders' Ted Hendricks is asked, "What question that's asked the most do you dislike the most?"

"That one there," he says.

"The same questions, over and over again," the Raiders' Lester Hayes said last Super Bowl. "You'd think they'd figure out some new ones. I try to give 'em what they want. I give 'em crazy stuff, nonsense, anything that comes into my head. They look at me with their serious faces and say, 'Uh-huh, uh-huh,' and write it all down."

Last year L.A.'s Howie Long, surrounded by a numbing crush of interviewers in the special tent set up at the Raiders' hotel, drew a deep breath and rolled his eyes heavenward.

"Give me a day to die," he said. "Are we in Kansas yet, Toto? I don't know where I am . . . Oh God, I'm in a tent. . . ."

Of course the game can never match the hype. Nothing could. "The writers spend two weeks building the game up and the next four weeks tearing it down," said NBC's Bob Griese, the Dolphins' quarterback in three Super Bowls.

I've always wondered about the media's fascination with itself, about the way they dwell on a player's reaction to interviews. It's an artificial situation at best, and it's got little to do with the person himself, either on or off the field, but it permeates everything. In one issue of the *Denver Post* (Friday, July 15, 1983) I saw the following.

From Buddy Martin's column about John Elway in camp: "John Elway isn't an easy interview. He's been around writers so much that he knows how to tender the 'safe' answers, and yet he never ducks controversy or evades the issue. He purposely keeps his answers short," etc., etc.

And this, the lead sentence of a piece on the USFL Michigan Panthers' Anthony Carter: "What was once a lighthearted conversation between reporters and Anthony Carter has become strained and uneasy. His eyes give it away. They stare down at the desk top, no longer seeking out each questioner during a reply. . . ."

At the end of his Elway piece, Buddy Martin wrote: "We have the media crush, then we have the media covering the media, saying there is media overkill. 'Why do we do this?' asked one writer. 'Why don't we just all agree to stop writing about John Elway?' "

I guess what disturbs me most about all this stuff is that while they're exhausting all these flimsy angles, much hard football reporting is forgotten. It's much easier to write the scene than to dig for a hard story. Writing the scene is the biggest cop-out in our business. It's easy, it gets you home in time for dinner. You write about what you see . . . the other writers, how a subject answers his questions, etc., and you're through for the day, leaving the tougher angles to the guys who want to work harder. Sometimes scene-setting is a necessity. If a player's head is drooping, and he's bleeding after a game, it has to be a part of the story. But not the whole story. What bothers me is that so few writers . . . in all sports, not just football . . . will take a crack at what many foreign journalists, particularly the English writers, do so well, and that is analyzing an event, giving you an idea of why things happened the way they did.

It seems to me that old-time writers were more apt to go this route. Maybe it's because they didn't cover the locker rooms much in those days, and quotes from anyone except the coach were a rarity, but you used to read some pretty good breakdowns. Sometimes they were way off the mark, too, but at least they gave it a shot.

Not that I'm a great apologist for football writing of the past. I think it's better today—much better—and the reason is the TV competition. Newspapers must provide insights that you don't get from TV coverage, in-depth interviews, good, solid personality pieces—yes, even exposés, especially in this drug-heavy era. Humor often comes from a good selection of quotes; in the old days the writers themselves were the humorists. But often their humor fell flat, too. And they didn't always work very hard. Even the famous names of the past, the Paul Gallicos and Grantland Rices, would get it up once or twice a week, and then, during the rest of the time, take a pass. You used to see whole stories devoted to the release of the weekly league stats; you'd see house pieces that were practically rewrites of releases. More writers were house men in those days, guys who were literally bought by the club they were covering. The Rams actually would hand the beat writers envelopes with cash for "per diem expenses" while covering the club on a trip. When the Professional Football Writers Association was formed in the 1960s one of the first complaints we had to deal with was from an L.A. beat writer who wanted us to get the club to raise the writers' per diem payments.

Owners or coaches such as Paul Brown or George Halas who were tight with the newspaper publishers and editors in town enjoyed a controlled press. If a beat writer started getting too uppity, he'd find himself mysteriously transferred off the club.

"I don't know how Paul Brown did it, but he sure managed to control the press in Cleveland," Weeb Ewbank once said when he was coaching the Jets. "I wish I could have that in New York, but it's impossible. The guys here are too interested in sensational stories."

"How would you like to be an editor and have a 'controlled' writer covering the club for the paper?" someone asked him. "Don't you think the readers deserve better than that?"

"It's just that in places like Cleveland, the newspapermen were more community-minded," he said. "They didn't want to do anything to hurt the club."

In the early days of the Oakland Raiders, Al Davis enjoyed almost complete immunity from embarrassing questions. He paid his locals back by laughing at them.

"We'll make a decision on McCloughan later this week," the

Raiders' coach, John Rauch, told a Bay Area press luncheon four days before Oakland played Kansas City in the '68 playoff.

"They're so dumb I've got to laugh," Davis said later that day. "Kent McCloughan was operated on for torn knee ligaments this morning."

No, I don't long for a return to the good old days of journalism; there are plenty of good tough football writers around nowadays, such as the *Boston Globe*'s Will McDonough and the *Buffalo News*'s Larry Felser. But I'd still like to see more stories analyzing the game itself, and leaving the hoop-te-do to the columnists. I'm still waiting, for instance, to read something that will tell me exactly how the American hockey team beat Russia in the 1980 Olympics. The event has been immortalized in print, every tear and every proud heartbeat has been duly registered, but I wish someone, somewhere, would have explained, technically, how we won the game.

Some coaches prefer to keep their writers in the dark, the theory being that the less they know the more secure the coach's job remains. When I first started covering the Jets Ewbank used to show us game films if we wanted to see them. I took it for granted at the time; I didn't realize what a bonanza this was. Very few of them will do it nowadays. Hey, we might get smart, even as smart as some coaches.

After the Jets lost to Oakland in the *Heidi* game in 1968, Weeb told us the game was one of the roughest and dirtiest he'd ever seen. We wanted to see for ourselves, so he let us look at the close-up films, and a whole new world opened up, a world of cheap shots and late hits and unparalleled viciousness . . . still vivid in my mind is the sight of the Raiders' Dan Birdwell putting a rush on Joe Namath and whipping a right-hand punch to his groin as he released the ball. We all wrote very colorful stories that afternoon—and the Jets got fined $3000 by the AFL for letting the writers know what was going on.

We are at a great disadvantage, not being allowed to see the films the coaches see. I wonder how many of them could come up with a coherent story about a game, based on only one look, as we have to. Often the players themselves, plus the coaches, don't know exactly what happened on a play until they've seen the films—for instance, whose responsibility a receiver was on a touchdown pass. You know the old joke . . . the coach gets married, and after his wedding night a buddy calls to ask him how it was. "I won't know," he said, "until I've seen the films." Hey, show those films to us, too. Give us access to the waiver wires. The league office itself likes to keep us in darkness. Often they'll announce a trade "for a draft choice," and we won't find out how high a pick it was until the actual draft day itself.

So players and coaches bitch about the dumb writers who don't really know what's going on out there, and yet the farthest thing from their minds is trying to educate those dumb writers. We might find out, for instance, that maybe the coach is playing a guy who has no business playing, who might be a personal favorite.

For some reason a familiar gripe seems to be "How can they write about a game when they never played it themselves?" You know the traditional answer—someone doesn't have to be able to sing soprano to be an opera critic. Playing experience might give you a little extra insight, but a careful observer who's been around the game long enough can describe it accurately to his readers. I will agree with the dumb-media theory, however, when it comes to most radio and TV guys.

They are the writers' worst enemies. Most of them have little knowledge about the sport—or anything, actually. You're in the middle of an interview, a plausible angle is being developed, and all of a sudden a guy will shove his mike under the player's nose and say, "Tell me about the game," after it's already been discussed in detail. The guy only needs one quickie quote, something . . . anything . . . to show he was there, a brief, five-second snapper. But it can kill an interview stone dead. They'll also leech off your questions, shove their mikes in and steal the quotes you're developing for your own story. Once, during an interview session with Vince Lombardi, someone reached over and shoved his mike under Lombardi's nose. The coach glared at him.

"You'd stick that thing in a coffin," he said.

To many of the players, though, we're all lumped together, the legitimate writers, the columnists, the one-shot radio guys. We're all Media to them, and sometimes, when the crush gets too bad, they'll shut us all off and simply refuse to talk to anybody. Redskins quarterback Sonny Jurgensen was always great at ducking writers after a game. During the cooling-off period before the locker room opened up, he'd dress and shower and duck out the back door, leaving an empty locker for the interviewers. He's a radio and TV analyst now, a familiar figure around the media lounge during Super Bowl week, buttering up the writers he once stiffed. Which brings to mind an old Frank Graham line: "They learn to say hello just when they should say good-bye." I remember a Jurgensen piece that Joe McGinniss once wrote for the *Saturday Evening Post* that showed a remarkable insensitivity to our business.

"Sonny Jurgensen does not like to talk about a game right after it has been played," wrote McGinniss, an ex-newspaperman. "He prefers to wait a day or so and sort things out in his mind. It is a sensible approach, and undoubtedly leads to more intelligent conversation, but sportswriters want quotes for their stories, and want them right away."

Yes we do. But when a quarterback throws a winning pass in the last two minutes, how do you explain to your readers, "Sorry, dear reader, but Mr. Jurgensen will not comment on that pass. He's busy sorting things out in his mind."

I was very surprised when John Riggins began a self-imposed ban of silence with the Washington writers in 1981. He had always been one of the most colorful talkers on the Jets, and there was universal mourning among the beat guys when he went to the Redskins.

"It surprised me, too," his brother, Billy, said. "John always used to say how much he enjoyed the give-and-take with the writers. He even thought he might be a sportswriter when he retired."

I asked Riggins about it after the Skins' first Super Bowl.

"I figured it this way," he said. "I'd caught heat in the papers, and if I was going to catch heat I wasn't going to throw any fuel on the fire. Sometimes when you're sitting in the locker room after a tough game, trying to organize your thoughts, you can be baited into saying something you don't want to say. Then it becomes like a fission thing. When the first atom explodes, the whole thing goes.

"You're going to say things that will cause trouble . . . but then again, the other side of it is that as a reader, those are the things I like to read."

Many times the athlete who has been burned by an unfair story will never get over his negative feelings toward the press in general, and no amount of positive feature pieces will undo the damage. When a team is going bad a natural hostility seems to exist between players and writers; you can feel it in the air. Questions that normally would be brushed off now become irritating or take on another meaning.

One of the toughest jobs in journalism is that of a beat writer on a perennial loser. I went through an awful lot of years like that with the Jets. The best you can hope for is an eventual change in fortunes. Your most sensible policy is to buckle up, write the truth without copping out and live with the fact that you're not going to be making any friends. Journalism shouldn't be a friendly occupation anyway. If you want to be loved, go into another business, but unfortunately many young writers can't handle the pressure of constantly being around a team that's morose and hostile.

So they make mistakes. One of the biggest mistakes is to become involved in the factional fights within a team, to ally yourself on one side or the other, to become "married" to a ball player and become a mouthpiece for everything that's bugging him, in return for which he'll be your pipeline and supply you with clubhouse gossip . . . always under the "unnamed player" label. Another mistake is to become a perennial whiner in print, a "fire the coach" redhot. If the coach doesn't get fired, if the team eventually straightens itself out, then the writer is stuck. He becomes a dark reminder of the time of troubles.

Ball players' evaluations of writers are mixed. Experience, plus intelligence, often plays a part. To some of them, writers hardly exist at all. A couple of seasons ago, Jet linebacker Stan Blinka, noticing the abundance of press in the locker room one day, said, "There are more nonpeople in here than people."

Some of them are appalled by writers' lack of compassion when they're interviewing key figures in a losing game. It bothers me, too, but newspaper writing is a deadline business and quotes must be gathered without delay. I've seen offensive guards or tackles stare at a writer in wonderment when asked to evaluate and break down an opposing team.

"Well," they'll say, "I can tell you about the guy I'll be playing against. . . ."

Once the Steelers' Jack Lambert had to explain to writers that he had actually made a mistake in a game. They didn't think it was possible.

"We don't get a chance to proofread what we do," he said.

Bengals punter Pat McInally keeps his sanity by constantly putting the writers on. Once he planted a story that he was going to buy an island for retired woodcarvers, "because they'd always been neglected artists." Only one writer bit on this one. He showed up at McInally's apartment with a tape recorder.

"I talked for an hour about woodcarvers," McInally said. "I didn't know what I was talking about. I guess in the 16th century they were very popular. This guy was eating it up."

All heroes are fair game these days. The exposé has become common. In *The Vineyard of Liberty*, James MacGregor Burns wrote, "Our heroes of years ago, say, Charles Lindbergh and Babe Ruth, were really accepted as heroes. There was no cynicism about it, no digging up the other side of their lives. Nowadays hero worship is followed by exposé. We can hardly wait for the exposé."

But Jim Bouton, author and former Yankee pitcher, says the negative, as well as the positive, should be written about.

"I think it's healthy," he says. "If you're going to be asked to buy their cereal and buy their clothes, it's fair to ask, 'Who is this guy?' "

It unhinges coaches, though. It goes under the label of "disruptive influences."

"Sometimes what writers write about a problem on something that's not a problem," says Notre Dame coach Gerry Faust, "could lead to it being a problem."

Once when the Cowboys played the Giants in Yankee Stadium there was a bomb scare in the press box. Reporters asked Tom Landry how he'd feel if all the writers had disappeared in a puff of smoke and flying typewriter parts.

"I suppose we'd have observed 30 seconds of silent prayer," Landry said. "Then we'd have continued to play—with enthusiasm."

I've always found San Francisco coach Bill Walsh very interesting to deal with, and extremely cooperative, and I assumed he enjoyed a cordial relationship with the Bay Area writers. But he once told me about the apprehension he experienced when he went into a regular press conference.

"You walk into the room," he said, "and you're staring at 20 good people and one criminal, a guy with a need to rip, to express himself. It's not personal animosity. You know he's in the room. You know he's plotting. So everything's addressed to him. You know he's gunning for you and working at trying to get you, but if I show it, then it seems that I'm paranoid. What I have to fight, like any coach, is: Don't let that interfere with your relations with the public, i.e., the press."

People on the outside often don't have the foggiest idea of our business. Players and coaches complain about the headlines, so you patiently have to explain to them that we don't write the headlines, or the picture captions either, just the stories. Lawyers are the dumbest when it comes to trying to understand our work . . . but they're never above trying to use us when it suits their purposes. Here's something I cut out and saved, an excerpt from the Brief in Opposition to Motion for Separate Trial of Equitable Claims in the Oakland Raiders' suit against the NFL. It was written by the lawyers for the Oakland-Alameda Coliseum, describing Al Davis' insistence on secrecy in his talks with the Coliseum and the Los Angeles architect: "Thus Davis avoided objective public scrutiny of the course of the discussions, and prevented the press, the league or the public from assessing the merit of Davis' manufactured claim of intransigence on the part of Oakland Stadium officials. . . ."

Sharp bunch of lawyers there. The press is always invited to sit in on all your talks, too, right?

At one time contract figures were guarded with utmost secrecy. Now any diligent writer can find out basic numbers through either the Players' Association or the agents. Agents love to gossip. They will spill all; they will make you their whores. All you have to do is protect them. Many of the major scoops these days come from agents who have cultivated certain writers. And the scoop is a newspaperman's bread and butter. It makes us all crazy. Many writers are measured by their superiors not on their depth of knowledge or their talent at writing a particularly tough story, but by how many stories they break, how many scoops they get, even if the story proves to be without foundation. It can lead to some wild things.

On the Tuesday before Super Bowl IV, when the story broke that Kansas City quarterback Len Dawson might be associated with a Detroit gambler, one of the first reporters to reach Dawson at the Chiefs' hotel, the Fontainbleu, was Ken Denlinger of the *Washington Post*. He wrote down Dawson's denial . . . "I have not been served with a subpoena . . . I am absolutely innocent of any wrongdoing . . ." and drove back to the main press room to call his story in to the desk. *Post* columnist Shirley Povich overheard the conversation, but he got the quotes slightly mixed up. He thought Dawson had dropped the word "absurd" into his denial. He mentioned it to someone, and his remark was overheard by Gene Ward, the columnist for the New York *Daily News*, sitting in the next seat. He thought it over for a while, took a deep pull on his pipe, tilted his chair back and called his desk to dictate the lead for his Wednesday column: " 'It's absurd,' Len Dawson told this writer in confidence last night. . . ."

Actually talking to athletes is a luxury unknown in some countries. No one gets to talk to the players in major European events, such as the World Cup soccer tournament. The press box itself is an invention of the 1920s.

In the old days, the writers were right down on field level. They couldn't watch the plays open up, but they could hear the curses and the hitting; they got a feel for the flavor of the contest. When the Giants played the first game in the Polo Grounds, on Oct. 11, 1925, the morning-paper writers got seats in the baseball press box, in the lower deck behind home and first base. But when the Chicago Bears brought the barnstorming Red Grange in at the end of the season, a press box was set up on the upper deck, at midfield, and that became the standard for future press boxes.

At one time writers could visit a locker room before the game—up till an hour before kickoff—but gradually that practice ended. The Jets were one of the last teams to discontinue it, and certainly none of the writers thought the locker room would be open before the 1969 Super Bowl game, but no questions were asked as they got off the team bus with the players and walked into the dressing room with them, the usual procedure for any game. They were treated to some memories that will always remain—Johnny Sample's strange, lonely ritual in the empty shower room as he "psyched" himself for the game; George Sauer lying on his back with his feet in the air, pretending he was a "frog upside down"; Don Maynard desperately trying to work the soreness out of his leg, right up until he had to go out onto the field.

We all thought it had been an oversight on the part of the club, letting us in like that, but Weeb Ewbank was one step ahead of the game.

"I didn't want the players to feel too much tension," he said afterward. "So I tried to make everything seem like just another road game, all the conditions. And that included having the writers around, as usual."

Weeb always was unique in his dealings with the writers. I never saw him close his locker room to the press, as so many coaches do now. His practices were always open, with the understanding that no strategic items would be written about. Even the opposing team's beat writers were welcome. Before a Houston game one Wednesday—offensive day—I saw him putting in a weird formation that split both running backs out wide, past the receivers. He actually used it in the game, on the first series, and got a touchdown out of it.

After practice I asked him, "Suppose I were a Houston writer and I asked you about that formation. What would you say?"

"I'd tell you," he said, " 'We're getting our defense ready for that crazy stuff the Oilers use.' "

Teams are getting tighter about writers in the locker rooms. The free-and-easy access of the past has given way to such stifling formalities as the Media Interview Room in places like Detroit and Baltimore. Supposedly you request a subject for an interview, and he shows up. Except that sometimes he doesn't. And if you want to do a piece on a group of players, such as the offensive line, it's impossible. They won't wait around. Some coaches, such as the Colts' Frank Kush and the Lions' Monte Clark, simply say, "That's our policy and that's the way it's going to be." Others lay it off on the players, i.e., "The players prefer it this way." So you remind them, "The players prefer not to have two-a-day practices in camp, too," but it falls on deaf ears. The presence of women reporters also offers a convenient excuse for closing the lockers, although some of the more enlightened teams have gotten around the problem simply by issuing minirobes for the players to wear.

In 1975, in a "Memorandum to Club Officials," Pete Rozelle set down a league policy for dealing with the news media that was to remain "standard operating procedure." Section 3 reads as follows: "Each member club will open its locker room at specified times to accredited members of the media during the practice week."

We've reminded the league office about that rule, and the answer is always the same: "We'll look into it." The real answer is: "What are you going to do about it?" And the only answer to that is to go to war, to withhold coverage until the league shapes up and enforces its own rule, but you could never get your editor or publisher to back you on that. So it remains a nasty situation . . . which bothers the league office absolutely zero.

"We amended that rule a couple of years ago," they'll tell you.

Every writer who has been around for a while learns to wade through much of the nonsense that is fed to him, whether under the guise of club releases, league releases or simply quotes from the coach, who often likes to use writers for his own purposes.

In 1966 I spent a week in Green Bay, doing Packer advances for a game against the Bears. On Tuesday I was granted an audience with Lombardi. We chatted about New York for a while, and mutual acquaintances. Finally he said, "You're from New York, so I'm going to give you a good story. This is the week I find out about my million-dollar rookies, Jim Grabowski and Donny Anderson. I've got to find out if they can play."

I couldn't wait to get to the phone. My heart was thumping . . . a young writer on the track of a major scoop . . . as I called my paper and told them to hold the back page, I've got a scoop from Lombardi. And sure enough, Wednesday's *New York Post* led the sports section with "Lombardi to Unveil Million Dollar Rookies."

P.S. Neither Grabowski nor Anderson played a down in the game, but the wire services had picked up the story and spread it around. It's what is known as the education of a young writer.

PR departments still don't understand how a team lines up on the field. For years their releases, and subsequent program lineups, would designate the safety positions, for instance, as LS and RS—left and right—when any fan could tell them the true description was strong and weak, and had been for some time. They still don't recognize the difference between strong and weak inside linebacker, preferring the old, comfortable L and R designations. Some coaches clearly differentiate wide receivers as flanker and split end, and runners as fullback and halfback, but you'll never see this indicated in a starting lineup. They're all just WRs or RBs. The '82 Dolphins' PR staff reversed the positions of their ends, Kim Bokamper and Doug Betters, all year. When the Dolphins made the Super Bowl the club printed a statistical review . . . 300-yard passing games, 30 best rushing performances, etc. . . . except the PR staff was too lazy to bring it up to date and include '82 figures. The Redskins, not to be outdone, issued a weekly fictitious lineup, right up through the Super Bowl, that had John Riggins and Joe Washington starting in the same backfield—an alignment that never took place. The Redskins used a one-back offense. When I would ask Joe Blair, the PR man, why he didn't correct it, he would say, "It would confuse the fans" . . . or "The league tells us to do it that way." Does anyone really care about all of this? Well, yes, I care. Why not be accurate?

There are some things I read in normal football coverage that make me a little nauseous, such as the cutesy reference to a bawdy expression, with the operative word replaced, e.g., "horsefeathers" for, well . . . you know . . . and "Going from the Penthouse to the Outhouse" and "You can't make chicken salad out of chicken feathers." Some clichés you read without pause are downright silly when you think about them, such as "the finest pure passer" (impure passer?) or "raw speed" (cooked speed?). But if I had to award a prize for the single piece of writing that caused me to have the most seri-problems digesting my dinner it would be this one, a Washington Redskins release dated January 26, 1983, four days before their Super Bowl game against Miami. The writer is anonymous, but it bears the unmistakable style of Jack Kent Cooke:

> Call them the Nation's team or call them the pride of Wash-ington, but call them. For the Washington Redskins staff is an-swering their Westin South Coast Plaza office phones this week with a response only they may give: "NFC Champion Red-skins!—May I help you?"
>
> Unique. Personable. And cheery. And why not? It's Super Bowl Week! The Redskin spirit does not stop in California. It transcends the entire Nation. Back in Virginia, at a place called Redskin Park, they are preparing a tape for incoming phone calls when everyone is departed for Pasadena. It reads:
>
> "The office is closed. Sorry we're gone. We're off to see the Wizard, the wonderful Wizard of Super Bowl. We'll be back Tuesday. Call us then—will you?"
>
> And now that the telephone rings have been tended to, the Redskins can turn their full attention to picking up some equally important rings—Super Bowl rings.

And you wonder why some writers end up with a drinking prob-lem.

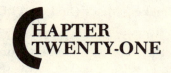

CHAPTER TWENTY-ONE

The Lost World: Football's Minor Leagues

God, I don't want to go back down there again. They tear your shoes off down there.

—Jimmy (The King) Corcoran, July 30, 1968,
two days before he was cut by the New York Jets

BENEATH the magic and glamour and hard-rock solvency of professional football lies a hidden world, a kaleidoscopic network of shifting franchises and unfulfilled promises that the ordinary fan knows nothing about. If you live in a big city with an NFL or USFL franchise, you may be dimly aware of the existence of this substratum that is loosely termed the minor leagues of football. If you come from a smaller community, you might have a more intimate picture.

At the top of this world there are leagues like the Atlantic Coast Football League and the Texas League, populated by the NFL's near-misses, players who were just a step too slow or a little too small, or too disorganized, to make it in the big time. Working your way down, you come to the regional leagues, representing fair-sized communities that don't mind supporting some local favorites—for a while.

And working your way down from there you come to the fly-by-nights, the lost and the hopeless, with an ever-shifting cast of players and owners and general managers and coaches. It is this world that I know more intimately.

There is a drawer in my desk marked "Important Documents," and somewhere in the middle of the confusion are two pieces of paper that I prize above all others. One is a letter that bears the heading "Greater Morristown Sports Association, Inc; Also Known as

MORRISTOWN COLONIALS." And the other is a check for $2.50, made out to me by the Paterson Pioneers, Inc.

The letter is signed by Charles W. Frost, secretary of the Morristown Colonials, and it goes like this:

> We have finally concluded arrangements with the Equitable Life Assurance Society in which it has been determined that only a very small percent of our players were covered for loss of income during the last season. With this no coverage decision, we, the Association, are entitled to rebates of those premiums unused.
>
> For some reason the company made a check out to your order. Rather than request them to reissue the drafts we thought the endorsement of the check to the Association would be the quicker approach.
>
> Please sign the enclosed draft on the back where provided and return to us. We naturally are planning on these funds to help liquidate some of the Association obligations.
>
> Your cooperation would be appreciated.
>
> Very truly yours

I keep it as a sort of microcosm of minor league football's lower depths. We were supposed to cover all our players by insurance, Mr. Frost was telling me, but we didn't. But the insurance company sent you some money by mistake ($25), since you weren't covered, and could you please let us have that money back, so we can bail out quicker?

I wonder what Pete Rozelle's lawyers would say about that one.

The Colonials represented my last fling at semipro football. (No minor league ever uses that term. From biggest to littlest, they call themselves "professional football.") When I was 35 I played a few games for the Colonials, just for kicks. Like most teams in this kind of world, the club began with high hopes and lofty aspirations that "the Colonials will create better business opportunities for all of you throughout the Morris County and Northern New Jersey area."

And of course the club went broke after one season, and there was the usual round of frantic phone calls in December. . . . "Could you please get the equipment back to us as soon as possible? We're trying to get what we can for it." Until I felt an ominous twinge in my right knee on one kickoff play, and clearly read the message that I was too old for this kind of nonsense, playing for the Colonials was a lot of fun.

The check for $2.50 from the Paterson Pioneers represented the sum total of payment for my services as offensive guard for the Paterson, N.J., representative in the Eastern Football Conference in 1960.

The Pioneers were the brainchild of a couple of local dreamers who persuaded a young Leonia, N.J., realtor to sink his money into the venture. Bob DeMarco, a northern New Jersey hero who was on his way up to the St. Louis Cardinals, was a regular figure at those early practices, which were supervised by Russ Carroccio, the old middle guard for the Giants. The whole operation was notarized; we signed legally acceptable player contracts, and everyone felt sure he was on his way to the NFL (there were vague hints about a mysterious tie-in with an "unnamed NFL club").

The fans turned out to see us in our league opener in Paterson's Hinchcliffe Stadium. We lost, 8–6, to the Union County All-Stars in a dull, miserable game, and the fans of Paterson had seen enough. They didn't come out anymore.

We had some fair ball players and some poor ones and some local hotshots such as Bob (Tootie) Harrell and Ralph Vigorito, whose son, Tommy, now plays for the Miami Dolphins. Ralph and Tootie, our halfbacks, were supposed to draw the fans into the stadium every Saturday night. We had one or two men like Dick Dalatri, our 240-pound center and defensive tackle, who were clearly better than the competition. Dick was one of the few players who actually did move up—four years as a starter with the Montreal Alouettes in the Canadian Football League.

After our third game no one had seen a dime in wages and half the team was ready to pack it in. The owners made an impassioned plea one night after practice . . . "Stick with us a little while longer." We had a team meeting and Dalatri, our captain and player rep, stood up on a bench and said, "What do you say? Let's give these guys a break."

That was enough. No one quit, although I did have a private session with the paymaster and asked him at least to reimburse me for the toll money I was spending crossing the George Washington Bridge from New York for practice two nights a week (my contract called for $25 a game). He wrote out a check for $2.50 on the spot, and even signed it.

We lost a couple more games, and by now it was obvious that only a miracle would get us any of our money. But we had a good little drinking group and no one wanted to break it up. There was Red Mosca, the 235-pound quarterback, and Big Artie Ackerman, who worked as a skip chaser for a loan company in Newark, and Dalatri, and 260-pound George Parozzo, the horse player, who had once been named AP Lineman of the Week for William & Mary, and a 270-pound tackle named Doug Hinton who had been the county half-mile champ but had eaten his way out of a track suit and into a football uniform. Doug used to show up at practice in a little kid's beanie hat.

After the workouts we'd get our beers in Benny's Bar in Paterson, a little place overlooking a softball diamond. Someone would always pick up the tab for us. In Paterson we were big men.

"So what if we go broke," Dalatri used to say. "We're having a helluva time, aren't we?"

One night one of us staggered over to the phone and called up our fullback, Reggie Powe. "This is Paul Pioneer, the owner of the Pioneers," he was told. "Just wanted to tell you that you're cut from the team." Reggie stayed away from practice for two nights until the coach personally drove by his house to find out what was wrong.

We played a game in Swedesboro, N.J., and four of us nearly missed it because we had fallen asleep at the beach that afternoon in Atlantic City, about 60 miles down the Black Horse Pike. We spent the first half sobering up, and even Sam Stellatella, our left linebacker (who had once kicked the extra point that won the Liberty Bowl game for Penn State over Alabama), was too groggy to play his usual game on the bench—checking the stands for the girl friends of the offensive players. When the offensive guy was in the game and Sam was out, he would make his play for the girl.

After our sixth loss, the owners got the clever idea of saving money by cutting the high-salary boys, the $50-a-game players, even though no one was getting paid anyway. Ackerman got the ax and so did Parozzo and Hinton.

"Aw, hell," Doug said that night down at Benny's. "There's lots of stuff I can do. I had a good job on a garbage truck back in the city. I can get that again."

He sat there and talked and the tears were rolling down his face. And it was a hell of a sight, the tears and the big moon face and the little beanie.

"I'll be all right," he said.

The team officially folded after our eighth loss, 33–6, to a Jersey City team called the Alvicks on a cold, damp night, with the fog rolling in and obscuring the lights. There were 200 people in the stands. Nineteen of our players showed up. An old Army buddy of mine came down with me to see the game, and Dalatri grabbed him outside the locker room.

"You ever play offensive tackle?" Dick asked. The guy shot me a wild look and moved up to the stands in a hurry.

Officially, the Pioneers were kaput, but Dalatri managed to wangle an exhibition game in his hometown, Spring Valley, N.Y. The Fire Department sponsored it, and Dalatri got the powerful Franklin Miners, led by the legendary Gunderman brothers, to play us. Somehow, somewhere, he managed to round up 35 assorted Pioneers, including a lantern-jawed, punchy little quarterback we'd never seen before. The guy brought an old helmet with a crack down the middle. None of us knew his name. We called him Cannonball.

We lost to the Miners, 35–0, but our game plan was to steal the Miners' guarantee money of $300 and use it for one final, grand farewell party. Unfortunately Sol Rosen, the Miners' owner, got there first.

Sol, who until 1968 was the commissioner of the Continental League, had been over the route before. He had one of the trainers stuff the money in the equipment bag and take off with it as soon as the game was over. We came away blank.

While we were showering, Frankie Fero, our general manager, grabbed all the uniforms out of our lockers and hustled them out to a truck. But someone caught him and made him give them back to us.

"It's funny, seeing Sol commissioner of our league," Dalatri said in 1966, the year he played for the Continental League's Brooklyn Dodgers.

"He still laughs about that night in Spring Valley. I played for him at Franklin the next year, before I went up to Canada. We beat the hell out of somebody one Saturday and drank all night. Next morning, about eight o'clock, Sol called us up and said that the Marines had canceled out of a game with Fort Dix and there would be $50 apiece for us if we'd drive down to Dix and fill in.

"Somehow we managed to get down there. The guys who were sober started the game, but then Fort Dix drove down to our four-yard line, so all the drunks went in. We stopped them and won the game, 32–14, and the soldier across the line from me said, 'Would you please breathe in some other direction? I'm getting drunk.' "

Next year I played for Mount Vernon, and the star of the team was Johnny Counts, who went up to the Giants a year later and finished second in the NFL in kickoff returns. The coach was Bill Elder, the old Notre Damer, who told us he scouted the enemy by "reading every newspaper clipping about them I can get my hands on."

Two years later I gave it another try—the Westchester Crusaders in the ACFL, and the highlight of our season was when our 260-pound right tackle, Fred Hovasapian, got thrown out of the league for assaulting a referee in a game against the Mohawk Valley Falcons in Utica, N.Y. That night I had the honor of lining up against 300-pound Ron Luciano, a former Syracuse tackle who later became famous as a baseball umpire. What was he like? Like a typical semipro 300-pound tackle. He'd anchor himself in a four-point stance and throw punches.

Strange memories come back. I remember standing in the tunnel one night in Mount Vernon, waiting for the introductions. I was standing between Alan Webb, who played for the Giants for five years and is now the 49ers' director of pro personnel, and Al Puryear, who was Calvin Hill's line coach in high school, and the announcer was introducing the other team (was it Bridgeport? Hartford?). When he came to their two gigantic tackles, he said, "Here they come, folks! Tons of fun!"

Puryear shook his head. "Tons of fun," he said. "Tons of fun."

Two days later we showed up at practice and found a locked gate. That was their way of letting us know the team had folded.

I remember a rough game against the Boonton (N.J.) Bears when I was playing for Morristown. There had been a lot of fights in the game, and the cops had to chase the hometown Boonton fans back in the stands a few times, and afterward the coach told us to be sure to keep our helmets on when we headed back to our bus. Out of the corner of my eye I saw a Boonton player following me.

"Number 64!" he yelled. "Hey, number 64!"

"Keep walking," the guy next to me said. "Don't look around."

But it was too late. The Boonton guy had caught up to me and had his arm around my shoulder.

"Hey, man," he said, and when I wheeled around it was Jerry Hamilton, a defensive end who'd been my teammate on the Pioneers eight years before that. We put away a lot of beers that night.

The names of some of those old minor leaguers might surprise you. Coy Bacon played for the Charlestown Rockets, John Unitas for the Bloomfield Rams. Half of the Raiders' Super Bowl backfield of 1976 played in the minors, Ken Stabler for the Spokane Shockers and Marv Hubbard for the Hartford Knights.

Bob Kuechenberg, who finished his 14th season as a guard for the Dolphins in 1983 and made the Pro Bowl for the sixth time, once played for the Chicago Owls of the Continental League, after Atlanta and Philly cut him in 1969.

"I figured that if I can't fly with the Eagles I'd play with the Owls," he said. One night I heard him talking about his Owl days, and it brought back many memories.

"I was supposed to make $200 a game," he said. "I signed on with nine games left. They paid me for the first three and stiffed me for the last six. They said, 'Don't worry. At the end of the year we'll change stockholders and you'll all get paid.' I'm still waiting for it.

"We played in Soldier Field and drew 3500 a game, and in that place they were invisible. It was like playing in an empty stadium. It was before they renovated the place for the Bears, and there were rats in the tunnels—big rats. To kill the rats they had cats, and to keep the cats around they had a big, square piece of wood with raw meat on it. I can shut my eyes and see it now, that big old pile of raw meat outside the stadium door.

"But it was fun. Pain and pain-killers and speed to get you up for the games, 300-pound garage mechanics punching you in the head, get drunk, have a pizza—that's what it was all about. I remember we flew to places like Omaha and Little Rock in little planes with wings that literally flapped. We'd reserve a hotel room—one room for everybody. We'd leave at 9:00 A.M. and arrive at 3:00 P.M. for a seven o'clock game. You'd check in and they'd hand you a little box lunch with a sandwich and a banana and a bag of pretzels and that was it.

"You know something? Nobody cared. Tonight we play a ball game. And it was fun."

The minors had their legends, like the Pottstown, Pa., Firebirds' Jimmy "The King" Corcoran, a quarterback who'd been up, briefly, with the Jets, Eagles and Patriots.

"Everyone knew The King," Kuechenberg says. "He'd drive up to the games in a black Lincoln Continental with a chauffeur and a loudspeaker that would announce, 'The King is here!' He'd hire a guy to hand him his towel when he came out of the shower."

When he was cut by the Jets, and he was on his way back to Pottstown, Jimmy called a press conference, attended mostly by rookies—out of curiosity.

"Come look me up in Pottstown," he told them. "I'll have jobs for all of you."

A year later I drove down to Pottstown to catch his act.

"Get this picture," he told me before the show began. "The stadium lights go dim. It's time for the intros. Now's the big moment, the moment they've all been waiting for. They introduce The King. The King comes running out between the goal posts. I give the fans a wave. The flags go up. The cannons go off. Ten thousand fans go out of their minds.

"It's like wrestling. When we go out of town I'm the villain. That's all the papers write about for a week. Pictures, quotes; half the stuff I don't even say, but who cares? It makes the fans crazy. They're all out there yelling for me to get killed.

"I'm not in Joe Willie's class yet, but I'm eating, man. I'm eating."

In 1981 Gino Malattia wrote a paperback about semipro football. It was published by the Triton Press in Morro Bay, Cal., which seemed just right to me. I read it with nostalgia. The message was the same throughout—high hopes, sagging attendance, another league folds, another one starts up.

George Sauer, the Jets' former pass-catching star, coached Charlotte, N.C., in the American Football Association for two years. In 1981 I read a story about how the team folded under him and AFA Commissioner Billy Kilmer, the old Redskins quarterback, declared the franchise "completely, absolutely dead."

"I probably won't coach again," Sauer said, "unless someone threatens me at least with death."

When some NFL teams actually had minor league farm systems, in the late sixties, the Raiders sent their backfield coach, Bill Walsh, down to take over the team they were cosupporting with the 49ers, the San Jose Apaches of the Continental Football League. It is a virtually unknown part of Walsh's coaching career.

"We had 49er and Raider taxi players," he says. "We finished 8–4, second in the league. We'd put on donkey basketball at halftime, dog shows, anything to bring people in. The problem with that league was the same the USFL is facing now. There are always overambitious people who try to get a competitive edge, like George Allen in the USFL, and in so doing they destroy the whole concept. In the end the weak teams bring it down."

In 1968 the NFL ruled out minor league tie-ins and the Apaches were gone and so was Walsh—back to Cincinnati and the big time.

I'll read anything about minor league football, the occasional feature pieces about the New York Rams or the Brooklyn Golden Knights, the guys with their perpetual aspirations. . . . "All I need is one break" . . . or the guys with none at all, the beer drinkers. Last year I read about a brand-new league called the Atlantic Football League that was opening up shop in the Northeast and was just a step away from a major league tie-in. I read that Paterson, N.J., would have a franchise. The publicity pitch was made at Toots Shor's. It should have been at Benny's.

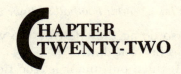

CHAPTER TWENTY-TWO

The Numbers Racket: A Look at Statistics

I can prove anything by statistics except the truth.

—George Canning, 1826

There are three kinds of lies: lies, damned lies and statistics.

—Benjamin Disraeli

EVERY time I hear a ball player tell me, "Statistics are for losers," or use the other maxim, "The only statistic that matters is win or lose," I wonder why everyone crowds around the bulletin board when the league stats are posted. The punt-return men look and see if they've gone up a couple of spots or slipped a few. So do the kickoff returners.

The stars pretend they don't care, but they'll sneak looks when they think nobody's watching. And after a game, the stat sheets are the first things grabbed up. Everyone tells you that statistics don't matter, but those stats have a strange way of making an appearance during contract talks—on both sides of the table.

The basic things you have to remember about the statistics you read in the paper every week are (1) they're not accurate . . . almost, but not quite; and (2) they are not as meaningful as they could be.

Statistics are not accurate because there is a human element involved. During a game the yardage is entered on a master sheet, or a work sheet, by the crew the home club hires to handle its stats. At the end of the game, it's tallied up and wired to Seymour Siwoff and the Elias Sports Bureau, Inc., in New York, a baseball statistics bureau that Pete Rozelle hired in 1960 to bring some order to the statistical chaos.

Seymour and his staff used to have 15 hours to get everything added up and prepared for release, so the papers and the clubs could get it for the Tuesday editions. (Monday night football has made that impossible, though, so Wednesday's paper is the new target date.) But often the crew in the press box is in a hurry to go to dinner that Sunday night, so they don't recheck their stats with the official play-by-play sheets, and an error in addition remains an error—forever, or until the Elias Bureau has enough breathing time to spot it and fix it. It doesn't always happen.

Plays often are forgotten in the excitement of the game. The most common error involves two running backs or two receivers with similar-looking numbers, e.g., 35 and 36, or 87 and 89. Number 35 might get Number 36's 10-yard gain, and 87 might get credit for the pass that poor Number 89 caught. These errors are never apprehended, and they happen in almost *every* game. Players seldom notice the mistakes, and even if they do, they rarely do anything about it. But there are exceptions.

Late in the 1966 season, the Jets' George Sauer was battling San Diego's Lance Alworth for the AFL pass-catching lead. In one game the Jets' statisticians credited Sauer with a catch that tight end Pete Lammons had made. Sauer brought the play-by-play sheets to the team's PR man and showed him the error—which was corrected. Sauer finished second to Alworth that year—but by more than one catch.

In a January 1983 playoff game between the Jets and Bengals in Cincinnati, New York's Freeman McNeil was credited with 22 carries for 211 yards, five yards better than Keith Lincoln's old record for yards rushing in a postseason game. But the stats crew had fouled up, which is not uncommon in Cincinnati. On the press-box mike Jim Blount incorrectly announced one nine-yard gain for McNeil (Number 24) that was really made by Bruce Harper (Number 42). The statistician, Howard Lewis, wrote it down as a nine-yard gain for McNeil. One man spotted it, Mike Graham of the *Cincinnati Post*. He reported the error to Blount, who waved him off, and there the matter stood—until the next day, when Graham alerted the NFL office, which corrected the error. So McNeil wound up four yards short of the record. The game was a 44–17 blowout by the Jets. McNeil was yanked early. He could have come back in to pick up his five yards. He brushed it off at the time but in the off-season it bugged him. "Hell, I could have just fallen for those five yards," he said.

The error was threefold. The announcer blew the call. The stat man should have been going with what his eyes told him, not what the announcer said. But the guy I hold most responsible is Graham. No true stats lover would allow himself to be waved off so easily. He should have fought for those yards, especially in a keynote situation like that. And he should have gone directly to the stats crew instead of the announcer.

Not that it would have done much good. The Cincinnati crew ranks with New England's as the worst I've seen, covering games around the NFL. Slowest, least organized, least familiar with the rules. How many times have I gotten gray hair arguing with the guys in New England, for instance, that a quarterback scrambling for zero yards gets a sack, not a rushing attempt, or trying to explain to the Bengal guys that if a holding penalty is called two yards downfield, and the net loss is eight yards, the whole play isn't wiped out—the runner gets credit for a two-yard gain. They yell at you, they snarl, they say, "Get the hell away from here or we'll call Security." So why do I care? Only because statistics are like love; you're either hooked or you're not. I happen to be a statistics nut, and I wouldn't wish it on other people. I try to keep my game stories relatively uncluttered with numbers, although if I do happen to come up with some particularly meaningful stats, I'll drop them in . . . gently.

Some stat crews are composed of dedicated, efficient people: the Miller family, who do the Rams' stats, the Jets' crew of Pat McDonough, a veteran of many years with the old New York *World-Telegram & Sun*, and ex-Columbia football star Ron Szypkowski. I rank San Francisco's number one in overall competence, but my favorite crew of all is the Dallas team led by Freddie Graham, the former sports information director at Texas Tech. Freddie's terrific . . . a little, wizened guy with a big, booming voice, a man who sneers at meaningless, subjective stats like "tackles and assists," as one should, a guy who can accurately spot the ball on its proper yard line before the refs can. A true stat lover, like yours truly.

Exhibition game stats are scanned, noted and then thrown away. They are completely unreliable. Sometimes the regular crew is on vacation. Backup crews are bad. Everyone's kind of laid back in August, anyway. No records are kept.

Once I was very curious to know who holds the record for most yards rushing in an exhibition game. No one could tell me, so I had my 12-year-old son, Michael, send in a letter to the "Ask Tex" column in the *Dallas Cowboys Weekly*. That's the one in which their GM, Tex Schramm, answers fans' questions. It must have stumped Tex, too. Mike never got a reply. I'd still like to know.

"Meaningful statistics" include anything that can give you an insight into a player's contribution in a game, or his worth at his position. For instance, if you read that John Riggins gained 82 yards on 23 carries for a 3.6 average, you know nothing. Ten other backs in the league might have done the same thing that Sunday. But if you are told that he carried the ball eight times on third-down, short-yardage situations, and picked up the first down on seven of those eight tries, you've learned something about the kind of day Riggins had.

Number of plays is a more meaningful statistic than time of possession. It's what you're doing on the field, not how long you're out there, that tires you out. Tackles and assists are rather silly stats. For one thing, statisticians are always more liberal about awarding them to their own guys . . . seldom will you see a visiting team's "assists" outnumber the home team's. The Broncos, whose releases always say that "tackles and assists are compiled from the coaches' films," must have an awful liberal set of coaches. If you believe them, then Randy Gradishar was the greatest defensive player in history. His tackles-and-assists figures are usually double those of any other linebacker in the NFL—every year. The Broncos' total numbers are always much higher, too.

"Let's say a cornerback gets credit for 12 tackles," Dallas secondary coach Gene Stallings says. "Well, it looks like he's had a super game, but it may be that they're catching the ball in front of him and he's tackling them. Somebody else may make only four tackles, but they're all right there at the line of scrimmage."

Some plays should be removed from the realm of statistics entirely, such as quarterback falldowns at the end of a half or the game. Roger Staubach hated them. "They just kill my rushing average," he used to say. And he was right. They're not rushing plays, they're zips, *nadas*, *nientes*, *nitchevos*. Ugly things. All they do is cloud a true interpretation of rushing yardage. And they penalize the better teams, because the losers don't call falldowns. How much can they affect a team? Well, two of them in a game, for minus five yards, can knock a team's stats on a normal rushing day, say 35 carries for 140 yards, from a 4.0 average down to a 3.6. And say a team is involved in eight games a season in which it's killed the clock at the end with those two falldowns; then its season average will drop from 4.0 to 3.8. And a quarterback's true rushing stats are knocked all to hell.

Last year I suggested to Steve Hirdt of the Elias Bureau that falldowns be lifted out of the realm of rushing stats and put somewhere else, like the garbage can . . . no, check that . . . like in a separate category, to figure in the team's overall yardage and plays, if necessary, but not to dilute a fairly meaningful statistic.

"You can't do it," he said. "Once you start throwing out plays . . . like the zero yards rushing you give a punter when he fumbles the snap . . . there's no end to it."

Well, throw 'em out, man, throw 'em out. Give us more meaningful stats!

Another stat that bugs me, and I see it in the agate box score every Monday, is "return yards." Now what the hell does that mean? Kickoff returns, punts, fumbles, interceptions, what? What does it tell you? Nothing. I realize that there are space limitations, and it would make the summaries too long to list each separate return category, so just get rid of this meaningless line and add something really nifty, such as the names of the players who sack the quarterback. You could do this under "Individual Statistics."

Granted, the agate summaries have come a long way in recent years. In the old days they wouldn't list individual stats, then only the one or two leaders. Now most papers give you a complete rundown, plus missed field goals, sacks, time of each score, and all sorts of niceties they didn't used to bother with. Remember that while baseball box scores have been virtually unchanged for the last 80 years, football stats are relatively new. Bert Bell had to beg them into the papers in the 1940s—mostly for publicity purposes.

Other people have their own statistical peeves. For years the Giants' punter, Dave Jennings, pestered the league office to list "net" punting average (gross yards minus return and touchback yardage), and finally they listened to him. Bud Wilkinson hates "third-down conversions." He says it's a bad stat because it doesn't indicate long or short yardage. The Cowboys' defensive people can't understand why team pass defense is figured on aggregate yardage, whereas a quarterback is rated on a compounding of four separate categories. Their own defensive stats are an average rating of all enemy QBs they've faced, and to me this makes a lot of sense. Why should an individual be rated one way and a team another way? The answer is that to figure the weekly offensive and defensive passing stats of the 28 NFL teams by the quarterback rating formula would take hours and hours of drudgery, and then you'd also have to include sacks and sack yardage (which don't figure in rating individual QBs), because they're so vital. I know. I did it. The Cowboys are right. It's a much better indication of which teams are more effective, in both passing and stopping the pass.

San Diego and Kansas City, for instance, which finished 1–2 in aggregate yardage in 1983, would be replaced by Washington and San Francisco. That seems sensible. The two best pass-defense teams, New Orleans and Philadelphia, would give way to Kansas City and Pittsburgh, and Philly would drop to 24th, which makes sense because the only reason why the Eagles finished high in pass defense was because everybody ran at them. Baltimore would retain its ranking as the worst passing team, and Pittsburgh, the second worst, would be replaced by the Giants. It's a tossup there. In replacing Washington and Dallas as the two worst pass-defense teams with Atlanta and San Diego I think you're really presenting a fairer picture of what happened. The Redskins would move to 11th, incidentally, under the new system, the Cowboys to 15th.

Don't ever expect to see this stuff take hold in the NFL, not in our lifetime, anyway. Too complicated. Too logical. It's only for nuts like me and anyone else who's read this far in the chapter.

I have my own statistical shorthand for keeping track of a game, plus a pass-frequency chart I invented myself. The purpose is to list every pass thrown, to which receiver and against which defender or combination of defenders, if it's a zone. Everything is included, even interference penalties, and if there's a badly thrown thrown ball, indicated by a small *o*, I try to indicate what kind of a misfire it was—underthrow, wide, etc. At the end of the day I have a pretty good idea of (1) which receivers are getting the action, (2) which defenders and (3) if the QB is off, what's his basic problem? I've reprinted my chart of the first half of the 1984 Super Bowl . . . Washington's offense versus the Raiders' defense. (See Fig. 17.)

Most successful statisticians are in love with their work. A statistic isn't just a cold number, it's a little story. And a good statistician can usually spot something that doesn't sound right.

"I can look through the old books and smell a phony statistic," Siwoff says. "Beattie Feathers, the old Bear halfback, gained 1004 yards rushing in 1934. No one had ever gone over 1000 before, and

FIGURE 17

WASHINGTON REDSKINS   Offense

SE 87 Brown	FL 81 Monk	TE 85 Warren	TB 44 Riggins	U-Back 88 Walker
X o ls out rt slot Hns X d RCHns √ & McEl X rt post Hayes √ INT PL 13 Hayes curl rt	X out left-motion Hns √ alm n X up 1 forced Hns √ X up left throw away Hns √ X out rt throw away Barnes √ & Hayes	89 Garrett 3d WR +17 in & out rt McK & Hayes	25 Washington +10 c-in left Millen msd +5 out left Mtn X c-in rt Davis √ & Martin √ bracketed N 5 Squirek (TD) screen left Alzado √ spy	86 Didier X o over up rt. Davis √ +8 out rt McKny & Squirek X o wd out rt Mil & Davis +18 scr 1 Martin +20 cross 1-r Dvs & McElroy 30 Giaquinto X wd out left McK bump √

L.A. RAIDERS   Offense

SE 21 Branch	FL 80 Barnwell	TE 46 Christensen	HB 32 Allen	FB 33 King

Field Chart Translation

BROWN	X (incomplete) o low on an out-pattern from slot right vs. Haynes X (inc.) d (dropped) right corner pattern vs. Haynes, who made a good play (√) and McElroy X (inc.) right post vs. Haynes' (√) good play INT PL 13 (13-yard interface penalty) on Hayes, curl pattern right
MONK	X (inc.) out left from motion, vs. Haynes (√), who almost intercepted X (inc.) up pattern left vs. Haynes' (√) good play—pass was forced by the rush X (inc.) up left—deliberately thrown away vs. Haynes' (√) good coverage X (inc.) out right—thrown away—vs. Barnes' (√) good play and Hayes
GARRETT	+17 — caught a 17-yard pass, in and out pattern right vs. McKinney (nickel back) and Hayes

Defense

LC 28 Green	SS 48 Coffey	FS 29 Murphy	RC 24 Washington	LLB 55 Kaufman	MLB 52 Olkewicz	RLB 57 Milot

Defense   Linebackers

LC 37 Hayes	SS 36 Davis	FC 26 McElroy	RC 22 Haynes	L Outside 83 Hendricks	Strong IS 55 Millen	Wk IS 51 Nelson	Rt. OS 53 Martin
	X o Didier				X o Didier		+5 Wash
		X Monk out		+10 Wash		+18 Didier
	+20 Didier	X Monk up				√
	X Wash √					
			X Monk up √			
			X o Brown	56 Barnes		23 McKinney
			X Monk √		—Nickel—
X Brown			X Brown d		58 Squirek	+17 Monk
int pc 13 Brown					+8 Didier
					N 5 Wash (TD)	X o Giaq

WASHINGTON +10 — caught a 17-yard circle-in pass left, Millen missed the tackle
+5 — caught a 5-yard out pass left vs. Martin
X (inc.) circle-in right, Davis (√) and Martin (√) had him bracketed between them
N5 TD intercepted by Squirek for a 5-yard TD on a screen left, Alzado (√) good play, dropping off into "spy" coverage

DIDIER X (inc.) o (overthrown), up pattern right, Davis (√) good coverage
+8 — caught an 8-yard out pass right vs. McKinney and Squirek
X (inc.) o (overthrow) wide, out pass right vs. Millen and Davis
+18 — caught an 18-yard screen pass vs. Martin
+20 — caught a 20-yard crossing pass, left to right, vs. Davis and McElroy

GIAQUINTO X (inc.) wide out pass left vs. McKinney (√) good play—bumped him out of the pattern no one did it again for 13 years, and in 51 years of statistics-keeping no one came remotely close to his average of 9.94 yards per carry. You see a statistic like that and it shakes you. It's like a bolt of lightning. I have a sneaking suspicion that some punt and kickoff runbacks were added into Beattie's rushing total."

Merle Hapes and Frank Filchock, two Giant backs who got in trouble for failing to report a bribe before the 1946 NFL Championship game against the Bears, had been wiped out of the record books.

"I went back and researched them," Siwoff says. "You don't pass moral judgments with statistics."

Ah, but if so, then why were all the old All-America Football Conference records wiped out and the AFL numbers retained? The AAFC was on a par with the NFL; some people, such as me, think it played a better brand of football, as Cleveland's 35–10 runaway over Philly in the 1950 opener (the first year of the merger) might indicate. Such great stars as Otto Graham and Marion Motley and Frankie Albert saw their most productive years ignored. The official reason given is that in 1970 the NFL absorbed the entire AFL, whereas in 1950 only three of the seven AAFC teams, and half of a fourth, were incorporated. I don't buy it. The same players came over anyway; the remainder were just taken by different NFL teams. No, the real reason is that bitter feelings existed between NFL and AAFC people, right up to and after the merger. So the way they were punished was through the stats department. Sad, isn't it?

Steve Hirdt says the bulk of the phone calls the Elias Bureau receives from coaches themselves concern special teams statistics. " 'Why didn't this guy get a punt return?' . . . 'He returned it six yards before the penalty, not four yards' . . . that kind of stuff. The et cetera department," he says. "I've got a feeling that some incentive bonus clauses in assistant coaches' contracts are tied in with those special teams statistics."

The most complicated statistic, and the one I was violently opposed to when it first appeared in 1973, is the quarterback rating system. My argument at the time was that statistics shouldn't serve to evaluate people; they should merely list things . . . they should be signposts, indicating the most, the least, etc. But since then I've gotten more and more interested in meaningful stats, so the argument is kind of washed. Besides, it's so much fun to figure out. It works like this.

Four categories determine a QB's rating—completion percentage,

percentage of interceptions per passes thrown, percentage of TDs, and yards per attempt. You consult a chart the league provides, and give a man points. The most points you can get for any single achievement is 2.375. Then you add up the total points in the four categories, divide by six, multiply by 100 and you've got his rating. A rating of 100 is considered the standard of true excellence in the NFL. It's only been done 12 times. The best ever for one year is Otto Graham's 112.1 for 1946 (that's right, I'm including AAFC stats). In a single category, 1.5 points equal a 100 rating (1.5 times four, divided by six, multiplied by 100, get it?). To get 1.5 points in each area the passer must complete 60 percent of his passes, average nine yards per attempt and 7.5 TDs and 3.5 interceptions per 100 throws.

My complaint with the system is that it's too wired into completion percentage. The low-risk, high-percentage, "dink" quarterbacks are going to be helped in three categories. The more daring guys who throw downfield are going to suffer. John Unitas never led the NFL, and in 1983 both he and Otto Graham, two all-time greats, were knocked off the lifetime top 10. The 60 percent completion and 3.5 interception percent standards of excellence are no big deal anymore. Eight quarterbacks accomplished each last season, whereas the nine-yards-per-pass figure and 7.5 TD percentage were achieved by, respectively, one (Lynn Dickey) and zero in '83. Which is as it should be.

"A team can pad the stats for its passer," Bill Walsh says, "by letting him throw a lot of dink passes at the end of a game. I know Seattle used to. Usually it's an offensive coordinator who wants to be a head coach. I've been through it. I know. I did it for Ken Anderson in his first few years, when I was the Bengals' offensive coach."

Unfortunately, few fans see the quarterbacks' ratings, because when the papers print the weekly stats most of them cut the column off just before you get to the crucial figure—the rating points. Without them the list of numbers is meaningless. *The New York Times*, for instance, drives me crazy. I keep telling them, "Why don't you just run your stats two columns wide instead of a column and a half, so you can include the rating points?" and they mumble something about not enough space. The *Boston Globe*, bless 'em, prints the rankings in full.

The system drives some quarterbacks nuts, too. "If they're trying to rate quarterbacks," the Patriots' Steve Grogan says, "why don't

they rate his entire game? Stuff like rushing yardage should figure in
. . . everything you're doing to help your team win."

Buffalo's Joe Ferguson has another complaint. Quarterbacks who
play in miserable weather conditions, such as in Buffalo, will never
have the ratings the warm-weather or domed-stadium QBs have.

"In Buffalo you'd just better forget about your stats," he says. "You
can keep 'em up in the first half of the season, but after that it's a
struggle to complete 50 percent."

Last year the weather wasn't too bad, but in '82 the cold and ferocious winds destroyed every quarterback who came into Rich Stadium. Mike Pagel went 3-for-17, for instance, David Woodley
6-for-16, Cliff Stoudt 2-for-10, Terry Bradshaw 2-for-13. No visiting
QB completed 50 percent of his passes in Buffalo that year, and Ferguson himself only did it in two games, both in September.

How important can one completion be in a guy's overall rankings?
Well, look at the 49ers versus the Cowboys in the final 1983 Monday
night game. In the first quarter Joe Montana threw a little screen
pass to Freddy Solomon. Dennis Thurman got blocked by Bubba
Paris, and Solomon raced 77 yards for a TD. Here's what that 77-
yard TD pass did for Montana: raised his rating from 93.2 to 94.6 for
1983, raised his lifetime rating from 89.7 to 90.1, making him the
only player in history to score over 90, lifetime. He ought to buy
Freddy and Bubba a dinner.

Even the most blasé statistics-minded player will tune in after he's
been out of the game for a while. Jim Brown used to sneer at numbers. "Every time I break another record I become more of a statistic, less of a person," he would say, and the world applauded. But last
year, when Franco Harris started closing in on Brown's lifetime
rushing mark, he threatened a comeback—to protect his numbers. It
was more of a protest than anything else, an outcry against modern
runners who go out of bounds, who "are skating their way into the
record books," according to Brown. A 1000-yard season is no big deal
these days, not with the 16-game season, and the record of Brown's
that I find the most amazing is that he never missed a game in nine
years. Besides, even if Jim came back, he'd be outlasted—not by
Franco, who might be nearing the end of the trail, but by Walter
Payton, who's only 30—with plenty of giddyaps left in his legs.

Sooner or later they all start thinking about numbers. Not as heavily as Seymour or me, maybe, but it's infectious. Once you're hooked,
you can't help yourself.

CHAPTER TWENTY-THREE

The Image-Makers: A Look at the All-Alls

I wanted to vote for offensive linemen, but they wouldn't let us. They said only the defensive linemen could vote for them. But what's the difference? All they're voting for are the best holders, anyway.

—Jack Reynolds

WRITERS vote for All-NFL, players and coaches vote for the Pro Bowl squads, a special committee votes for Hall of Fame nominees. These are the bonbons at the end of a season—or a career. "Lollipops," Walt Michaels calls them. Selection can bring joy to a dismal season, often it can bring cash (if All-Pro selection is built into a player's contract as one of the incentive bonuses).

"I learned that you have to be very careful what you spell out as All-Pro," the Giants' general manager, George Young, says. "Do you mean All-Pro or All-NFC or All-AFC or the Pro Bowl squad? And you have to make sure you define the pickers. I've had an agent come in demanding an incentive bonus because his guy had made one All-Pro team, picked by his hometown paper in North Carolina or someplace like that. If you look hard enough you can manage to find someone, somewhere who will pick any player."

The end of an era seems to inspire an outbreak of All-All picking. The end of a decade did it for the AFL, which chose its All-Time team in 1969. A positive milestone, like the NFL's 50th anniversary, simply drives the pickers wild.

Remember the furor with which the Associated Press greeted the end of the first half of the 20th century? The wire service picked its "Greatest Athlete of the First Half of the 20th Century" in all sports, finally rolling all the greatests into one greatest, Jim Thorpe, who happened to be destitute at the time. The AP picked its Greatest Upset, Greatest Sports Thrill, Greatest Game . . . I can't remember the full list of Greatests, although I've got them all written down somewhere.

The Pro Football Hall of Fame commemorated the NFL's 50 years of existence by picking its All-Stars of each decade, and then boiling them down into one All-Star team, which is perfectly all right with me, because I happen to enjoy all this All-All picking, and most other people do, too, even though it's fashionable to scoff at it.

Oh, there are inconsistencies. Four members of the Cleveland Browns made the All-Star squad of the 1940s, even though the Browns were strictly an All-America Football Conference team and not part of the NFL during that period. The reasoning was that the AAFC was incorporated into the NFL in 1950, so its history had a right to come along with it. Which is fine, except that the AFL, which became part of the NFL in 1970, got totally neglected on the All-Star team of the sixties. But that's the way it goes with All-Star picking. You make a dozen friends and 100 enemies.

The worst, positively the worst, All-Star teams are the ones picked by the fans after their team undergoes a notable success. After the 49ers won the '82 Super Bowl a San Francisco paper ran a poll to pick the all-time 49er team, a very foolish thing to do, in the wake of all that hysteria, and an insult to history. You need time to let things settle down when you're talking about historical perspective. Predictably, the fans, most of them youngsters with no feel for the past, loaded their ballots with the names of 1981 Forty-Niners. First-year people, such as defensive end Fred Dean and middle linebacker Jack Reynolds, made it even though they were "situation" people who didn't play every down. I felt very bad for old-timers such as Norm Standlee, the Big Chief, whom I'd seen have so many great years as middle linebacker for the Niners.

The yearly All-Pro picking is left to the wire services and the players and the coaches. The Hall of Fame started picking a combined AFL-NFL team in 1968, and so did the Professional Football Writers Association.

The NFL used to pick its official All-Star team from 1931 through 1942, at which time the wire services (AP, UPI, and the now defunct INS) took over. In 1955, NEA (Newspaper Enterprise Association) joined the group, and although this was probably the most highly respected team, since the players did the selecting, it took six years for the NFL to recognize the picks in its annual *Record Manual. The Sporting News*'s All-AFL team was a players' poll team, and its All-NFL divisional teams were picked by its own staff.

Both AP and UPI follow the same technique. Two or three writers who regularly cover a team are designated as official pickers from that city. When there's a scarcity of regular reporters, the wire service uses one of its own men who covers the club. The ballots are tabulated and the choices are made accordingly. Negligent writers, or people whose picks are erratic, are replaced. ("One Dallas guy had 10 Cowboys on his 1969 team," reports a UPI official).

The only drawback to this system, unless you figure that writers are not qualified to judge talent, is that a man may not get to see all the teams in the league. He has an intimate knowledge of the club he travels with, but he only gets one or two looks—sometimes none at all—at the players on other clubs. But it's expected that the reporters will go heavy on the men of their own team, and when all the ballots are in, the whole thing is supposed to balance out.

The NEA, or NFL players' team (coaches picked the NEA's All-AFL teams), had its weaknesses, too. Murray Olderman, the NEA's executive editor and formerly its sports editor, originated the idea and handles the whole thing, and he said that only 60 percent of the players used to send in ballots, despite repeated prodding.

For years this was probably the best team of all, and history bears it out. Men like Merlin Olsen, the Rams' defensive tackle, Green Bay safetyman Willie Wood, and Green Bay and Philadelphia center Jim Ringo were all picked by NEA one year before the rest of the world discovered their greatness.

"Ringo told me that he was flying home from Green Bay after the 1956 season," Olderman said, "and he stopped off at O'Hare Airport in Chicago. Our picks had just come out, and Ringo was the center even though the Packers had finished 4–8 that year. He had never been picked before, and no one else picked him that year.

"I remember I led off the story with something about how the players weren't impressed with a big reputation or a team's record. They selected according to pure talent. Ringo said that he looked over the shoulder of a man reading a newspaper in the airport, and he saw the story and tears came to his eyes."

The coaches' ballots, which many a general manager would use around contract time, showed Olderman one thing. Coaches were lousy spellers. "There's no predicting how they'll spell even a name like Smith," he said.

"But the players weren't much better. We have an award called the Third Down Trophy that we give out every year. A team votes for its own MVP, and one year the Boston Patriots picked Gino Cappelletti, the flankerback and kicker. We counted it up, and Gino's name was spelled 17 different ways."

Before 1977, the NFL Pro Bowl and the old AFL All-Star game selections were handled by the coaches. Under the terms of the 1977 collective bargaining agreement, players took a hand in the picking for the first time. It was an improvement on the old method, because the coaches' primary aim was to put a team on the field, not to pick a collection of All-Stars. (The AFL, in fact, used to have its All-Stars play the defending league champion, a loose counterpart to the NFL's college All-Star Game.) The selections had to be made strictly by position, i.e., the selectors had to pick a man who regularly played left defensive end and one who played right defensive end, left offensive tackle and right offensive tackle, etc. So if there were, for instance, four outstanding left defensive ends in the division and no decent right defensive ends, only one of the outstanding left group will get picked, to be joined by the best of the mediocre right group.

The players weren't officially told about this, though, and sometimes they were deeply hurt by the obvious injustices. It hurt financially, too.

The rest of the squads were supposedly filled in by the runners-up in the balloting, but a lot of horse trading went on. And if a player came up injured before the game—or if he was merely worn out from the overlong season—the coach of the particular All-Star squad could fill in as he saw fit, usually with men from the team he coached during the regular season. Hence, seven members of Van Brocklin's 6–8 Atlanta Falcons showed up on the West's 1970 Pro Bowl squad, also coached by Van Brocklin.

When the players stepped in in 1977, each team was given two ballots by the league, one to be filled in by the coaches, one by a consensus of the players; teammates were not eligible for selection. An AFC team could only vote for AFC players, an NFC club for the NFC—a practice that annoys some players.

"It should be an all-opponent team, period," Joe Jacoby, Washington's All-Pro offensive tackle, says. "The best end I played against, by far, was Lyle Alzado of the L.A. Raiders, but I wasn't allowed to vote for him. And then I had to turn around and try to rate some NFC guys I hadn't faced."

Some teams let all their players vote for everybody, others allow only defensive players to vote for offensive opponents, and some define it even more narrowly by restricting it only to people in the picker's own immediate area, a designation that breaks down when it comes time to picking a quarterback.

Some players don't take it very seriously. "You vote for who the coaches tell you to vote for," Reynolds says. "They pass around ballots with two weeks to go," says much-traveled kicker Fred Steinfort, "and when it comes time for selecting kickers, the players just look at who has the most points. They don't understand things like weather conditions. Guys who kick in domed stadiums have it made. But kickers on teams like San Francisco and Buffalo and the Giants and Jets have it the worst. They really have tough conditions."

The Redskins probably do it in the most legitimate manner.

"We'll sit down in a classroom, by groups," offensive guard Russ Grimm says, "and we'll put the names up on a blackboard. Each guy mentions the toughest guy he's faced, or seen on film, if that guy happened to have an off day when he played against us. There's some discussion, and then that player becomes the unanimous choice for our team. The ballot our group fills out only mentions defensive linemen and linebackers, and that's it. I mean it would be foolish for me to start rating the secondary. My choice is always easy. Randy White's the best guy I've played against for the last three years."

"Sometimes it's like an old-boys club," Jacoby says. "Offensive linemen have no statistics to help in the judging, and it's tough for a newcomer to crack in. It's like a fraternity. Once a guy makes it, he's on forever."

Personal popularity helps. In 1982 the Packers' J. J. Jefferson was asked if he was surprised at making the Pro Bowl team, even though he hadn't caught a touchdown pass in the regular season.

"I'm popular," he says. "I've got a lot of friends. I always shake hands after the game. I'm respected."

When Jet defensive end Mark Gastineau started doing his sack dance in 1981 his teammate, quarterback Richard Todd, took him aside and tried to explain the facts of life.

"Don't forget," he said, "that those tackles you're dancing over are the ones who'll be voting for the Pro Bowl."

It didn't matter. They picked Gastineau anyway, and they've done so ever since.

"New players usually get neglected and old ones generally make it a year or two after they should," Giants' punter Dave Jennings says. "In 1981 Mark Haynes had a great year as cornerback for us, but he didn't make the Pro Bowl because he hadn't gotten much publicity. I told him, 'Don't worry, at the end of your career you'll get one you don't deserve and it'll even out.' "

Until the game was moved to Hawaii on a more-or-less permanent basis in 1980, participation in the Pro Bowl game was spotty, especially by players who had been in the Super Bowl the week before. But the idea of a week in the sunshine did wonders for player attendance.

The game itself means different things to different people. "I remember we were playing in the Pro Bowl one year," says coach Walt Michaels, who was a linebacker on a few of the Eastern Division teams. "Jim Parker was the West's offensive guard, and Ernie Stautner was our defensive tackle playing over him. Jim just wanted to take it easy, but Ernie was playing like a madman.

" 'Pro Bowl, Ernie—Pro Bowl,' Jim said.

" 'You're getting paid ain'tcha?' Ernie told him. 'Shut up and play.' "

The selection to the squad usually means more than the actual game itself. Herb Adderley, the Green Bay cornerback, was furious when he found out that the Packers' coaching staff hadn't voted for him for the 1970 Pro Bowl game. He demanded to be traded all winter. Finally he was.

For Gino Marchetti, the Colts' defensive end, the Pro Bowl was a chance to get even.

"When we beat the Colts, 27–0, in the 1964 Championship game, Frank Ryan was throwing the ball at the end," says former Cleveland guard John Wooten, who's now a scout with the Cowboys. "I think Frank was trying for a fourth TD pass or something, but Gino went wild. He kept screaming, 'I'll get you, Ryan! I'll get you for this in the Pro Bowl!'

"Dick Schafrath, our tackle, told me that in the Pro Bowl next week Gino kept begging him, 'One shot, just gimme one shot at the guy,' and Dick said, 'I can't do that, Gino,' and Gino said, 'The hell with you, I'll get him on my own.' Sure enough, he got him on the first series of the second half. Sacked him and turned him upside down and drilled him into the ground. Screwed up his shoulder."

For the last 15 years I've been picking my own All-Pro team, first for the *New York Post,* now for *Sports Illustrated.* I have my own set of prejudices, naturally, and one of them is in favor of people who have had long and distinguished careers but never were picked to anything—for example, Jon Kolb, the Steelers' offensive tackle, and San Diego guard Ed White, both of whom made my team in, respectively, 1980 and '83.

I, along with many of my fellow writers, am guilty of one of the greatest injustices of modern times, never having picked Dallas quarterback Roger Staubach. Oh, he made a few All-NFC teams in his career, and they sent him to the Pro Bowl four times, but he was never picked to a combined All-NFL team, despite the fact that his archenemy, Redskin coach George Allen, named him as the "best quarterback I ever coached against." It seems that every time Roger had a good year, someone else picked that time to have a slightly better one. It's sad.

Coaches and players generally sneer at newspapermen's efforts to pick all-anything. But in 1969, *Sports Illustrated* tried polling the assistant coaches of each team, since these men look at more miles of film than anyone in the game, and the results were hilarious.

The coaches couldn't vote for their own players, which was supposed to encourage objectivity, but somehow two Dallas offensive centers, Dave Manders and Mal Walker, wound up with one vote apiece, Minnesota cornerback Bobby Bryant received one vote as a safetyman; San Diego's Ron Mix got two votes, placing him among the top six offensive tackles in the AFL, even though he had been out for the whole season with a pulled leg muscle. Sam Walton, an offensive tackle for the Jets, received a vote, even though he had been cut from the squad in midseason, so *Sports Illustrated* frantically called the coach who had voted for him, and the answer was, "No, I meant the other guy on the Jets." Fourteen different NFL guards got votes; and on one NFL team four different assistant coaches picked five different cornerbacks. Maybe Atlanta's head coach, Norm Van Brocklin, had the right idea. He forbade his assistants to pick anybody.

The most serious picking of all is done by the Hall of Fame committee in its annual review of candidates. A player who has been out of the game five years becomes eligible. So does a recently retired coach, or a current owner or administrator. Every year during Super Bowl week 29 selectors—one writer covering each NFL franchise, plus one from the Pro Football Writers Association—review some 40 to 60 names supplied by the Hall itself. There's also a separate list of Old-Timer candidates, players who completed at least 60 percent of their careers 25 years or more before the selection date. Five of them are proposed by a special Old-Timer Committee.

"The 40 to 60 names we supply," says Hall of Fame vice-president Don Smith, "come from writers' nominations, as well as from letters by the fans. Anyone legitimate is considered."

The big list is whittled down to 14 finalists, based on a vote for 14 names, and there is one Old-Timer candidate. A finalist makes the Hall of Fame if he carries 24 of the 29 votes. The meeting lasts two-and-a-half hours, and each name is discussed before the vote is taken. The list of Hall of Fame selectees cannot exceed six, plus one Old-Timer.

"When we called the old Chicago Bear guard George Musso to tell him he'd made it, he didn't believe us," Smith says. "He said, 'If you don't mind, I'll call and double-check. People have pulled my leg about this before.' When I called Lance Alworth he took it very calmly. Then he called his father and cried. Telling someone he's made the Hall of Fame is the best part of my job."

Oh yes, in the vast history of postseason honors, one list should not be neglected: a runner-up bowl for teams that got beaten in the play-offs. Thankfully, the event has been shelved forever. Miami used to host this game.

"A hinky-dinky football game, held in a hinky-dinky town, played by hinky-dinky football players," Vince Lombardi once called it. "That's all second place is, hinky-dinky."

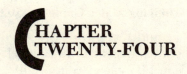

CHAPTER TWENTY-FOUR

Strictly Personal:
The Greatest Player

Paul Brown once had been asked, "How'd you like to have that Doc Blanchard?" And he replied: "The man I've got in mind is called Marion Motley and he's better than Blanchard."

> —*Sport* magazine, November 1952,
> History of the Cleveland Browns.

He was the greatest all-around football player I ever saw. The man was a great, great linebacker. Believe me, he could do everything. He had no equal as a blocker; yes, he could do it all.

> —Blanton Collier

Nothing devastates a football team like a selfish player. It's a cancer. The greatest back I ever had was Marion Motley. You know why? The only statistic he ever knew was whether we won or lost. The man was completely unselfish.

> —Paul Brown

I first became acquainted with Marion Motley when I bought a copy of *Pro Football Illustrated*, 1947 edition. It cost a quarter, but it was one of those giant-sized magazines they used to put out in those days and it was loaded with pictures, so I figured it was worth it.

I was thumbing through it on the subway home from school, and there was this picture that stopped me dead. It was a full-page shot of Motley, running right at the camera, with his face sort of sqwunched together and his lower lip sucked in, and what looked like a scar running down one side of his cheek. I thought he was the toughest-looking man I'd ever seen in my life.

A couple of weeks later, when I saw Motley's Browns play the Yankees in the Stadium, that first impression was confirmed. He was the toughest football player I'd seen. I didn't keep stats in those days, but I seem to remember that Motley averaged about 10 yards a carry, which is fancy stepping for a 238-pound fullback, and I know for an absolute fact that he scored three of the Browns' four touchdowns.

He backed up on the line on defense, and I can still see him on one play, reaching out with one hand and grabbing the Yankees' little Buddy Young by the seat of his pants and holding him up in the air for the crowd to see.

A few weeks later I went to the Stadium again, this time for the Browns against the Yankees for the All-America Football Conference championship. I was sitting in the upper deck, above home plate. My binoculars caught Motley coming right at me, 51 yards on a direct handoff over the middle, the last 10 or so with the Yanks' Harmon Rowe riding his back and slugging him in the face.

The papers next day had a quote from Motley, answering a photographer who asked him to smile.

"I can't," he said. "My teeth were knocked out."

The record books show that he gained 109 yards in 13 carries that day, which was a typical kind of day for Motley—a lot of yards, not many carries—the kind of day that left you wondering what kind of stats he could have run up if Paul Brown had decided to build his attack around him in those days, instead of around Otto Graham's passes.

I watched Motley right up until his last, hopeless days when he tried a comeback with the Pittsburgh Steelers in 1955, and if there is a better football player who ever snapped on a helmet, I would like to know his name. There's a statistical table at the end of this chapter, detailing the numbers that made up Motley's professional career, but it's a kind of meaningless way of evaluating this remarkable player. It would be like trying to describe a waterfall in terms of gallons per second, or a sunset in terms of light units.

Never has there been a set of statistics to measure the force and intensity of a man's hitting power, or his effectiveness as a pass blocker, unless you use a seismograph, and that would probably run into too much money. And until they start playing football with adding machines, I have to believe that the force of the blow is still what the game is all about.

Giving a quick look at the table, though, you'll note that Motley averaged 5.7 yards a carry during his pro career, which is half-a-yard better than the lifetime average of Jimmy Brown, the greatest running back who ever lived.

Brown was the best pure runner I've ever seen, but Motley was the greatest all-around player, the complete player. He ran, of course, and he caught flare passes and turned them into big gainers, and he backed up the line in an era in which the rest of the world was switching to two platoons, and he pass-blocked like no other back who ever played the game.

"That young fella, Jimmy Brown, has been getting a lot of heat because he didn't block," Motley said when Brown was in his prime. "Let me tell you something about that boy. When he first came up to the Browns, he asked me to show him a few things about pass blocking. We were pretty good friends, used to play golf together.

"Well, I showed him, and he seemed eager to learn, but the system just didn't call for it. That was Paul Brown's way. He had you helping him where you could help him most, and he didn't want to hear anything else."

I talked to people who were connected with Motley in the old days, and tested their reactions when I told them that I thought he was the greatest player I'd ever seen.

"The people who talk about Motley are talking about the Motley who played in the NFL—on two bad knees," said former Buffalo and Denver coach Lou Saban, who was the defensive captain of the Browns during their AAFC years.

"The Motley they saw was just a shadow of the old Motley, even when he made All-Pro in '50 and led the league in running. Don't forget, he was 26 years old in his rookie year—in 1946."

"I think you've made a very wise choice," said old Jets coach Weeb Ewbank, who was on the Paul Brown–Blanton Collier staff that had Motley as its fullback at Great Lakes Naval Training Center and then Cleveland.

"You know, you think about those old days of pro football, and you wonder about some of the great stars then and how they could stand up nowadays. Take Bill Willis, for instance. One of the great middle guards in the game, but where would he play today—at 210 pounds?

"But Motley would be the same now. He weighed 238 and he could keep up with any back except maybe Buddy Young. He just might be the greatest player at that."

"We had a scrimmage between Great Lakes and the College All-Stars," Collier once recalled. "We finally went into a seven-man line, with Marion as the linebacker, in an effort to hold them. Pretty soon it developed into a struggle between Marion and the All-Star offense—and you can believe me when I say it was a standoff."

"Marion lived right near me," said New Orleans line coach Joe Spencer, who was a young tackle on the '49 Cleveland team. "One day after practice I was counting my pennies and trying to figure out the cheapest way to get home. Marion didn't say a word—except 'Get in,' when he pulled up in his car.

"So every day we used to drive to practice together and drive home, one of the greatest stars in the game and a guy just fighting to stay on the club. But that's the way he was. If you were his teammate, he would do anything for you."

About 10 years ago I decided to hunt up some old movie film on the Browns' early games and see for myself whether the recollections of a 14-year-old high school kid would stand up. It's generally a bad play to make, messing around with the cherished memories.

I remember Cus D'Amato telling the story about how he forced Jimmy Jacobs, the fight film collector, into showing him old movies of George Dixon, the featherweight champ.

"When I was a kid," Cus said, "all my father would talk about was George Dixon, the greatest fighter that ever lived. It was George Dixon this and George Dixon that. Before every meal, he'd lift a glass of wine to George Dixon.

"So I asked Jimmy if he had any old films of Dixon and he said he did, but that I wouldn't want to see them. I said show them to me anyway. I watched one, and I said, 'That's not George Dixon,' and he said, 'I'm afraid it is.' The guy fought like a zombie.

"I got this terrible pain in my stomach, watching that film. It really hurt. I said, 'Jimmy, for Christ sake, shut off that projector.' "

The films of Motley didn't break my heart. They just showed me that my vision had been remarkably clear in those days, probably better than now. He was dynamic and terrifying, but it was his pass blocking that really lifted him into a different dimension.

"Why is the Cleveland passing attack so good?" a radio interviewer once asked Gail Bruce, San Francisco's fine pass-rushing end of 20 years ago.

"Well, you rush Graham, and put on a move and beat your man, and there's Motley waiting for you," he said. "Next play, you beat your man with a different move, and there's Motley waiting again. Pretty soon you say, 'The hell with it. I'd rather stay on the line and battle the first guy.' "

Motley's style was a numbing, paralyzing head-and-shoulders shot that would lift defensive ends and tackles and dump them on their behind. People usually gave up early on trying to shoot their linebackers in when Motley was back there, or as Ewbank said, "Marion took the romance out of the blitz."

I finally met Motley the day before the Jets-Colts Super Bowl in Miami. He was down there to help with a fund-raising campaign for the NFL Alumni Committee. The idea was to try to get some kind of pension installed for some of the old players, the ones who were broke and could use a little help.

I told him I wanted to do a story on him, and he gave me a kind of uh-huh look.

"I've talked to guys who said they were going to do stories," he said, "and somehow I don't get to see those stories. They say they'll send them, but they never do."

We were in his room in the hotel, and aside from a slight bulge around the midsection that a green golf sweater didn't quite hide, he looked formidable, still the Motley from *Pro Football Illustrated*, 1947.

He had been burned by Paul Brown, who discarded him after his value was exhausted. He had been burned by Otto Graham, his old teammate, who turned him down when he had asked him for some kind of a scouting job in the Washington organization. This was when Graham was the coach of the Redskins. He had owned a bar in Cleveland and lost it, and he had gone along with a weird idea about coaching a girls' football team in the Cleveland area, a scheme that also went down the drain. His most recent job is supervisor in the Ohio lottery system.

"I was in the Yankee Stadium," I told him, "the day you knocked Tom Casey out of football."

Casey had been a 175-pound defensive back for the Yankees. He was probably the only man I ever saw stop Motley head on when

Motley was going full tilt. Casey woke up in Bronx Veterans' Hospital, and he never played any more football.

"I see him every now and then," Motley said. "He's Dr. Thomas Casey now and he lives in Shaker Heights, right outside of Cleveland. We kid each other about that play and he'll say, 'You S.O.B., you ended my career.' And I'll tell him, 'I couldn't help it if you got in front of me.' "

I told Motley that I was in Kezar Stadium in San Francisco the day Norm Standlee tackled him near the 49er bench, and I remember Motley crawling all the way across the field and out-of-bounds so that the Browns wouldn't have to take time out. I mentioned this, too, and the old fullback warmed up a little.

"Young man," he said, squinting at me, "you've got a good memory. I pulled a muscle in my leg on that play. I would have scored if not for that. I liked old Norm, though. Always did. He was another guy who played linebacker and fullback at the same time."

Motley's legs were the saddest story of all. If not for a couple of crippled knees, he probably could have had five more great years.

"The first time I hurt my knee was in college," he said, "at the University of Nevada. I had started at South Carolina State in Orangeburg, and transferred to Nevada in 1940. I spent three seasons there, hurt my knee, and went back home to Canton, Ohio.

"My knee was pretty bad, but I got a job with Republic Steel. I was a pieceworker. I burned scrap iron out of the steel with a torch, and it'd get awful hot up there on top of the steel where I worked. I honestly think that all that heat mended my knee. The muscles around the knee had been torn. When I hurt it, I played the next week, but it would get stiff and swell up on me. But that heat fixed it up."

On Christmas Day 1944, Motley entered boot camp at Great Lakes. The coaching staff had Ewbank and Collier and Paul Brown, who had coached Massillon High when Motley was the rival fullback for Canton McKinley.

"I was about 210 or 215 at Great Lakes, but I was fast," Motley said. "Just how fast, I couldn't say. I'd been timed in 10-flat for the 100 in college, but it was only an intramural meet, and I don't know how good the timers were. In high school I once raced the best 220 man in the school. He gave me 20 yards, and when the race was over I still had that 20 yards he gave me.

"Paul Brown was a little different at Great Lakes. In the beginning he didn't call all the plays. I think he was a little leery of it.

"Anyway, I wrote to him when I got out of the service and he was coaching the Browns. He wrote back that he had enough backs at that particular time and he couldn't use me. But then they got Bill Willis in camp, and in about a week they decided they were going to keep him. He was the only Negro in the league. The AAFC sort of had this unwritten rule about keeping the league all white, but rules like that didn't mean anything to Brown.

"About a week later I got a phone call from Bob Voigts of the Browns. I was all set to go back to college and get my degree, but he asked me, 'How would you like to try out for the Browns?' I said I'd like it fine. Later I found out that the only reason they called me was that they needed a roommate for Bill Willis for the road trips.

"Gene Fekete was the fullback and I worked at linebacker. One day we had this scrimmage and I was making a few tackles and shaking a few people up and someone asked Willis, 'What's the matter with Motley today? He trying to kill somebody?'

" 'No,' Bill said. 'He's just trying to make this football team.' "

Fekete hurt his knee in the league opener against the Miami Seahawks, and Motley became the Browns' fullback, as well as their linebacker.

"People knew the players pretty well then," Motley said. "Most of the ballplayers came from Ohio State, and Brown had gotten a few off the Cleveland Rams, which had become the Los Angeles Rams. But they couldn't place me. They didn't know I was colored and they'd ask each other, 'What's that, a French name, or what?' They figured out the story, though, the first time they saw my picture in the paper.

"You know, black kids in those days just never thought about professional football. It was just too farfetched. But I remember I used to read the stories about the old pros in *Liberty* magazine. I remember there was once a story that the old star Dutch Clark wrote himself about being approached by gamblers who wanted him to throw the game. He turned them down and they threatened him. And then he went out and played his best, and he wound up in the hospital with broken ribs. But he scored the winning touchdown, right through the goal posts.

"He was fighting and squirming, but he made it through those posts. That was my impression of professional football, fighting your way through the goal posts."

Motley's first contract was for $4500 ("I signed the first thing they

put in front of me"). His last one for Brown—for the 1953 season—
came to $11,500. In between he had spent a few years averaging 55
minutes a game; he had lost a few teeth when he misjudged a tackle
on Frankie Albert; and he lost a few more in that championship
game in 1947, not to Harmon Rowe's fists, but to an elbow.

"It was on an extra-point play," he said. "I was setting to block,
and someone caught me with an elbow. It drove my teeth right back
up into the roof of my mouth. I didn't even catch his number.

"We had four plays for me and that was all: an end run, a buck up
the middle, a trap and a screen pass. I'd only carry the ball eight or
nine times a game, and inwardly I'd have the feeling that I should
have carried more. But Paul Brown was a winner, and he didn't need
any advice from me."

Brown was once accused of running a pass-and-trap offense, which
was kind of a silly rap to hang on a coach who had won the league
title every year it was in existence, but Brown answered his accuser
normally.

"All right, so I'm a trap-and-pass coach. But any coach having
Graham and Motley would do what we do. He'd be crazy not to."

The beginning of the end came in 1951 when Motley collided with
linebacker Tony Adamle in a scrimmage. Once again, the damage
was to his knee.

"He hit me with a reverse body block with a leg whip," Motley
said. "I'd never teach that kind of block to anybody."

He dragged through the 1951 season, but by 1952 he'd run into
something new. The Giants' Steve Owen had devised a defense that
assigned one man, linebacker John Cannady, to Motley, on a permanent basis.

"One time I ran over to the sidelines, and there was John, right
alongside me," Motley said. "I said, 'John, what the hell are you
doing over here?'

"He told me, 'Coach Owen said that if Motley goes home, you go
with him. If he goes in the stands, you go along with him. So here I
am.'

"Anyway, what that accomplished was that it took away my trap
play."

By 1953 Brown had a new fullback, a chunky blond-haired kid
from Indiana named Chick Jagade who yelled and screamed when he
ran. "The most reckless football player I've ever seen," Coach Brown
said of Chick.

"I had some kind of a bonus clause in my contract in '53," Motley said, "Something about $1000 extra if my yardage was up with the leaders. I was doing OK in the beginning of the season, and then I could feel myself getting eased out. I finally got the picture in Chicago, when Brown said to me, 'Well, Motley, this is Chick's hometown, so we're going to let him play today.'

"I said to myself, 'You son of a bitch,' but there was nothing I could do about it. I just let it roll. Next season in early camp I was running downfield on a kick team and I felt something tear in my knee. I came back from the injury, but I knew I was finished in Cleveland. They had all those backs like Curley Morrison and Maurice Bassett and Dub Jones and Chet 'The Jet' Hanulak. They didn't need old Marion anymore.

"When he traded me to Pittsburgh in '55, I still thought I could play some good football. I felt my speed coming back when I ran the sprints. Then I hurt my knee again, and that was it. I told them I was through. After I retired I asked the Browns if they could find a job for me. They told me, 'Have you tried the steel mill?'"

You have to wonder what kinds of records Motley would have set if he had carried the ball 20 to 30 times a game, like Jimmy Brown did half-a-decade later. Or what he would have been like if he would have come into the league with a heavy bonus and a no-cut contract.

"I think it takes something away from these kids now," he says. "They just don't have the same desire to make the club. It's like a job to them, an easy job, and they don't seem to be putting out the way we were."

He was standing up, buttoning his sweater.

"I've got a meeting to go to, with that NFL Alumni Committee. Do me a favor. If you're writing an article, mention somewhere that it would be a good thing if Rozelle could find a way to lay aside a little pension money for some of the old-timers who are needy now, guys like Jack Manders. He had the cartilage taken out of his knee this year, and he's on crutches. How much do these kids have in their pension kitty now? Ten or 15 million? Maybe they can turn some of it loose for us old guys."

Marion Motley: Career Record

Year	RUSHING				PASS RECEIVING				TOTAL POINTS			KICKOFF RETURNS		
	Games	Attempts	Yds.	Avg.	TD	No.	Yds.	Avg.	TD	TD	Pts.	No.	Yds.	Avg.
1946	13	73	601	8.2	5	10	188	18.8	1	6	36	3	53	17.7
1947	14	146	889	6.0	8	7	73	10.4	1	10†	60	13	322	24.8
1948	14	157	964°	6.1	5	13	192	14.8	2	7	42	14	337	24.1
1949	12	113	570	5.0	8	15	191	12.7	0	8	48	12	262	21.8
1950	12	140	810°	5.8	3	11	151	13.7	1	4	24	—	—	—
1951	11	61	273	4.5	1	10	52	5.2	0	1	6	—	—	—
1952	12	104	444	4.3	1	13	213	16.4	2	3	18	3	88	29.3
1953	12	32	161	5.0	0	6	47	7.8	0	0	0	3	60	20.0
1954	Did not play													
1955	7	2	8	4.0	0	0	0	0.0	0	0	0	—	—	—
Totals	107	828	4720	5.7	31	85	1107	13.0	7	39	234	48	1122	23.4

° Indicates league leader.
† returned one intercepted pass for touchdown.

MOTLEY IN HIS PRIME: THE AAFC CHAMPIONSHIP GAMES.

	Attempts	Yards	Avg.	TD
1946	13	98	7.5	1
1947	13	109	8.4	—
1948	14	133	9.5	3
1949	8	75	9.4	1
Totals	48	415	8.6	5

Index